Critical Praise for this Book

'French certainly knows his stuff, and there is no shortage of good arguments and facts.... This is a book packed with information without being emotional or rhetorical as the subject tends to make people.'

Asia Times

'North Korea stuck with Stalinism and is now on the point of collapse, with millions suffering from starvation and the remainder overworked and underfed. Explaining how and why this has all come about and what might happen in the future is French's task in this book.'

John Walsh, *Asian Review of Books*

'Throughout the book, French is careful to consider the role of historical events and outside state actors in shaping North Korea ... [the book] serves as an excellent introduction for anyone hoping to develop an understanding of why the world deals with this isolated regime the way it does, and how the regime continues to survive despite failures that seem obvious from the outside.'

Ethnic Conflict Research Digest

'This is a refreshingly different look at North Korea. Too many books on this strange land are partial: either excoriating or excusing Kim Jong-il's regime. Others focus narrowly on the nuclear issue, usually from a US viewpoint. Paul French, by contrast, covers the waterfront with no axe to grind. Fact-packed and readable, this is a fine introduction for the general reader to a troubling land. Once again at the cutting edge of a post-colonial hot spot, Zed tells it like it really is.'

Aidan Foster-Carter, author of *Korea's Coming Reunification*

'Paul French's book on North Korea is a comprehensive look at one of the world's most secretive countries. It is a miracle that he has been able to find out so much about a country that publishes no data, severely restricts visits by foreigners and bans its people from talking to them without official approval. I praise his objective and documentary style, about a country that lends itself easily to polemics. Thirty years from now, or possibly sooner, North Korea will not exist in the form it is today. Paul French's book gives us a well-documented record of an extraordinary country that exists in our time despite a thousand reasons why it should not be as it is.'

Mark O'Neill, Shanghai correspondent, *South China Morning Post*

'Rich in detail, well researched, Paul French's thorough yet readable book is a fascinating and valuable addition to our scant knowledge of this singularly secretive, scary country.'

Catherine Armitage, China bureau chief, *The Australian*

'French's new book on North Korea should help educate and entertain anyone interested in this subject.'

Journal of Asian Studies

About this Book

This new edition of Paul French's acclaimed introduction to North Korea provides an up-to-the-minute overview of the politics, economics and history of the DPRK, with added chapters dealing with recent events. A new foreword examines why North Korea remains an issue in world politics and argues that an understanding of the country is more important now than ever. A new in-depth postscript offers analysis of recent years, why Pyongyang felt compelled to test a bomb and revert to blatant nuclear diplomacy, and how the crisis can be resolved peacefully.

About the Author

Paul French is the Chief China Representative of Access Asia, a market research and business intelligence company specialising in China and North Asia's economics and markets. He was educated in London and at the University of Glasgow. He is the co-author of *One Billion Shoppers: Accessing Asia's Consuming Passions* (1998) and author of *Carl Crow: A Tough Old China Hand: The Life, Times, and Adventures of an American in Shanghai* (2006). He lives in Shanghai.

North Korea

The Paranoid Peninsula – A Modern History

_____

PAUL   FRENCH

ZED BOOKS
London & New York

To my father, who first introduced me to a love of history

'Isn't it a pleasure when you can make practical
use of the things you have studied?'
CONFUCIUS, first line of *The Analects*

North Korea: The Paranoid Peninsula – A Modern History was first published
in 2005 by Zed Books Ltd, 7 Cynthia Street, London N1 9JF, UK, and
Room 400, 175 Fifth Avenue, New York, NY 10010, USA
www.zedbooks.co.uk

Second edition published 2007

Designed and typeset in Monotype Jansen by Illuminati, Grosmont
Cover designed by Andrew Corbett
Printed and bound in Great Britain by Biddles Ltd, King's Lynn, Norfolk

Distributed in the USA exclusively by Palgrave Macmillan, a division of
St Martin's Press, LLC, 175 Fifth Avenue, New York, NY 10010

A catalogue record for this book is available from the British Library
Library of Congress Cataloging-in-Publication Data available

ISBN 978 1 84277 904 0 (Hb)
ISBN 978 1 84277 905 7 (Pb)

Contents

Acknowledgements

This book is the culmination of watching the Democratic People's Republic of Korea (DPRK) for many years and writing about the country from a business perspective for Access Asia and a variety of other publications. It has to be stated at the start that many people who fed ideas and experiences into this book cannot be mentioned by name. Such is the nature of the DPRK that securing entry visas and building relationships are hard enough without being associated with a book that will probably not be warmly greeted in Pyongyang. Those people know who they are and will I hope recognise their contributions. Naturally, any mistakes made with the information they provided or differences in interpretation are entirely the author's responsibility.

A number of people can be mentioned, though. Primary thanks must go to my two colleagues at Access Asia: Matthew Crabbe (who provided the title) and Chris Torrens, both of whom share my interest in the DPRK and contributed to the debates around the changing nature of the country. Both colleagues were also gracious enough to indulge me patiently in pursuing this book. Thanks should also go to Barry Colman in Shanghai for his comments on the original proposal and encouragement.

Thanks must go to Joe Studwell and Arthur Kroeber of the *China Economic Quarterly*; Stephen Green, the head of the Asia Programme at the Royal Institute of International Affairs at Chatham House; Professor David Wall of Cambridge University's School of International Relations; the staff of Reference Asia at Proquest in Cambridge; Randal Eastman and the Shanghai Rotarians; Andy Rothman, Chief China Strategist with CLSA; Hugh Peyman of Research-Works and Tom Toback of Pyongyangsquare.com. Thanks also to Mark O'Neill of the *South China Morning Post* for comments on Sinuiju, and to Richard McGregor of the *Financial Times* for his thoughts on the DPRK.

Other thanks go to various Pyongyang and East Asia observers including Josh Green, Keith Bennett, John Swenson-Wright of Cambridge University and the Royal Institute of International Affairs, Amit Chanda of World Markets Research Centre in London, Aidan Foster-Carter, Fons Tuinstra in Shanghai, Sam Chambers and Turloch Mooney in Hong Kong, Sara Rance of Conville & Walsh in London, and Stuart Doig at Dialog Asia Pacific in Hong Kong.

Information on the DPRK is hard enough to dig up, though made easier by the helpful staff of the Shanghai Public Library, the British Library, the London Library, Hong Kong University Library, the RIIA's library, London School of Economics Library, the Russian State Library, Shanghai's Fudan University Library, the Marx Memorial Library in London and the New York Public Library. I also acknowledge the work the Nautilus Institute does in supplying regular updates and thoughtful essays on the situation in the DPRK (www.nautilus.org), CanKor for its DPRK clippings service (www.cankor.ca) and Pyongyangsquare.com for its database of DPRK-related information (www.pyongyangsquare.com).

At Zed Books in London thanks must go to Robert Molteno, Senior Editor, who enthusiastically took up this project, and Anna Hardman, my editor, who suffered having to communicate with me on the manuscript between North London and Shanghai's Changning district. Thanks are also due to Robin Gable, who invested a lot of energy in pulling the manuscript into shape, to Andrew Corbett for cover design, and Farouk Sohawon and Mohammed Umar for foreign rights and distribution.

Last but not least thanks to Lisa (Xu Ni), who had to endure endless half-formed thoughts during the writing of this book and was never anything less than totally supportive.

Abbreviations, Spellings and Figures

AC	Administrative Council (DPRK)
ACF	Action Contre la Faim
ADB	Asian Development Bank
ADRA	Adventist Development and Relief Agency International
AFTA	Asian Free Trade Association
AMC	asset management company
APEC	Asia Pacific Economic Cooperation
AREP	Agricultural Recovery and Environment Plan
ASEAN	Association of South East Asian Nations
CAP	Consolidated Appeals Process (UN)
CBMs	confidence building measures
CBW	chemical and biological weapons
CCTV	China Central Television (Chinese state broadcaster)
CDMA	code division multiple access
CFSAM	Crop and Food Supply Assessment (FAO/WFP)
CIA	Central Intelligence Agency (US)
CNKR	Commission to Help North Korean Refugees (ROK)
CNN	Cable News Network
Comecon	Council for Mutual Economic Cooperation
CPC	Communist Party of China
CPSU	Communist Party of the Soviet Union
CSRC	China Securities Regulatory Commission (stock market regulator)
DCRK	Democratic Confederal Republic of Koryo

DMZ	demilitarized zone
DPRK	Democratic People's Republic of Korea (North Korea)
EBRD	European Bank for Reconstruction and Development
EU	European Union
FALU	Food Aid Liaison Unit
FAM	Food Administration Ministry (DPRK)
FAO	Food and Agriculture Organisation (UN)
FDI	foreign direct investment
FDR	Federal Republic of Germany (West Germany)
FDRC	Flood Damage Rehabilitation Committee (DPRK)
FIFA	International Federation of Football Associations
GDP	gross domestic product
GDR	German Democratic Republic (East Germany)
GNP	gross national product
GNP	Grand National Party (ROK)
GSM	Global System for Mobile Communications
HEU	highly enriched uranium
HKSE	Hong Kong Stock Exchange
HKSFC	Hong Kong Securities and Futures Commission
HPRS	Household Production Responsibility System (PRC)
IAEA	International Atomic Energy Agency
ICBM	intercontinental ballistic missile
IMF	International Monetary Fund
IRBM	intermediate range ballistic missile
ISI	Inter-Services Intelligence (Pakistan)
JSA	Joint Security Area
KAL	Korean Airlines (ROK)
KCIA	Korean Central Intelligence Agency (ROK)
KCNA	Korean Central News Agency (DPRK)
KEDO	Korean Energy Development Organisation
KGB	Committee for State Safety (former USSR)
KITA	Korea International Trade Association (ROK)
KPAF	Korean People's Air Force (DPRK)
KPA	Korean People's Army (DPRK)
KPN	Korean People's Navy (DPRK)
KSM	Korean Sharing Committee (ROK)
KWP	Korean Workers Party (DPRK)
LDP	Liberal Democratic Party (ruling Japanese party)
LWR	light-water reactor
MDP	Millennium Democratic Party (ROK)
MOU	Ministry of Unification (ROK)

MPS	Ministry of People's Security (DPRK)
MSDF	Maritime Self Defence Force (Japan)
MTCR	Missile Technology Control Regime (US)
NEACD	Northeast Asia Cooperation Dialogue
NEM	New Economic Mechanism (Laos)
NEP	New Economic Policy (USSR)
NDC	National Defence Commission (DPRK)
NGO	non-governmental organisation
NHK	Japanese television news channel
NIE	National Intelligence Estimate (US)
NKRAF	North Korean Refugees Assistance Fund
NKW	North Korean Won (DPRK currency)
NLL	Northern Limit Line
NNSC	Neutral Nations Supervisory Commission
NPL	non-performing loan
NPT	Nuclear Non-Proliferation Treaty
OCHA	UN Office for the Coordination of Humanitarian Affairs
OECD	Organisation for Economic Cooperation and Development
OPEC	Organisation of the Petroleum Exporting Countries
PBoC	People's Bank of China (China's central bank)
PDS	Public Distribution System (DPRK)
PRC	People's Republic of China
PVOC	Private Voluntary Organization Consortium (US)
RDA	Rural Development Agency (ROK)
RMB	renminbi (Chinese unit of currency)
ROK	Republic of Korea (South Korea)
RPR	Revolutionary Party for Reunification (ROK)
S&P	Standard & Poor's
SAR	special administrative region
SARS	severe acute respiratory syndrome
SDF	Self-Defence Forces (Japan)
SEZ	special economic zone
SMEs	small and medium-sized enterprises
SMS	short messaging service
SNCC	South–North Coordinating Committee
SOE	state-owned enterprise
SPA	Supreme People's Assembly (DPRK)
SSD	State Security Department (DPRK)
SSE	Shanghai Stock Exchange
TMD	Theater Missile Defense (US)
TPM	total particulate matter

TRT	Three-Revolution Team Movement (DPRK)
UN	United Nations
UNDHA	United Nations Department of Humanitarian Affairs
UNHCR	United Nations High Commission for Refugees
UNDP	United Nations Development Programme
UNICEF	United Nations Children's Fund
UNSCOM	United Nations Special Commission
USAID	United States Agency for International Development
USDA	United States Department of Agriculture
USFK	United States Forces, Korea
USSR	Union of Soviet Socialist Republics (Soviet Union)
WFP	World Food Programme (UN)
WMD	weapons of mass destruction
WTO	World Trade Organisation
YMCA	Young Men's Christian Association

A Note on Spellings and Names

On 1 July 1996 the political representatives of Korean-speaking countries signed a common declaration about the reform of Korean spelling rules. The reform took effect on 1 August 1998. There is a transitional period until 31 July 2005, in which the old and new spellings will coexist. After that only the new spelling rules will be valid. Many place names have undergone transformations. Gone are capitals to denote different syllables; gone too are special marks to represent sounds.

In Korean the family name comes first, followed by the given name or names. The practice is followed in this book with the given name hyphenated, hence Kim Il-sung and Kim Jong-il. An exception to this rule is Syngman Rhee. There is also extensive repetition of certain family names, notably Kim, Park and Lee. It should also be noted that traditionally Korean women keep their maiden names after marriage; hence former ROK President Park Chung-hee was married to Yook Young-soo.

Spelling of Chinese names follows the pinyin style of Romanisation as two separate words, for example, Mao Zedong.

A Note on Figures

Statistics and figures from the DPRK are highly unreliable and patchy at best. The author Joseph Bermudez, who wrote a study of North Korea's armed forces, summed up writing about North Korea best when he stated,

'The catch words probably, estimated, or believed to and apparently must appear frequently in any work of this type', while Marcus Noland, a Senior Fellow at the Institute for International Economics who has written extensively on North Korea's economy, sensibly warns 'not to trust any datum on North Korea that comes with a decimal point attached'. This is not a new problem. In the 1970s the former CIA Director Robert Gates described North Korea as a 'black hole' and the 'toughest intelligence target in the world'. Indeed many economic, military and health statistics remain classified as state secrets, while all available official data are questionable at best. An additional problem is that the DPRK's political system releases comparatively few policy documents and has a tradition of relying on oral rather than written agreements in dealings with organisations such as NGOs, meaning that much of the data becomes unverifiable, as Pyongyang often makes a decision on statistics based on what is politically acceptable to release.

There are a number of reasons why North Korean statistics are problematic. These include the fact that statistical methodology in the DPRK is rarely explained and thought to be relatively basic; that centrally planned economies notoriously have dubious statistics; that the DPRK has its own internal security reasons for not making all figures known internationally; and that there may be some official underreporting in order to attract aid. Additionally, politics remains paramount in North Korea, including in terms of the gathering of statistics. Where possible the problems with verifying statistical data are explained and the possible differences in calculation commented upon in the text.

While some of the figures from this report are from official North Korean sources such as the Korean Central News Agency and the Census Department they are treated with extreme caution and compared to estimates from other sources where possible. There are a number of other sources that have provided figures on the DPRK and all urge the user to exercise extreme caution. These sources include the European Union (EU), the various embassies and consulates in Pyongyang, the international aid agencies and NGOs operating in North Korea including the World Food Programme and the UN Food and Agriculture Organisation, as well as the US Department of Agriculture. There are also a number of Chinese academics watching the DPRK, as well as China's Customs Bureau and National Bureau of Statistics, that provide some insight. Various international bodies including the United Nations, the World Health Organisation, the International Monetary Fund, the World Bank, the Asian Development Bank and ASEAN, as well as various other universities and academic institutions, also collate data to varying degrees.

Problems abound particularly when considering the state and depth of the food shortages in the DPRK. NGOs and state aid agencies still do not have open and unfettered access to the entire country and are, despite some progress, still largely unable to conduct unannounced site visits or effectively monitor aid shipments from arrival in the country to final disbursement; while other projects are prevented from collecting follow-up data to assess their effectiveness.

There are also a number of South Korean organisations releasing data on the DPRK, some of which may have their own agendas for inflating or deflating figures. The most reliable among these is generally considered to be the Bank of Korea and its North Korea Economic Studies Division, the Ministry of Unification, the Korea Trade-Investment Promotion Agency, the Korea Development Institute, Seoul National University and the Korea Rural Economic Institute, as well as the National Statistical Office. In Japan the External Trade Organisation's Institute of Developing Economies is also useful.

Essentially no reliable statistics have been published by the DPRK since 1965. Those that are available are problematic, for instance using Soviet-era statistical and accounting methods or, as with figures on food consumption, not accounting for spoilage (which is considerable) or supplying only aggregate production levels that cloud discrepancies across various sectors of the economy. The decline in statistical release accelerated in the 1970s as economic stagnation set in, while in the 1980s the country went so far as to withhold totally the growth/decline rate for industrial production and key agricultural statistics.

All sums of money are expressed in US dollars or local currencies at the exchange rates prevailing at the time.

Foreword

Still Paranoid after All These Years

On the border with North Korea in the Chinese city of Dandong every day a stream of trucks make the crossing over the bridge that spans the Yalu river, forming a bottleneck entering the bustling Liaoning town. Dandong is typical of China; a city of 2.4 million people expanding fast, conscious of its own rapid growth, full of energetic traders, fast-talking deal-makers and ever-proliferating middlemen glued to their mobile phones keen to cut a deal, reach an agreement and move on to the next bit of business. Across the Yalu river, known as the Amrok river in Korean, lies the Democratic People's Republic of Korea (DPRK), North Korea. The contrast couldn't be starker – and growing ever more so on a seemingly weekly basis as the North's economy spirals downwards and China's appears to soar inexorably higher. The view is virtually barren from the border as far as the eye can see, and the eye can see as far as the city of Sinuiju, once slated to be a special economic zone, but, since that plan was shelved after it collapsed in a series of almost comic disasters, for now a forlorn, desperate and frankly clapped-out industrial relic on the horizon, where life is grim and economic activity sluggish, to say the least. From Dandong the view of Sinuiju includes seemingly derelict buildings, with no glass in their windows and a few blue-jacketed peasants working in what appear to be barren fields close to the town. The largest structure is a dormant Ferris wheel that hasn't turned in years.

Dandong is the most active hub for cross-border trade between the DPRK and the PRC along the two countries' 880-mile shared border. The trucks arriving from the DPRK tell a story. The story they tell is one of economic collapse and desperate survival tactics – many are loaded with freshly cut timber or scrap metal. This is North Korea now – reduced to asset-stripping its few vestiges of remaining industry and selling its precious raw materials with little or no value added. With China so notoriously resource- and commodity-hungry, as its own economy continues to expand and consume, there is no shortage of buyers in Dandong ready to pay cash or barter food or goods for the metals and wood. In this border town between the two countries the economic eclipse of the DPRK is palpable and startlingly obvious.

The first edition of this book argued that in order to understand the DPRK, its economy, politics and diplomacy, it was necessary to understand the country's misguided economic policies. These have seen the North economically underperform the South to a point where the North's economy is a fraction the size of the South's, with the South's gross domestic product (GDP) in 2005 approximately US$965 billion while the North's was at best US$40 billion, according to the OECD, while the average income in the South is now at least fifteen times that of the North. The gap between the two Koreas is widening in just about every applicable metric – life expectancy, calorific intake, incidence of disease and even average height.

Despite repeated rallying cries from the regime in Pyongyang, economic 'Speed Battles', mass exoduses of the urban population to the countryside to engage in agricultural work, and intense sloganising, the North's economy has been unable to imitate the country's neighbour and closest ally China by reforming and marketising to any significant level. Though Beijing has repeatedly urged Pyongyang to follow its reform blueprint, albeit with North Korean characteristics, the North has chosen not to. The detailed reasons why this process has not occurred are one of the core arguments of this book; it should always be remembered that in North Korea politics, the national religion of self-reliance, Juche, remains paramount.

Since the first edition of this text was published in early 2005 the world's attention has largely focused on Iraq, Iran and Afghanistan. Yet periodically North Korea has been a significant story, suddenly leaping up the media agenda, only to recede again soon afterwards. Then in early October 2006 it became *the* story when North Korea conducted a nuclear test. The four-year game of show-and-tell that had been played since Pyongyang admitted secretly restarting its nuclear programme was over. Pyongyang showed and told dramatically, capturing the world's attention in the process. Even for the regime's harshest critics around the world it was clear that President George W. Bush's January 2002 State of the Union 'Axis of Evil' speech had got it back-to-front – Iraq and Iran did not have nuclear capabilities while

North Korea, as we now know, does. Pyongyang has joined the international nuclear club and, in the process, left Washington's global non-proliferation strategy in tatters. The Korean peninsula has gone nuclear; the East Asian region now has two nations with the bomb: the DPRK and China.

The region and the world have changed. How did we get to this point? Why did Pyongyang see no alternative to nuclearisation? Why does the country stubbornly refuse to reform? Those questions are the meat of this book, and the road from the attempted economic reform process in 2002 to the nuclear test and reactions to it in late 2006 and early 2007 are considered in the new postscript.

Yet despite all the news coverage, op-eds and diplomatic flurry around North Korea – the international community's 'outrage', China's 'final straw' – has the world come to know North Korea any better than it did a year ago, five years ago, a decade ago, or fifty years ago for that matter? Perhaps the most crucial question concerns America's Korea policy: is it any more sophisticated and advanced than previously? This book argued originally, and still does now, even more vocally, that 'the DPRK is a failed state and therefore liable to become unstable unless engaged enthusiastically and strategically' and that understanding and accepting this is the only way forward that avoids an inconceivably horrific and bloody endgame on the Korean peninsula. The former *Washington Post* journalist Don Oberdorfer wrote: 'Korea's fate was often to be an afterthought, subordinated to the more immediate or compelling requirements of larger powers, rather than a subject of full consideration in its own right.' Has this changed? The evidence would suggest not.

The Korean peninsula, and particularly Pyongyang, is still paranoid. Korea remains an 'afterthought' in Washington's geostrategic thinking, which is still invariably reactive rather than proactive. At the same time the role of China in the Korean crisis has heightened and moved centre stage. North Korea has become an urgent issue for Beijing, an unstable state on their border that is now nuclear. Beijing still fears an exodus of refugees from the North across the porous border into China; Beijing is frustrated by Pyongyang's continuing diplomatic bluster and economic stagnation while it is grudgingly forced to send food, fuel and finance to the North at a time when income and social disparities in China threaten stability and Beijing feels it needs to focus its efforts and resources on its own people. However, China is unable simply to disengage with the North no matter how frustrated it may become. Some 1,300 miles away from Pyongyang is the Chinese city of Guangzhou, the steamy capital of the economic powerhouse of Guangdong province, close to Hong Kong. In the city's Revolutionary Martyrs Park senior citizens kill time playing mah-jong, students cut classes and young lovers covet the shady benches for the afternoon. Among the park's attractions is a two-storey horseshoe-shaped structure called the Sino-North Korean Peoples Blood Condensed Friendship Pavilion. A quick survey of young Chinese sitting holding hands on the steps of the memorial and the senior citizens sitting in the shade sipping tea revealed that attitudes to North Korea now range from a vague sadness for the people of the DPRK to bemusement that Pyongyang doesn't follow a path of economic reform similar to China's. The two countries, whose close relationship was once likened to that of lips and teeth, have grown apart economically, politically and socially but they remain, like it or not, neighbours.

The contrast between Dandong and Guangzhou, on the one hand, and Pyongyang and Sinuiju, on the other, is clear: the former are thriving, thrusting cities where people's living standards are improving fast while political change is developing at a slower pace, but is moving; the latter two cities remain mired in economic decline with no sign of any political reform apparent and little sign of change in the immediate future. In Dandong and Guangzhou ordinary people are buying apartments, cars and plasma screen televisions; they are going shopping, having family meals at restaurants and thinking about perhaps taking a holiday in Thailand. In Pyongyang and Sinuiju this sort of life is barely possible for even the most privileged of the elite. For ordinary people life will continue to revolve around food rationing, long work hours and constant political sloganising.

Politics and political theory continue to determine North Korea's disastrous economic policy, which in turn prevents the country and the regime from attaining food security, foreign currency reserves, international loans or economic growth. Consequently a regime fearing economic reform but reliant on foreign aid for survival falls back on a policy of nuclear brinkmanship and international isolation in a desperate bid simultaneously to retain power and to secure urgent supplies of food and energy to feed its people and maintain the last vestiges of its industrial base. The fundamental key to understanding North Korea remains not primarily the nuclear capability estimates from the Pentagon or the debates over the current state of mind of Kim Jong-il, as endlessly speculated in the media, but economics.

Introduction:
The Paranoid Peninsula

Paranoid *adjective.* 1. Characterized by or resembling paranoia; a tendency on the part of an individual or group toward excessive or irrational suspiciousness and distrustfulness of others. 2. Characterized by suspiciousness, persecutory trends, or megalomania.

This is a book about a country – the Democratic People's Republic of Korea, or the DPRK. North Korea occupies 55 per cent of the total land area of the Korean peninsula, approximately the size of New York State, and contains 22 million people. North Korea is a country that is changing – not through political will, but because it has to, if its leadership is to survive in power.

The reclusive DPRK has often been described as the 'Hermit Kingdom', and there is undoubtedly a truth to this. President Clinton described the Korean peninsula as 'the Cold War's last divide' in 1997, while President Bush infamously included the DPRK in his 2002 'Axis of Evil' speech. Japan's prime minister called North Korea a 'disgraceful' country and his chief cabinet secretary described it as a 'crazy' country.

North Korea effectively closed itself to the outside world after Kim Il-sung took control, with Stalin's blessing, after World War II. The state became seen as largely a Soviet satellite, though this was an overstatement; while in the Cold War era Pyongyang and Moscow appeared close, a longer lasting and in many ways more influential relationship has existed between Pyongyang and Beijing.

North Korea has emerged into the current century as a relic of the last. It is effectively the only unreformed Stalinist-style command economy left in existence, while most others have crumbled or begun reform programmes.

While the other remaining socialist states have tended to downplay their military capacity in recent years, North Korea still publicly and vocally adheres to a military-first ideology of 'putting the army before the working class'.

It is certainly true that the history of the DPRK has been one of retreat from international politics. The country remains outside most international or regional forums, as well as remaining outside the World Bank and the International Monetary Fund. Pyongyang follows its own path in many respects: it has developed its own political theory that encompasses North Korean life in Juche theory; it operates its own calendar; until recently it retained few official diplomatic ties with foreign nations. Few of the North's citizens, even those in privileged positions, ever travel outside the country, and the nation restricts access by the outside media.

While the DPRK has largely shunned the outside world and pursued its own path, the outside world in return has, until recently, largely ignored North Korea except at intelligence agency levels and, since the mid-1990s, through aid donations to deal with the famine ravaging the country. Tourism to the DPRK remains small-scale and business delegations rarely visit.

The division drawn across the Korean peninsula at the 38th parallel in 1953 remains in force with the world's most heavily militarised border between the Koreas. Given the history of the peninsula and the states that have grown up since 1953 a little paranoia is perhaps forgivable. However, it has been the fate of the North to be the least understood of the two halves. Misconceptions regarding the DPRK abound – hopefully this book doesn't add to them.

Observers of Planet Pyongyang

Former US vice-president and ambassador to Japan Walter Mondale once observed that anyone claiming to be an expert on North Korea was either a liar or a fool. For the whole of the DPRK's history the role of Pyongyang watchers has been akin to that of astrologers: gazing in largely from outside, acquiring snippets of knowledge and occasionally gaining highly restricted access to the country itself. Pyongyang watchers are a strange breed, invariably repelled and fascinated by the country in turn. They marvelled at the access their counterparts were gaining in the Kremlin-watching and Sinology communities, relying on small fragments of speeches and rhetoric-filled policy statements along with other snatches of information that could be pieced together to comprehend Pyongyang's reasoning and strategy.

Any information was valued, as the country itself has been effectively closed to Western observers. Though it is not so common these days, the country often used to describe itself as a 'paradise' in the heady days of the 1960s and early 1970s when development was rapid and before economic stagnation, starvation and isolation set in for a prolonged period.

This has led to an excess of qualifying terms to describe the North. The country is invariably autarkic, sclerotic, schizophrenic, Orwellian, anachronistic, a pariah or suicide state. In part all of these epithets are accurate yet not overly helpful in understanding the country, its people, politics and economy. North Korea's insistence on positing every issue in a historical context makes the nation appear a fixed entity, yet its unpredictability makes it a movable feast for those studying East Asian politics. It is also true that the regime's constant referrals to the past – to the Korean War, to the Japanese occupation of the peninsula, to the withdrawal of Soviet aid and American imperialism – do make the DPRK appear to be a country with a past but no future. It does also appear to be committing suicide with no meaningful economic answers to its industrial and agricultural stagnation, a diplomatic policy of belligerence and a rigid political system that is maintained despite famine and collapse. North Korea is in this sense a prisoner of its own history and apparently has no way to exit itself from this cycle of decline and collapse.

Many, not least the US government, have believed that if left to its own devices North Korea will simply implode. This may be true, but the same was said in the late 1980s when the USSR and Eastern bloc collapsed, severing Pyongyang's economic lifeline, and again in the mid-1990s when Kim Il-sung died. It didn't happen. Additionally the consequences of leaving the DPRK to implode of its own accord are not strategies that most of the major regional and international powers can pursue. Aside from the obvious human rights issue of allowing a country to starve to death without aid, regional powers are faced with numerous other problems – the South Koreans with an unstable neighbour, the Chinese with a potentially massive refugee problem, Japan neighbouring a 'nuclear unstable state'.

Somehow North Korea must be dealt with through either engagement or containment – a debate still raging in the US. At the same time the world's last Cold War divide remains along the Demilitarized Zone (DMZ), where 1 million North Korean troops face down 700,000 South Korean and 37,000 US troops. As the GI saying goes, 'there ain't no "D" in the DMZ'.

The most recent nuclear crisis was precipitated by Pyongyang's decision to restart its nuclear programme. However, that decision is rooted in the long US refusal to abide by the only international agreement ever signed between the two countries – the 1994 Agreed Framework. The agreement was never really taken seriously by Washington and, it would seem, Pyongyang has reached the conclusion that the cancellation of scheduled oil shipments in December 2002, and the late arrival of two promised civilian-use reactors from the Korean Energy Development Organisation (KEDO), were an effective withdrawal from that treaty, leaving the DPRK with no choice but to respond. It has to be noted that none of the countries expressing concern over the present problem, including China and Russia, has seen fit to raise the issue of US responsibility or, as one commentator noted, 'sees anything roguish in the US refusal to honour its commitments'.[1]

Tentative Reform

In the spring of 2002 North Korea began a tentative economic reform process that raised awareness of the country to many outsiders. Certainly 2002 had promised to be a different year. Traditionally the Pyongyang government issues its broad policy objectives annually at New Year through the state news agency, KCNA. There is invariably talk of economic growth and improving international relations, but 2002 saw a significantly more strident tone emanating from the hermit kingdom. The editorial expressed an interest in opening to the outside world and modernising the economy, announcing a new era of 'advance, great turn and broad opening'.

Pyongyang indicated several ways in which it might do this, including 'Restructuring the economy through enhancement of the existing infrastructure and the development of up-to-date technology, in particular in the power, coal, metal industry and railway transport sectors; implementing the June 2000 North–South Joint Declaration; improving relations with the outside world and making a positive contribution to global independence and peace.' To realise these objectives, the government had previously announced a budget for 2001 that at US$9.9 billion was nearly 3 per cent up on 2000. Perhaps paranoia was about to give way to an outburst of reform.

The Problem of the Command Economy

The central thesis of this book is that the DPRK is a failed state and therefore liable to become unstable unless engaged enthusiastically and strategically. The DPRK has failed not primarily because it is run by a leadership obsessed with the cult of personality or because it is a one-party state entirely devoid of democracy, though neither of these truisms about North Korea has helped its development, but because it subscribes to the failed concept of the Soviet-inspired socialist command economy that insists on a centrally planned system. As Dennis O'Hearn has noted,

Soviet style centralised planning is neither *socialist* planning nor even effective planning. Since it is not socialist or democratic planning, the preferences of society (much less of individuals) are not met.... As a result, the plan is not effective – it is violated at all stages of the economy.[2]

The issues that revolve around North Korea – famine, excessive military spending, the nation's crumbling infrastructure and industrial base, the propagation of the country's guiding Juche philosophy – are all subordinate to the existence of a centrally planned state and an economy that has failed under the weight of its own contradictions. Industrial collapse, a failed agricultural policy, famine and exorbitant levels of military spending all take place within a political context heightened in North Korea through the all-embracing nature of economic planning.

Whatever attempts are made at economic reform to introduce elements of marketisation and mercantilism are doomed to failure while the command economy remains in place and dominant. Under this system a DPRK with or without a Kim or nuclear weapons cannot survive except by relying on the drip-feed of international aid. The inherent contradictions of the command economy, enshrined in the philosophical mixture of Marxism–Leninism, Maoism, Confucianism and traditional Korean heritage that is Juche, cannot successfully undertake any rust-to-riches transformation without jettisoning its core economic theory. It cannot reject this economic theory without admitting the failure of Juche and the regime created by Kim Il-sung and Kim Jong-il. As the personality cult around the Kims is built on their infallibility, any truly radical restructuring of the economy to deal with the current spiral of decline would destroy the ruling elite's legitimacy and strip them of the Mandate of Heaven.

Ultimately the demise of the USSR was not about Gorbachev, the legacy of Stalin's purges or Khrushchev's de-Stalinisation, but about the failure of the command economy to deliver economic growth and prosperity. In Eastern Europe the leaders bolstered by personality cults fell away, from Romania to Albania. Again, it was ultimately the failure of the command economy to deliver growth rates and living standards equivalent to Western Europe that brought down the regimes. In both cases the one justification that the ruling regimes used to secure their position – the elevation of the position of the working class – was not achieved, as the economic system was unable to drive growth. China has realised this, as to varying degrees have other command economy states, such as Vietnam and Cuba, where rigid political regimes have begun to shift away from the politically administered economic plan to balance the preservation of the legitimacy of the ruling Communist Parties with new, more liberalised, mixed economies. Where this shift is real, such as in China's coastal cities, the ruling regimes have managed to remain dominant while delivering growth. In those regions, such as the inland provinces of China, where the reforms have largely been illusory and the command economy still dominates, economic failure continues to deepen and the Party's legitimacy is being more widely questioned.

In the last two years the world has seen three separate though interlinked strategies employed by North Korea to try to maintain the legitimacy of the ruling regime, force concessions from other nations, guarantee the vital inflows of aid and attempt to resuscitate the economy. These strategies have emerged as an attempted process of diplomatic engagement with regional powers to achieve a normalisation of relations, followed by a highly limited economic reform programme, which ultimately failed and led finally to a reassertion of the military-first theory and its tangential nuclear weapons programme as Pyongyang's primary tool of leverage in international negotiations and the giving of priority to military issues to ensure regime survival.

North Korea: Paranoid Peninsula

This book is structured in such a way as to provide the reader with an overview of the society, philosophy, economics and possible future of the DPRK. Juche (self-sufficiency), the guiding theory of North Korean life, combines politics, economics and social control in one philosophy. Therefore to understand the basic failing of the nation one has to consider all elements of the society and cannot separate politics from economics from social development. In Juche-led North Korea all are planned, all are interlinked and all are collapsing, while politics remains paramount.

The first part of this book looks at the society that fifty-five years of the DPRK has created. Daily life, its structure, routine and purpose, are little understood outside the country, still less the highly politicised nature of the society that reaches down into the minutiae of daily life. This is followed by an examination of Juche itself, its theoretical roots, 'borrowings' from other philosophies and more all embracing traditions, such as Confucianism and traditional Korean thinking. As Juche seeks to underpin theoretically the position of Kim Il-sung and Kim Jong-il at the head of the society and perpetuates their personality cults, the theory itself is examined in some detail.

The second part of the book concerns the DPRK's economic system. Though North Korea remains a Stalinist-style command economy, it has adapted certain tenets of the planned economy to its own needs and requirements. Therefore the DPRK's economy is examined in contrast to the Soviet and Chinese models, in terms of their similarities and differences, adaptive influences and differing roads to development. Central to the failure of the DPRK's planned economy has been the inability, for a decade now, to feed itself. This failure in the agricultural sector highlights the unsuitability of the command economy's form of collectivised farming as well as revealing a lack of success in meeting Juche's goal of self-sufficiency. Consequently both the famine and the inability to reform fundamentally the agrarian sector reflect starkly the failure of the system in North Korea and the human cost of that failure. There is therefore a discussion of North Korea's agricultural system and an examination of the root causes of the famine and its effects on the nation, as well as of the efforts of NGOs and Pyongyang to solve the food crisis. Two primary questions are raised here. First, how did North Korea's economic and agricultural system reach a point of collapse whereby mass famine ensued? Second; why did the government fail so completely to deal with the famine that a country guided by Juche was forced to lose face and request international aid?

As indicated, an economic reform programme of sorts has been started. The basic tenets of this reform process and its lack of success are examined. This programme includes both reform of the command economy's control of the distribution process, which for most of the country's history has entailed rationing as the major form of food and goods distribution, and financial reforms designed to kick-start economic activity. The results, given that these were relatively minor measures occurring within a rigid political system, have been far from impressive; the process has been mostly mishandled and has led to further impoverishment and decline in the economy, as well as potentially causing a major rift in the ruling regime between Kim Jong-il and the military.

There has also been an attempt by the government to follow the Chinese path more overtly and open up to outside investment through the creation of an economic zone in the north of the country, Sinuiju. This experiment was an unmitigated disaster and revealed the almost total lack of understanding in Pyongyang of economics, fiscal policy, the law of supply and demand, or international business practice. This episode is covered in detail.

The unravelling of the nuclear crisis is discussed in some detail, as it involves the DPRK's relations with its closest allies, China and Russia, as well as South Korea and Japan. DPRK–US relations are considered in the context of the historic failure of the US either to successfully contain or to engage the DPRK. It eventually developed a policy that fell between two stools, to be followed by each succeeding American presidential administration. Historically there has been a US policy failure in dealings with both Pyongyang and Seoul. American policy towards the peninsula has always been one of reaction and not anticipation, of last-minute compromise in place of deeper consideration.

The reassertion of the military-first line is discussed in some detail as a major policy shift following the failure of the regime's plans, first for engagement and then for reform. This necessitates a discussion of the role, size and capabilities of the Korean People's Army (KPA) given their restated paramount position in society.

The final part of the book looks at the possible outcomes for the DPRK by positing several potential scenarios for change, as well as considering the prospects for Korean reunification. The division of the Korean peninsula for over fifty years has been one of the most tense international standoffs of the modern era. The division has affected the form and shape of the development of both the Koreas, their Cold War allegiances, their post-Cold War alliances, and consequently their economic systems, international relations, social development and national psychologies.

PART I

The Juche Nation:
Beloved Leaders, Brilliant Thoughts,
Power Cuts and Empty Shelves

I

A Normal Day in Pyongyang

North Korea's capital remains one of the least known places on earth. For more than half a century the government of the DPRK has carefully managed the availability of images and reporting from Pyongyang, meaning that for people outside North Korea the city remains unknown. Those images of Pyongyang that do emerge are carefully stage-managed and usually reflect only highly organised processions or parades during ceremonial events. Rarely if ever is the life of the ordinary residents shown. Similarly, within the country Pyongyang is shown by state media as the capital of the revolution; hence many North Koreans have little idea either of the reality of daily existence in the capital.

This lack of familiarity with Pyongyang has gone a long way to hiding the nature of daily life in the capital. Life in Pyongyang is highly politicised and regimented; yet increasingly, as the economy has collapsed and food shortages have continued, attention has been fixed on daily survival, coping with shortages and maintaining something approximating a normal life.

Pyongyang: Capital of Our Revolution

The day starts early in Pyongyang, the city described by the government as the 'capital of revolution'. North Koreans emerge from bed at around 6.00 a.m., dress and head off to work, where many arrive by 7.30. Most Pyongyang residents (the city's name means 'level ground') live in high-rise buildings, hastily erected over the fifty years since the end of the Korean

War. The blocks are lined up along the city's wide boulevards and house most of Pyongyang's 2 million-plus population. The apartment blocks, and the noticeably few office blocks, which were erected fast to house a massive homeless population devastated by war, are now showing signs of their age. They were mostly built in the 1960s when Pyongyang was rebuilding after being almost completely flattened by American bombing during the war. There are still a few narrow single-lane and some two-lane roads, though most streets are boulevards of uniformly utilitarian high-rise blocks – what the nation's founder Kim Il-sung liked to think were the hallmark of a city of the future. The war-induced necessity of rapidly rebuilding Pyongyang, and the political policy of resettling many rural people in cities and towns, have given North Korea a relatively high population density of approximately 185,000 people per square kilometre, similar to Italy or Switzerland.

Those who live on higher floors may have to set out for work or school a little earlier than those lower down. Due to the chronic power shortages affecting the entire DPRK, many apartment-building elevators have long stopped operating, or work only intermittently. As many buildings are between twenty and forty storeys tall, this is an inconvenience. In general the major problem is for the older residents, who find the stairs difficult. Many senior citizens are effectively trapped in their apartments; there are stories of old people who, having moved in, have never been able to leave. Even in the better blocks elevators can be sporadic and so people just don't take the chance. Families make great efforts to relocate their older relatives on lower floors or in houses but this is difficult and a bribe is sometimes required.[1] With food shortages now constant, many older people share their meagre rations with their grandchildren, weakening themselves further and making the prospect of climbing stairs even more daunting.

Keeping warm is also problematic. Apartment buildings are largely heated by boiled water, houses by charcoal briquettes. However, if the electricity supply is suspended – a not uncommon event given the ongoing fuel crisis – then no heat is available. Most residents stay in their winter clothes all day, even sleeping in them. People who manage to obtain chicken or duck feathers use them to make warm quilts to see them through the icy winters.

Every day people liaise with their neighbours on the current electricity situation. At times a large proportion of Pyongyang operates an 'alternative suspension of electricity supply' system, meaning that when buildings on one side of the street are blacked out the other side of the street gets power. Neighbours monitor the situation, often sending children or older relatives to watch television in a friend's apartment across the road. When the power supply alternation time arrives there is a mad rush of children as they head for their friends' apartments across the road. Even 'prioritised'[2] buildings can suffer these interruptions of supply; this was not uncommon in the late 1990s, and occasionally happens today.

Apartments cut off use candles, carbide and kerosene lights, though many families are too poor to afford these alternative power sources, which are anyway in short supply and relatively expensive. Those with access to dollars and connections might have a tank battery to supply electricity, and thereby avoid the worst of the power cuts, but they will have to spend tens of thousands of DPRK won (NKW) to get one. Some apartments and houses have no problem with regular power cuts such as those of the more senior party cadres (defined as above primary party secretary level), leadership's guards and senior army personnel. On the other hand, the power never gets cut to, for example, the Mansudae Statue, to the Juche Tower on the banks of the Taedong river, which flows through central Pyongyang; or to the numerous neon propaganda signs on top of buildings. If nothing else Pyongyang residents can console themselves with the fact that the situation outside the capital is invariably much worse.

A Roof over Your Head

Worrying about the electricity supply means you have a house or apartment, though privacy is not always guaranteed. It is common for two households to have to share in Pyongyang. For a small family in a house with three rooms, it is not unusual for another householder of the same age to be moved in. While people don't like surrendering valuable living space, it is often dictated by the work unit. House and apartment shortages are serious throughout North Korea and in Pyongyang in particular. According to the Korea Institute for National Reunification's White Paper on Human Rights in North Korea,[3] the supply of housing in the DPRK is around 56–63 per cent of demand. All housing is apportioned by the state, and quality and location are dependent on social rank – the DPRK's social ranking system of fifty-one political classifications assigns everyone a place in the national hierarchy. With a growing population, the overcrowding is not about to improve.

In Pyongyang, it can take two or three years for a newlywed couple to be allocated a one-room apartment attached to a communal kitchen. As the shortages have worsened many newly married couples continue to live with one set of parents for as long as a decade. The quickest way to escape this situation is to have a contact in the housing allocation section, under the jurisdiction of the People's Committee Urban Management Bureau, which handles housing allocations. For Korean Workers Party (KWP) cadres, the party headquarters assigns housing. The very senior benefit from the few luxury compounds.

So long as a person is employed by the same work unit their allocated dwelling is usually theirs until they die. They invariably live close to co-workers, thereby increasing the self-monitoring of society. If reassigned to a different work unit, they may have to move. However, people do not expect anything much bigger or better, as virtually all Pyongyang apartment buildings are the same size and quality. Outside the city you might get a so-called 'harmonica' house, Korean-style row houses invariably consisting of three or four single-story buildings of one room and one kitchen each. These are mostly suited for newlyweds or families with just one child. They have the additional luxury of a small garden, which means the couple can grow vegetables to supplement their diet. Senior cadres, military officials, favoured academics and enterprise managers can get more – typically two rooms, a veranda, shower, flush toilet and hot running water. Rural workers on collective farms can typically expect two rooms and a shared kitchen in a smaller apartment building or possibly a more traditional two- or three-room Korean-style farmhouse.

In both the capital and the provinces, complaints about noise from the neighbours are common as apartment walls are thin. Buildings are invariably freezing cold in the winter and very hot in the summer, as central heating and air conditioning are rare. People have been known to weep on the day they move in to a new apartment and immediately start decorating with wallpaper and oiled paper for the floors. (A house-warming party is obligatory and guests all take small gifts.)

As the housing shortage worsened, so many people have started to bypass the official route. Clandestine house transactions have been reported in Pyongyang since the mid-1980s. One famous story concerns Pyongyang's Kwangbok (Liberation) Street, which was built for ordinary workers with 25,000 family units, though deemed to be of superior quality compared to Pyongyang's regular housing stock. Apparently a group of wealthier North Koreans who used to live in Japan and some senior KWP cadres bribed the urban management officials with foreign currency and electronic appliances and obtained the apartments for themselves. This story got around Pyongyang and caused some disquiet, leading to a government crackdown on illegal transactions. However, others have found ways around the system, and people who have left the DPRK report that a one-room apartment in Pyongyang can be 'bought' for US$400 and a three-room one for US$1,500, though prices are now reportedly skyrocketing.

As an unofficial housing market emerges in Pyongyang, in the countryside in the late 1990s many families sold their homes to raise money either to start some sort of bartering business, buy black-market goods or escape to China. At this time houses were reportedly trading for as little as US$15. For those who need currency to buy housing, an informal foreign currency loan will require the payment of 20 to 30 per cent in annual interest – perhaps even as high as 50 per cent per month. With the food shortages worsening, cases have been reported of families becoming homeless in the provinces after swapping their accommodation rights for food.

Badges, Bicycles and Fashions

In Pyongyang a growing number of women work in white-collar office jobs; they make up an estimated 90 per cent of workers in light industry and 80 per cent of the rural workforce. Many women are now the major wage-earner in the family – though still housewife, mother and cook as well as a worker, or perhaps a soldier. Make-up is now increasingly common in Pyongyang, though is rarely worn until after college graduation. Skin lotion is popular but still sometimes frowned upon by the local Socialist Youth League. Local brands have appeared from the Pyongyang and the Sinuiju cosmetics factories. Products include ginseng liquid cream, though rumour has it that it contains no actual ginseng (ginseng toothpaste is also ginseng-free). Chinese-made skin lotions, foundation, eyeliner and lipstick are available and permissible in the office. Many women now suffer from blotchy skin as the national diet has deteriorated and in consequence they are wearing more make-up. Long hair is common but untied hair is frowned upon.

Men's hairstyles could not be described as radical. In the 1980s, when Kim Jong-il first came to public prominence, his trademark crewcut, known as a 'speed battle cut', became popular, while the more bouffant style favoured by Kim Il-sung, and now Kim Jong-il, in their later years, is also popular. Hairdressers and barbers are run by the local 'Convenience Services Management Committee'; at many, customers can wash their hair themselves. Economic pressures have seen many hairdressers close down, as more people cut their hair at home to save money. Women often buy Chinese-made permanent wave and hair-dye kits at farmers' markets and perm each other's hair.

Pyongyang is the fashion capital of North Korea, offering greater access to foreign, often Japanese-inspired, styles. This was how bell-bottoms became fashionable; and how wearing Japanese sunglasses became a sign of being connected and in style. A Japanese watch denotes someone in an influential position. The increasing appearance of Adidas, Disney and other brands, usually fake, indicates that access to smuggled goods from China is growing. Most branded clothing is smuggled in and sold for cash. Jeans are fashionable though risky – occasionally they have been banned as 'decadent', along with long hair on men, which at times has led to arrest and a forced haircut. Fashion as such is not really an applicable term in North Korea, as the Apparel Research Centre under the Clothing Industry Department of the National Light Industry Committee designs most clothing. However, things have loosened up somewhat, with bright colours now permitted as being in accordance with a 'socialist lifestyle'.

Clothing – including socks and underwear – remains in short supply, while winter clothing is now increasingly provided by the aid agencies. Socks have been a perennial problem, with foot wrappings often substituted to save socks for best occasions. One unique contribution to fashion is the still commonly seen Vinalon – a synthetic textile manufactured from limestone exclusively in North Korea – which, though hard to dye and with a tendency to shrinkage after washing, is made into the North Korean version of the utilitarian Mao-style grey suit worn by many men (though the new uniform of white shirt and black tie is becoming increasingly popular). Despite the efforts of the Textile Industry Management Bureau, Vinalon has never been an export success; neither has the North's other textile development, Tetron. In highly stratified North Korea, clothes represent status. Possession of an overcoat or leather shoes, for example, indicates rank.

One daily ritual of all North Koreans is making sure they have their Kim Il-sung badge attached to their lapel – one of the few social delineators in the DPRK. The ubiquitous badges both denote social status and are a fashion item. Schoolchildren and teenagers use the badges to perk up their school uniforms. Increasingly Kim Il-sung badges have been replaced by the newer Kim Jong-il badges. The former have been in circulation since the late 1960s when the Mansudae Art Studio started producing them for party cadres. They slowly became a status symbol indicating rank, as well as testifying to the growing personality cult around Kim. Now the badges are worn universally and desirable ones can change hands on the black market for several hundred NKW. In a city where people rarely carry a significant amount of cash and don't wear jewellery, and where credit cards are unheard of, Kim badges are one of the most prized targets of Pyongyang's pickpockets.

What badge you wear depends on who you are. Fashions and campaigns change but, for instance, students at Kim Il-sung University wear Kim Il-sung badges; non-party, non-student young people usually wear youth vanguard badges; while the general public usually sport general badges. Kim Jong-il and combination badges portraying both the Dear Leader and the Great Leader are also increasingly seen. Badges are supplied free of charge, but losing one can be a problem as people have to explain what happened to it and prove they had no politically malicious intent before being given another.

Breakfast usually involves corn or maize porridge, possibly a boiled egg and sour yoghurt, with perhaps powdered milk for children. After breakfast it is time for work. North Korea has a large working population: approximately 52.4 per cent of the total in 2000. Many workers travel by bicycle, though these are prized possessions; most walk. Despite being a cheap form of transport, bicycles are not an overwhelming presence on the streets as they are in Chinese cities. Only about 50 per cent of households have bicycles, though demand is high. For cycle-less Pyongyang residents the alternative is the cheap, though overcrowded, public transport system. However, trolley buses and subway train services suffer from power shortages. For those outside the capital the major alternative is walking.

Those who have a bicycle usually own a 'Sea Gull' unless they are privileged and own an imported second-hand Japanese bicycle. Even a Sea Gull costs several months' wages and requires saving. Cheaper brands are available, such as the Songchonggang. Very recently more Japanese-made bicycles have been spotted. Pyongyang residents do have standards, and anyone arriving on a gleaming Sea Gull to pick up their girlfriend on a date will be considered a relatively good prospect. The other way round doesn't work: women riding bicycles are still often looked down on. In 1999 DPRK TV denounced 'bicycle-riding women in trousers' as a practice running counter to good morals and manners.

Pyongyang's street scene remains constant though the remaining fruit trees blossom in the short-lived spring to add some colour. While street hoardings and advertising are non-existent, propaganda posters are common, as are loudspeaker systems along major streets and within housing complexes, as well as roving trucks with loudspeakers broadcasting political news, slogans and music. Fads in slogans come and go – 'Long Live the Revolutionary Sovereignty of Labourers and Farmers Led by Kim Jong-il' and 'Everybody Must Take Part in Consolidating Revolutionary Sovereignty' are two traditional slogans that have endured. In the current political climate slogans praising the military and denouncing the US are in vogue. On an election day there is more activity, with youth-guard singing teams and brass bands, as well as performances of a 'socialist dance' which resembles a polka. On election day voting is compulsory; hence the near 100 per cent voting and approval rates. Kim Jong-il's reelection with 100 per cent support in September 2003 reportedly saw scenes of dancing housewives and loyal soldiers 'wildly clapping their hands and shouting hurrays' while 'women in colorful dress and children wearing red scarves sang songs and danced on streets decorated with flags and flowers'.[4] In fact there were some absences, but the authorities put this down to people being overseas, sick or out fishing.

Looking for the Rush Hour

Pyongyang has traffic and some people do drive to work but congestion is hardly a major problem. Despite the relative lack of cars, police enforce traffic regulations strictly and issue tickets. Fines can be equivalent to two weeks' salary. Most cars belong to state organisations, though are often used as if they were privately owned. All vehicles entering Pyongyang must be clean; owners of dirty cars may be fined. Trucks are banned from the city centre during the day; night passes are required between the hours of 22.00 and 05.00. Those travelling out of Pyongyang require a travel certificate. There are few driving regulations; however, on hills ascending vehicles have the right of way, and trucks cannot pass passenger cars under any circumstances. Drunk driving is punished with hard labour. A striking peculiarity for some years was that North Korea was unique in having four-colour traffic lights (the fourth for turning right). However, most traffic control is now peformed by female traffic directors (reportedly handpicked by Kim Jong-il for their beauty), as the lights are switched off to save electricity. The odd oxcart can still be seen trundling around Pyongyang's suburbs.

Cars in the North are estimated to number only around 260,000 (compared to over 12 million cars in the South). Most are under the control of the Party, executive committees, the State Security Agency, the Ministry of Public Security or the Ministry of People's Armed Forces. Traffic fines rarely apply to cars – invariably older model Mercedes, Volvos or Soviet-era Volgas and ZILs[5] – owned by these organisations. Smoking while driving is banned on the grounds that a smoking driver cannot smell a problem with the car – a sign that reliability is questionable in North Korean vehicles. (Many drivers keep a bottle of alcohol and some cigarettes for emergency bribes.) Petrol and diesel rationing is in force and many petrol stations remain closed due to the fuel shortages. Fuel is bought with coupons to ration supply, though much of what is available is of low octane.

People going outside of Pyongyang usually travel by train, and require a travel certificate, ID card and must purchase a ticket in advance. Express trains, known as first-class trains, serve the provinces and major cities. Away from the main lines, poorly maintained track has increased journey times considerably, with the 120-mile trip between Pyongyang and Kaesong taking up to six hours. Shortages of serviceable rolling stock and lack of fuel have meant that trains are generally dilapidated and invariably crowded, with the exception of key express services. Recent defectors have reported that it has become possible to move about with fewer restrictions if drivers are bribed, though checkpoints remain on roads out of Pyongyang.

Shopping

Shopping is an as-and-when activity in Pyongyang. If a shop has stock, then returning later is not an option as it will be sold out. The recent opening up of more farmers' markets has provided a source of food and other goods. A new market in Pyongyang's Tong-il Street that opened in 2003 quickly became a popular destination.

Newspapers occasionally advertise various goods such as wool jumpers, oilstove wicks or baskets, and occasionally consignments of various products appear including mirrors, tools, rubber bands or Taekwondo uniforms, as well as other everyday items, referred to as '8–3 products' in North Korea. Higher-ranked citizens can enter the few department stores meant for foreigners, tourists and senior cadres. Since the mid-1980s a wider sector of society has been able to shop at these establishments, though often foreign currency is required. These stores usually have supplies of rationed goods such as clothing, sports goods, cigarettes, beer, cutlery and plates, though people generally consider them expensive.

According to defectors, North Koreans want the 'five chests and seven appliances'. 'Five chests' are a quilt chest, wardrobe, bookshelf, cupboard and shoe closet, while the 'seven appliances' comprise a television, refrigerator, washing machine, electric fan, sewing machine, tape recorder and camera. Most ordinary people only have a couple of appliances, usually a television and a sewing machine, though cadres usually manage to accumulate a larger range of electrical appliances. School notebooks and textbooks are always in short supply. Possession of a range of appliances and a number of warm blankets is often an indication that a relative has worked abroad in Russia's far east in logging camps or construction projects, or in other locations, such as Libya, where workers can earn up to US$100 a month, or that the family has access to the black market or receives remittance money from relatives in Japan.

Food shopping is equally problematic. Staples such as soy sauce, soybean paste, salt and oil, as well as toothpaste, soap, underwear and shoes, sell out fast. The range of food items available is highly restricted. White cabbage, cucumber and tomato are the most common; meat is rare, and eggs increasingly so – these are often distributed by NGOs. When available from butchers, meat is invariably sold by weight and is reportedly usually tough and sinewy. It is impossible to request individual cuts – it is widely believed that the best go straight to the party hierarchy. The quality of the meat is such that most people mince it to make it more digestible. Fish is available, though is rarely fresh and stocks are often pre-packed. Fruit is largely confined to apples and pears. The main staple of the North Korean diet is rice, though bread is sometimes available, accompanied by a form of butter that is often stale and rancid. Corn, maize and mushrooms also appear sometimes.

In the late 1980s more goods were appearing in department stores, which attracted record numbers of visitors, who went largely to window-shop and criticise the high prices. Though more products appeared, the vast majority of new goods were beyond most people's disposable income. They had largely disappeared from the shelves by the early 1990s.

Work and School

For a high percentage of North Koreans the working day starts around 7.30 with a daily thirty-minute reading session and often exercises before work itself begins. The reading session includes receiving instructions and studying the daily editorial in the party papers. This is followed by the allocation of directives on daily tasks and official announcements. Work starts at 8.00 a.m. Pyongyang is the centre of the country's white-collar workforce, though a Pyongyang office would appear remarkably sparse to most outsiders. DPRK banks, industrial enterprises and businesses operate almost wholly without computers, photocopiers and modern office technology. Payrolls, inventories and accounting are invariably done by hand.

At midday factories, offices and workplaces break for lunch for an hour. Many workers bring a box lunch, or, if they live close by, go home to eat. Many larger workplaces have a canteen serving cheap lunches, such as corn soup, corn cake and porridge. The policy of eating largely in work canteens, combined with the lack of food shops and restaurants, means that Pyongyang remains strangely empty during the working day with none of the busy lunchtime periods seen in other cities around the world.

Work finishes at 5.00 p.m., but not social commitments. Most people are required to remain in the office or factory for the daily 'Community Session' and 'Learning Session'. At the Community Sessions there is a discussion of the results of the day's work, an evaluation of progress and an anticipation of the next day's tasks. The Learning Session is more overtly political and can include a 'Political Ideology Learning Session' to outline and disseminate Party policy. Self-criticism is still popular, as is mutual criticism in so-called 'colleague criticising sessions'. Criticisms can range from consistently being late for work to wasting national resources. All criticism is based on the 'Ten Principles for Firmly Establishing the Party's Unique Thought System'. Solidarity, Learning and Community Sessions are held by the Agricultural

Working People's Union, the Women's Union and the Children's League. In December longer meetings are held to take stock of the year. As well as these formal political sessions, occasional 'spontaneous demonstrations' or marches often require attendance.

North Korean defectors report that although political sessions remain a major part of life, their strictness and enforcement have lessened somewhat since the economic situation deteriorated sharply in the 1990s. Non-attendance rates have grown among non-party members, who face less censure for failing to appear. Many believe that the Party accepts that people's spare time is now mostly absorbed in trying to find food and queuing. Illness is also a growing reason for non-attendance, as rates of tuberculosis, hepatitis and other diseases associated with the food shortages have grown.

For children the school day starts with morning exercises to a medley of populist songs before finishing with a session of marching on the spot and saluting the image of Kim Jong-il. The education system provides one year of preschool, four of primary school and six of senior middle school. The curriculum is based around Kim Il-sung's 1977 Thesis on Socialist Education, emphasising the political role of education in developing revolutionary spirit. All children study Kim Il-sung's life closely. However, politics overlays everything: learning to read means learning to read about Kim Il-sung; music class involves singing patriotic songs. Rote learning and memorising political tracts is integral and can bring good marks, which help in getting into university – although social rank is a more reliable determinant of college admission. The children of KWP cadres get priority admission to university. Kim Il-sung University specialises in training KWP cadres and describes itself as the 'supreme seat of Juche science', offering courses in economics, history, philosophy, mathematics and biology among other disciplines. Around 14–16 per cent of children go on to some sort of further education. Invariably after graduation the state decides where graduates will work.

Most people have returned home before 8.00 p.m. and are in bed by 10.00. The scarcity of cars, the early nights, the almost total absence of entertainment places, combined with the electricity shortages, mean that by midnight Pyongyang is effectively a ghost city until 6.00 the next morning.

Love, Marriage and Fun

Returning from work in winter most people first take off their street clothes and don layers of underwear and shirts to retain body heat. Pyongyang's apartment buildings don't retain heat well and are generally draughty, forcing residents to cover the windows with plastic sheeting in an attempt to retain some warmth if they are staying in for the evening. Organised activities and a social life are alternatives, though they are strictly controlled.

Football is popular, as is athletics and boxing. New sports are gaining popularity, perhaps due to Kim Jong-il's rumoured liking for American sports on satellite television. Baseball is back in vogue, and basketball too has become popular since the mid-1990s, with a men's and women's league supported by Kim Jong-il as part of his 'height-increase campaign'. A song entitled 'Basketball is Exciting' became popular, as did the Pyongyang Beer Factory Basketball Team, comprising only housewives.[6]

Social communication is problematic. Most telephone calls are made through operators – an important job. This is a prime occupation for women (all of them are women), and a way to gain access to rumour and information before other, ordinary, workers. Personal telephone ownership remains low, although the Korea Posts and Telecommunications Ministry has a goal to install a phone in almost all households within five years. At present phones are only installed for high-ranking cadres and senior enterprise officials, and are thus technically official rather than private. To boost phone installations requires increasing the number of automatic switchboards, which will make monitoring calls more difficult. In the meantime those who need to make a call can go to a telephone bureau or post office, or, if they can, use the telephone at work. Pyongyang has few public phone boxes. Making a call from Pyongyang to the provinces is reportedly likened to speaking over a 'walkie-talkie'. Calling overseas is even more problematic, and in any case few destinations are available to most people. Being kind and flattering towards the operator can smooth the process a little. A call to relatives in California or Seoul is impossible. Local calls are expensive, to discourage abuse of the system. It is possible to submit a written application for a home telephone, containing your workplace details, position, the reason for wanting a phone installed and indicating who will pay the bills. One way round this process, though it is risky, is to buy a mobile phone smuggled in from China and connected to a Chinese network. This development has caused alarm in Pyongyang, as with such phones people can make unmonitored international calls.[7]

Many other low-cost activities in Pyongyang are impossible for most people. Despite some new churches built to give the appearance of religious freedom, worship is strongly discouraged, and is punished as 'superstition', along with fortune-telling.[8] Pets are rare and the authorities have banned dogs in the home to keep Pyongyang clean, though senior cadres have dogs. Dogs are allowed in the countryside, and some people make extra money raising pups for sale. Cats are more common, though again usually kept only by senior cadres. Pet ownership is susceptible to changes in the political wind

– Kim Il-sung was apparently fond of dogs, and those he personally raised were moved to Pyongyang Zoo when he died. When the 13th World Youth and Student Festival was held in Pyongyang in 1989, Kim Jong-il publicly permitted dogs, as well as allowing women to wear necklaces to demonstrate how liberated North Korea was.

There is some street crime in Pyongyang, though incidence is low by the standards of most capital cities. While the authorities regularly clear the city of 'undesirables' – which means that illegal salesmen, beggars and prostitutes are not seen – Pyongyang has a criminal underclass that dates back to the days of the Japanese occupation. Among the Koreans resident in Japan who moved to North Korea in the 1960s were a number who belonged to yakuza or other gang organisations, and these gangs have existed ever since. The authorities have cracked down on them, with most criminal families reportedly having been 'relocated' to mining areas in Hamgyong province and other provincial cities. Hamhung, the capital of South Hamgyong province, is the crime capital of the DPRK, where gangs apparently mug people regularly and where several deaths have been reported. Travelling to Hamhung is reportedly a risky enterprise, as the gangs watch the train station for likely victims. Bag-snatching and violence are not unknown. However, muggers are generally low-ranking criminals; black-market currency exchange and smuggling are more profitable criminal enterprises. The rural farmers' markets have been reported to be centres of operation for a new breed of extortionists who force the stallholders to pay protection money. In Pyongyang crime is seen largely as a provincial problem, even though it is now affecting tourists and visiting cadres.[9] These provincial criminals, who have exploited their distance from the more closely monitored Pyongyang, have a saying that 'The law is far away, but the fist is close by.' With persistent food shortages the activities of smugglers have grown: gangs are known to exist in Sunchon, Chongjin, Nampo, Sinuiju and Anju, as well as Hamhung. Occasionally it is reported in the official media that a convicted murderer or thief has been executed.

Criminals, who have a better income than many ordinary people, aren't that worried about politics. They have better clothes, often Japanese-made jeans, with the universal symbol of outsider status and rebellion: long hair. However, while they may smoke foreign cigarettes like Marlboro and Mild Seven they still wear the obligatory party badge – though for criminals the most expensive Kim Il-sung badges are often sported as symbols of wealth and power. The gangs have names such as the Weasel Family, the Owl Family and the Cockroach Family. While they live in the provincial cities, they are increasingly travelling to Pyongyang to target the subway and bus stations. With the economic situation worsening, these gangs are reportedly growing in number, forging links with Japanese–Korean smuggling rings and Chinese black marketeers along the border areas.

Smoking is a cheap pleasure. As shortages have grown many people roll their own. Smoking can be a small act of resistance, as the best rolling paper is considered to be the Workers' Party daily paper. Loose tobacco can be bought from old ladies in the street who claim that their tobacco is stronger than the next seller's. Some rural residents grow their own form of weed tobacco for personal use or sale for extra income. Party leaders get a ration of 30–35 packs of filter cigarettes a month. Foreign cigarettes have to be paid for on the black market or at a foreign goods store. The Rothmans brand has traditionally always been a bit more expensive on account of the popular rumour that, before he publicly gave up in 1999, Kim Jong-il smoked Rothmans; a copycat version of the brand is produced called Paektusan.

At night women largely continue working in the home. Despite being politically 'communist', North Korea is also hyper-traditionalist. Consequently, women in North Korea are workers, mothers and housewives. After a day's work they still have to take care of the children, the housekeeping, the cooking and other chores. Outside Pyongyang, gardening and tending domesticated animals are women's responsibilities. Though women are officially described as the 'wheels propping up the revolution', they usually have lower-grade jobs, with limited promotion prospects. On the other hand, women do a high percentage of the farming in North Korea. Single women above a certain age are rare and spinsterhood is frowned upon. The responsibility for making a match and supplying a dowry rests with the bride's family. Usually weddings are arranged and politically motivated, though in Pyongyang marrying for love is a growing concept and matchmaking is less common now. Pyongyang natives can be snobbish – marrying a 'country man' is considered impossible for most women, as this would involve them leaving Pyongyang for the countryside as well as being a step down socially. The Party has run a campaign to encourage more love matches, and has officially censured party cadres for criticising those seen dating in broad daylight. However, in some areas of the countryside where the preference for male heirs means that men still outnumber women, there has been a long-term shortage of available brides and arranged marriages remain common.

For a married woman, divorce is a major decision. Divorced women are discriminated against and courts usually favour husbands. Remarrying is problematic, though women in the higher echelons of society are increasingly divorcing and living independently. For most women spinsterhood is unthinkable. Nevertheless, North Korea did run a number of Spinster Boarding Houses for such women, who were unable to get a housing allocation as singles.

Women accounted for three-quarters of all North Koreans who fled to China in 1997 and declared themselves. They are still leaving and still make up the majority of refugees. Many end up in China's sex industry but still declare they do not want to return to the DPRK. Bride snatching is a growing problem, with organised gangs kidnapping women as wives for Chinese farmers; the women are reportedly traded for US$275–300.

Another area of personal life resistant to government control is sex. The government wants continued high rates of childbirth but, with the present economic situation, food shortages and overcrowding, the number of women wanting abortions is growing.[10] Condoms are hard to obtain (although black-market Chinese ones are available) and other contraceptive devices are rare, often substandard and ineffective, such as the locally produced 'loop'. Contraception is seen as the woman's problem. However, they receive only minimal sex education, called 'sanitation common sense', at school. The most effective form of contraception is the fact that many people live with their in-laws and the walls are paper-thin. Abortion is discouraged. However, illegal abortions are available, along with a host of 'farmer's wife' cures for unwanted babies. Women nevertheless remain politically active – 40 per cent of Party members are female (compared to 12–15 per cent of the total population) – and they do become doctors, professors and cultural workers.

Formal entertainment options are limited in Pyongyang. The city has around eight cinemas, although many shut early due to lack of power. The Yongdae Funfair also remains closed, as do many theatres. The cinemas all screen locally produced movies, the quality of which is improving as film studios, like the Chosun Artist Film Studio, increasingly try to compete with the South Korean film industry. Domestic movies are shown on television and some larger enterprises screen films for their staff. In more cosmopolitan Pyongyang it is occasionally possible to see a foreign film, invariably an old Chinese or Soviet movie; tickets tend to be distributed to key workers and are not widely available. Normal fare at the cinema is heavily propagandist, such as *Sea of Blood, The Fate of a Self-Defence Corps Man, Flames Spreading over the Land, The County Party Chief Secretary, Notes of a Woman Soldier* or the recent hit *Beyond Joy and Sorrow*, which included the first on-screen kiss seen in North Korea. The usual plots describe South Korean or American perfidy and end with a victory for the KPA.

For refreshment, a growing number of street kiosks sell locally produced drinks such as cola from the Kyongryon Aeguk Carbonated Drink Factory, and Calpis, a sweet milky water, as well as Taedonggang Beer. Fruit flavoured drinks are popular, including pear, as is *omija*, a milky drink made from beans; in addition, locally produced and somewhat flavourless ice cream is available.

Holidays are rare events despite a long list of anniversaries and commemorative occasions. Four or five days' annual holiday appears to be the norm around Kim Jong-il's birthday, the anniversary of the DPRK's founding and Kim Il-sung's birthday, when children are given biscuits and confectionery by their parents. One year many residents of Pyongyang were given winter blankets and clocks, while soldiers were given wristwatches.[11] On these rare occasions Pyongyang's parks and riverside are crowded and street kiosks do good business. Sunday is 'walking day', with public transport schedules curtailed. Live music is often performed by Art Propaganda Troupes singing popular ballads (*pansori*) espousing revolutionary sentiments. In 2003 the government launched a walking campaign, urging students to walk to school and people to walk to work for 'health reasons'.

Home entertainment consists largely of television, which has become more widespread though it remains strictly censored by the powerful Propaganda and Agitation Department of the KWP, which issues monthly guidelines for media coverage. Citizens are required to report purchases of radios and television sets. The authorities control the channels, and have been known to make inspections to ensure sets are not tuned to anything other than official programming. With the exception of certain social categories, possession of foreign books, magazines and newspapers is forbidden. However, some news of the outside world does filter through in a limited way via illegal short-wave radios. The popularity of South Korean songs and older Japanese ballads, dismissed by the leadership as 'crooning tunes', and their distribution in recent years is one sign of this.

There are other signs that DPRK society may be changing. The Japanese newspaper *Sankei Shimbun* obtained a leaked sixteen-page KWP document[12] circulated to senior officials in 2002, which contained ideas to be drawn upon in public speeches. The document stated: 'Women are putting foreign-style make-up on their lips and eyelashes, and wearing "short skirts".' It added that divorce was increasing and that fortune-tellers were becoming popular. The document also revealed that those with radios were increasingly listening to broadcasts from South Korea and other neighbouring countries, while young people were memorising South Korean songs and bragging about it.

Sometimes change can be small but revealing. In 2003 Kim Jong-il officially raised the bun allocation to North Korean universities so they could introduce hamburgers onto the menu.[13] Additionally, in October 2003 Pyongyang's first chewing gum factory opened. Gum had been seen as a useless capitalist product but the new factory claims to be producing 1,200 tonnes annually. Other signs of change include reports that a GSM mobile phone network will operate nationwide by 2007 and now covers Pyongyang, Nampo and Rason Free Port. The DPRK claims that 2,000 mobile handsets were sold in Pyongyang between November 2002 and August 2003.[14] And after several years of virtually no Internet access (despite some connections via Shenyang in China) KCNA announced the launch of a new Internet service in 2003 to be operated by the North's International Communications Centre and supposedly guaranteeing secure email for no charge.[15]

While changes such as lipstick, chewing gum and pop songs may be signs of a more divergent society, the fact that use of mobile phones and the Internet is restricted solely to the elite, rather than demonstrating structural reform, merely reflects how an entrenched elite can sidestep the collapsing state infrastructure as their needs become acute.

Living in the Land of Perfect Bliss

Clearly North Korea is a country of hardship and deprivation for most citizens. In October 1962 at the First Session of the Third Supreme People's Assembly Kim Il-sung stated that 'everyone will live in tile-roof houses with a hot bowl of rice and beef soup every meal after the completion of the following seven-year development plan.' Kim also stated in 1979 that the DPRK was a country where 'our people are enjoying a happy life to the full, without any worries about food, clothing, medical treatment and education. There is no better "paradise" and no better "land of perfect bliss" than our country.' Clearly these aims have not been realised. Pyongyang remains orderly, as indeed does most of North Korea compared to the crowds that throng China's increasingly market-driven and sophisticated streets. Generally quiet and clean streets are the hallmark of Pyongyang in contrast to Beijing, Shanghai and Guangzhou, which, while remaining nominally communist, have massive commercial centres with a plethora of small businesses and bustle. The contrast with Seoul is even starker. Democracy is, of course, completely absent; though people may know their own local representative, they rarely have much idea who governs even neighbouring districts.

Health care in Pyongyang is a growing problem, with a lack of antibiotics and basic medical equipment such as stethoscopes and bandages. Although hospitals are reported to be generally clean, supplies are low and equipment is antiquated. Traditional and herbal medicine has become increasingly relied upon, with modern pharmaceuticals scarce. Power shortages affect hospitals too: the Red Cross estimates that only 50 per cent of essential operations are carried out during the winter months, when temperatures in Pyongyang can reach −20°C. Most hospitals are overburdened. Sariwon Hospital near Pyongyang, for example, which covers a catchment area of 1.6 million people, is reportedly short on energy, medicines and ambulances.[16] In the 1990s, as well as famine, North Korea saw tuberculosis and cholera epidemics, along with rising rates of hepatitis, malaria, dysentery and general problems associated with vitamin deficiency and what aid agencies call 'severe nutritional distress'. Poor drinking water means the level of waterborne diseases is high, as is that of respiratory and other diseases associated with pollution.

That personal hygiene is also becoming an increasing problem due to the shortages is apparent in the government's 'Cabinet Decision No. 20', calling for the eradication of fleas and lice, apparently a major problem. Also, hygiene is affected by water shortages and the closure of many public baths, which were once common across the country. According to the UN Office for the Coordination of Humanitarian Affairs (OCHA) in North Korea, only 25–50 per cent of the population can rely on piped water, with many pipes broken or contaminated and community wells not functioning.

For those who do question the system in North Korea the penalties are stiff. For North Koreans political re-education camps are a real threat, along with torture and forced labour. Estimates of the number of such camps range from ten to fifteen large-scale institutions holding in total between 200,000 and 250,000 prisoners. In 2002 the *Far Eastern Economic Review*[17] revealed satellite photos of one camp, the No. 22 Camp near Hoeryong, it claimed held 50,000 people, whose crimes ranged from not showing appropriate respect for the leadership to flaws in their family history. Pyongyang does not admit the camps' existence. The vast majority of prisoners are held on politically related charges, and engage in agricultural, factory or mining work. Execution has reportedly increased in the 1990s, partly as a response to the breakdown in social order during the famine. According to the US Bureau of Democracy, Human Rights, and Labor, 'an estimated 200,000 political prisoners [are] detained in the DPRK'. The report notes that

> Female prisoners underwent forced abortion, and in other cases babies reportedly were killed upon birth. Execution is a common punishment for petty crimes. Capital punishment and confiscation of assets are used for a wide variety of 'crimes against the revolution', including defection, attempted defection, slander of the Party or State, and listening to foreign broadcasts.[18]

The overall effect of the repressive atmosphere is that it is impossible to be silent in the DPRK and not show overt support for the regime, nor is it possible to create an obviously private realm – all life must be lived within the socialist Juche consensus. The punishment system is further strengthened by the policy of *yongoje*, or family purging, whereby any individual crime leads to discrimination against the family and close colleagues of the transgressor. This reinforces an atmosphere of self-censorship. Defector testimonies indicate that the degree of self-censorship exceeds that in other states, such as China, where people still have two modes of expression: one for talking with family and friends and another for talking with anyone else – the so-called standard political talk, or what the Chinese call *biaozhun shuyu.*

The Sinologist Perry Link has described the situation in China as 'an essentially psychological control system that relies primarily on self-censorship' whereby the authorities can carry out arrests and punish but intimidation and control rely largely on the fear of this happening. While this system may be starting to break up in China, it remains rigid and enforced in North Korea, with informing on family and colleagues still encouraged.[19] It is also more extensive, often stretching back several generations in a family to search for 'unreliable traits', with everyone divided into one of three groups: the core class, the wavering class and the hostile class. Within each class are numerous subclasses. Moving class definition is difficult while rations, education, work, health care, housing and access to goods all depend to a greater or lesser extent on your designated class.[20]

Society is constantly monitored by the Ministry of People's Security (MPS) and the State Security Department (SSD), both the effective prae-torian guard of the regime, and at a local neighbourhood level by *bans* or street committees. The result is that most people keep their head down and look after themselves and their family as far as possible. This is the pattern of life for most people despite periodic reports of attacks on cadres, the plotting of army coups and the stoning of elite cars in Pyongyang; others simply decide to leave and walk to China.

No government in the world is currently more reclusive, more suspicious, more averse to international contact than Pyongyang. Overarching the entire social system is the national political concept of Juche. To understand fully the theoretical rationale of the North's economy, its emphasis on military tradition and its relationship to the wider world, it is crucial to appreciate Juche's theoretical underpinnings, application and effect on the country's development.

2

The Juche State:
Political Theory in North Korea

The Politics of Self-Reliance

The guiding philosophy of the DPRK is Juche (self-reliance) theory, known as Kim Il-sung's 'original, brilliant and revolutionary contribution to national and international thought'. Juche permeates every aspect of North Korean life and is officially the ruling creed of the country, forming its national mythology and reinforced by a dynastic succession from father (Kim Il-sung) to son (Kim Jong-il). An understanding of the basic tenets and theories of Juche, as well as its theoretical antecedents, is necessary to understand the DPRK today, its world-view and its economic system. Though originally seen as a progression of Marxism, currently Marxism–Leninism as a political philosophy is barely mentioned. Instead all ideological efforts are focused on promoting Juche, which is deemed to be uniquely Korean and yet adaptable to all developing countries. Consequently Juche has taken on a universalist tendency that echoes elements of the pre-modern Chinese concept of the Great Systemic Whole (*da yitong*).[1] Juche elevates Kim Il-sung, Kim Jong-il, the guerrilla fighters of the liberation struggle, the military and the KWP to the highest positions in society.

Juche is seen as the way the nation will move to *chaju* (independence) in a process that is equatable with the Marxist–Leninist notion of socialism as a transitional stage to communism. This process towards independence involves the development of an independent national economy through *charip*, or self-sustainability, and a nation capable of its own self-defence through *chawi* (literally 'self-defence'). *Chaju* also dictates that each nation has equal rights in relation to other nations, and this has clearly affected the DPRK's international negotiating style, while the need for *chawi* has led to the development of the military-first policy, which gives primacy to the military over the proletariat. Simply put, the military-first line guarantees political independence, which in turn guarantees the conditions for economic self-reliance.

The notion of *chawi*, which is crucial to Juche, positions the military as the primary social grouping above the working class and the peasantry. This adaptation of classical Marxism–Leninism reflects the origins of Kim Il-sung in the guerrilla struggle and the prevailing situation on the Korean peninsula since 1953. In Juche thinking, as long as imperialist countries continue to exist so the military-first line will remain paramount.

Upon the foundation of the DPRK, the guiding political philosophy was largely Marxist–Leninist and built mainly upon the Stalinist system developed in the USSR. In the 1950s, as the strains in Sino–Soviet relations intensified, Kim Il-sung's thinking became less overtly pro-Soviet and leant more towards Maoist thinking. However, since 1955 and then more overtly since the mid-1970s, the idea of Juche (Kim Il-sungism) was developed as an indigenous revolutionary doctrine fusing the basic tenets of Marxism–Leninism with elements of Maoism and Confucianism and traditional Korean social systems. Juche, then, was partly an adaptation of the 'universal truth' of Marxism–Leninism to a Korea that for centuries had looked ostensibly to China as its major frame of reference, but it also represented Kim Il-sung's bid to be recognised as a prominent – indeed, the pre-eminent – ideological figure in the communist world.

Juche was also an assertion of the DPRK's independence from the USSR after Pyongyang's refusal to join Comecon[2] and submit to Soviet-dictated prices for goods and materials. In the 1970s, when Comecon proposed greater integration among its members, the DPRK moved further away from the organisation, seeing the so-called Comprehensive Programme for integration as another means for the USSR to dominate the socialist world further. Juche managed to anger both Beijing and Moscow, bringing upon Pyongyang both the wrath of the Red Guards, who described Kim Il-sung as a 'fat revisionist', and of Moscow, who feared Pyongyang was setting itself up as an alternative theoretical centre. In part both analyses were correct. Juche did revise some aspects of traditional Soviet Marxism–Leninism and reject many ideological elements of Maoist theory and practice. However, the coding of relations was ultimately less about theoretical wrangling over interpretations of Marx and Engels and more to do with unease at the DPRK's growing dependence on the USSR for technology, energy and raw materials.

Juche was offered, often fanatically, as a 'third way' for underdeveloped non-aligned nations; though ultimately the requirement to submit to the Kim Il-sung personality cult, and to North Korean arrogance, alienated most nations, such as those in the Bandung Group, with the exception of some followers such as Mengistu in Ethiopia. Even the Albanians described North Korea as 'an unbelievably closed society', while the Chinese foreign minister, Qian Qichen, visiting Pyongyang in 1991, described the country as 'left deserted by some invisible plague'.[3] Though Juche quickly came to dominate totally the life, politics, economics and foreign relations of North Korea, it has been an exclusively North Korean philosophy, with no international following worth mentioning.

A Creative Application of Marxism–Leninism

Juche is described by Pyongyang as superior to all other systems of human thought, including Marxism, though it admits that its basis is Marxist–Leninist theory and that it was, at first, officially a 'creative application of Marxism–Leninism',[4] even though now all references to Marx, Engels and Lenin have been expunged from official Juche texts. The purer form of Juche was formally introduced in the 1970s; to have attempted to supplant traditional Marxism–Leninism earlier could have led to a break with the USSR, upon which North Korea was still dependent for aid. With the thaw in the Cold War, post-Stalin, there was a greater flexibility to develop national socialist ideologies without suffering isolation within the socialist bloc, as had happened to Yugoslavia and Albania. Kim's experiences with Marxism–Leninism as a guerrilla in the USSR and Manchuria led him to consider the theory especially suited to the DPRK, as it sought to explain colonialism and imperialism scientifically, provided an apparent blueprint for economic growth similar to that achieved by Stalin in the USSR, and offered the opportunity to resolve the inequities of capitalism.

Essentially, Juche is based upon the classic works of Marxism from Marx and Engels through Lenin, Stalin and Mao. It is dogmatic in essence and operates on the basis that the facts should fit the theory. As well as antagonising the USSR by claiming to be an advanced form of Marxism–Leninism, Juche also annoyed other Marxists with its insistence that the capitalist stage could be skipped completely and an economy and society could move directly from feudalism to socialism. This revision flew in the face of the accepted experience of the USSR with the New Economic Policy (NEP) of Lenin[5] and the emerging Marxist theories of Western Europe.

The Marxism–Leninism that Kim understood and introduced to North Korea was a theory developed for Western developed industrial nations and not East Asian semi-feudal agrarian nations (which included most of Russia in 1917). Despite the Japanese occupation, industry was not widespread on the Korean peninsula; so there was consequently little proletarian class struggle despite an ongoing independence struggle and an antagonism towards landowners typical of a largely agrarian country. As in the USSR, the creation of collective farms was part of an attempt to proletarianise the peasantry. Kim also adopted Stalin's tactic of purging. Although Kim accepted the correctness of Leninism in the USSR, he saw Juche as a specific interpretation applied to Korean reality, a country that had not experienced a capitalist period but that had existed as a colony and then been destroyed in the Korean War. The forces of production were not developed in the way they had been in the Russia of 1917, and consequently differentiations between workers and peasants would remain after the socialist phase of the revolution.

This was a major revision of Marx's belief that there were essentially no differences between industrial and agricultural workers and that society was simply divided between the capitalist and the proletarian classes. Kim saw no need for a capitalist phase to emerge in Korea. The coming to power of the working class in the form of the KWP was sufficient to bypass the capitalist period and move straight to socialism with no class struggle between workers and capitalists in North Korean society. Class struggle under Juche involved merely turning the peasants into workers (proletarianisation) through collective farms, using new industrial techniques (however ultimately unsuitable) for agricultural production, with the use of central planning and heavy use of inputs such as chemicals, fertilisers and pesticides.

Further, Kim's creative application of Marxism–Leninism stated that the dictatorship of the proletariat would remain in any one country while there were still capitalist nations existing. Kim never saw these theoretical changes to Marxism–Leninism as revisionism (still a highly charged term in the communist world when Juche was first developed) but rather as an adaptation to North Korean reality. For their part the Soviet Marxists saw Kim's reinterpretation of Marxism–Leninism as outright heresy.

While Kim revised many Marxist concepts, he was happy with many of Lenin's ideas, including the difference between bourgeois and Soviet republics, democratic centralism and the dictatorship of the proletariat, as well as the Soviet leader's notion of War Communism, which seemed ideally suited to the situation in North Korea. War Communism dictated the subordination of all industry and economic distribution to the state, complete nationalisation, and the introduction of a rationing system to handle supply and distribution; pricing and money circulation were also dealt with at the highest state level. Later, as the USSR's collapse neared and relations with Gorbachev soured, and while China embarked on its reform programme under Deng Xiaoping, Pyongyang moved away from the two major Marxist powers by speaking of 'Socialism in Our Own Style' – an echo of Lenin's 'Socialism in One Country'. Originally Juche was seen as an internationalist and not a nationalist philosophy, in much the same way as Stalinists argued that 'Socialism in One Country' was internationalist – as proletarian internationalism started by building the revolution at home. In other words, the primary internationalist objective was first to create the communist system in Korea.

With Juche's adaptation of War Communism and Socialism in One Country, Pyongyang actually used core Marxist–Leninist concepts to distance and differentiate itself from what, by the 1980s, was a failing system in the USSR and an increasingly market-oriented system in China. With practical knowledge of the Marxist–Leninist classics almost obliterated by the 1980s and the Juche notion of the leader as the final embodiment and arbiter, there existed neither the intellectual understanding nor the political space to challenge this development, which was in any case supported by the elite as it justified regime survival during a time of domestic economic collapse and the falling away of former allies and supporters.

Where Kim deviated from orthodox Marxist thinking most dramatically was in his approach to free will. Marx believed that people were shaped by the prevailing social and economic conditions and that this social structure gave rise to the 'historical contradictions' that propelled society inevitably towards socialism. Kim, perhaps harking back to his family's Christian roots, emphasised in Juche that free will motivated people's actions independent of the economic imperative. This strand of Juche has been further stressed during Kim Jong-il's reign. The notion of free will in Party-dominated North Korea is almost as absurd as the notion of self-reliance. However, it is politically useful in establishing that philosophically North Koreans, through Juche, are capable of independence as contrasted to the servility of the South Koreans dominated by American imperialism. Within this theoretical paradigm the DPRK appears the free country and the ROK the enslaved chattel of the US.

Marxism–Leninism's contribution to Juche was almost totally derived from Stalinism and largely in the realm of economics and party structure. However, Kim's embracing of Marxist–Leninist theory gave him a theoretical system that allowed him to be simultaneously anti-colonial (and later anti-Western) and apparently progressive. The 1998 revised version of the DPRK's constitution, which reinforced Juche, stated unequivocally in Article 20 that, 'the means of production are owned solely by the State and co-operative organisations'.[6] As we will see, the notion of creating a truly egalitarian society was soon abandoned in favour of a revolutionary reworking of traditional

Korean social structures, while political rejuvenation through Maoist-style constant revolution was rejected as unsuitable for DPRK society. Though equality may have been only a political phrase in the USSR the rhetoric of equality remained. By contrast in North Korea Juche has served to create and reinforce a hierarchical system.

Selective Borrowings from Maoism

Juche borrows heavily from Maoism, though without overtly admitting it, in regard to the need for a mass line and the requirement for the national leader to be a guider of policy at all levels. Hence the frequent and heavily reported visits to factories and the countryside by Kim Jong-il and other leading cadres to provide 'on-the-spot' guidance.

In the DPRK's early days when Juche was first being developed, Kim, though tied to the USSR through patronage, military relations, fraternal aid and increasingly debt, was covertly admiring of Mao's China, even adopting the Chinese slogan *zili gensheng* (self-resuscitation) as a motto; he felt a greater affinity with this new, seemingly more independent, nation. When Kim first announced Juche in 1955 it went hand in hand with an obviously Maoist-inspired political rectification campaign and a call for newspapers to stop copying headlines directly from *Pravda*.

In part this reflected the historic relationship between Korea and China, but it was also an expression of the growing inequality in the trading relationship with the USSR compared to the apparently greater equity in relations with China – the so-called closeness of 'lips and teeth'. Maoism appeared attractive to Kim, a Korean with a long history of relations with China, which he felt he knew well. Like Maoism, Juche strongly emphasises formal political study, criticism and self-criticism as well as the role of public campaigns in mobilising the population for specific goals. The theory also involves a standing people's army, prepared to fight a people's war; this 'military-first' policy pervades national life. The concept of a people's war is taken almost verbatim from Mao (who took it from Sun Tzu's *The Art of War*). Juche also, at least until the end of the 1970s, encouraged the practice of senior officials engaging in mandatory periods of manual labour to get closer to the people, in a similar vein to the Maoist concept of 'going down' among the masses. In the 1960s and 1970s most officials, except the highest ranking, were expected to contribute one day a week to manual labour on a construction site or similar. As the separation of the elite from the mass of ordinary people has grown and privilege has become an ingrained part of the system, so this practice has died out.

However, Juche theory differs from Maoism in accentuating the three-class alliance of workers, peasants and intellectuals, whereas Mao downplayed the role of intellectuals and emphasised that of peasants and workers (in the early years of the revolution the Korean equivalent of *kulaks* were purged). This was largely a reaction to the fact that after the DPRK's establishment a large number of intellectuals left for South Korea and Japan, creating a brain drain and skills shortage that has never truly been filled since.

For many centuries the outside world that the Koreans knew and experienced was dominated by China, and naturally the country has imitated much in the Chinese experience. Under Juche the role of the supreme leader is enshrined: Kim Il-sung is held up as the 'iron-willed, ever-victorious commander' and the 'respected and beloved Great Leader', along with many other honorific titles. Talk of Kim Il-sung as father of the national family of North Koreans would pave the way for the announcement that his son, Kim Jong-il, would succeed him in 1980. In addition North Korea's Chollima mass mobilisation movements were clearly modelled on China's Great Leap Forward.

Nevertheless, North Korea, with its persistent cult of personality and rigid Juche theory, has not imitated Chinese communism in its ability to reconsider decisions and adapt to circumstances. While Maoism was able to adopt and then jettison campaigns, such as the backyard furnaces of the Great Leap period that ultimately were found to be a waste of resources despite their function as an agent of social cohesion, Juche has been marked by an attitude of perseverance in the face of disaster. Juche has demanded that North Korea stick with centralised economic planning and collective farming despite their being a major element in the state's failure and a cause of the famine. While Mao was able to undertake periodic revitalisations through his notion of permanent or constant revolution, North Korea has not embraced this aspect of Maoism. Even more unimaginable are the sort of repudiations of one-time theoretical absolutes that Deng was able to make after Mao died.

Although the personality cult of Kim Il-sung resembles those of Stalin and Mao, there is a subtle difference. While Mao and Stalin were venerated as revolutionary leaders and national protectors, in the DPRK the underlying theme of Juche is that Kim Il-sung bequeathed a nation to the people and that they should repay his benevolence with unquestioning loyalty and devotion. This is essentially a revolutionary spin on the Confucian value of repaying debts of gratitude.

The Maoist element of Juche is essentially derived from the period in Mao's theoretical development between the 1949 liberation and shortly before the Cultural Revolution of 1966–75. In 1958 Mao launched the Great Leap

Forward, which followed the 'Let a Hundred Flowers Bloom' campaign. These two related movements were most instructive to Kim. Both Hundred Flowers and the Great Leap were not the result of collective decision-making within the Communist Party's higher ranks but simply products of Mao's own visionary inspirations. The basic principle of the Great Leap was to make up for China's industrial and economic underdevelopment by utilising the nation's vast human resources. The people were to be galvanised by one unanimous and massive burst of revolutionary enthusiasm that would make up for the technical deficit in society. Essentially the Great Leap was an attempt to overcome a lack of material resources with spiritual resources while also reinforcing Mao's rule.

Mao is not openly studied in the DPRK now and any Chinese influence in Juche is vehemently denied by Pyongyang as part of its campaign to be seen as independent. Additionally, the early calls from the 1950s by Kim to replicate Maoist-style rectification campaigns have been officially expunged from the historical records in the DPRK. Indeed, the erasing of the debt to Maoism is so all-encompassing that many people even in the upper echelons of North Korean society have little knowledge of Mao and Maoist theory. While pictures of Marx and Engels remain in Pyongyang, Mao's image is conspicuously absent. This downplaying of Mao reflects the fact that while in the DPRK's formative years Kim was able to employ some Maoist guerrilla tactics, he traced his rise to power most directly to Soviet patronage. During this period of ascendancy and after the formation of the DPRK, Kim had struggled against several opposing groups within the Korean communist movement. Primary among his competitors were the group of communists who had worked and fought most closely with the Chinese communists. The so-called Yan'an Group[7] were more closely aligned to Maoism than to Stalinism. Kim eventually distanced himself from them and obliterated their influence from the official histories of the DPRK, having first purged them in a series of show trials.

Kim, like Mao, was forced to absorb experts and intellectuals into the cause of rebuilding the country. Just as overseas Chinese returned to the 'new' China, moved by patriotism, likewise ethnic Koreans returned to the North, largely from Japan, imbued with an idea that a new sort of post-colonial socialist Korea was being built. However, both Mao and Kim distrusted these elites in the same way Stalin had distrusted anyone who had spent time abroad. In the DPRK these returnees were eventually to be largely persecuted after a brief period of being fêted by the regime, just as those with overseas connections were largely penalised during the Cultural Revolution in China and suffered under Stalin's purges in the USSR. Mao distrusted these returnees and tested them in the Hundred Flowers campaign. Kim observed that Hundred Flowers essentially ended the notion that there was room for a multiplicity of ideas in China, and around this time undertook the repression of Japanese Koreans in the DPRK.

Juche, with its adoption of elements of Maoism, is a theory essentially developed by communists raised and schooled in guerrilla struggle. The Great Leap encapsulated three main ideas of Mao – all rooted in the guerrilla struggle and the Long March period in Yan'an. Mao concluded, first, that China's strength lay in her poverty; second, that village and peasant wisdom were important (or at least by acknowledging this importance Mao raised his status and legitimacy among the peasantry); and third that revolutionary fervour alone could effectively overcome material obstacles and transform matter. This third idea of Mao's from the Great Leap was the one that Kim adopted most radically. Naturally this idea finds a receptive audience among guerrilla leaders who have known long years of struggle, been seemingly outnumbered, outgunned and in desperate situations, when often ideology is all that has kept their forces moving, fighting and eventually winning. Hence Juche, like the Great Leap and the Cultural Revolution, elevated the 'red', or the revolutionary, over the expert. This form of 'red thinking' to overcome natural disadvantages or shortages became a hallmark of Juche.

Confucianism:
Tapping into Traditional Thinking

In addition to elements of Marxism–Leninism and Maoism, Juche has also incorporated Confucius. As a belief system Confucianism has long provided a set of core values, a social homogeneity and a national spirit that interconnect with a wider Asian spirit that can be traced back to a series of ancient books known collectively as the Chinese, or Confucian, classics. The influence of Confucianism has been widely seen across the Korean peninsula. Though Confucius is not cited by name in North Korea, his influence dates back to pre-division Korea and the traditions of centralised authority that characterised the ancient Korean dynasties, with family achievement extended to produce a sense of national self-confidence. Article 63 of the Constitution states that 'Citizens' rights and duties are governed by the principle of collectivism, where the individual exists for the collective, and the collective for the individual.'

Confucianism in North Korea is used as a binding force for society, to provide a sense of belonging and a way to achieve a broad consensus that social order (under the Party) is in everyone's best interest. Confucian ideas are integrated throughout Juche theory in order to emphasise a cultural propensity to put the group first and individual needs second. Through this Confucian influence the command economy concept is reinforced. Long-term growth is strengthened as a guiding principle of the economy and people are asked to defer personal gratification in the present to build for the future.

From the beginning it was argued that personal gratification would have to take second place. North Korea was devastated during the Korean War. After the establishment of the DPRK the primary aim was to get industry moving again, restart the agricultural cycle and get roofs over people's heads. Initially most available funds were diverted to building factories and developing heavy industry as well as infrastructure; little was left for housing. Thus, by direct experience the population became used to seeking personal gratification second.

Confucianism is used in the DPRK to reinforce the idea of a homogenous society – one, of course, run by the KWP in the person of, first, Kim Il-sung and now Kim Jong-il. The use of Confucius allows the regime to reinforce a sense of national belonging that combined, within Juche and Marxist–Leninist notions of class struggle as well as Maoist notions of national restoration, maintains social order. To employ a term much used by Western liberal economists, this combination of class, nation and society is used to reinforce the notion of individuals as 'stakeholders' in the country, in its system and in its perseverance in the face of enemies and those that the government determines seek to destroy the nation. In this sense an attack on the nation, either verbal or physical (in the sense of military action, embargo or a boycott), becomes an attack on the whole society. This interlinked thinking goes a long way to explain why the government in Pyongyang finds it so seemingly easy to mobilise millions of people in 'spontaneous' demonstrations and to declare any proposed boycott against the DPRK as an act of war. While there is clearly an element of coercion, this alone cannot explain the genuine outrage felt by many citizens.

Confucian concepts also suit Juche theory inasmuch as they involve feelings of group loyalty and encourage a group orientation within the society. Employees become members of their workplace group even if they are outside the leadership cadres or the Party. Like other highly Confucian societies – such as Japan, China or South Korea – inter-factory sports and social activities assume great importance. In the case of North Korea, though, the Confucian influence on society works both ways. The government in effect promises full employment and a basic standard of living; the worker promises loyalty.

North Korean workers have been provided with lifetime employment and a salary, or access to goods through the government rationing system.

In return most workers feel extremely loyal to their workplaces, though perhaps not motivated enough to care about their enterprises' profitability. In this sense mass reductions in the workforce at many state-owned enterprises (SOEs) are impossible as the Confucian two-way trust would be broken.

Although Juche clearly utilises elements of Confucian thought that are deeply ingrained in the Korean psyche, the government does not encourage the study of Confucius or his writings or commentaries. The Confucian ethic, such as it is interpreted by Pyongyang, is wrapped up in Kim Il-sung-ist thought. Of course political corruption or coercion are perversions of Confucianism, which argues that leaders should rule by example and that moral principles flow downhill like water. North Korea's leaders realise that leading by example is central to Confucianism, but they tolerate no dissent. The influence of Confucianism is felt in the regular 'on the-spot' guidance sessions, a concept that feeds into the general perpetuation of the personality cult. Both Confucius and Mencius argued that, though one should never disobey parents, the state is changeable and can be overthrown if it abuses its power. Although the Confucian element of Juche is rarely admitted openly, Kim Il-sung did once berate a foreign communist for criticising the cult of personality around the Great Leader by telling him 'we live by Confucian culture'.[8] Juche reinforces the concept of a supreme leader using Confucian and Korean traditional thought to establish the notion of a leader that embodies unity of thought and action. To question Juche is to question the leader, while loyalty will lead to success.

Underpinnings of Korean Nationalism and Traditionalism

The final element of Juche is a hyper-traditionalist reading of traditional Korean culture. Clearly much of this is also derived directly from the general Confucian ethic but also includes methods by which to regulate society's behaviour – including marriage, child-rearing, family (known as the 'cell', or basic unit of society) and the position of women. Traditional thinking – essentially a blend of Confucianism and specific Korean attributes – is evident in all aspects of life, not least the fact that Kim Jong-il waited fully three years before officially adopting his dead father's title of General Secretary of the KWP. Kim Jong-il was merely following the Confucian-inspired tradition of showing prolonged respect. Indeed Kim Jong-il never took the highest post his father held, that of President, instead declaring the deceased Kim Il-sung 'President for Eternity'. This was certainly an act of extreme

Confucian filial piety (*hyo*), raising Kim Il-sung to the level of Confucius and showing, once again, that North Korean society was not going to follow the Maoist tradition of constant reinvention and revolution. Rather, Juche presents a substantially more fixed, rigid and hierarchical ethic, based to a significant degree on the ancient systems of organisation and caste structure in Korea but in communist clothing and with new gods.

Kim Il-sung's communism was always closely intertwined with Korean nationalism and traditionalism (what Juche calls 'social patriotism'), despite the fact that to all intents and purposes history begins in 1945 in the DPRK, with everything before being characterised in terms of Japanese imperialism. In the early days of Juche's propagation as the national creed Kim did acknowledge that its roots lay not entirely with him but with early-twentieth-century Korean academics. The majority of Kim's early life had been centred around the struggle against Japanese colonialism and reclamation of the Korean homeland. Therefore the struggle for Kim, though communist in theory, was nationalist in essence. Indeed, for all the individuals that were influential in the early DPRK, 'nationalism' and 'communism' were virtually interchangeable terms. The Korean communist movement, due to its fractured and disparate nature, was not that ideologically advanced or dominated by ideologues. It had relatively simple aims: the expulsion of the Japanese and the establishment of a communist-led government. Little thought was given to the society that was to be created after liberation.

The Korean communist movement's disparate nature meant that by 1945 they had never had a Party Congress. Essentially the movement was a collection of groupings: the Soviet Koreans, Kim's Red Army-linked guerrillas, the Yan'an Group and a small collection of communists who had remained in Korea itself. This was an almost unique situation in world communism: a leadership that had no traditions, no clearly defined theoretical strands, no newspapers or journals, not even a party HQ. The Party and the movement were in need of a unifying force and a theory to bring the movement together at a grassroots level in some form of political coherence. Further, Kim used calls for greater study of Korean revolutionary history, including events such as the June Tenth Movement and the Kwangju student incident, to marginalize further, and then completely eradicate, the role of the Soviet Koreans and the Yan'an Group.

The traditionalist element of Juche reinforces the idea that although humankind is the master of its destiny, it is guided by a collective consciousness embodied in a great leader. The notion that Korea is somehow a chosen land and a starting point for world civilisation, though not emphasised, is still implicit in the tone of Juche's theoretical pronouncements that equate the nation as being defined essentially by the party-state. Additionally, traditional elements of Korean thought and behaviour continue to extend themselves through national life. Despite having absorbed influences from both China and Japan, Korea clearly still has a strong domestic traditional culture embodied in numerous forms, from female Korean national dress (the *hanbok*, a flowing gown), which is still a common sight on the streets of Pyongyang; to sitting, sleeping and eating on the floor; to national cuisine. However, these traditional elements of society are not practised universally.

Korean traditionalism allows the DPRK to accept inequality and a very apparent and enforced social hierarchy, despite the rhetoric of equality. This is largely a harking back to Korean tradition, most notably the Yi dynasty.[9] The use of the socially equalising term 'comrade', used in most socialist countries, has been largely jettisoned in favour of two more traditional Korean terms: *damu*, which is used for subordinates and between people of equal rank; and *dongshi*, which is used for superiors. Therefore Juche enshrines a token conception of socialist equality while reinforcing one of the most hierarchical and elitist states in the world. There are three main political categories in North Korea to divide society: the 'core class' of loyal cadres; the 'wavering class', which is suspect and monitored; and the 'hostile class', which is politically unreliable. A further fifty-one subcategories exist, based on family background and performance in political tests, among other criteria. The 1980 Party Congress identified 25 per cent of the population as being core class, 50 per cent as wavering and 25 per cent as hostile.[10]

While traditional Korean philosophy has been used to reinforce theoretically the divisions in society and maintain the ruling elite, Kim defended the inclusion of traditional Korean thought within Juche as a way of dealing with what he saw as many negative aspects in the recent Korean past that had given undue credit to things non-Korean. In this sense it was another way of asserting the DPRK's independence from the socialist great powers and the recent history of subjugation on the peninsula. However, Kim was always aware that giving too much influence to Korean tradition could threaten the Party's ruling position, and so tempered the elements of traditional thought Juche promoted with a warning against 'restorationism', by which he meant a return to any uncritical acceptance of traditional thinking. Most telling is the fact that Korean history is more often alluded to than actually studied. More than half of the thirty-three volumes of official Korean history that are taught in the DPRK and start at the creation of a separate and identifiable Korean nation deal with events after the formation of the DPRK. This rewriting of traditional history has continued, with landmark events in Korean history such as the June Tenth incident and the March First Movement being largely omitted from syllabuses in favour of the supposed founding of Kim's guerrillas in 1932 and the foundation of the DPRK.

The Architects of Juche

Officially Juche theory is a creation of Kim Il-sung and his son Kim Jong-il. They are the fathers of Juche, according to the official record, which states that Juche is a 'gift bestowed by the Kims to North Korea's people'. Clearly, others were involved in Juche's creation. Nevertheless, North Korea tries to demonstrate that Kim developed the ideas of Juche as early as the 1930s; some official documents have been rewritten to reflect this. One biographer of Kim claims that completely invented speeches, such as one supposedly made to a regional youth group in June 1930 (when Kim was 18) calling for Juche-like principles, have been inserted into the official DPRK historical record. At least fifteen such fictitious speeches, all published in the 1970s and claimed to have been given in the 1930s, have been uncovered.[11] Conversely, statements made by Kim in the 1940s about learning from Stalin and the Soviet experience have been deleted from the records.

Kim first mentioned Juche around 1955 to declare North Korea's independence from the USSR. Along with the announcement of Juche went both purges against the Soviet Korean group and what Kim saw as the slavish copying of Soviet techniques in education and propaganda.

Despite the announcement in 1955 little more was officially said on the subject until 1963. Between 1955 and 1963 Kim undertook a form of shuttle diplomacy between Moscow and Beijing trying to gain a stronger position during the Sino–Soviet split. Self-reliance was clearly not something Kim wished to raise as he tried to play Moscow and Beijing off against each other. In 1961 at the Fourth Party Congress, both Chinese and Soviet Communist Party delegates attended and Juche was not mentioned. The tipping point for Kim was 1963 when the USSR temporarily ceased economic and military aid, effectively deciding Kim's position in the Sino–Soviet dispute for him. From then on Juche was constantly referred to in the DPRK. The end of military assistance from Moscow at a time when Beijing was unable to offer similar levels of aid led to the formal introduction of the *chawi* concept and the military-first line. In 1965 Kim effectively declared full independence from Moscow and Beijing as well as restating Juche, during a speech in Indonesia. Kim used Juche as a third way between the USSR and China, engendering Soviet rage at causing splits in the Third World, and also leading to Chinese anger, expressed in the attacks on Kim during the Cultural Revolution.

Today Kim Il-sung is officially seen as the sole architect of Juche, with some advances having been made by Kim Jong-il. However, another figure credited with being a major influence on the theoretical foundations of Juche is former DPRK Secretary for International Affairs Hwang Jang-yop.[12] His role is known because he has admitted it: Hwang defected to South Korea in 1997, at the age of 74 – the first high-level official to seek asylum in the South. His name has since been expunged from all DPRK official histories. He had earlier voiced concerns over the succession of Kim Jong-il to the leadership. It is known that he was a member of the Central Committee of the KWP, chairman of the Foreign Relations Committee of the Supreme People's Assembly and a confidant and private tutor to Kim Jong-il, and responsible for his education at Kim Il-sung University. This position did not prevent Hwang's influence from waning considerably after Kim Il-sung's death. Since defecting Hwang has described the DPRK as a 'feudal state' (though 'semi-feudal' might be a more accurate description).

Born in 1922, Hwang studied philosophy at Moscow University and was then a philosophy professor at Kim Il-sung University. He began cooperating with Kim Il-sung on developing a more rigorous theoretical basis for Juche. He was de facto the chief political philosopher of Juche and guided many of its principles of foreign engagement. Hwang was also for many years the official most closely identified with Juche overseas, travelling extensively and covertly visiting Japan and meeting American and South Korean scholars. It was also reportedly Hwang who informed America and South Korea that Pyongyang actually desired that US troops remain in the ROK in the 1970s.

Hwang eventually came to believe that Juche was being undermined by elements in the military hierarchy who had become more important due to having formed an alliance to secure Kim Jong-il's accession to power. The emergence of the 'Red Banner' philosophy in 1996 that re-emphasised revolutionary and pro-military ideals alarmed Hwang. He eventually declared, after being effectively expelled from the KWP's inner core, that the new Kim Jong-il leadership had nothing in common with the genuine Juche ideal, declaring: 'Anyone who conducts demonstrations or shows the slightest anti-government color, anyone who says or does anything humiliating the authority of the leader, is secretly shot.... From the intellectuals' standpoint it can be said without hesitation that the entire country is a large prison.'[13]

The other major architect of Juche has been Kim Jong-il. As the son and heir of Juche's creator it is essentially Kim's specialist subject. He has no background in the military, as a political theorist or as an economist, yet as the interpreter of Juche he accrues power. As Kim Jong-il came to assume greater power throughout the 1970s and 1980s and was designated the official heir (in 1980), so his input into Juche's development grew. Kim Jong-il is thought to have been largely responsible for ending official references to Marxism–Leninism. He also emphasised that the best way to implement Juche was for people to follow more closely the guidance of the Party and the leader. Hence Kim took a philosophy and turned it increasingly into 'an article of faith rather than a guide to practice', in the words of Oh and Hassig.[14]

However, at the same time Kim Jong-il was introducing subtle changes to Juche that sought to make it appear more responsive as the DPRK's economic situation was deteriorating. These sought to emphasise the 'mass line' and disperse any pent-up grievance, across the entire population and not just the elite and leadership, regarding the economic situation. At the same time it called for greater elevation of the leader's position and more trust in the Party. Juche interpreters had by this point effectively decided that Kim Il-sung was divine and that there was no form of social contract between ruler and ruled, thereby transcending even the Confucian relationship enshrined in the Mandate of Heaven, which required loyalty but only to a virtuous ruler. The element that permitted a ruler to be overthrown if he abused the Mandate was effectively removed. Justifying regime change on Confucian grounds was out.

'Original, Brilliant and Revolutionary'?

Juche ideology is currently undergoing another revision in the face of the ongoing economic crisis and, consequently, 'the changing needs of the ruling elite'.[15] There has been talk of 'new thinking', which translates into the stimulation of local economic initiatives. However, a contradiction exists between this new localised thinking and the requirement for central planning enshrined in Juche theory, as well as the need for the Party and its leadership to provide guidance. Furthermore, the dominance for generations of the command economy has severely reduced the ability of most North Koreans to take individual initiatives, act in an entrepreneurial manner or even make suggestions. Throughout the period of the economic reforms in 2002 and 2003 social discipline through adherence to Juche has been re-emphasised, as the regime feared social unrest. Currently there is an increase in reference to Songun politics, the more army-centred policy of Kim Jong-il that elevates the military-first policy.

Essentially Juche has been a theoretical tool that has allowed North Korea to maintain an independent and isolated stance, first from the warring ideologies of Stalinism and Maoism during the Sino–Soviet split, then to distance the DPRK from the collapsing USSR and now from the US. Additionally, as Juche became officially distanced from Marxism–Leninism in the 1980s so it became seen as completely distinct from its Marxist heritage, which ultimately proved useful in explaining why the USSR and the countries of

Eastern Europe collapsed: Juche theory was officially a major advance on Marxism–Leninism; those countries that stuck with Marx and Lenin alone and failed to embrace Juche were eventually destroyed by capitalist imperialism. There was therefore no theoretical reason for maintaining that North Korea would follow this pattern.

However, ultimately the rigidity of Juche has not allowed North Korea to change course even slightly, notwithstanding the obvious failure of much of the system. To explain why Juche has not yet brought communism to North Korea the leadership has identified three political factors: lingering individualist tendencies of the masses; domestic agents spreading rumours; and imperialist agents working among the masses. The KWP's answer to all three problems is further study of Juche, greater political commitment and greater trust in the leadership and the Party. It has also had to come up with answers to increasingly tricky questions, such as the seeming wealth of the West and of South Korea. Despite the media clampdown some news does filter through. Juche's answer has been to take a basic 'looks can be deceiving' approach to life in the West and to claim that images of Western cities represent the life of the lucky few and that even they live lives of spiritual emptiness. How many people there are in North Korea who do not believe this argument, and instead can see that the sheer volume of cars and number of buildings indicate that the lucky few might not be so few, is one of the great imponderables.

Juche remains the governing creed of North Korean society and is taught to its citizens from their first day at school. Even the most advanced university courses require 20 per cent of study time to be devoted to Juche theory, while for many higher-education courses the percentage is far greater. Workplace and farm study groups are also required to study Juche and it is a constant feature in the media – Korean Central Television's founding principle is 'Continuation of the revolutionary spirit of the Great Leader Kim Il-sung, and contributing to the dissemination of the theory of self-reliance and the victory of the Juche ideology based on Juche guiding principles on reporting and broadcasting.'

The Contradictions of Self-Reliance

In light of the current economic collapse of North Korea and its growing reliance on international aid to feed its people and to power what is left of its industrial base, the notion of self-reliance appears ridiculous. It arose, however, as the guiding theory of North Korea partly to justify the existence of the regime in a Cold War world, one that also featured the schism of the

Sino–Soviet dispute, and to create a unifying theory in an organisation that was largely devoid of ideologues. It is conveniently forgotten that the practising of self-reliance and independence in a state that was largely brought into being by – and is led by a party that owes its dominant position to – Soviet and Chinese patronage is something of a contradiction in itself.

However, Juche has become, in effect, the state religion and thus major revisions are unlikely. As is shown in Part II of this book, which looks at North Korea's economy, without a fundamental reassessment of Juche significant economic change cannot occur, and therefore continued economic decline is assured. Juche has become the DPRK's straitjacket preventing the country from moving away from the rigid central command economy and military-first line. High military spending, disastrous economic policies and the freeze on political change will persist as long as Juche is the dominant theoretical force in society.

Juche was the creation of Kim Il-sung and subsequently Kim Jong-il. While Kim Jong-il is held to be the only true interpreter of the faith, everyone else in North Korean society is vulnerable to the charge of revisionism or deviation. It follows, then, that we must examine the DPRK's leadership in more detail.

3

The Revolutionary Dynasty:
Leadership in North Korea

Birth of a Personality Cult

Overwhelming personality cults surround the only two leaders the DPRK has ever known. It is necessary to examine these cults, and to understand the roles of Kim Il-sung and his son and heir Kim Jong-il, the Great Leader and the Dear Leader, as they are central to the North's interpretation of it's own political history, economic development and social system. The two men have also often defined the way the DPRK has interacted with the outside world and, in return, the way the international community has responded to the North. On occasion opponents of the DPRK have levelled insults at its leaders, thereby making the antagonism between the North and its opponents very personal. For example, in 2002 at a meeting with Republican senators, President Bush compared Kim Jong-il to a 'pygmy' and described him as 'a spoiled child at a dinner table', while US Deputy Secretary of State Richard Armitage has described him as 'unstable'.[1] Notwithstanding the extreme personality cults applied to these men, it is crucial to understand who they are, and why the party–state apparatus they have built has remained in power.

Although other major personality cults in the socialist world have been similar to that in North Korea, arguably none has been so total and complete as in the DPRK, or has had such blatant theoretical justifications as those enshrined in Juche. During the lifetimes of leaders such as Mao and Stalin, details of their youth, early careers and everyday lives remained shrouded in mystery; North Korea, however, has taken its elevation of the individual to another level. The cult of Stalin largely expunged his time at the Tiflis Theological Seminary and exaggerated his role in pre-1917 Russian revolutionary politics, as well as the closeness of his relationship to Lenin. Kim Jong-il, for his part, was apparently born under a rainbow on a sacred mountain. While the cult around Mao has overly proletarianised his origins and forgotten such inglorious times as his stint as an assistant librarian in Beijing, the Chinese leader's role in the guerrilla struggle was real and crucial. Kim Il-sung's guerrilla experiences, on the other hand, have been greatly exaggerated and mythologised.

The personality cult around Kim Il-sung was constructed for a number of reasons, most of which also account for its extension to Kim Jong-il. Among these was the need for Kim and his political faction, one of several in the Korean communist movement, to secure undisputed control of the DPRK. Kim was heavily exposed to the Soviet system as a young man, through his time as a guerrilla fighter, to the creation of the DPRK. For North Korea to survive following the mass destruction of the Korean War, and in the environment of the Cold War, Kim sought to cement the new revolutionary government in a mixture of Soviet Marxism–Leninism, Maoism, Korean nationalism and Confucianism, as we have seen. From a Confucian standpoint the concept of an all-powerful leader with the Mandate of Heaven was a legitimate one. The transfer of power to the son guaranteed the perpetuation of the cult around Kim Il-sung as well as ensuring maintenance of the regime by creating a similar cult around Kim Jong-il.

The first decades of the existence of the DPRK saw Kim Il-sung's personality cult grow, first to secure power, then to motivate the population, and finally to dominate the country. The cult was then effectively enshrined in Juche. It is now such an integral part of North Korean society that to end the cult in the way that Khrushchev was able to with Stalin, or Deng with Mao, would be impossible; it would be likely to hasten the total collapse of the country, endangering the regime's survival. While Khrushchev was able to de-Stalinize and China was able to reconsider decisions made by Mao (the famous 70 per cent good, 30 per cent bad formulation) the scale and nature of the personality cult in North Korea, with its rigid Juche thinking, makes such a course impossible.

In many ways North Korea – its creation, development, politics, economic form, negotiating style, foreign relations and society – is the creation of Kim Il-sung and Kim Jong-il. The personality cults of Lenin, Stalin and Mao were so powerful that they spread beyond national borders, inspiring millions around the world; lesser global cults have built up around other socialist leaders such as Castro and Che Guevara. Other cults in the socialist world remained largely national affairs – the 'little Stalins' of Tito, Ceausescu and Hoxha. However, the cult of the Kims has been almost entirely a national affair with few outside adherents, notwithstanding the fact that it is stronger by far than any previous such cult.

The cult status of Kim Il-sung was established while he was still a guerrilla leader in the war against the Japanese colonial power, and during the Korean War when he commanded the Northern forces. Clearly Kim had learnt from his time in Stalin's Soviet Union (as well as from autocratic traditions in ancient China and Korea) how the power of the cult of personality could be used to mobilise the masses. Indeed the Soviets played their part in engendering the legends and myths around Kim when they selected him as their preferred leader in North Korea.

Whereas Stalin stood second in line to the legacy of Lenin, Mao, as he had no predecessor as leader of the Chinese Revolution, was perhaps the better role model for the DPRK. As with Mao, Kim's apparent military triumph and role as a galvaniser of the anti-colonial struggle and guerrilla leader helped generate the mythic legacy of a 'people's war' led by one overwhelmingly heroic figurehead.

Kim's cult became so complete that all other revolutionary and guerrilla leaders, the other men and women who formed the KWP, have been sidelined by official North Korean history at best or were purged and executed at worst. Kim remains the only figure in the official histories of the DPRK before liberation and during the guerrilla struggle. There are no official equivalents of Trotsky or Bukharin in the Soviet Union or Lin Biao in China, no former close colleagues who were set up to show the hidden reactionary forces that the leader defeated. Most other cults have needed these figures – Hoxha had his Mehmet Shehu for instance.[2] Equally, no one has survived in the official North Korean records to be passed down in history as a loyal ally of Kim's – as Zhou Enlai was to Mao, or Che was to Fidel. There are not even any minor figures like those that managed to survive the purges in the USSR such as Lazar Kaganovich.[3] No one has been allowed to take credit for anything in North Korea expect Kim Il-sung. When opponents of, or challengers to, Kim were purged in the early year of the DPRK, in contrast with the USSR and most East European countries, their show trials were not public – which might have had a negative effect on South Korean public opinion. Thus the cult of personality is total around Kim Il-sung; even Kim Jong-il is still forced to live within it.

From Guerrilla Leader to Leader of a Nation

Kim Il-sung's entire history is purposefully shrouded in mystery. Born Kim Song-ju[4] in the village of Magyongdae near Pyongyang, on 15 April 1912 (the day the *Titanic* sank), he was the oldest of three sons and though officially it is claimed he hailed from peasant origins, it appears that in reality Kim's father, Kim Hyong-jip (1894–1926), was never actually a farmer but a practitioner of traditional Korean herbal medicine. The official history also makes no mention of the fact that Kim's parents were practising Christians and that his mother was the daughter of a leading local Presbyterian family, whose father was an elder of the church and had attended a missionary school while his uncle was a preacher. However, it does note the more unverifiable facts that Kim warmed his mother's cold hands with his own breath after she returned from work each day in the winter, and that he gave up the pleasure of playing on a swing because it tore his trousers, which his mother then had to mend.

The family were involved in the struggle against the Japanese colonial authorities within the Korean National Association. Kim Hyong-jip was imprisoned in 1917 for a year. In 1919, following the March First Movement,[5] the family moved to Manchuria, where Kim's father would run a herbal pharmacy; Kim Il-sung was just 7. Kim would live in Manchuria, except for two years of schooling in Pyongyang, until he was nearly 30. His father died in 1926 and his mother in 1932.

Kim entered the Chinese school system, which he left after barely three years of middle school, being expelled for revolutionary activities, to become involved in communist organisation full time at the age of 14 in Jilin.[6] By 1932 he had passed through the communist youth movement and was a guerrilla in Japanese-occupied Manchuria, having already spent two years in prison for anti-Japanese activities when he was just 17. His notion of the Korea he was fighting to liberate was hazy, and in this sense, as was the case with Mao and his guerrillas on the Long March, the formation of Kim's revolutionary ideals also involved the formation and inculcation of a concept of Korea. However, life in Manchuria was not necessarily a handicap for Kim. The extent of the Japanese colonial repression in Korea meant that most effective resistance was based outside the country. The guerrillas Kim eventually led never numbered more than a couple of hundred. They received some support from the USSR and China but in the main were isolated; this informed Kim's later ideology of self-sufficiency, which became enshrined in Juche. His military record may not have been outstanding, notwithstanding the later rewriting of his heroic struggles, but the Japanese did notice him and put a price on his head.

In 1941 Kim and part of the Chinese army were forced to retreat across the Manchurian border and join Soviet Red Army training camps, where they spent the rest of the war. Kim married a fellow guerrilla, Kim Jong-suk, had two sons (the elder being Kim Jong-il) and during this time was selected by the Soviets to be the future leader of an independent North Korea.

The protracted amount of time the guerrillas, whether working closely with the Soviets or the Chinese, spent outside Korea naturally impacted on their conceptions of the homeland they were fighting for. China offered additional support after Zhou Enlai's 1941 statement that 'We should sympathise with independence–liberation movements of other nation states and assist anti-Japanese movements in Korea or Taiwan.'[7] The guerrillas naturally adopted theoretical tendencies from their hosts and supporters. This all played a part in Kim's view of the world post-1945 when he eventually took power in North Korea. Also Kim (like Mao) was a product exclusively of Asia; he had not, like many other socialist leaders in the region, such as Deng Xiaoping and Ho Chi Minh, spent time abroad. Nevertheless, his time in Manchuria and with the Soviet Red Army did leave him fluent in Chinese and Russian. Overall his education was sporadic, although in later life he was to use his knowledge of Confucianism and Marxism–Leninism to develop Juche.

Officially Kim fought guerrilla skirmishes against the Japanese, though more probably he remained largely in Siberia. Retired former Soviet army colonel Gujimin Gregory, who met Kim's guerrillas during the war, claims they spent much of their time just 'wandering about'.[8] In the Second World War Kim is thought to have attained the rank of captain, or perhaps major. Although Kim may not have been the military and guerrilla leader his cult would raise him to, he did spend a protracted period under arms, moving around waging guerrilla-style 'hit-and-run' raids. It is fair to say that Kim never lost the outlook of a guerrilla fighter and that this sensibility was reflected in both the highly regimented North Korean state that eventually emerged, a state that demanded unswerving and unquestioning loyalty from its citizens, and in the core of Juche theory and its exhortations to self-reliance and self-sufficiency. Kim's peacetime leadership style and politics were those of the demobbed guerrilla fighter. They go a long way to explaining why the Stalinist-style command economy was favoured as an economic model, with its strictures, intricate plans and inflexibility, as well as its emphasis on rapidly creating an industrialised state capable of defending itself militarily for prolonged periods.

When Kim eventually took power in the North in February 1946 it was with Soviet acquiescence, though Stalin had agreed with Roosevelt at the Yalta Conference in 1945 exactly when the USSR would enter Korea. When the Soviets presented Kim to the crowds in liberated Pyongyang as their leader, dressed in the uniform of a Soviet army captain, many reports have it that the crowd was shocked and surprised. Here was a leader, short in stature, slightly chubby and not much over 30. He looked young and fresh beside the Soviet command on the rostrum and many Koreans did not at first believe that this was their leader, who was already being mythologised in Soviet and Korean communist propaganda. The Soviet Union felt that a younger leader was needed in the North, and Kim's loyalty to the USSR and Stalin was considered to be strong. Despite some misgivings among the crowd that day in 1945, the pro-communist *Pyongyang Times* displayed none, describing Kim as 'the incomparable patriot, national hero, the ever victorious, brilliant field commander with a will of iron ... the greatest leader that our people have known for the last several thousand years ... a man equipped with exceptional powers.' The cult of personality had begun. The KWP was formed in August 1946. However, Kim was not elected leader; instead Kim Tu-bong,[9] a member of the more Chinese-leaning Yan'an Group, took charge, with Kim as one of two vice-chairmen. Yet by 1949 Kim Il-sung had manoeuvred himself into the chairmanship, a post he held until his death.

Keen to reunify the peninsula under a communist system, Kim managed eventually to gain the support of Stalin and Mao for launching the Korean War in June 1950. His forces achieved an early string of military successes but the expected rising in the South did not materialise. Kim had also reckoned without American involvement. His army was saved by the intervention of the 300,000 Chinese Volunteer Forces, who also assumed control of military tactics until the end of the war, as part of Mao's policy of extending China's foreign sphere of influence after securing power in Beijing. As soon as Chinese forces recaptured Pyongyang, Kim began a process of purging Korean military leaders. Throughout the 1950s he purged all his political opponents, while forging the myth of a great military leader who single-handedly led the defeat of US imperialism.

Consolidation and Dominance

Immediately after the cessation of hostilities in 1953 Kim showed that he had learned from the experiences of Stalin in the USSR by holding a show trial for a dozen party officials accused of aiding the Japanese and plotting to replace him as leader with Pak Ho-yong, the former leader of the communists in the South. All twelve were found guilty and executed. Two years later Pak himself was also executed following a show trial. These trials, which continued throughout the 1950s as Kim secured his position, included accusations against all those in the party who had close links to Moscow and Beijing, and even some of Kim's former guerrilla comrades. The people Kim trusted most were the members of the so-called 88th Brigade, who had spent World War II with him. Kim first reinforced the position of these ex-guerrillas at the expense of all other groups, ensuring the dominance of former Brigade members over other guerrillas. Periodic purges of high-level cadres continued up until around 1977, ensuring that Kim effectively retained the total control over the KWP he had largely secured by the 1958 Party Conference.

The reality of Kim's domination over the Party was evident at the Fourth Party Congress of the KWP in 1961, known as the 'Congress of Victors'. Kim was effectively beyond challenge; those remaining in the senior leadership of the Party were little threat to him as he consolidated his position. The guerrilla tradition was emphasised as the true and only history of the Korean revolutionary movement, with Kim as the undisputed leader with no obvious factions to oppose him. Kim was also playing off the USSR against the Chinese while trying to stay on comparatively good terms with both (Deng actually attended the 1961 Congress as head of the Chinese delegation), and around this time Kim also began to emphasise the non-aligned and independent nature of the DPRK as a way of safely treading water around the Sino–Soviet dispute while looking for new allies in the Third World. Throughout the late 1950s and 1960s Kim was at his most active politically, conducting on-the-spot guidance visits and giving long speeches to a wide variety of political organisations around the country.

The Sino–Soviet dispute was a major challenge of diplomacy for Kim, who received briefings from high-placed officials on both sides – Zhou Enlai and Deng from China and Aleksei Kosygin and Frol Kozlov from the USSR.[10] Kim travelled to both Beijing and Moscow. Privately he tended to favour the Chinese against what he saw as the blatant revisionism of Khrushchev, and his policy of peaceful coexistence with the West and de-Stalinisation. However, Kim largely kept his own counsel, never once publicly criticising Stalin during the de-Stalinisation campaign even though he attended the CPSU's Twentieth Party Congress in 1956, which launched Khrushchev's attack on Stalin, and the Twenty-first in 1959 and the Twenty-second in 1961. In 1960 Kim managed to negotiate treaties of friendship with both countries, remaining nominally neutral though precariously balanced between the two warring factions. During the 1962 Cuban missile crisis, Kim did not comment on the capitulation of the USSR; while during the 1962 Sino–Indian border war Kim supported China but stayed silent on Moscow's tacit support for Delhi. Kim's answer to questions on where he stood on the spat between Moscow and Beijing was simply to declare non-commitally that he was on the side of 'the socialist camp'. The USSR may have believed that Kim should have offered them more support given their position as his primary backers after World War II, but as one of Kim's biographers, Suh Dae-sook, has noted, 'The Soviet Union may have put Kim in power, but they were not able to remove him.'[11] Later all Kim's speeches regarding the dispute were expunged from the official records of the DPRK.

Kim maintained relations between the two factions, meeting Brezhnev in 1965 in an attempt to repair relations with the USSR, though the previous close bonds were never fully renewed, and became even more problematic during the Sino–Soviet border clashes of 1969. However, this didn't stop Brezhnev awarding Kim the Order of Lenin in 1972 on his sixtieth birthday. Kim recognised that an alliance with Moscow was necessary given the stronger ties that existed between the US and the ROK, Seoul's new rapprochement with Tokyo, and the rapid growth of the South Korean economy. This was also the time of China's Cultural Revolution when the Red Guards began openly attacking Kim, culminating in a Beijing newspaper article in 1968 entitled 'The Korean Revisionist Clique of Today'. This angered Kim, who ensured that no copies of Mao's *Little Red Book* ever circulated in North Korea. The animosity between China and the DPRK remained until the CPC's Ninth Congress in April 1969, when the Chinese moved to restore more cordial relations with Pyongyang. In 1970 Zhou Enlai visited the DPRK to repair the damage further. However, Kim's independence from the USSR was maintained throughout the late 1960s and 1970s, as was revealed when secret files in Moscow were released after the fall of the Soviet Union. For instance, Kim had never consulted with Moscow over the capture of the USS *Pueblo* spy ship in 1968 or about the secret visits by senior South Korean officials to Pyongyang in 1972.

With the introduction of a new Constitution in 1972 Kim completed his total domination of the DPRK's political life, holding all positions of power with the ability to issue edicts, grant pardons and sign treaties. He oversaw political, economic and military life, all senior appointments and all diplomacy. Kim was re-elected president at the Seventh Supreme People's Assembly (SPA) in 1982. However, he then went into a form of semi-retirement, increasingly transferring duties to Kim Jong-il. From 1982, by which time Kim was 70 and had rapidly failing eyesight, he rarely undertook on-the-spot visits anymore and largely receded from public life, with the exception of a mid-1984 train trip to Moscow to visit new CPSU General Secretary Konstantin Chernenko, soon after Brezhnev's death, further to repair Soviet–DPRK relations, followed by a tour of Eastern Europe by train, meeting leaders of the socialist bloc – all of whom would be out of power by the end of the decade. The balancing act continued with China responding to this new warmer relationship by despatching CPC general secretary Hu Yaobang to Pyongyang in May 1984. Kim's last meeting with the Soviets was with Gorbachev in 1986, shortly after the reform-minded general secretary had locked horns with Reagan over nuclear weapons at the

Reykjavik Summit. Gorbachev saw Kim as a dinosaur, though he continued to supply weapons to Pyongyang as his dispute with Reagan grew.

The Undisputed Great Leader

Ultimately Kim Il-sung surpassed both Mao and Stalin in terms of longevity of rule. He died of a heart attack in July 1994, shortly before he was due to sign the groundbreaking Agreed Framework with the Americans. He had seen six ROK presidents, nine US presidents and twenty-one Japanese prime ministers come and go. By the time of his death Kim's personality cult had arguably exceeded that of Stalin or Mao, and he had survived to be the world's longest ruling leader.

Despite the fact that he came to dominate completely the life and politics of North Korea many who met Kim described him as 'normal', at least in the early period of the DPRK, and there is little of the reporting of a sense of awe and distance that is associated with records of those who met Stalin or Mao. However, as the DPRK developed and his power became increasingly absolute so Kim retreated into reclusiveness inside massive palaces, such as the Kumsusan Palace, summer retreats in the coastal foothills near Pyongyang, and particularly his favourite villa in the Myohyang Mountains, becoming increasingly cut off from daily life. Indeed, Kim only travelled twice outside the communist world – to Algeria and to Indonesia.

As the privileged life of the Great Leader grew so the mythologising process was at work. Kim Il-sung began a routine of undertaking sealed train trips to Russia, which Kim Jong-il has continued; he established special prerogatives for himself and the leading KWP cadres, including private car lanes and escorted motorcades; and he would only meet with pre-arranged and prepared groups of citizens. Gradually he began to live the life of an emperor, with special medical institutes dedicated to his health and welfare (for example, research was undertaken into the causes of the benign tumour that Kim had on his neck from the 1970s). This status necessarily was also bestowed on most members of the immediate Kim family, including his second wife (the first died in 1949 following an ectopic pregnancy) Kim Song-ae, a typist and daughter of one of Kim's bodyguards, whom Kim married in the early 1950s though she remained out of public view for many years.

What set Kim apart from most other leaders of socialist bloc countries was his fiercely independent streak, which to a degree accounted for North Korea's perceived diplomatic arrogance and led to the creation and elevation of Juche as the dominant creed of DPRK life. He has been described as an 'Oriental Talleyrand', becoming known for making promises but then breaking them and pursuing his own line once back in Pyongyang. Kim was unable to delegate decision-making, working late at night and demanding reports from senior cadres and military leaders. This led to the institution of on-the-spot guidance visits, derived from the Maoist period, reflecting his obsession with micro-managing all aspects of DPRK life. These guidance visits often led to the countermanding of aspects of the economic plan, undermining Kim's own personally instituted industrial and agricultural system. If the advice from Kim was bad, wrong or just plain stupid, as it reportedly often was, it was still obeyed. If it wasn't obeyed, then officials could expect to undergo lengthy self-criticism sessions at best or be ousted and punished further at worst. Kim Il-sung, like Stalin and Mao, became obsessed with identifying and preventing 'deviationism' in the country.

During his lifetime Kim Il-sung presided over, first, the rapid growth and then the terminal decline of the North Korean economy. However, he died at 82 before the worst excesses of his economic policies were fully revealed in the famine. This legacy, along with his unassailable cult, he left to his son.

The Successor and Dear Leader

The extent of Kim Il-sung's role as a guerrilla leader, communist theoretician and military campaigner may be questionable but he was at least directly involved in the liberation struggle and then the Korean War. Kim Jong-il was obviously not, being at most only 12 years old at the end of the war. Consequently a personality cult was built into the younger Kim's official biography from the start to make up for this deficiency. The official story is that Kim Il-sung and his wife were leading the resistance to the Japanese from the border area between Korea and Manchuria in China when Kim Jong-il was born. Kim was reputedly born on Mount Paekdu, traditionally Korea's highest and most sacred mountain, where legend has it that Korea came into existence 5,000 years ago. As he came into the world a new star appeared in the sky, a double rainbow appeared, an iceberg on a nearby lake cracked, strange lights filled the sky and a swallow passed by overhead to pass on to the world the news of his birth. Kim, as a baby, remained by his father's side until the Japanese were defeated, expelled from Korea and Pyongyang was liberated.

The truth of Kim Jong-il's birth is thought to be somewhat different. He was probably born on 16 February 1942 after Kim Il-sung had fled across Manchuria to the Soviet border pursued by the Japanese. He was born in Vyatskoye on the Amur river near Khabarovsk in Siberia. Kim spent part of his youth in Vyatskoye, where he was known by the Russian name Yula.

This story is more plausible, because it is known that Kim Il-sung's guerrillas did join with the Soviet Red Army's 88th Special Rifle Brigade based in Vyatskoye. A second son, Kim Pyong-il, later to drown in a Pyongyang swimming pool in 1947, was born in Vyatskoye in 1944. Accounts of life with the Korean rebels and the Russian soldiers in Vyatskoye vary but many indicate that though Kim was in command of several hundred men, he didn't enter Korea during the war and remained largely secure in Soviet territory. It is also suggested that rather than personally liberating Pyongyang, Kim waited until this was done by the Red Army and was then flown into the city via Vladivostok and then taken by boat to Korea in time to take the podium at the victory celebrations in October 1945. Kim Jong-il himself does not subscribe to this version of events. Reportedly, when Kim passed close to Vyatskoye on his train trip across Russia in 2001, the Russians somewhat mischievously suggested he may like to visit his home town; Kim declined the offer. During the Korean War Kim Jong-il was sent to Manchuria for his safety and returned to Pyongyang in 1953.

In North Korea the official version of Kim Jong-il's birth still holds. Though it sounds bizarre to outsiders, it makes more sense in the context of the Korean tradition of deploying mythology as a tool to perpetuate tradition and inspire the people. The story is allegory, and is probably understood as such by most ordinary North Koreans, even though it serves to raise the stature of Kim Jong-il and perpetuate the personality cult that surrounds him. For a leader not to be enshrouded in such allegorical myths would be a break with Korean tradition, which is a crucial element of Juche.

Kim attended No. 4 Pyongyang Primary School and then the prestigious Mangyondae School for the Children of Revolutionaries and Pyongyang's Namsan Senior High School, where most of the ruling elite's children are educated. In May 1964 Kim graduated with a degree in political economy from Kim Il-sung University. As the personality cult around his father grew, he was already being referred to officially as the 'The Premier's Son', and treated with a high degree of respect by the university faculty. Stories appeared that he 'corrected' his teachers' errors and took part in construction work. During Kim's university days he was personally mentored by the head of the philosophy department, Hwang Jang-yop, who was later to defect to the ROK. After graduation he initially worked within the Central Committee of the KWP, first as a ministerial assistant, rising, at 31, to be a senior official in the powerful Propaganda and Agitation Department.

Kim Il-sung officially decreed that Kim Jong-il would succeed him in 1980, awarding his son senior posts in the Politburo, the Central Military Commission and the Party Secretariat. However, the decision regarding the succession was probably taken as early as 1971, though not publicly intimated until 1977 when Kim Jong-il was first referred to as the 'Dear Leader'. Rumour had it that another son, Kim Yong-ju, was preferred but that he disgraced himself in the late 1960s; he disappeared from view until 1993. From the 1980s onwards Kim was regularly referred to as 'Dear Leader', and a personality cult was constructed around him to prepare for a smooth and legitimate transition of power. From around 1975 Kim was officially being referred to as 'Party Centre' (*tang chungang*) and his portrait began appearing in classrooms and magazines. In 1980 he was ranked fourth in the KWP Politburo; he began on-the-spot visits in 1981. He is thought to have been directly involved in ordering the 1983 bombing in Rangoon that killed 17 visiting ROK officials. However, some defectors claim that Kim was given little influence over foreign affairs and was unconnected with either the Rangoon bombing or the 1987 shooting down of a South Korean airliner that killed all 115 passengers on board.

Kim's inheritance was officially sealed in February 1982 when he was awarded the title 'Hero of the DPRK' on his fortieth birthday, and he published an essay 'On the Juche Idea'. That he got the inheritance at all, being the first individual to be promoted outside an obvious clique within the party, was down more to Confucian tradition than to ability, though his father attempted to portray his son's rise as a merit-based progress through the Party ranks rather than his own decision. Confucian tradition dictates that the eldest son should inherit and obey the father's wishes.

It appears that Kim Il-sung retained a firm control over international affairs until his death; nevertheless Kim Jong-il was highly influential in domestic matters and covert operations. The evidence is contradictory, though. Some high-ranking defectors and Pyongyang watchers believe that from the 1980s Kim was actively manoeuvring to secure his power base in various ways. These included his undertaking an official visit to Beijing, although he had no 'official' position, as well as allegedly imprisoning opponents and arranging 'accidents' for them. Other reports claim that the younger Kim was regularly late, or hungover, at Politburo meetings. This would anger his father, who would occasionally berate him in front of the senior leadership and make him sit in the corner. Despite this the grooming process continued, with Kim publishing treatises on Juche in the mid-1980s and in 1991 being appointed Commander in Chief of the Army, clearly the number two position to his father. Portraits of the Great Leader also began to appear with Kim Jong-il next to him and of similar stature.

Kim Il-sung's sudden death, in 1994, led to an incredible nationwide outpouring of grief. The mourning for the dead Great Leader appeared genuine and intense, as the majority of people did see the elder Kim as the leader of the resistance to Japanese colonialism and then to American imperialism, as well as being the founding father of the nation. There has never been an overt anti-Kim Il-sung mood in North Korea in the way that there was an anti-Stalin mood in the USSR after 1953. He remains a 'spiritual father' to the nation in a society accustomed to looking upwards for guidance. Kim's death occurred at a time when the big problems for the DPRK were just beginning, as the effects of the ending of Soviet subsidies and climatic disasters combined with the inefficiently organised economy to create economic decline, food shortages and famine. It also occurred on the eve of the signing of the breakthrough 1994 Agreed Framework, which marked the first major diplomatic exchange between the US and the DPRK since the 1953 armistice. Within a year of the Great Leader's death Pyongyang was forced to call on international agencies to provide humanitarian aid.

Initially following Kim Il-sung's death Kim Jong-il disappeared from public view, apparently distraught after his father's emotional funeral and observing the traditional Confucian period of mourning (the entire country observed an official Confucian three-year period of national mourning). However, it is generally believed that Kim was simply taking time to consolidate his new leadership team.

Kim Jong-il re-emerged announcing that he would take the official title of General Secretary of the KWP, leaving the title of President to be retained by his dead father for eternity. This ensured that Kim Il-sung's cult as the founding father and guiding force of the nation would be maintained. Kim also became Chairman of the National Defence Commission, a group of ten that includes the heads of the army, navy and air force. Despite this, rumours have persisted that the military hierarchy in particular were not supportive of Kim Jong-il's ascendancy to power (he was at the time the youngest member of the KWP Politburo by at least thirteen years, with most members in their seventies and eighties) and believed him to be an indecisive leader at a time that would largely determine the future of the DPRK.

It has been suggested that Kim formed an alliance with the military hierarchy that allowed for the theoretical reassertion of martial values. This was the opinion of the highest ranking defector from the DPRK, Hwang Jang-yop, who believed that the Juche theory he had largely helped develop was undermined by the emergence of Kim Jong-il's 'Red Banner' (*songun*) philosophy that accentuated revolutionary commitment and military values and was seen as the theoretical realisation of the compromise between Kim Jong-il and the military leadership. Additionally, Kim has conspicuously visited a large number of military bases, reportedly accounting for 45 per cent of all on-the-spot visits, urging the KPA to be alert, and still regularly visits army outposts, meeting troops in what is seen as a constant effort to keep the military onside. He has, furthermore, manoeuvred his supporters into positions of leadership of important social groups, including the 4-million-strong Socialist Youth League and the 80,000-strong Three Revolution Teams movement that sent students into the countryside. There have also been unconfirmed reports that he has purged and executed several non-military Politburo members thought to be against the growing role of the military.[12] Many in North Korea were willing to suppress their doubts about Kim in order to ensure a smooth succession during the signing of the Agreed Framework with the US.

'Expect No Change from Me'[13]

The popular Korean phrase 'tiger father, dog son' is one that has been invoked frequently by Pyongyang watchers, defectors, and probably disgruntled North Koreans. While Kim Il-sung was alive, Kim Jong-il was in a position as the effective 'Party Centre' to make and verify many appointments to senior posts and was able to promote allies, while outmanoeuvring his stepmother, her promotion of his half-brother, his uncle and the generals.

Kim Jong-il rarely travels, except for known trips to Russia and China; he is thought to speak basic Russian and a few words of English. Little that is verifiable is known of his life, though he has probably lived in comfort and luxury for most it. However, various rumours have emerged about his lifestyle and habits, which have served to create a strange image. These include reports of a collection of over 20,000 videos (sent to Pyongyang in diplomatic pouches), of which he is apparently particularly fond of Rambo, James Bond, horror movies and Hong Kong action films; an apparent fascination with Harley Davidson motorcycles; indications that he is the largest private buyer of Hennessey Paradis Cognac in the world, on which he spends between US$650,000 and US$720,000 a year; his tendency to work very late, firing faxes off to the various ministries and sleeping no more than four hours a night. There are tales regarding his taste for Scandinavian and Japanese women, who have reportedly been flown into Pyongyang to entertain him. He is said to play the violin and piano, and to be a gourmand and wine aficionado. Cho Myung-chul, a defector who knew Kim from childhood, has described him as a fine pianist, an accomplished table tennis player, as well as a keen recreational swimmer.[14]

Various other details have come to light, though they are difficult to verify. Kenji Fujimoto, who worked in the 1980s in Pyongyang as Kim Jong-il's sushi chef, preparing his favourite dishes of shark's fin soup, fatty marbled tuna and caviar (though officially Kim prefers plain Korean food), claimed that in 1988 he went horse riding (apparently Kim prefers Orlovs, a Russian breed), shooting and water-skiing with Kim. Fujimoto also claims that Kim had a serious fall from a horse in 1992, resulting in a broken collarbone and head injuries. Again according to Fujimoto, Kim keeps a 'Joy Division' of beautiful young women who sing, dance and bathe the leader. His closest female companion, Koh Young-hee, is a former dancer who was born in Japan of Korean parents.[15] She was reportedly seriously injured in a car crash in 2003, and it is thought that she has an unidentified chronic disease. Kim is also considered to be generous with those he favours, lavishing them with gifts including cars and luxury goods.

Lee Young-kook, a former bodyguard who defected to Seoul, has claimed that Kim has a hundred Western luxury cars kept in a five-storey building. He reported that a member of Kim's security detail was banished to a coal mine after he was caught smoking one of Kim's cigarettes in one of his fourteen luxury villas. The man was apparently stoned to death by fellow miners, who were in turn killed when Kim found out.[16] Long-time North Korea watcher Aidan Foster-Carter has written that, when his father died, Kim the younger was distraught and stayed in his room with a loaded pistol.[17]

Kim is thought to be self-conscious about his height (1 metre 57) and wears platform shoes. He is reportedly a lover of the theatre and cinema and personally was involved in the campaign to make the DPRK a 'Kingdom of Art'. While at university Kim directed a number of plays, including *Fate of a Member of the Self-Defence Corps* and *True Daughter of the Party*. Kim allegedly kidnapped the prominent South Korean actress Choi Eun-hee in 1978 and kept her under house arrest in Pyongyang for eight years, along with her film director husband, making movies reportedly financed by the proceeds of Kim's personal goldmine concession.[18] There is a popular image of Kim as something of an ageing lothario, although heavy drinking and gambling among political allies is not exactly unheard of in Japan or South Korea. Kim appears to be fascinated by the media and is apparently an avid watcher of the BBC, CNN, Japan's NHK, China's CCTV and, more recently, Middle East television news channels. He is thought to be a regular Internet surfer and computer buff.

Kim's leadership style within the upper echelons of the regime has been described by his former mentor Hwang Jang-yop as 'strong willed ... short-tempered and ruthless when it comes to punishing anyone who questions his policies'.[19] Nevertheless, diplomats who have met Kim say that he can be charming and also that, despite the human rights abuses of his regime, he has never been known personally to raise a weapon. He is also said not to be a 'people person', as his father was, when undertaking on-the-spot guidance visits. Where Kim Il-sung at first sought out as many people as possible, Kim Jong-il prefers smaller gatherings and less close contact with ordinary workers. This is also evident in his taste for drab military-style clothes and dark colours, whereas Kim Il-sung would occasionally appear in more adventurous and extravagant clothing. Kim has never been seen in a Western suit the way his father often was. This awkwardness appears to have eased a little in recent years as Kim embarked on his charm offensive with Russia, China, the US and Japan, though he appears to lack the charisma of his father. The military garb Kim Jong-il favours may also reflect his determination to keep the military hierarchy onside.

Kim is often lampooned and parodied in the Western media though others report that he is knowledgeable. According to Peter Maass in the *New York Times*, when Madeleine Albright went to Pyongyang in 2000, 'Kim was presented with a list of 14 technical questions related to his missile programme; the Americans expected him to pass the list to advisers who would respond later. Instead, Kim went down the list, one question after another, and answered most of them himself', reinforcing his image as a micro-manager. South Korean President Kim Dae-jung met Kim at the 2000 North–South Summit in Pyongyang and described him as a 'man of intellectual ability ... the type of man we can talk with in a common sense fashion', while the former Soviet defence minister, Dmitri Yazov, simply called Kim 'lucid' after he met him in 1995.[20]

As well as being the heir of his father to the highest positions in the land, Kim Jong-il also inherited the right to be the sole interpreter of Juche, which gave him the useful political tool of declaring any potential political enemy to be deviating from or contradicting Juche and therefore liable to be purged. Kim has been presented more in terms of a Confucian-style benevolent leader than a national founder, as he lacks the guerrilla credentials of his father. Kim has increasingly involved himself more directly in the economy. Consequently he is sometimes portrayed as a more technocratic leader than his father. For example, he has launched various seemingly benevolent campaigns, such as the 'August Third Consumer Goods Production Campaign'. This aimed to stimulate local production of basic consumer goods, to redress the shortages that were leaving North Korean citizens with very little in their houses and nothing to buy with their meagre wages. Few consumer goods did find their way into the system when the campaign was launched in 1993, at a time when the domestic economy was in an advanced state of collapse; nevertheless, through the prism of the Pyongyang propaganda machine it appeared that Kim's first priority was the people's welfare.

The handing down of power from Kim Il-sung to Kim Jong-il was viewed with disdain by many traditional Marxist–Leninist countries. The concept of the revolutionary dynasty, a communist monarchy headed by the Kim clan, is more understandable in light of the Confucian influence in North

Korea and the idea that a family be entrusted as the defenders of a secular, though orthodox, faith. However, revolutionary dynasties are not an unknown concept in Marxist-oriented (or post-Marxist) countries. Ceausescu in Romania was looking to establish a dynasty, while in Cuba all indications are that Raul Castro, the younger brother of Fidel, appears set to become the next leader of the Caribbean island.[21] Similarly in once Marxist regions where revolutionary ideology has been historically mixed with traditional beliefs and kinship patterns, dynasties have also appeared. A prime recent example is Azerbaijan, where Heydar Aliyev (1923–2003), who dominated Azeri politics for thirty years as KGB leader, Communist Party leader and (from 1993) president, was intent on handing over power to his son, prime minister Ilham Aliyev. Another example was the attempts of Saddam Hussein to advance his sons and other members of the al-Tikriti clan into positions of power in Ba'athist Iraq.

Tiger Father, Dog Son

Although the personality cult may seem strange to outsiders, it makes sense when understood as an aspect of the Confucianism and traditionalism of the DPRK. The creation of a clan-dominated society with a hereditary succession is consistent with this philosophical tradition. After all, if Kim Il-sung truly held the Mandate of Heaven and could do nothing but good, then who else could he pass it on to but his eldest son? To pass the leadership to anyone else would be to admit that the Kim family had somehow erred.

The Kim family revolutionary dynasty is about more than just the father and the son. Kim Il-sung's ancestors have all been effectively beatified as revolutionary heroes, helping to create a dynasty of leaders that runs back into history including fighting the Americans in the 1860s and founding various anti-Japanese associations. One of Kim Jong-il's first public campaigns after succeeding his father was to make his mother, Kim Jong-suk, a revolutionary immortal. (Kim Il-sung's second wife remains a non-person in North Korea because Kim Jong-il apparently never forgave his stepmother for favouring her son over him – or indeed his father for remarrying.) Kim Jong-suk is now also recorded as having conducted on-the-spot guidance sessions, and has been described as a 'great strategist' in her own right. Her home town of Hoeryong has a museum, a library, a statue, a square and the house in which she was born devoted to the 'Mother of Korea'.

Kim Il-sung promoted his younger brother Kim Du-nam to the rank of general and to be his military secretary. Another brother, Kim Yong-ju, was a senior official in the KWP and appointed to the Politburo in 1993.

Kim Il-sung also made his second wife, Kim Song-ae, chairwoman of the Democratic Women's Association of Korea. She reportedly held considerable power in the DPRK while her husband was alive and, according to the former Swedish chargé d'affaires in Pyongyang, when she attended any formal function she would be accompanied by an inner circle of ten ladies and a woman general, as well as twenty further female attendants and their drivers and security.[22]

While Kim Jong-il was groomed to succeed his father, his half-brother Kim Pyong-il (whose mother was Kim Song-ae, and who was named after the son born in Vyatskoye in 1944 who drowned in 1947) has been an ambassador in several European countries. One of his sisters, Kim Kyung-hee, is married to a general and is often referred to in the DPRK media as the North's 'First Lady', while her husband Chang Song-taek heads the KWP's Organisational Department as a Vice Director of the KWP Central Committee and has visited Seoul. Chang Song-taek's brothers are also important: Chang Sung-woo, who commands the army district that defends Pyongyang; Chang Sung-kil, who is commissar of another KPA corps in the capital; and Chang Sung-u, who is a senior official in the Public Security Bureau. Another of Kim Jong-il's sisters, Kim Kong-hui, is a member of the KWP Central Committee and heads the party's light industry bureau. Other extended family members remain in positions of power or hold unofficial power through their membership of the extended Kim clan.

All the current members of the extended Kim family are members of North Korea's 'Core Class', which includes Party, military and government officials as well as descendants of independence fighters and relatives of the military and civilian dead from the Korean War. Core Class members are permitted to live in Pyongyang and other major cities and receive preferential treatment within the party, employment in the bureaucracy and service as military officers, as well as preferential treatment in education, ration allowances and medical care.

Primary among the Kim family members are Kim Jong-il's sons: Kim Jong-nam, born illegitimately in 1971 to Sung Hae-rim, a former actress not formally recognised by Kim Jong-il or the official media; Kim Jong-chul, born in 1981 to to Koh Young-hee, a former star with Pyongyang's Mansudae song-and-dance troupe; and Jong-woon, his second son with Koh Young-hee. Little is known about Jong-woon, who is said to resemble his father and is now in his early twenties.

Kim met Sung Hae-rim when he was in his twenties. Although she was married with a son, Lee Il-nam, Kim reportedly forced Sung to leave her husband and live with him; this is according to Sung Hae-rang, Sung Hae-rim's sister, who defected in 1996 and published a memoir. Sung Hae-rim is thought to have died after being sent to Moscow for treatment at a sanatorium in 2002. The son, Lee Il-nam, attended the same private school in Geneva as Kim Jong-nam and later defected to Seoul. He also wrote a memoir about his life in the DPRK. He was killed in 1997 in what the ROK intelligence agency claims was an assassination by North Korean agents. Kim Jong-il never married Sung, both because of her previous marriage and because she was six years older than him, both frowned upon in the Confucian tradition. Kim is also thought to have adopted Sung Hae-rim's niece, Li Nam-ok, whom he sent to be educated in Moscow and Geneva. She likewise defected, in 1992, eventually moving to Paris where she too wrote a memoir, *The Golden Cage*, in which she described Kim as a 'modern thinking man'.[23]

Kim Jong-il also has a 29-year-old daughter named Kim Sol-song, from his marriage to Kim Jong-sook in 1974 (apparently at Kim Il-sung's behest after risking scandal with the married Sung Hae-rim). Kim Jong-il has also lived with Hong Il-chon, an ex-president of the Kim Hyung-jik Teaching University in Pyongyang; an unconfirmed story claims they have a 35-year-old daughter named Kim Hye-kyung. It is thought that Kim Jong-il has fathered at least six sons by four different women.

While rumours have long circulated among dissidents that Kim Jong-il is not a man of his father's stature, the same can be said of his sons. From an early age the illegitimate Kim Jong-nam had reportedly been groomed to be his successor, even becoming the public head of the Korea Computer Centre, thought to be the DPRK's cyber-warfare headquarters. However, Kim Jong-nam ruined his chances when he was arrested at Tokyo Airport in April 2001 trying to enter Japan illegally with two women and a 4-year-old boy, on a Dominican passport. A strange incident became farce when Kim Jong-nam claimed he was taking some of the Kim clan on a trip to Tokyo Disneyland, a trip he had apparently made several times before on his fake passport. Kim Jong-nam was initially banished to Beijing; he is now reported to be seen regularly in the casinos of Macau, afraid to return to Pyongyang.[24] According to Hwang Jang-yop, 'The fate of Kim Jong-nam is finished.'[25]

Due to the scandal involving Kim Jong-nam, and Jong-woon's lack of a public role, the signs are that it is Kim Jong-chul who will be Kim Jong-il's heir. Kim Jong-chul was educated at a private school in Geneva and, though still in his twenties, is already serving in the KWP's Propaganda and Agitation Department. His mother Koh Young-hee has been referred to as 'The Respected Mother' since August 2002 – though it is unclear whether or not she and Kim Jong-il ever officially married. According to Hwang, 'An heir must be the child of a woman a king loves, and it is true that Kim Jong-il loves Koh Young-hee most.' Whatever the truth of this possible succession, it does appear that at present the political elite, the military hierarchy and, more obviously, the Kim family all wish to see a continuance of the revolutionary dynasty in the DPRK beyond Kim Jong-il.

The Lodestar of the Twenty-first Century

It is a crime to question the personality cult in North Korea. According to defectors the criminal courts deal with what are referred to as 'No. 1' cases – involving the offence of defaming the prestige of Kim Il-sung or Kim Jong-il. A 'No. 9 case' involves the same offence against any of Kim Jong-il's family tree. People have apparently been imprisoned for criticising the leaders or defacing their images. The personality cult is perpetuated in myriad ways through the state's total control of the media – everything from the mass rallies held to mark anniversaries of one of the Kims' birth or the Great Leader's death to popular songs that extol the Kims.

The universal lapel badges, worn next to the heart, and the portraits of the Kims that hang in every household to show that the Great Leader and the Dear Leader effectively watch over every family in the land, extend the cult into the private realm. There are approximately 34,000 monuments to Kim Il-sung in the DPRK (though few if any statues of Kim Jong-il), the main Kim Il-sung Square in Pyongyang, Kim Il-sung University, the Kim Il-sung Party School and numerous other institutions and places named after him, not to mention the Museum of the Revolution, one of several sites dedicated to venerating his life and work. These include Magyongdae where Kim's supposed ancestral farm has been restored as a tourist attraction.

Other methods include indoctrination right through the educational process, in the political dimension of working life, in the mass media and culture; and then there is the national flower – the Kimilsungia begonia. Pyongyang's major memorial to Kim Il-sung is the 20-metre bronze statue of Kim, the Mansudae Grand Monument, where North Koreans and all visitors to the capital pay their respects, and where Deng Xiaoping apparently noted with disgust that the statue was coated in gold.[26] People overseas are also expected to appreciate the greatness of the North Korean leadership – in 1997 the North Koreans took a full-page advert in the *New York Times* to celebrate the rise to power of Kim Jong-il, describing him as 'The Lodestar of the Twenty-first Century'. Kim officially has over 1,200 titles, including The Sun of the 21st Century, The Ever-Victorious General and The Guardian Deity of the Planet.[27]

According to Dr Balazs Szalontai of the Central European University, 'With the possible exception of Tito's Yugoslavia, nowhere did a leadership cult emerge as quickly as in North Korea.'[28] The cult of personality of Kim Il-sung and now Kim Jong-il are central to legitimising KWP rule. To admit to flaws in the leadership would be to concede vulnerability on the part of the entire regime and question the correctness of Juche. Kim Il-sung remains the *suryong*, or Great Leader.[29] At the 1998 KWP Party Congress Kim Il-sung's last report to Congress was simply rebroadcast. When Deng took power in China he started a process of demythologising Mao. Khrushchev did the same with the cult of Stalin. Much later Gorbachev extended this historical reassessment. In North Korea the monopoly the leader enjoys as a moral exemplar and national guide has precluded the emergence of any organised internal opposition, such as has been seen in most socialist bloc countries.

As with other notable cults of personality, that in North Korea has developed its own internal dynamic – it is a central part of everyday life and is incorporated within every aspect of society. Habits of excessive flattery and obsequiousness are universal and people from all strata of society feel compelled to outdo their compatriots in manifesting their loyalty to the regime, while the state perpetuates the myth that the DPRK has allies and admirers internationally. Consequently one generation indoctrinates the next and the system perpetuates itself. The other way in which the cult of personality around the father and son leadership continues is through repression. At its mildest level this is Confucian self-repression – needing to conform to the group. To be different is to invite isolation and exclusion. At its harshest level some form of punishment is involved, such as demotion or reduced rations, and at worst death.

Consequently the political debate in North Korea, such as it is, is played out in direct relation to the leader. Since the formation of the nation, purges, political reorganisation, variations in economic policy, foreign relations and social measures have all taken place through the direct intervention of the leadership or following debate framed only in terms of support for the leadership. From the start, Kim Il-sung worked to create a mass party subservient to him.

Yet, while Kim Il-sung came to dominate the DPRK totally, he never managed to achieve his objective of extending his cult overseas and becoming a major figure of adulation and leadership in the developing world; nor did he become a rallying point for the non-aligned movement. Indeed, as the world turned against him, so he increasingly turned against the world. Other leaders who have become closely identified with their nation's development and have built cults of personality have managed to become a focus for millions outside their borders – for instance, Stalin, Mao and even Saddam

Hussein. Kim Il-sung and Kim Jong-il have not been able to achieve this broader international support.

In Part II we see how, in essence, proxy power in the DPRK was all that Kim Il-sung gained in 1945 and that power was the only tool he could wield to change society. This task has been beset by constant and, in one way or another, constantly renewed economic difficulties. The absolute rule and unquestionable power of the leadership in North Korea involved the imposition of an economic system that is not necessarily well suited to the country's conditions and has become ossified and incapable of sustaining the nation. Indeed, it is the economy that has revealed the failings of the leadership and its political ideology most visibly.

PART II

The Economics of North Korea: Chollima, Speed Battles, Collapse and Famine

4

Economics Pyongyang Style:
Command and Control

The Possibility of Perestroika, the Impossibility of Glasnost

The current period in North Korea's political-economic history can be described as being all about the possibility of perestroika but in the absence of glasnost. That is, that there have been signs of a potential opening up, or nascent liberalisation, of the economy, yet no accompanying liberalisation of the political system, which remains as rigid as ever. In this sense the DPRK may be seeking to start out along a path of economic reform similar to that China embarked upon under Deng Xiaoping in the early 1980s with Deng's theory of 'one centre and two bases' – the centre being economic construction and the two bases being adherence to socialism (taken to mean one-party rule by the CPC) and furthering economic reform. This is distinctly different from the path taken by the USSR under Gorbachev of attempting to liberalise both society and economy simultaneously. This delineation between the two socialist superpowers is quite clear in North Korea. Pyongyang openly rejects the Soviet reform path, believing that it ultimately led to collapse and the fall from power of the CPSU. While Pyongyang has often been critical of marketisation in China, it does recognise that the country has prospered economically and that the Party has retained power.

To date the DPRK has maintained a rigid centrally planned economy (or 'command economy' or 'administrative economy') that directs economic life from top to bottom. It has consistently suppressed markets and monetisation, preferring an all-encompassing rationing system called the Public Distribution System (PDS) and state control of industrial and agricultural production.

Central planning is enshrined in Article 34 of the DPRK's constitution: 'The State shall formulate unified and detailed plans and guarantee a high rate of production growth and a balanced development of the national economy.' Power and control of distribution are seen as more important than money, the currency remains non-convertible, and all aspects of official economic life are controlled by the party-state.

Pyongyang has studied the Chinese experiment in economic reform. Indeed it has been forced to do so, as the Chinese have insisted on taking both Kim Jong-il and his senior officials to liberalised and economically successful areas such as Shanghai. The images of Kim Jong-il being guided around Shanghai were shown extensively on Chinese television – the sight of a bewildered-looking man in a hooded parka being escorted by leading officials around an ultra-modern foreign-invested car plant made for strange viewing. In effect Kim was receiving a lecture from the Chinese leadership on the benefits of economic reform. Beijing had been giving these lectures to visiting Pyongyang delegations for some time. In the late 1980s Deng told a visiting delegation of DPRK military officials that 'We [China] have no choice but to carry out price reform, and we must do so despite all risks and difficulties.' The North Koreans, on hearing this and then receiving a lecture on the Marxist law of value, were apparently 'bemused'.[1]

Blaming the collapse of the USSR on weaknesses in political ideology has largely been a smokescreen to conceal the contradictions of the Soviet-style planning system that the DPRK instituted shortly after its inception. Kim Il-sung's early life, guerrilla experiences and communist allegiance were largely Soviet-influenced and it is not surprising that in the Stalinist command economy of the 1930s, and then again after World War II, Kim saw a suitable, applicable and transferable economic model that would allow the DPRK rapidly to construct a self-sufficient industrialised economy with a strong military base. The lesson was that Stalin's command economics had allowed for the rapid industrialisation of the USSR in the 1930s, which in turn allowed the country to resist and defeat Hitler, while the country's second rapid industrialisation, carried out again within the framework of the command economy, after the devastation of World War II, allowed the USSR to survive in the hostile Cold War environment as a bulwark against American global power. Despite its having adopted various tenets of Maoism and Confucianism, within Juche the DPRK's economic system is more akin to the Soviet economic system than to the Maoist version.

Nevertheless, Pyongyang has also borrowed liberally from China and from other socialist states in developing its economic system. The Chollima period[2] of intense reconstruction and emphasis on mass mobilisation, which started in August 1958, following the final collectivisation of all land in the

DPRK, was not dissimilar to the Stakhanovite movement in the USSR or the Great Leap Forward in China; many of the guiding tenets of Juche and its politicisation of daily life mirrored the use of Mao's *Little Red Book* in China. Additionally, the country's isolation and self-sufficiency drive borrowed tactics from Albania, while the idea of permanent war, if not borrowed from George Orwell, was inspired partly by Castro's Cuba.[3] Initially many looked to the DPRK as a successful example of socialist planning. However, the model country was soon perceived to be a chimera and disillusion rapidly set in among most foreign observers.

The Chollima Spirit

Self-sufficiency became an obsession in North Korea's version of the command economy, with all production subordinated to the most urgent needs of the state. Classical Marxist economics does not stipulate self-sufficiency and isolationism; indeed it encourages the import of goods not manufactured domestically. Despite the almost total devastation of large areas of the North during the Korean War, particularly Pyongyang, the reconstruction programme emphasised the Chollima spirit. Although the North borrowed liberally from the USSR and China, it also sought to plough its own furrow and kept its distance from Comecon, believing that it could not be relegated to being simply a supplier of raw materials and inputs to Comecon countries and had to develop its industrial and agricultural base independently.

Why did North Korea opt for the route of self-sufficiency? It was a matter of ideology rather than economics, and in this sense the DPRK was similar to China. Just as China attempted to limit contact with the outside world during the Great Leap and the Cultural Revolution as a response to 150 years of bad experiences with foreign capitalism, so Pyongyang developed a form of xenophobia towards the outside world that dictated an isolationist path and in turn bolstered Kim's leadership. This extreme political nationalism became a form of economic nationalism too. In fairness to the North its initial experience of 'socialist cooperation' was not positive. From the formation of the DPRK the country complained that Moscow abused Pyongyang's situation to sell to the regime at high prices while dictating low purchasing prices for the North's raw materials in return. North Korea remains largely agriculturally barren but has rich mineral deposits,[4] and the USSR exploited this fact to try and purchase cheap minerals. It was also true that, unlike some other socialist countries, the DPRK did not 'inherit' any developed industries that it was able to expropriate, as, for instance, the Cubans did with the sugar and tobacco industries.

However, the economic principle most prevalent in the DPRK, cen-
tralisation (essentially a political rather than an economic principle), was
imported from the USSR, accompanied by the establishment of the North
Korean equivalent of the powerful Soviet State Planning Committee agency
Gosplan. This was the command economy that Stalin imposed on all the
Soviet satellites in the wake of 1945; it followed the basic model seen in
all the 'Peoples' Democracies' – Albania, Bulgaria, Czechoslovakia, East
Germany, Hungary, Poland, Romania – and later in countries such as Vietnam and Cuba. The command economy replaces the political market with
'democratic centralism', and the economic market with central planning and
a state-run economy, the collectivisation of agriculture and centralisation
of economic decision-making, emphasising rapid industrialisation and the
priority of heavy industry. The system was adopted in the DPRK in the
1950s at a time when many economists, even in the West, still suspected
that administrative allocation of resources might be a more efficient system
of industrial organisation than market allocation.

This was the result of Bolshevik-inspired Marxist–Leninist theory, and
also of distrust of market economics by many on the political left following
the Great Depression of 1929. To the communists in Pyongyang the USSR's
rapid industrialisation and recovery from the ravages of war seemed appeal-
ing and applicable. It was also the case that the Sino–Soviet dispute allowed
Pyongyang to play the Chinese off against the Russians on price. Ultimately
Pyongyang remained closer economically to the USSR and saw it as a closer
military ally and 'donor' of subsidies than the then economically deprived
Chinese of the Great Leap period. China responded by retaining low-level
economic contacts with the DPRK throughout the 1950s, 1960s and most of
the 1970s, while openly allowing the Red Guards to criticise Kim Il-sung. In
the meantime, the Soviet model was applied throughout the Eastern bloc
and to fraternal nations – consistently, uncritically, and with no allowance
being made for traditional, cultural or developmental differences.

Initially it appeared that this rapid development of North Korea's industrial and agricultural base was successful, along with campaigns to
improve public health and literacy. Following the Korean War the DPRK
had inherited over 75 per cent of the peninsula's mines, 90 per cent of its
electricity generating capacity and 80 per cent of Korea's entire remaining
manufacturing plant. Until the mid-1970s North Korea was wealthier than
South Korea in terms of per capita GDP and, according to some estimates,
the twentieth richest country globally, while the South's economy was frequently described as a basket case.

The North's 1947–48 One-year Plan reported a 54 per cent growth in
industrial production while the 1948–49 Plan reported a 38 per cent increase.

By the end of 1950 industrial growth was 3.4 times greater than in 1946. In the late 1950s the annual per capita income in the DPRK was double that of the ROK, and by the end of the 1950s Kim had complete control of the country and economy while the ROK was dealing with student protests and an impending military coup, as Seoul's economy continued to grow slowly with per capita GNP in 1961 of just US$100.

The North's early acceleration was in large part due to the encouragement of a Chollima spirit (introduced during the 1957–61 Five-year Plan) – a massive human mobilisation and effort in the spheres of construction and the development of heavy industry. Chollima was a form of industrial advance to which the communist command economy is suited for an initial period, with its inbuilt ability to drive production through ideological support and basic industrial techniques. In the late 1950s Chollima had become the dominant form of organising economic and human resources, with its strange new concepts such as the 'drink no soup' movement that encouraged workers to remain on the factory floor rather than go to the lavatory. The Chollima period was preceded by the 'Maximum Production with Evincing Thrift' campaign in 1956, which grew into the more rounded political mobilisation campaign of Chollima. As Chollima accelerated in 1958 the North saw the institution of a Stakhanovite-style rewards system with medals and praise for the so-called 'Chollima Riders', groups of workers who surpassed their targets, while the press was full of reports of super-human construction efforts and the role of Kim in personally micro-managing the economy through the 'intensive guidance' (*chiphung chido*) programme.

However, by 1961 the extra reserves of labour were dwindling and growth was increasingly due to a large-scale spending programme by the North Koreans to acquire technology (though not technique, which was perhaps more urgently required) and machinery. Little technological development took place in an economy where R&D spend could not be measured effectively by the planners, and where the vast majority of R&D was concentrated in the military sector, which was divorced from civilian production. The quantitative growth of the economy was less urgent by this point. At the same time, the military component of the national budget leapt from 2.6 per cent of GNP in 1961 to 5.8 per cent in 1964 and 10 per cent in 1966, a year in which the overall economy actually contracted by 3 per cent. Chollima achieved results in terms of propaganda, but as early as the late 1950s Kim was expressing concern that many manufactured goods were of inferior quality, unsellable internationally and therefore not capable of providing the government with much needed foreign currency. The attempts by the USSR to charge the North Koreans high prices backfired when Pyongyang found that it could purchase better-quality, more advanced and reliable technology and machinery in the West – on credit – without depleting the country's mineral deposits at bargain prices to the Soviets. Additionally, where possible, as with tractor production, the North Koreans simply set up their own plants, copying Soviet tractors or other pieces of technology through reverse engineering.[5] The North Koreans argued that their reverse-engineered machinery was superior in quality to that purchased at above market price from the USSR.

By the end of the 1957–61 Five-year Plan it was becoming obvious that an economy run on the muscle of poorly educated workers was not sustainable, but the rise of the cult of personality and Juche meant that the country either had no economists who realised a change was needed or none who was able to find a way to voice their concerns in safety. Consequently the command economy persisted. By the time of the Fourth KWP Party Congress in September 1961, Kim had assumed total political power and had an opportunity to change the economic system. However, he chose to retain the command economy and rely largely on Chollima to spur growth, despite some attempts to replace the guerrilla generation with younger, supposedly more economically able, technocrats. This largely failed as they were invariably Moscow-trained and consequently too imbued with the Stalinist system, being specialists at mass mobilisation techniques and statistical manipulation rather than economic management.

At the December 1962 KWP Plenum, Kim claimed massive growth rates in grain production, steel, coal and textiles manufacture and fish catch, but he had no new policies to refine the economy beyond a new 120-day Chollima campaign, which led to so many medals being awarded that their symbolic value was seriously reduced in terms of conferring real status on workers. At the same time Kim introduced the concept of 'Equal Emphasis' (after observing the Cuban missile crisis and interpreting it as a Soviet capitulation to American military might), linking high economic growth rates to equally high levels of armaments production, a linkage that was to add to the multiplicity of drags on the economy later. Despite the supposed growth of the economy, Kim's promise at this time that everyone would wear silk, live in a house with a tiled roof and have three square meals a day was still an empty one. By 1968 Kim was forced to admit that lack of manpower meant that Chollima-inspired growth was of limited capability (as had Brezhnev in the USSR where a similar problem was encountered), despite a new policy to employ additional female workers in light industry and to involve the army more closely in industrial work as well as utilising prison labour.

The Great Leap Outward

Buoyed by what he believed was strong growth in 1962, Kim began to increase the rate of investment in order to attempt both to modernise production and to further the 'Equal Emphasis' policy that required a more advanced industrial base. The rate of investment in heavy industry rose from 40 per cent to in excess of 65 per cent of total state investment by the mid-1960s. Consequently in the 1960s and 1970s North Koreans travelled to the West to buy, and Western businessmen travelled to Pyongyang to sell, encouraged by the annual published growth rates of over 40 per cent in the 1950s and over 36 per cent in the 1960s. This was the high point in North Korea's brief experience of international trade, which was prompted by the North's growing concern at the ROK's economic progress under General Park Chung-hee's rapid industrialisation programme. Pyongyang launched its so-called 'Great Leap Outward' policy of buying up plant and machinery from the West and Japan – close to US$1 billion worth in total from Japan alone.[6] Certainly Pyongyang's seeming independence from the USSR was attractive to Western business.

The DPRK acquired the world's largest cement factory as well as a watch factory, paper mill, steel mill, fertiliser and chemical plants, among many other assets. Yet their potential was never fully realised in the rigidly planned economy, despite the fact that trade with the Western nations as a percentage of total trade rose from near zero to over 40 per cent. Western vendors were keen to see new business, though the credit honeymoon was relatively short-lived as it soon became apparent that Pyongyang was either unwilling or unable to pay for most of what it had received. This situation worsened during the 1973 Middle East oil crisis and global commodity price collapse despite the repeated use of neo-Chollima techniques, including Speed Battles and the 80,000-strong Three-Revolution Team Movement – a form of Red Guards where students went to the countryside to help introduce new techniques they themselves knew little about, to increase production, though at the inevitable expense of quality. Nevertheless, the oil crisis was not catastrophic for the DPRK as most of its oil supplies were subsidised by a USSR that had abundant supplies. Western business hoped that, like the Eastern European socialist bloc, North Korea would at least attempt to pay. However, debt negotiations eventually became bogged down and endless.

Erik Cornell, the Swedish chargé d'affaires in Pyongyang 1975–77, believed that much of the problem over debt repayment was due to the North Koreans believing that anyone who did business with Pyongyang tacitly supported them and consequently saw it as a version of aid, meaning that late payment was not a problem.[7] All debt repayments to the West stopped in 1976 when the DPRK effectively declared itself bankrupt, even though the press still reported annual industrial production growth rates of approximately 16 per cent. By that point the estimated debt was US$5.2 billion. Conversely the South had also looked to gain new technology and plant and had also incurred debt, but was seeing rising exports creating earnings to pay their bills. Crucially, the ROK signed mostly licensing agreements with Japanese firms rather than buying whole production lines.

To many, North Korea appeared to be a success story. It had undeniably managed to re-create an industrial base and become largely self-sufficient in agricultural production. There was also no denying the massive residential construction projects that had managed to house many North Korean citizens left homeless after the Korean War.

Additionally, visitors could see tangible progress up until the mid- to late 1970s, when arguably the North still had a higher standard of living and a more even wealth distribution than South Korea, even though by 1971 military spending was absorbing as much as 30 per cent of GNP. Even during the 1978–84 Second Seven-year Plan, launched without discussion, as Kim had by then absolute authority, the DPRK was claiming an economic growth rate in excess of 12 per cent. The state was also declaring that it could tangibly improve people's lives through initiatives such as the 'August Third Consumer Goods Movement', which aimed to produce more products for domestic consumption, despite the need to extend the Plan by a further two years and launch a new Chollima campaign of working at 'Pyongyang Speed'. The consumer goods movement was doomed to failure. The problem with poor-quality production is that it creates additional demand for goods to replace broken ones, a demand that can become insatiable, even in a largely cash-starved consumer economy like that of North Korea. There is also a concomitant rise in demand for spare parts and repairs, both of which are in turn invariably substandard in execution, thereby ensuring that shortages remain. There was some apparent progress during this period, such as the rebuilding of the Panmunjom to Pyongyang road, which before the late 1970s was in extremely poor condition. The road was upgraded by the 1980s to a major highway, giving a faster journey. Today it is a multi-lane expressway.

As the DPRK's economy slowed to a halt, energy capacity dwindled and agricultural production stagnated, the West switched from a policy of trade with the DPRK to one of primarily debt negotiation. Export credits ceased and the DPRK was forced to reach an accommodation with Comecon through its barter system and to rely increasingly on Soviet subsidies. Although it did not entirely forgive the DPRK for going it alone, Moscow came increasingly to prop up the North Korean economy. China was also a major trading partner though on a more equal basis. The Soviet Union was also useful to North Korea in a multitude of other ways. For instance, in 1974, shortly after the first OPEC oil crisis and the collapse of world copper prices, Moscow sponsored Pyongyang's entry into the International Atomic Energy Agency (IAEA), which allowed the Soviets officially to help North Korea develop civilian nuclear-power-generating capacity.

The DPRK rapidly changed from being an admired state to another failing socialist state supported by the Soviet Union. Meanwhile its closest neighbours, Japan and the ROK, moved rapidly ahead in their own industrialisation processes and China began its reform programme under Deng. Japan's growth had begun earlier and its *sengo kiseki*, or post-war miracle, became the model for both South Korea and China, which largely adopted the state-controlled export-driven growth strategies of Tokyo with their own national characteristics attached. By the mid-1970s Japan was no longer desperately poor, though per capita incomes were approximately a third of those in the US.

The DPRK became essentially a vassal state of the Soviet Union. It was forced into the straitjacket of the command economy as much by its own Juche theories and economic history as by its need to conform to Moscow's criteria for receiving aid. Pyongyang may have appeared to be independent but was in fact largely dependent on Soviet subsidies by the mid-1970s.

The Impregnable Fortress of Socialism

The economic model of the command economy as practised and developed in the Soviet Union emphasised investment over consumption, heavy over light industry, any industry over agriculture, and farming over services. The DPRK introduced central planning officially in 1947 with the nationalisation of all industry and the introduction of the first state plan. At the end of the 1961–67 First Seven-year Plan, despite praise from the leadership and the claim that the DPRK was now an 'impregnable fortress of socialism', the decision was made to extend the plan by another year, which indicated that problems were mounting.

The limitations of the Soviet economic planning system meant that the levels of wastage in the DPRK economy rendered the system overcostly in terms of resources and inputs. The inadequacies of Chollima, or crash industrialisation, and the command economy became apparent relatively quickly. Despite the belief that Juche would lead to North Korea attaining an economic and industrial parity with the West that would be reflected in living standards, the plans were often uncoordinated and newly purchased equipment was wasted through lack of use as factory construction and energy capacity lagged behind plant purchasing. Product quality remained below international standards, meaning export orders were rare. In 1969 Kim lashed out again at the workers, this time ignoring the lack of Chollima spirit he had previously criticised and turning his attention instead to the growth of speculative activity and pilfering in the system, a hallmark of all command economies.

For decades, first Soviet economists, then Chinese, and today North Korean, have claimed that planning was a rational and scientific form of economic management. The fact is that, even in a relatively basic industrial economy, planning to the levels envisaged by the Soviet system, and supposedly practised in North Korea, is impossible even with the aid of supercomputers. Even in a mid-sized economy, over a million variants in terms of size, shape and purpose will be needed in just the rolled steel sector. Though steel is a major industry in the DPRK, producing over 6 million tonnes annually, most of the major mills were constructed during the Japanese occupation and now suffer from outdated technology, a lack of coking coal and the low purity of domestic iron ore. The situation has created serious problems for the industry, and led to a scaling down of the crude steel target by the end of the Third Seven-year Plan (1987–93), in place of the planned increase of 4 million tonnes. Predicting how much of each type of steel is required in advance is impossible and therefore simply doesn't happen.[8] Yet the planning system gets around this by ignoring issues of quality and customer satisfaction, instead evaluating and predicting the performance of the steel industry in terms of the aggregate weight of output. Ridiculous situations then arise, an example of which is the sale in the USSR in the 1980s of titanium badminton rackets at cheaper prices than wooden ones.

Local enterprises must accept the steel that is produced, even if it does not match their specifications exactly. Hence the notoriously heavy tractors, cars and refrigerators produced by the Eastern bloc. To fulfil the ever-expanding plan, more and more materials are used, leading to waste and multiplying the absurdities. Enterprises are not able to re-route unused or unsuitable steel to other factories, as there is no effective inter-enterprise payment system in place, and because enterprise managers tend to hoard materials even if they are unsuitable or substandard. The impact of this wastefulness and squandering of materials in the command economy cannot be overestimated. Even if the machinery produced is arguably more functional and long lasting, the absence of a concomitant spare-parts and maintenance industry means that products rapidly become useless. As well as wasting resources, the process also wastes the power used in producing it, the workers' time, additional transportation costs, and so on.

The existence of the state planning mechanism meant that, apart from the most basic goods and materials, socialist countries could not operate successfully as exporters, and consequently the DPRK's exports have been minimal. While domestic enterprises were either not permitted to import or lack the hard currency to transact purchases and therefore had to accept, say, the wrong steel or rubber, foreign companies are not in this position. The result was that when steel was exported from the command economies it was as a virtual raw material, priced cheaply due to the lack of value-added and the fact that accounts are expressed in physical or material units in a planned economy. The Soviet Union at one point produced over 20 per cent of the world's steel output, yet, despite exporting virtually none, suffered a steel shortage. As was the case with most other products, little of the steel produced by the Eastern bloc was of an international standard. This left socialist countries, and leaves the DPRK today, attempting to export its mineral base in raw form with little opportunity for value-added profit.

Another inherent absurdity in the planning system is that enterprise managers – essentially the administrators of state property and ground-level enforcers of the output plans – have learnt to ensure they never manufacture at full capacity despite creating the illusion of doing so. Managers who have grown up with an intimate knowledge of the planning system and its mechanisms know that if they produce to their full capacity (rare nowadays in the DPRK due to the scale of the industrial collapse and the energy shortage), their plan targets will simply be increased, forcing them to find a way to produce more – the ratchet effect. Managers therefore devise ways to run at under full capacity; this allows for the increase in the next plan period. This manoeuvre accounts for the ability of enterprises to cope with the periodic campaigns of intense production announced by the leadership. Again these campaigns are a feature of the Soviet-style system that has been adopted by Pyongyang. In the Soviet Union they were referred to as 'storming' and in the DPRK as 'Speed Battles'; they can last from a period of a few weeks to over 70 days. If the DPRK's state-owned enterprises (SOEs) were operating at full capacity then ramping up production significantly during these Speed Battles would be near impossible. Yet, according to the official press, it does occur and virtually all SOEs manage it, at least in the newspapers.

The Industrial Crown Jewels

With a rigid centralised planning system controlling the economy there has been no space for the development of private enterprise. While the development of private enterprise was initially thus restricted in China, it was the growth of this sector that largely propelled the reform process as well as winning a certain amount of public support for the reforms among key constituencies.

A central failing in the command economy is that SOEs, the so-called 'industrial crown jewels' of Stalinist economies, or, as Lenin described them, 'the commanding heights' of the economy, do not purchase from each other. The manager of a rubber gloves factory cannot simply telephone the manager of a rubber factory, explain his requirements and then negotiate a price and delivery date. In the DPRK firms invariably do not purchase directly from one another but go through government agencies. These agencies 'allocate' resources according to the national plan. To avoid getting less than the factory needs to fulfil its plan, the manager orders more, effectively over-ordering, to compensate for the inherent discrepancies in the planning system as well as making sure there is additional supply in case of a sudden Speed Battle or wastage. This naturally leads to the under-utilisation of capital through maldistribution of resources. Government planners, although aware of this tactic, allocate less than requested.

In this situation being honest is not an option and the planners assume a lie. Supplies are anyway invariably interrupted leading to slowdowns, stoppages and shutdowns when reserves of raw materials or energy expire. Ultimately the demand for any material or product becomes unlimited regardless of use, sale or need. In such a planned system with these built-in contradictions the concept of cost is immediately lost. Political connections are also a factor in procurement, which further distorts the system. For example, if the manager of one plant has more leverage or stronger connections with the allocation agency than another manager, he may achieve a greater allocation; this can lead in turn to a wasteful system of bargaining between industrial units and the planners rather than active cooperation and feedback. The result is that some SOEs end up hoarding a surplus – stockpiling – while other enterprises suffer a shortage.

Given the problems identified with SOEs caught within the central planning system, it is no surprise that they inevitably become insolvent, go bankrupt and production stops as the contradictions mount up along the chain of production and supply – as is the case in the DPRK now. SOEs are, after all, not just economic units but representatives of the political-economic theory of the party-state. However, it is not always easy to establish the final profitability of an SOE. The SOEs, by their nature, operate in a command economy that fixes prices, subsidises various costs from distribution to wholesaling to advertising, and may receive yet more direct subsidies in the form of power supplies and other utilities at below market rates. Additionally, SOEs have various responsibilities that are hard to calculate or serve to obfuscate the picture – workers' accommodation, pensions, sickness benefits and various assets, as well as (in many cases) basic welfare provision such as schools, clinics, medical care, a holiday resort for their workers, local transport and payments for retired, sick or disabled former employees. These imposed social functions means that the SOEs are inevitably overstaffed by Western standards, with many of the excess staff underutilised – what has been termed 'production for employment's sake'.

The nature of the planning system in the DPRK means that many SOEs are in the costly position of having not only to manufacture a product but also to maintain an assembly shop to make the equipment they need for production – lathes, conveyor belts, tools and all the attendant spare parts required to keep everything operating. Naturally this usually means that factory plant is substandard and dated while the need to produce these items boosts the payroll. The payroll is further increased by the need to maintain what is often referred to as a 'padded workforce' composed of extra hands to be called upon should a Speed Battle suddenly be unleashed.

The highly centralised command economy makes reform extremely problematic for Pyongyang. The DPRK may cast a glance towards China when it talks about special economic zones, but to begin a reform process similar to China's is nearly impossible, notwithstanding Kim Il-sung's praise for Deng's 'Four Modernisations' in 1984. North Korea's economy is more closely modelled on the Soviet version than on the Chinese. The economies of the USSR and Eastern Europe were highly industrialised and nationalised when initial reforms were attempted. Over 90 per cent of the workforce were engaged by SOEs, and all enjoyed social welfare benefits. This situation is mirrored now in the DPRK. However, China was quite different. At the beginning of the Dengist reforms 80 per cent of China's population worked on the land – China was (and still is) an overwhelmingly agrarian economy in employment terms with a per capita GDP of under US$100 per annum. Less than 20 per cent of Chinese were covered by welfare payments, the so-called 'Iron Rice Bowl'. It can therefore be argued that economically at least China was never more than 20 per cent socialist and the vast majority of the rural population did not enjoy social benefits. Politically, of course, the system was rigid and did not tolerate dissent and stated officially that the economy was socialist. Yet because economically China was in reality neither highly industrialised nor highly nationalised, the reform process was arguably easy to kick off, enabling growth to be generated in incomes and the economy as a whole – what some Chinese economists have described as 'realize growth while problems exist, solving them in the process of growth.'

China did encounter problems. Former Premier Zhao Ziyang's own think-tank, the Economic Reform Institute in Beijing, which largely conceived the mechanics of the reforms and put a Chinese spin on what had been

Hungarian and Yugoslav policies, noted some of the problems with SOE reform. These included a tendency for managers to boost consumption and make bad investments, which led to a loss of profitability. SOE managers tended to overcompensate themselves and their workforces through large bonuses which, although they created happier workforces, were not profit- or performance-related but rather plan-target-related. They also managed to further inflate their own bonuses and those of their workers through housing allocations and other social benefits. Zhao's Institute came to the conclusion that managers felt little risk or sense of economic reality as ultimately the party-state underwrote their actions and guaranteed to bail them out. Thus had begun the period of politically motivated 'policy loans', which created huge amounts of debt and non-performing loans (NPLs) within China's state-owned commercial banking sector. It remains a major negative factor in China's financial system.

The problems were not surprising as the reforms of 1984 gave most Chinese managers a greater level of control without any retraining. Though few management teams were familiar with the term, they operated within a system of 'soft budget constraint' where output was emphasised over price stability, fiscal responsibility was jettisoned, and investment levels were determined by how much cash managers could persuade the banks (i.e. the government) to hand over rather than according to business criteria. This idealised form of managerial control is not possible in North Korea, where, though some additional powers have been ceded to SOE managers, the collective nature of management decreed by Kim Il-sung in 1961, the Taean Work System (after the Taean Electrical Machine Plant), whereby higher-level functionaries are supposed to assist lower-level functionaries and workers in a comradely spirit, still officially forms part of Juche economic theory.

The Lack of Investment

The rigidity of the DPRK at both economic operational and political levels has meant that there have been few opportunities for foreign investment in the country. Indeed foreign investment flows have been among the lowest in the world and for the most part actively discouraged, notwithstanding North Korea's laws permitting joint ventures and independent accounting, introduced in 1984 during the Second Seven-year Plan (1978–84) and extended during the Third Seven-year Plan (1987–93). Despite this legislation, Kim Il-sung still declared that the North was a self-sufficient socialist economy with no need for foreign capital, which could lead to national subordination, while acting as if the debts incurred in previous decades had ceased to exist. The 1984 joint venture law duly became little more than a vehicle to secure easier access to funds sent to the North by pro-DPRK ethnic Koreans in Japan.

The North's first tentative experiment with an economic zone designed to attract foreign inward investment was the Rajin–Sonbong Free Trade and Economic Zone, established in 1991, located on the Russian–Chinese–DPRK border. It was a complete failure due to a lack of infrastructure, no state support and political stubbornness. Pyongyang's attitude at that time was the somewhat arrogant one of 'build it and they will come', or rather 'declare it to exist and they will come' (an attitude again exhibited in 2002 when the Sinuiju zone was announced as part of a renewed package of reforms). The DPRK authorities built virtually nothing; those who invested in Rajin–Sonbong found totally inadequate, or even non-existent, facilities in terms of water, power and other utilities to support their inward investment, while little or no official encouragement was given. Pyongyang's history of defaulting on Western creditors since the 1970s did not offer foreign investors much incentive to trust the government either. Rajin–Sonbong, like Sinuiju, more than a decade later, was too little, too late.

Pyongyang's preoccupation with ensuring the regime's survival and its fear of losing control over the populace were such that ready and available workforces were not forthcoming as they had been in southern China in the Special Economic Zones (SEZs), such as those in Guangdong province. Facilities were noticeably substandard compared to many of the SEZs in China. While the Beijing bureaucracy often frustrated foreign investors, the process seemed smooth and transparent compared to dealing with Pyongyang. Early examples of foreign investment in the DPRK had been highly problematic, and advertising and marketing opportunities have remained non-existent. The persistent problem of the bad debt hangover from the 1970s also made attracting investment difficult. In 1996 Kim Jong-u, the DPRK's Director of External Economic Co-operation, travelled to Washington to try to interest potential investors, and he again appealed for foreign direct investment (FDI) at the annual Davos World Economic Forum in 1997. Little came of these efforts.

China's reform process was characterised by massive inflows of FDI, which were initially strictly controlled. Following the country's entry into the WTO in 2001, foreigners were able to majority-own businesses in an ever-growing range of sectors. FDI flows into Pyongyang, on the other hand, have remained paltry. This has meant that whereas China has grown into an economic powerhouse, attracting increasing amounts of FDI while exporting manufactured goods to earn foreign currency to fund massive infrastructure projects, Pyongyang has remained economically backward and has fallen into serious economic decline with minimal foreign currency reserves. Despite a commitment to prioritise light industry in the mid-1980s, the sector most likely to generate exports and to attract investment, the policy was never acted upon; consequently the light industrial sector, which comprises approximately 4,500 enterprises, has remained secondary to loss-making heavy industry.

Pyongyang has not been willing to allow the use of material incentives to improve economic efficiency or international trade to promote and modernise industry. A policy similar to Hua Guofeng's[9] in China in 1978, which sought to accelerate growth through capital accumulation and massive importation of technology from abroad to retool and overhaul industry, is still unthinkable to the economic planners in Pyongyang. At the early stages of the Chinese reform process this investment flowed largely into basic, but necessary, industrial sectors such as oil, gas, coal and steel, but it provided a foundation from which to consolidate the reform process right across industry. Not that Hua's policy was guaranteed to work; after all, Hua borrowed it from experiments by Gierek[10] in Poland and Ceausescu in Romania – not normally held up as models of industrial success. Without concomitant reforms across the board the contradictions of the planned economy soon ensured that any new plant was wasted.

The Doublethink on Foreign Trade

A major problem for North Korea has been its inability to develop into an exporter of any substance, and the consequent failure to build up reserves of foreign currency. In contrast, China has emerged over the last decade as one of the world's largest holders of foreign currency reserves internationally.[11] These large reserves are now providing a comfortable financial cushion for the economists of Beijing as they try to balance rapid development with a mounting welfare bill, which, they hope, will allow China to absorb the impact of the closure of outdated and bankrupt SOEs, and of the resultant unemployment, as well as encouraging a shift of labour from rural to urban areas, while also funding the recapitalisation of the banking system laden with NPLs.

Even if North Korea were to find additional export markets its constitution does not encourage foreign trade. The constitution stipulates, in accordance with Juche self-sufficiency theory, that foreign trade should be at most 10 per cent of GNP, significantly below the international norm (including the socialist economic norm). Juche maintains that a high level of reliance on foreign trade threatens national survival and independence, thereby clearly indicating that an economy such as South Korea's, with a high level of dependence on exports, is somehow not independent. Again political imperatives have adversely affected economic development. In the meantime the country has not entered into serious debt rescheduling negotiations with its foreign creditors, who are obviously loath to do further business; consequently the international financial community continues to treat the DPRK as a pariah state. An additional hazard is the almost total absence of transparent economic data, which means that estimating risk is impossible.

Since the collapse of the USSR and the loss of export markets in the Eastern bloc, North Korea has engaged in a process of doublethink on the question of exports. While continuing to argue philosophically that exporting leads to dependence on foreign markets, in 1993, in the face of a crumbling economy, the government announced the 'Trade First' initiative wherein it announced that engaging in foreign trade was now good. The fact remains, however, that even if trade were prioritised, few internationally saleable goods are being produced. Since the late 1950s, when Kim Il-sung first complained about poor-quality products, rigid planning, combined with a lack of resources, inputs and modern equipment, along with the politicisation of the economic process through the relentless and numerous Chollima campaigns, poor quality has remained a problem for the industrial sector. This failure to tackle the issue of quality is a hallmark of command economies. Take just one example in the USSR. Brezhnev first complained about poor manufacturing quality, notably of shoes (also a problem in the DPRK), in 1976. It was eight years later that Brezhnev's successor, Chernenko, passed a decree on quality in the Soviet shoe industry. That a country's leader, either in the DPRK or the USSR, should become personally involved in a debate on the quality of footwear reveals much about the political micro-management of command economies.

From Subsidy Junkie to Ailing Economy

A major factor in the DPRK's economic development has been the central role of economic subsidies. Originally the subsidies were due to the largesse (or political opportunism) of the USSR; they were a pawn in the larger chess game of the Cold War and Moscow needed Pyongyang onside. At the time the USSR was a stronger economic power than China. Following the Sino–Soviet dispute Moscow determined that the DPRK would stay within Russia's orbit and not be lost to Beijing.

Despite their maintenance of a fairly independent line in general, Kim Il-sung, and later Kim Jong-il, unabashedly continued to accept large subsidies from the Soviets in the form of oil and other essential inputs. Once amounting to around US$1 billion per annum, not including armaments, these subsidies were cut substantially by Gorbachev, who also demanded repayment of outstanding loans and future settlements in hard currency. When the Soviet Union collapsed in 1991, the subsidies dried up to a trickle and then halted as the new Russian Federation slipped into economic decline and hyperinflation. With the end of the Cold War, Moscow began to sell its fuel competitively on the world market and use its earnings to support its own ailing SOEs. The effect of ending the subsidies was catastrophic for the DPRK.

For all the former socialist countries, and for those still nominally socialist such as China, Vietnam and Cuba, dealing with the legacy of state-owned industry has been a major stumbling block. Now the DPRK is faced with this problem as its SOEs become a drain on the country's already severely depleted currency reserves, its fragile and underdeveloped banking system, and the rising social welfare bill. In socialist one-party states with crumbling economies, dealing with these industries is highly problematic; there is little hope of finding alternative employment in new industries, and political legitimacy rests on the ailing SOEs as well as little or no foreign reserves to fall back on.

Political ideology plays its part. In the socialist system 'state owned' is used interchangeably with 'workers' control', however incorrect this may be in reality. Add to this the fact that by the 1980s the socialist bloc had developed military–industrial complexes that had little success in transferring military technology to civilian use. In the DPRK Kim Il-sung, who was spending 30 per cent of GNP on the military, appeared not to realize that he was competing not just with ROK but also US military spending, as America was both selling and transferring arms and weapons technology to Seoul. With mounting debts and waste from the SOEs, as well as their general unproductiveness, it finally became clear that something had to be done before they dragged down whole countries with them – though in some cases they did.

Gorbachev tried to deal with the Soviet Union's SOEs through perestroika, although ultimately he would encounter too many political and ideological obstacles. Slimming, shutting or privatising Soviet industry couldn't work because the resultant unemployment and social deprivation was too much for a socialist country to bear politically. Subsequently, perestroika failed, Gorbachev was ousted and privatisations went ahead under Boris Yeltsin using a combination of public share offerings, direct sales and investment tenders, management and employee buy-outs, and an untested and ill-conceived voucher scheme that saw most of the profitable parts of Russian industry bought up by what became popularly known as 'oligarchs' while the rust belt stayed with the people and continued to collapse, with citizens' vouchers gathering dust.[12]

China has approached its SOEs from a slightly different perspective, though no less tentatively. Nearly twenty-five years after the reform process began, most of the SOEs remain in place, supported by politically motivated 'policy loans' sanctioned by Beijing and paid by China's state-owned banking system. China, though, has several advantages over the DPRK in dealing with its SOEs. First, some of the state enterprises are profitable and have managed to reinvent themselves, slim down and improve their operations, build brands, absorb other non-performing SOEs and enter profitable joint ventures with foreign companies. Second, China's growing private enterprise economy has served to absorb the unemployed, and its substantial currency reserves have allowed it to maintain a basic welfare system. The DPRK has no currency reserves, brands, potential foreign partners or private economy to speak of.

Other models of dealing with SOEs in socialist states may prove to be more suited to the DPRK's needs. One such is the 'equitisation' programme now ongoing in Vietnam. Another may be the New Economic Mechanism (NEM) being instituted in Laos, aimed at shifting the country away from central planning and towards limited free enterprise.[13] However, one important facet of both equitisation and the NEM is the close involvement of the World Bank and other international agencies – something not currently possible in North Korea.

Palaces Galore But No Socks

It is difficult to assess just how bad a shape North Korea's SOEs are in. Yet a description of the giant Magnitogorsk steel plant in Russia's Urals, written by a visiting American academic in 1988, may be indicative of the state of North Korea's heavy industry.

> Plaintive calls for the total overhaul of the Magnitogorsk plant began more than 25 years ago. But reconstruction was perennially postponed, and the factory was called upon to make do with what it had: shore up a bit here, patch things together there, in short, give itself a sort of artificial respiration. The factory complex employs many more repair workers than steel smelters.[14]

Failed SOEs also present a political problem for governments. Although enterprises are often praised in the state press and on television, it is usually painfully obvious to the workers at an ailing plant that the enterprise is a failure. In North Korea enterprises are subject to on-the-spot guidance visits (the *Chongsan-ri*, a system that began during the 1961–67 Five-year Plan under Kim Il-sung following his visit to the Chongsan-ri Cooperative Farm in South Pyngan Province). Guidance visits lead to elaborate preparations; the idea that a production line might be stopped due to electricity shortages or to a machine being idle for lack of a spare part during a visit by a leader is unthinkable. These visits create Potemkin Villages, fake yet elaborate scenes for an afternoon only.

Hence there is a contradiction. Workers in an obviously decrepit enterprise see the whole falsehood of government economic statistics and claims before them every day. However, workers employed in one of the few productive enterprises may well start asking themselves why they are working sixteen-hour days, six days a week, and still there are no goods available, rations are short, prices are rising and shops are empty, while they are exhorted to do still more. In most socialist countries key SOEs have been privileged places despite their lack of profitability, with workers rewarded in various ways, including higher wages, bonuses, holidays and better apartments. However, in North Korea, with the economy in such a state of collapse, the incentive system is worthless. One alternative has been to isolate key enterprises, such as in the Soviet Union or in China's secret cities, though these tend to be military complexes. The situation in North Korea today is as absurd as it has been in other socialist economies in the past. This account of a worker at Magnitogorsk in the 1980s gives an idea of the ridiculousness of the situation that undoubtedly exists in the DPRK today.

> How can it be that we have needs and yet no producer is in a position to fulfil them? It's no use appealing to the central trade authorities. The whole process usually culminates in one of their 'studies of demand'. They then include this in the reports of their work and receive bonuses for it! Our sewing factory is plastered over with posters of outstanding workers; you can't buy an article of clothing in our stores.[15]

A further drain on resources of the productive economy are the monumental construction projects in the DPRK. The grand schemes of the leadership appear to be more to do with internally legitimising the system – maintaining an aura of success for the population and curious foreigners – than with solid economic growth. They function as a form of architectural propaganda.

North Korea has built a large number of structures that have clearly been costly to construct and that have redirected resources, manpower and funds from the industrial and agricultural sectors. Pyongyang's Juche Tower, the

Grand People's Study House, the Arch of Triumph (taller than the original in Paris), the Kim Il-sung Stadium and the Kumsusan Memorial Palace where Kim Il-sung's remains are kept – all are expensive follies. Additionally, there are massive projects that have never been completed, such as Kim Jong-il's pet project, the 105-storey pyramid-shaped Ryugyong Hotel, started in 1992 but never finished due to lack of funds. The ambition behind these grand projects is grand indeed. The Kim Il-sung Stadium is the world's second largest. An estimated US$4.5 billion was spent on new facilities for the Thirteenth World Festival of Youth and Students in Pyongyang in 1989.[16]

In addition to these monolithic structures, which represent massive waste at a time of dire economic need, are the luxury cars for the Party elite, the elaborate theatres and museums that also act as propaganda centres, and, of course, the weight of military spending. The redirection of funds from the productive economy is very substantial.

The Economy Shows Its Cracks

After the period of rapid growth to rebuild the country following Chollima, the Great Leap Outward and Trade First, the command economy began to show cracks in 1976 and 1977, although already by 1968 the country had stopped officially publishing detailed economic statistics. Twenty years of massive human investment in the economy had raised it rapidly in a way that Marxist–Leninist economics had done in the USSR in the 1930s and again in China after World War II. The application of muscle, ideological drive, aid and subsidises from the USSR, as well as an initial period of easy credit from the West, had worked for a while; yet, as in other command economies, the system was not suited for longer-term economic development. Coupled with this, by the mid-1970s the gloss had worn off the DPRK's image inter-nationally and the country was retreating into an increasing isolationism governed by ossified Juche theory and a dominant personality cult around Kim. The inherent contradictions in the planned economy were becoming ever more obvious.

The Fifth Assembly of the DPRK's SPA, North Korea's parliament, revealed the failing state of the economy in April 1977. The reports of the senior officials of the government were, as usual, full of praise for the Great Leader and detailed growth in government revenues with expenditure less than planned. The SPA announced an annual growth rate for the 1971–76 six-year plan period of 16.3 per cent, despite the fact that the plan was extended by one year. The leadership praised the introduction of the local budget system, which claimed to delegate more financial responsibility to the provinces, though in effect it never did. However, later in 1977 it was announced that some administrative districts were not performing to target and that subsidies would be required. The fiscal year for 1977 (January–December) was declared to be a 'period of readjustment' prior to the launch of the new seven-year plan.

The plan was effectively extended by a year, indicating that targets had not actually been met. The budget for 1977 was set at NKW 13.7 billion in income and NKW 13.8 billion in expenditure, higher than the figures for 1976 of 10.6 and 12.3 billion respectively (the DPRK's budget is derived from turnover taxes, profits from SOEs and user fees for working capital). Mineral extraction and agriculture, two crucial areas of the economy, were identified as needing much additional work. In calling on workers to reduce the wear and tear on machinery, the government was admitting that a crisis was mounting in terms of spare parts, many of which required hard currency to purchase. With loan repayments still outstanding, spare parts clearly would not be shipped without some form of resolution to the debt problem or cash in advance. The government also called on workers to use energy and raw materials more sparingly, thereby indicating growing shortages, and to remit more surpluses to the government, despite an apparent fiscally prudent underspend. They indicated that the books may not be quite as balanced as the Budget and Finance Committee had claimed.

As well as making these changes the government virtually admitted that the plan was a failure by calling upon 'local industries' and foreign-currency 'Work Companies' to raise their profile. Local industries are those operating outside the normal planning regime; Work Companies are those, invariably small, businesses formed with the express intention of earning foreign currency for the government. The emphasis on this sector indicated that even if plan forecasts were met, or exceeded, this would not be sufficient to maintain economic growth and output. Kim Il-sung publicly intervened in the debate, berating enterprises for their excessive consumption of coal and urging them to meet their plan targets. Clearly the leadership was aware that the planning system was no longer meeting the needs of society.

A further indication that the situation was deteriorating was the strange ideas suggested by the leadership. These included substituting rice production for higher-yield maize, the construction of more mineral water plants, and criticism of the fishing fleet for catching fish that were too large. The Minister of the Fishing Industry bravely informed Kim Il-sung that fish stocks were depleted. The Great Leader's response was to highlight a fundamental problem of the command economy: that transportation had been underfunded; a consequence of which was that the wastage of fish was immense. He ignored the fact that fish stocks had been depleted, apparently with no restocking built into the plan. In another instance, Kim called for the generation of more foreign exchange earnings, ordering the mining industry to earn US$100 million by extracting and selling precious metals – far in excess of targets in the original plan. This drive for foreign exchange may also have had the effect of depleting the DPRK's gold reserves. While no reliable figures are available for the 1970s, it is known that between 1995 and 1997 Pyongyang exported US$193 million worth of gold bars to the ROK.[17]

Clearly the 1971–76 plan had not been fulfilled, yet the SPA was told that it had been. What occurred in fact was that certain areas of the economy had overfulfilled their targets, while others had fallen significantly short. The statisticians in Pyongyang then used a trick learned from the USSR, and replicated in China: they declared an aggregate production level that appeared to indicate that the overall plan had indeed been fulfilled, without making public the shortfalls in various sectors.

This tactic of using over fulfilled sectors of the plan to cover up under-performing sectors of the economy raises an obvious contradiction in the whole command economy process. Clearly those sectors that had fulfilled their plan targets had not then stopped production; they had carried on, exceeding the plan's targets. Yet, once the target had been reached, the additional production continued to use raw materials and energy – which clearly must have come from other sectors of the economy. The absurdity of the plan thus becomes apparent.

For instance, if the ceramics industry fulfilled its stated quota earlier than envisaged, it would continue producing until the end of the plan period and the subsequent issuing of new targets in the next plan. During this period the industry would continue to consume raw materials, energy and fuel. Now, assuming a certain level of co-ordination within the plan, the ceramics industry would have been allotted a certain amount of inputs to meet its target. It follows that all excess use would be at the expense of other sectors requiring these same raw materials and fuels. Additionally, the extra ceramics produced would require additional logistical resources, distribution infrastructure, warehousing and transportation – all at the expense of other sectors. Even if the energy and raw materials sectors were to exceed the plan too, this would still cause problems for other sectors such as mineral extraction and power generation, which would have additional demands placed on them.

The result of this mismatch between the sectors, the plan and available resources would mean that, while the ceramics industry may have exceeded its targets, another sector, say textiles, would be unable to meet its target due to shortages. The knock-on effect would be immense and compound, distorting the whole economy. In addition, ceramics, like most North Korean products, are rarely successfully exported, being destined largely for the domestic market. If they were being manufactured for export, the demand would have been finite; exceeding the plan would then translate into overproduction, in turn pushing down the price paid by the importer and depressing revenues and profit margins for the exporter. This would also explain why North Korean consumers have to cope with a retail-rationing system that may have a surplus of ceramic products while the shops are empty of winter clothing or shoes. A similar process can occur in the agricultural sector, leading to the availability of, say, tomatoes but little else, thereby making balanced eating extremely problematic.

The continual exhortation to overfulfil quotas, the inherent rewards for exceeding the plan (or, conversely punishment for failure to do so), the constant Speed Battles and drives to raise production through local industries outside the plan, which could be competing with the ceramics plant and adding to overcapacity and energy use – all this means that instead of the smoothly oiled machine the plan claims to be, it is instead a mess of improvisation, unfair allocation and staggered production, not to mention the time wasted, while factories lie idle for want of energy or spare parts, or officials, who might otherwise be profitably employed, try to scrounge resources. Ultimately, in a command economy both over- and underfulfilment of the plan quota disrupt the system. Rather than cooperation between related enterprises, there is competition between factories, each aiming to exceed the plan faster and by more. The consequence in North Korea, as in other command economies, has been waste on a massive scale of resources, energy and labour. The results include, at best, inferior products, squandered human resources, wastage of fuel, energy and raw materials, and a consumer market forced to accept shortages and uncoordinated distribution (which in recent years has been subject to rampant corruption, meaning that a high percentage of goods are lost in unofficial or semi-official 'tolls'), and a complete lack of goods and famine at worst. As Hillel Ticktin, a specialist on the Soviet economy, has noted: 'The question is why is there this enormous waste in the producer goods sector. The answer lies in a conflict of interest between those who administer the economy centrally and those who deal with their instructions at the immediate or local level.'[18]

While the simple mass production of steel or ceramics may be suitable in the rapidly developing phase of an economy, such as during Chollima, to provide steel for construction when people are homeless, or ceramics for people who have no plates from which to eat, once a certain basic level of development has been achieved the plan becomes subordinate to the needs of the market and, as was the case in the DPRK in the late 1970s, rapidly undermines the economy and hastens economic collapse.

Despite these obvious contradictions and the admission that a year-long 'period of readjustment' was required, North Korea remained wedded to the command economy, due to its central position in Juche and in the leadership's conception of economic management. At the same time as the economy began to slow, and then enter into inevitable decline, the Equal Emphasis line remained in place with its consumption of resources that would otherwise have been channelled to civilian society. Finally, a degree of reform was attempted that conceded market realities and accepted the need to try to prevent – unsuccessfully, as it transpired – the country slipping into a state of permanent shortage, and ultimately famine.

The period 1976–77 was a tipping point for the DPRK economy, as the system's stagnation and decline reached critical mass and the regime triggered a renewed process of political isolation. By tacitly admitting the failings of the planning system but devising no real solutions to the problems except to redouble the physical human efforts used to drag the economy along, the country entered what Eric Cornell has described as a 'cul-de-sac'.[19] Relations with the West reached a new low, and the regime had isolated the non-aligned movement through its arrogance and insistence on the theoretical superiority of Juche while becoming increasingly dependent on the ailing economies of the Eastern bloc, which were neither overly well-disposed to North Korea, nor by this time able to provide substantial aid – for their own economies were entering cycles of terminal decline. The eventual collapse of the USSR only hastened the collapse of North Korea's economy.

The Arduous March Begins

By the start of the 1980s the DPRK's economic collapse was well under way, notwithstanding vague claims of annual economic growth of over 12 per cent, as the planning system continued to erode the industrial and agricultural base of the country while Pyongyang was forced to reschedule its foreign debts, almost immediately falling behind in promised interest repayments. The 'Ten Major Targets for Socialist Construction in the 1980s' were announced – in effect a partial reiteration of the aims of the Second Seven-year Plan (1978–84) halfway through. By the end of the plan period the government was claiming it had reached all targets, although it released no detailed statistics to back up the claim. The Third Seven-year Plan, announced in 1987, simply used 1986 statistics as base figures. It indicated that the previous plan had run two years over schedule, despite the claims of fulfilment. The new plan called for unrealistic increases in steel and grain production – the DPRK ceased production of statistics on actual grain production in 1984.

The role of the USSR as a prop to the economy became increasingly important as throughout the late 1970s and early 1980s the DPRK came increasingly to rely on subsidised fuel and other economic aid, although it was becoming increasingly apparent that Moscow now saw its interests as lying elsewhere, and indeed had severe economic problems of its own. A five-year trade agreement was concluded with the USSR in 1981, and a similar one with China in 1982. These eased the trade crisis, but only for a couple of years, after which exports to both countries fell again. By 1990 the DPRK was reliant on the USSR for most of its coal and oil as well as a third of its steel. The USSR accounted for over 50 per cent of the DPRK's two-way trade. However, 1990 saw the country's GNP begin seriously to decline.

The arrival of Mikhail Gorbachev in the Kremlin with his twin policies of glasnost and perestroika marked a sea change in the relationship between North Korea and the USSR. Glasnost led to a major questioning and rethinking of the history of the Soviet Union, the role of the CPSU and the country's relationships with its client states, fraternal partners and the West, while perestroika was largely a belated formal recognition of the shortcomings of the command economy. Gorbachev's policies brought about fundamental change within the USSR as well as reorienting the country's foreign policy, aid priorities and international alignments.

Gorbachev immediately urged perestroika on Pyongyang, hinting that the USSR now had to concentrate on its own ailing economy and lacked the resources to support client states. However, the USSR retained a military alliance with North Korea that saw joint naval and air force manoeuvres in 1986. For a time military aid to the DPRK also continued; in the late 1980s the USSR supplied at least fifty MiG fighters and forty warships to the North.

While Gorbachev looked for ways to reduce the USSR's financial and military commitments to the DPRK and extend the new détente with the West, Russia under glasnost was discussing North Korea. In 1989 the Soviet media, buoyed by a new investigative zeal, started reporting on the DPRK's faltering economy and its waste of resources and aid. A series of articles in the Soviet press highlighted the poor quality of goods imported from the DPRK. As TASS reported growing economic hardship among the North Korean population, Radio Moscow pushed for the establishment of official ties between the USSR and the ROK, as well as vocally supporting the ROK's entry into the UN. The Seoul Olympic Games of 1988 were a symbol of international recognition for the newly democratic South Korea. The North demanded a socialist boycott of the Games, a call unheeded by the socialist bloc.[20]

The rapprochement between the USSR and South Korea was of major concern for Pyongyang, and forced Pyongyang to recognise the changing world. In response, the North fell back into isolation, feeling betrayed by allies and fearful of losing ground to the South. The crunch had come when Gorbachev led a delegation to Seoul to establish diplomatic relations in June 1987 and to meet ROK President Roh Tae-woo. This new relationship subsequently forced Pyongyang to start its own process of engagement with the South, and in September 1990 the highest-level delegation ever of North Korean officials visited Seoul for talks.[21]

In the USSR media coverage of the DPRK became increasingly harsh. The influential liberal current affairs magazine *Argumenty I Fakty* published a negative profile of Kim Il-sung in April 1990, just prior to the Soviet–ROK summit that vexed Pyongyang. This was followed by the publication of an article by Soviet historian Mikhail Smirnov claiming, against CPSU orthodoxy, that the North Koreans started the Korean War. By the turn of the decade it had become clear that Gorbachev was recasting ties with the DPRK. Russia effectively cut all military aid to the North by insisting Pyongyang settle its bills in hard currency. While this removed the North as an active military client of the USSR, it was arguably the impetus for the DPRK's subsequent involvement in various illegal activities (drug dealing, counterfeiting, smuggling, illicit arms sales, etc.) in order to obtain hard currency.

Almost immediately after the collapse of the USSR in 1991 and the near total withdrawal of subsidies, North Korea's economic situation nosedived, reflecting the extent to which Soviet aid had been drip-feeding the country's economy and subsidising import costs. The decline was dramatic: in 1991 the USSR supplied over 40 per cent of North Korea's imports; by 1993 it had fallen to below 10 per cent. The government was forced to admit the failure of the Third Seven-year Plan (1987–93), stating that some major indices including electric power, steel and chemical fibre envisaged in the Third Seven-year Plan were not attained due to international events and the acute situation created in Korea. With much of the North's industry reliant on cheap imports, the loss of the trading relationship with the USSR precipitated a process of deindustrialisation. At the same time the cost of imports from other countries was rising – between 1989 and 1992 the price of crude oil rose by US$75 to US$135 per tonne, further exacerbating the situation.

Whereas the North had enjoyed a per capita income of approximately double that of the South, by the time of the USSR's collapse the situation had been dramatically reversed.[22] The government's remedy was predictable: further calls for production outside the plan, which simply further accentuated the command economy's contradictions. Several ambitious and ill-conceived plans were inaugurated to stem the decline, including the mass reclamation of coastal land for rice growing, which faltered when desalination and adverse climatic conditions caused flooding. The reclaimed rice fields (some 300,000 hectares) utilised significant resources and lay outside the central plan, thereby distorting the system. Several infrastructure projects were planned and then scrapped, including the Ryugyong Hotel. The decision to commit valuable resources of labour, materials and energy to such projects, which combined vanity and economic ignorance, reflected the obvious gulf between the elite and the rest of society while also demonstrating the further 'dissipation of resources',[23] as everything took longer to complete than intended, or was never completed at all. Social equality, still noticeable in the 1970s, gave way to chauffeur-driven cars, private restaurants for cadres and better housing and food rations for the elite.

Essentially the DPRK was unable to change its economic and trade orientation quickly enough to cope with the sudden shock of the USSR's demise. The result was an instant implosion as crucial inputs exited the economy. Within a few years, the global geopolitical situation had changed dramatically as the socialist bloc crumbled, China further embraced market reform, and other socialist command economies, such as Vietnam and Cuba, embarked on limited reform programmes of their own. Central planning and the command economy were out of fashion. By the mid-1990s North Korea was in a state of famine and industrial collapse; in 1995 it was forced to call on aid agencies and governments to help ease the situation. By the time of Kim Il-sung's death in 1994, strict adherence to the economic plan, though still maintained publicly, was forgotten; the government drifted and economic collapse became absolute.

The DPRK's rigid command economy and collectivised agricultural sector had both become reliant on Soviet power and material inputs. When the inputs ceased, the inability of the economy to adjust to a new reality led to collapse and food shortage – though Pyongyang protested that natural disasters were to blame. To give just one significant example: when the USSR officially ceased aid in 1987, the DPRK's daily grain rations, distributed through the PDS, immediately fell by 10 per cent. By 1992 rations had declined by a further 10 per cent, at which point Pyongyang launched a 'let's eat two meals a day' campaign to try to reduce consumption.[24]

The Energy Crisis: Grinding to a Halt

The major detrimental effect to the North's economy following collapse of the USSR was the deepening of the country's energy crisis consequent upon the ending of fuel subsidies. The shortfall in power output was a major factor in undermining the command economy and destabilising the plan

– the DPRK's 'Achilles heel'.[25] The situation was exacerbated by the DPRK's outdated generating capacity, lack of a maintenance system,[26] low reserves of traditional fuel and the underdevelopment of alternative energy sources. The result was that factories were unable to run, fuel for transportation was severely rationed and the public was forced to endure blackouts. In 1999 electricity generation was 40 per cent of that in 1990.

The North's economic infrastructure focused on heavy industry and collectivised agriculture; hence power requirements were considerable and consequently a priority. For instance, the main fertilisers used in North Korea, urea and ammonium sulphate, are both petroleum-based; low fuel stocks restrict supply, with only an estimated 40 per cent of requirements being met.[27]

The North inherited some power stations from the Japanese occupation; though they were modern when constructed, by the 1970s, outdated and poorly maintained, they were due for retirement. Other power stations were bought semi-constructed from the USSR. However, because they were completed with locally sourced parts that were substandard they broke down regularly. This has reportedly been a perennial problem with the Pyongyang Thermal Power Plant, which has consistently been unable to supply the capital with the power it needs. Ultimately it was the command economy that played a major role in undermining the DPRK's ability to provide energy. With the exception of some local energy markets, price plays little role in the DPRK energy system. There is no allowance made for repairs and upgrading, and the distribution system is in a state of near collapse. Waste too is a major factor. Indeed, Peter Hayes, executive director of the Nautilus Institute, claims that 'a significant fraction (often more than 50%) of scarce energy supplies are wasted by inefficient end use equipment.'[28]

From the beginning the DPRK sought to utilise its natural landscape and climate to generate hydroelectric power, though the same erratic climatic conditions that have bedevilled the country's agricultural system have also afflicted its hydropower-generation capabilities. Persistent drought has reduced reservoir levels to below the minimum needed to produce hydroelectric power, and currently 85 per cent of the DPRK's generating capacity is idle. To counter this unreliability the country constructed coal-fired thermal plants. The DPRK has coal reserves, the Mabong Trading Company alone used to export around half a million tonnes per year, mostly to Japan. However, by the mid-1970s the coal-mining industry was in crisis, with flooded mines and lack of power to transport coal to the stations, which in turn began to fall idle and into disrepair as supplies ran out and maintenance was not performed.[29] A similar problem has occurred in the magnesite sector, where there is insufficient power to operate kilns. Like other non-functioning capacity, power stations were responsible for enormous energy waste, with transmission and distribution losses increasing.

The next phase of power development was the building of small and medium-sized stations – the North Koreans claim to have built 5,000 in 1998 alone. Here again, though, the plan contributed to the collapse of the economy, with calls for additional power station construction without concomitant plans for maintenance. Hence many were built in the wrong locations, to poor standards, and quickly fell into disrepair. Many were thermal power plants designed to get round the DPRK's lack of oil reserves. Even the planners saw the stupidity of this waste of resources and reduced the number being built to a few hundred per year.

Although the DPRK has reserves of both oil and gas, it has not exploited them effectively and relies instead largely on supplies piped from China, in the absence of Soviet fuel.[30] The country has possible reserves in the Yellow Sea, where China's Bo Hai Gulf oil fields are already onstream. Foreign investors have been invited to help develop oil and gas reserves; these include Australia's Beach Petroleum in 1990, Sweden's Taurus in 1992, and a British company, SOCO International, in 1998. However, the companies have usually had to work with antiquated Eastern European drilling equipment, while much vital seismic data was in the hands of the government-owned North Korea Oil Exploration Company. North Korea has also made small-scale forays into alternative energy sources – wind, tidal and solar power – but, with a dearth of energy experts and little outside contact, these have as yet done little to stem the energy crisis. The other power source is, of course, nuclear.

Nuclear power generating capacity in the form of two light-water reactors (LWRs) was supposed to be provided to the DPRK by KEDO as part of the 1994 Agreed Framework. However, these have yet to materialise. Aside from the political issue of the two reactors, their impact on the DPRK's energy crisis is questionable. Maxim Kozlov of Korea Business Consultants in Beijing has stated that, though the two reactors would have a combined total capacity of 2GW, which would go some way to easing the country's power shortage, they could unbalance the country's ageing and poorly maintained grid system. If one reactor were shut down, according to Kozlov, the grid would need to be capable of taking the load until the reactor was reactivated. This is possible if the capacity of any single reactor is less than 10 per cent of the grid's total capacity. The DPRK's existing grid is thought to have a capacity of approximately 7GW and thus it cannot support 1GW LWRs. Kozlov concludes that the only course of action is for the DPRK to interconnect with other regional grids, a solution that has so far not been politically workable.[31]

The withdrawal of energy subsidies by the USSR – 506,000 tonnes in 1989 down to just 30,000 in 1992 – certainly worsened the crisis. Yet the major factor has been the command economy's inability to plan a workable national power grid. Efforts at extending the national grid have invariably been based on volume power station construction, which has led to ill-suited facilities in the wrong locations or tied to SOEs that allowed them to fall into disrepair. The situation has been further compounded by a lack of technical skill, the absence of hard currency to purchase spare parts, no foreign investment, and the failure of the economy to upgrade and maintain facilities.[32] As with industrial production and agriculture, waste has been a significant factor in the energy crisis – cities, towns and many factories still suffer regular blackouts, while workers walk to work because buses have no fuel. Factory managers also soon realised that the renewal of fixed capital was not rewarded and that incentives to raise production through the introduction of new technology were low and that any gains in productivity could not be offset through unemployment as the plan required the workforce to remain padded. So new plant was only acquired when administrative pressure forced the purchase.

The lack of dependable energy resources is crucial to understanding the economic collapse. It is estimated that in 2002 North Korea's power generation contracted after a small growth in 2001. A major cause of the contraction is the ever-worsening state of the country's coal mines while maintenance problems have reduced hydroelectric generating capacity, on which North Korea is now overreliant, while sudden fluctuations in voltage cause system overloads and damage machinery, reducing its working life and increasing the demand for maintenance and spare parts.

The Two-track Survival Economy

Although North Korea has stubbornly refused to jettison its command economy system of economic management, the new realities since the late 1990s have seeen the country create an identifiable two-track economy: the supply of materials and resources to the military and the leadership would continue, while the civilian economy came increasingly to survive on humanitarian aid. However, unlike other such two-track economies, most notably China in its forging of a middle way between the free market and command economy, North Korea has thus far proved unable to shed the straitjacket of Juche and abandon the top-down approach to planning whilst retaining total political control. Increasingly, any notion of a plan has been steadily eroded. As shortage and decline have become the keynotes of the economy, attempts have been made to create new industries with the possibility of reviving the economy. The hasty announcement of such initiatives has invariably meant that all resources and labour devoted to them are, by definition, outside the plan. Any 'new' industry must absorb or divert resources from other sectors within the plan. Even if these industries are partially backed by inward investment, such as the small-scale projects to produce IT and telecom products with Chinese partners, valuable and scarce energy resources have to be diverted. By sanctioning these interventions, the planners are in effect subverting the plan themselves.

Transforming a command economy into a market economy is a hazardous business, and Pyongyang has shown that as far as it does pursue economic reform this will be in a gradualist fashion, even though the consequences may be catastrophic for people's lives. Again the example is China and not the USSR. Pyongyang's assessment of the transition in Russia is not that different from most people's – Gorbachev failed because he didn't deal with entrenched ideologues and the resistance to loss of power among elements in the CPSU leadership and military. Into the vacuum stepped Yeltsin, who crashed out of the command economy into a market economy while at the same time presiding over the break-up of the Soviet empire, the collapse of the country's military power, mass impoverishment, the rise of resurgent separatist claims, of organised crime, of crony capitalism and a particularly unattractive class of newly rich entrepreneurs and oligarchs (albeit tempered by a series of new possibilities for more entrepreneurial Russians). Russia essentially ceased to be a superpower, lost its satellites in Eastern Europe and became, in the famous expression, effectively 'Upper Volta with nukes' – an epithet now increasingly applicable to the crumbling DPRK.

China is seen as the opposite example and greatly admired by many, for the right or the wrong reasons, for its ability to start and continue a transition towards a more full market economy. This view is encouraged by China's WTO accession in 2001, the awarding of the 2008 Olympics to Beijing and EXPO 2010 to Shanghai, all high-profile events that suggest world approval of Beijing's reforms. Nevertheless, China remains a nuclear power, with no democracy, has used tanks against protesting students; imprisons striking industrial workers and angry peasants while continuing to refuse to accept a free press, an unblocked Internet or a convertible currency; and continues to attract lobby group fury for its activities in Tibet while sabre-rattling over Taiwan and the Spratly Islands. Yet China remains one of the most popular destinations for multinational companies, tourists, trade delegations, visiting politicians and businesspeople.

China has created a two-track economic system. The first track is the one that China actively promotes internationally and likes to present to foreign investors. This is the coastal and southern China: the powerhouse cities of Guangdong; the skyscrapers of Shanghai; the tourist resorts and enterprise zone of Hainan Island; the growing ports of Ningbo and Xiamen; as well as the manufacturing centres of eastern China around Zhejiang, Fujian and Jiangsu provinces. The second track is the central rural belt of poor peasant farmers, the underinvested western regions of Xinjiang, Ningxia and Tibet, and the ailing industrial areas of northeastern China around Jilin and Heilongjiang provinces.

While the first economy is booming and privileged, with foreign investment and government support, the second economy is protected from total collapse by central government funding and something not dissimilar to the old-style command economy. When economists discuss how the WTO will change China, they really mean the first economy. The changes forced on the country by the WTO do not really touch the second-track economy. The first economy is the one propelling forward the much-talked-about Chinese middle class, car ownership, property buying and wine tasting. It is where China's exports that so vex American politicians originate, and where the growing inflows of foreign direct investment arrive and the growing incomes and retail sales occur.

In the second economy unemployment is spreading fast, overcapacity is the norm, bad debt is mounting, poor-quality goods are manufactured and bureaucracy dominates the economy. Where the first track has been increasingly integrated into the global economy and is subject to a more deregulated market and flexible pricing, the second economy is still rigidly controlled and supported by aggressive taxation on farmers and political loans to state-owned enterprises that instantly become non-performing, which are the bedrock of most communities. It is also where the burden of rising welfare payments is crippling local administrations and enterprises; where rural health care is in a dire state after the SARS outbreak and threatened by an HIV/AIDS explosion.

Nevertheless, the existence of a two-track economy, while problematic, offers Beijing a way out of the economic problems inherited from the total command economy of Mao's day. Conversely, the DPRK lacks this first track, which is a major problem in terms of both its current economy and the prospects for any future reform programme.

The first-track economy in China has no political power as such – that continues to reside in Beijing. Yet it does have the capacity to earn foreign currency, stimulate consumer spending and provide funds for the economic measures and infrastructure development needed in the areas of the second economy. The huge injection of central government transfers, Treasury bond issues and development funds have been generated by the first economy and by loans. It is this cash that has the potential to bail out the banking sector and to stimulate growth in key sectors of the second economy. Andy Rothman, China strategist with CLSA Emerging Markets in Shanghai, certainly believes in this scenario whereby track one generates enough activity and revenue to overhaul track two: 'What we can expect to see is a longer term improvement to [China's] rural infrastructure – with the building of farm-to-market roads, power and water supplies, schools and irrigation – that will lead to greater productivity and a higher standard of living.'[33]

This is not to say that there are not problems with the two-track approach. Unemployment is growing faster than Beijing expected. Consequently statisticians have had to revise their figures substantially, and these still do not account for the underemployed or the millions of rural migrants engaged in temporary work in the first-track cities. Government borrowing and investment in infrastructure projects are very substantial and must eventually be repaid; looming in the background too is the problem of the state banks and their non-performing loans (NPLs). These loans, which now act as subsidies, were made to support ailing SOEs, which can never hope to repay them. Notwithstanding all the asset management efforts, the government, in the form of the central bank, the People's Bank of China, remains the final underwriter and guarantor of all this debt – which will most likely never be repaid.

Whatever the problems for China, the DPRK is left without the options enjoyed by its neighbour. Farm-to-market and factory-to-port roads, for instance, remain largely inadequate. There has been little investment capital available for upgrading, while fuel shortages have reduced road and rail freight transport to below 40 per cent of their 1990 levels. While China's leaders can bite the bullet and face up to such problems, the leadership in Pyongyang has no room for manoeuvre. What Pyongyang appears to have done is created its own version of the two-track system: the first track is the terminally sick domestic economy and underproductive agricultural sector; the second track is dependency on foreign aid.

The DPRK as an Aid Economy

By 2000 the DPRK was faced with a collapsing economy reliant on ever-growing donations of aid from various international sources. This latest round of aid had begun with an appeal to foreign NGOs in 1995. There had been an initial appeal in 1979 to the UN Development Programme (UNDP), which led to a technical assistance grant of US$8.5 million and further aid totalling of US$73.8 million in the period up to 2000. In 1991, after severe food shortages that led to a lowering of the Public Distribution System (PDS) ration, Pyongyang called in the UN World Food Programme (WFP) to conduct a needs assessment. However, on the ground the WFP met with a lack of cooperation. In 1991 it was still impossible for the political elite to admit to a failure in government economic policy. Rations continued to be reduced throughout the early 1990s. Betwen 1995 and 2001, the international community has donated some US$591.96 million to North Korea.[34]

What North Korea is left with now is effectively an 'aid economy' on a par with certain African nations using aid to ensure regime survival. The aid economy keeps the country, its people and the political regime afloat on a drip feed, while the second economy, the domestic sphere, continues to drain resources and act as a counterproductive force. The longer the command economy continues to drain resources and energy, the more severe the economic collapse, and the more aid is needed to prop up the country.

Although few official statements on Pyongyang's attitude to aid exist, beyond highly rhetorical and political comments,[35] it is clearly a thorny issue for the leadership. The government's relationship with the aid agencies has long been described as 'adversarial'.[36] The sources of the aid are rarely made public to North Koreans, as large donations of aid from the US, Japan and South Korea, among others, clearly reveal inherent weaknesses in the system. Until the latest impasse over the DPRK's nuclear capability put an end to most official American government aid, between 1995 and 2002 the US donated almost 2 million tonnes of food aid and US$1 billion in energy and other aid to North Korea, making the country the largest single Asian recipient of US state aid.[37]

Relations with Japan have been, until recently, similarly paradoxical: the level of official anti-colonial rhetoric against Tokyo has remained high as aid inflows from the country grew. A similar situation exists in relations with South Korea. Non-nationally based NGOs have also encountered problems. The US Private Voluntary Organization Consortium (PVOC) pulled out in 2000. Médecins Sans Frontières discontinued its operations in September 1998 due to lack of access and suspicion that supplies of medicines were being channelled to children of the elite. World Concern has also halted relief supplies of food, claiming KWP cadres were profiting from selling food aid. Oxfam also pulled out in 1999, as did Action Contre la Faim (ACF) in 2000, both citing differences with the North Korean authorities. The obstacles posed by Pyongyang, such as obscuring the extent of the crisis, have frustrated many aid agencies. They say that if they were to believe the claims of the government and the evidence of the regularly presented healthy-looking children, then they would pull out as clearly the country would have no need of them. The process, then, involves Pyongyang dissembling to save face, while knowing that NGOs will not believe them and continue humanitarian aid shipments.

Assessing the scale of the famine has not been helped by the issuing of only limited visas to aid workers, restrictions on travel and the requirement of advance permission for controlled visits to rural areas, and no access to certain severely affected areas linked to military installations. Consequently, the list of NGOs that have pulled out either temporarily or permanently lengthens, America's CARE and Britain's Children's Aid Direct among them.[38] In consequence, the aid effort is largely organised and run by the UN and various national or supranational efforts. In effect, aid supply to North Korea has become a diplomatic issue rather than one of charity and famine relief. While this has meant that the North Koreans have been able to receive aid without ceding significantly higher levels of access and moni-toring – most UN- or government-sponsored humanitarian aid is subject to less rigorous tracking procedures than that from NGOs – it has also meant that aid has taken the form largely of humanitarian food shipments to ease the immediate situation rather than of longer-term NGO projects involving changes in farming techniques and methods. Although Pyongyang has failed to feed the population through the collectivised agricultural system, it is unwilling to change much, with the exception of turning a blind eye to the growth of barter and private plots.

The DPRK is now an economy centrally dependent on aid from overseas. Historically the country has received aid from the USSR, the Eastern Euro-pean socialist bloc and China since its inception. This, however, was 'fraternal' aid, and is distinct from the country's latter-day aid dependency. Formerly aid was military and industrially based; now it is humanitarian. The dependence on aid has also meant strings attached for Pyongyang, initially support for the USSR or China and latterly an increasing pressure to liberalise, enact political reform or get back into line on the nuclear question as an induce-ment to receiving further payments. In the same way that the DPRK was not keen to side with either the USSR or China, likewise today it is apparently no more willing to make concessions in return for aid, whoever the donor. As with earlier aid from China and the USSR, the DPRK has institutionalised latter-day humanitarian aid by including it as part of the annual budget or plan, thereby effectively integrating aid into the command economy.

Estimates of how much aid North Korea receives and of the scale of its needs vary. The United Nations estimated the country's needs at US$383 million for 2002, while the World Food Programme claimed to be feeding 7 million North Koreans already, approximately 30 per cent of the popula-tion. Notwithstanding the claims of Juche ideology, North Korea can only provide at best about 50 per cent of the cereals it requires to feed the population from its own agricultural base. Pyongyang has been forced to relax its attitude towards aid agencies by making visa applications easier and allowing NGO representatives longer periods of time in the country, though full cooperation, as seen in African or South Asian nations, is still rarely forthcoming.

With many other pressing cases for international aid, and in light of the DPRK's increasingly pariah status, aid levels have been hard to maintain. Many people may feel there is an ethical imperative to help feed the starving people of North Korea but not to help prop up what the vast majority consider to be a totalitarian regime. In July 2002 the UN claimed to have secured 61 per cent of the required aid of US$383 million for the DPRK for the full year and the Korea Rural Economic Institute stated that UN relief agencies had raised US$160 million. This was a rerun of 2001, when by April the UN had raised less than one-third of the amount required.

The growing aid economy in the DPRK has only added to the overall economic woes of the country. Pyongyang has increasingly concentrated on maintaining and increasing aid shipments to try to fend off the growing famine. This has also meant that instead of dealing with the dire situation in the agricultural sector the government has been able to divert funds into other areas. This has duly threatened the aid shipments, as many countries sought to tie aid to nuclear inspections, weapons limitation programmes, economic reform and enhanced levels of diplomatic dialogue. Aid has also meant that Pyongyang has been able to put off more meaningful levels of economic reform as the inflows have helped mitigate the famine and food shortages but not altered the fundamental industrial or agricultural economic system of the DPRK significantly. For instance, many NGOs keen to provide assistance in the most severely affected provinces, such as Hamgyong, have been told that they can only gain access after establishing projects in places such as the relatively unaffected Nampo, where the government is keen to improve conditions.[39]

A further question concerning humanitarian aid has been the alleged diversion of shipments of food aid to the armed forces. This issue has generated a lot of discussion. On the one hand aid workers wish to see the food distributed equally over the country to those most in need. The level of access aid workers from the various NGOs have managed to secure in North Korea through hard bargaining is not always appreciated. A fair degree of autonomy is now given for inspections, and aid workers increasingly have the ability to track aid shipments from arrival to destination. On the other hand some argue that the army is so all-pervasive in the DPRK, rather than the elite troop of most other countries, that food shipments destined for the army will ultimately be distributed widely throughout the country anyway.

The diversion of aid to the military and the elite remains a major problem for NGOs, with one UN official asked about the question declaring simply 'We don't know.'[40] Chung Ok-nim, an adviser to the Seoul government, has written that South Korean NGOs have pointed out that between 200,000 and 300,000 tonnes of food per year is required to feed the army. If the average domestic grain production of the North is still around 2 million tonnes, then this should not be a major issue.[41] However, the initial concentration of aid in the south of the DPRK, rather than in the worst affected regions in the northeast, also benefited the army as about 70 per cent of its strength is deployed south of Pyongyang.

Despite the relations with Russia, China and Japan having improved in the recent period, there is little likelihood of traditional subsidies returning to North Korea. Aid is, of course, a form of subsidy, but different in substance. Russia is unwilling to reinstate subsidies to the DPRK even though the Russian economic situation is stabilising and Russia is assuming a more forthright global role under President Putin. Simply put, North Korea is no longer high on Moscow's agenda. Putin may still agree to meet Kim Jong-il but only because of traditional ties and the current Russian realpolitik of balancing interests between the superpowers. North Korea remains the market for Russian arms and weapons technology despite its historical debt to the USSR, estimated at US$3.8 billion. Little is currently being done with regard to that debt, with the strange exception of North Koreans sent to work in Russia's far east, apparently in appalling conditions and with little say in the matter.[42]

The Chinese are also keen to reduce their aid to North Korea and divert these resources to their own rust-belt provinces. However, while the North Koreans are increasingly becoming a political and economic burden and a general embarrassment to Beijing due to embassy-wall-jumping dissidents and aid requirements, the prospect of a sudden Romanian-style collapse of the DPRK is alarming to Zhongnanhai.[43] Any collapse of the North that led to an erosion of the demilitarised zone without US guarantees of troop withdrawal could effectively put American troops on China's northeastern border. This is not a welcome prospect for military planners in China as, in addition to threatening the strategically important port of Dalian, it would see US troops on the PRC's northwestern borders in Afghanistan and Tajikistan.

Likewise, aid shipments are problematic for Japan while the anti-Japanese rhetoric continues. The Kim–Koizumi one-day summit in 2002 split Japanese public opinion on the principle of aid to the North following the confirmation that North Korea had abduced Japanese citizens in the 1970s and 1980s. A similar split in public opinion exists in South Korea.

While in China, as we have seen, the two-track economy means that Beijing can use the first, booming, economy to prop up and overhaul the second, North Korea's two-track economy is far less flexible. Some in Pyongyang may hope that the aid economy provides sufficient relief to allow the country to introduce reform or find some other way out of the current malaise, but the economy cannot be revived in this way. Little of the aid is designed to restructure industry or improve agricultural production, being instead short-term aid, which Pyongyang prefers.

The process of securing aid is itself a drain on any real reform; North Korea has grown used to its dependency. Negotiating the delivery, amount, arrival and distribution of aid is a time-consuming task, invariably undertaken by people who should be using their time to revive the economy; those suffering malnutrition obviously also lack strength, which reduces their productivity – if they are still able to work. As to those supplying the aid, they are increasingly suffering donor fatigue, as North Korea appears an unworthy recipient in a world of seemingly more deserving causes. In the longer term food aid will not solve the food security issue in North Korea; it is now simply too big to be papered over. The only answer is for aid to tide the country over until a reform process opens the DPRK up to trade and the earning of hard currency with which it can purchase food stocks. This requires the revival and overhaul of the industrial economy to a point where it can generate revenues through exports to provide the DPRK with food security.

The Command Economy Remains Firmly in Place

Since the heady days of reconstruction and Chollima following the establishment of the DPRK, the country's economy has gone through three major periods of shock and revision:

- 1976–77 It had become clear that Chollima was no longer yielding results and that muscle combined with planning was no longer sufficient to deliver growth. The attempts to introduce more advanced industrial and production methods largely failed, systemic debt accrued and waste mounted. De-Stalinisation in the USSR had rendered the aim of socialism increasingly opaque in economic terms and regime survival became paramount. Additionally, the Sino–US rapprochement of the 1970s left the DPRK feeling more isolated and it subsequently retreated into the planned economy. The government called on workers to produce more while urging conservation of energy. At the same time the practice of producing outside the plan further undermined the system. The rural workforce did, however, embrace this concept and concentrated on supplying their own needs as much as possible through private plots, thereby further reducing the output of the collective farms. In 1976 all debt repayment to the West ceased in what amounted to an admission of bankruptcy.

- 1988–91   Reforms and adjustments introduced in 1977 had failed to address the faltering economic situation significantly. Production outside the plan continued to weaken the system. Machinery imported in the 1960s and 1970s was now obsolete, either broken down for lack of spare parts or rusting away unused. DPRK–USSR relations changed: Gorbachev demanded hard currency payment while reducing 'fraternal' aid. Foreign debt exceeded US$6 billion. North Korea was becoming economically and politically further isolated from the West, to which it owed money; from its allies in the Eastern bloc, whom it could not pay and who were themselves crumbling; and from the non-aligned movement, which had become alienated by Pyongyang's arrogance. China was concentrating on its own reform programme and was forced to contain dissent at Tiananmen Square, while South Korea pulled away from the DPRK economically and became a global success story. The energy crisis intensified. Nevertheless, North Korea joined the nuclear age, commissioning a nuclear reactor at Yongbyon. Meanwhile food shortages became more serious. The only response was to urge the workforce to produce more outside the plan, which only served to fuel further overall decline.

- 1994–96   The full effects of the collapse of the USSR were now being felt, accentuating the energy crisis. In 1993 North Korea's debt was estimated at US$11.9 billion; its GNP was US$22.3 billion. North Korea became increasingly isolated internationally and was being described as a 'pariah state'. The country's situation was in stark contrast to that of South Korea, by now a fully fledged Asian 'Tiger' with average annual income in excess of US$10,000. The energy crisis persisted and deepened in the absence of oil supplies from Russia, and food shortages were aggravated by a series of climatic disasters. By 1995 Pyongyang had recognised the famine in the country and called on aid agencies around the world to help.

Throughout the period the command system remained in place, a central pillar of Juche and upheld by the leadership. Though disillusionment with the economic system had set in by the 1970s – if there was ever an opposition to the economic policy it was in the 1970s when there were reports of worker discontent, posters appearing, critical remarks and the first defections across the border to China – in the aftermath of the USSR's dissolution the command economy had collapsed to the degree that most people were absorbed in simply trying to feed themselves.

The DPRK's maintenance of the command economy ran contrary to the wholesale switch from the model in the former USSR and the gradual shift away from rigid planning by the Chinese, as well as the various reforms in Vietnam, Cuba and other socialist countries. Why has North Korea remained loyal to central planning?

The answer to this question lies in the DPRK regime's own belief that politics is paramount. Central planning is enshrined in the overarching political value system – Juche. To criticise it is to call Juche into question and hence to challenge the leadership. With the cult of personality all-pervasive, the trend is for officials to strive to outdo each other in showing loyalty to the leadership, rather than to question the plan or expose waste in the system. Thus the command economy and the havoc it has caused will last as long as Juche and its proponents remain the dominant force in society. In 1991 North Korea was forced to explain why the Marxist–Leninist command economy had failed in the USSR and Eastern Europe. Kim Jong-il's answer, reported in a talk given to senior KWP cadres, was that 'The imperialists and reactionaries, loudly advertising the "advantage" of private ownership, are urging socialist countries to abandon social ownership and restore private ownership.... The people in our country experienced through their actual lives that social ownership alone provides them with an abundant and cultured life.'[44] Essentially, Kim argued that Juche was a higher form of organisation than Marxism–Leninism and therefore North Korea would not follow the Soviet economy into the dustbin of history. Yet to describe the North Korean economy as providing an 'abundant' life for the people of the DPRK in 1991 was clearly a massive act of self-delusion by the leadership and the elite.

Thus it is that the DPRK media continue to laud the country's economic progress and to dismiss the economic dynamism of South Korea. Such an inversion is necessary to justify Juche and the plan, and can be done because there exists no comparative base upon which to judge the statements. Consequently they can claim improved agricultural yields, even when yields are poor compared to other nations'. A classic example is the official jubilation that met the state's announcement that North Korea had built a 20,000-tonne ship. Domestic readers lacked any point of reference and had no idea that ROK shipyards had for many years been driving their Western competitors out of business, building 200,000-tonne and larger tankers up to 400,000 tonnes. Indeed, things had moved on to such a degree that South Korea was no longer concentrating on shipbuilding; other nations, such as China, could now do it more cheaply and profitably. Even when the shipyards of the ROK had become a 'sunset' industry, the country was still producing ships totalling some 43 million tonnes annually in 2002. In the same period the DPRK was producing just over 1 million tonnes.[45]

Before examining how Pyongyang has attempted to reform its economic system, it is necessary to assess just how low the economy has sunk and to reflect on the repercussions of industrial decline, agricultural collapse and famine for the people of the DPRK.

5

The Worst of Times:
Food, Famine and the Arduous March

From Riches to Rags

The run-up to the announcement of economic reform in North Korea was a period of particularly bad public relations for Pyongyang – not that the regime has ever been too worried about its international image. The problems can be broken down into five major categories: economic collapse; persistent shortages and knowledge of the recent famine reaching the outside world; the collapse of Kim Dae-jung's 'Sunshine Policy' of rapprochement; the growing problem of defectors crossing the border into China, highlighting conditions inside the DPRK, and overwhelming embassy compounds in Beijing; and George W. Bush's 'Axis of Evil' speech, which ratcheted up the rhetoric between the US and DPRK.

The economic situation is currently dire but it was not always so; indeed North Korea's decline has been described as a process of 'riches to rags' or alternatively the 'march of misery'. In recent years an identifiable black market has emerged, with prices as much as ten times higher than those in the PDS. This has been accompanied by the emergence of a growing class of smugglers, many of whom regularly cross the border between China and the DPRK. In the current emergency economic climate some of this activity is semi-officially tolerated as a means to reduce shortages.

Since the late 1990s the North Korean people have been on an official long march that makes that of Mao look like a stroll. The period from the late 1980s through to the famine was described as an 'Arduous March'. As severe shortages continued into 1998 the slogan was adjusted to the 'Forced

March to Final Victory'. Then, despite no let-up in the economic situation, the slogan was again reworked to the hopelessly optimistic 'March to Paradise'. At no time did the state admit to any ideological, economic or systemic problems as causes of the industrial decline or famine. Rather, a host of other explanations have repeatedly been offered, including the after-effects of the Japanese colonial period, the Korean War, the rejection of socialism by Russia and China, and the unofficial blockade of the country by American imperialism. In North Korea the Arduous March continues, notwithstanding the rejection of the rigid plan and collective farming in both China and Russia.

As industry has collapsed, the inability of the agricultural system to provide sufficient sustenance for a sizeable percentage of the population has been the most disastrous consequence of the decades of fatally flawed central planning. The rural economy's collapse has led to famine, starvation and death on a massive scale. It has also forced the DPRK to call on international assistance, in effect admitting its failed policies to the world. Though the worst of the famine may now be past, food security is still far from guaranteed, with a large section of the population reliant on aid and severe shortages persisting nationwide.

Despite the obvious failure of the system, the collectivised nature of the agricultural economy remains officially in place even though it is increasingly fraying at the edges as people are forced to adopt survival mechanisms that conflict with official policy. Agricultural production remains extremely problematic, and hence feeding people without aid is impossible. Drought and flooding have persisted, further adversely affecting the rural economy. The longer Pyongyang refuses to make significant changes in the organisation of agriculture the more the risk increases of famine returning – what USAID's Andrew Natsios has called a possible 'second apocalypse'.[1] The continued adherence to collectivised Soviet-style agriculture combined with another major crop failure, compounded by donor fatigue reported by NGOs, would be truly catastrophic for North Korea, its people and its neighbours.

The Collective Agricultural Disaster

The majority of Korea's arable land, including most of Korea's rice-growing regions, lies in the south of the peninsula. For a decade now a major problem for North Korea has been famine. Although severe food shortages were experienced the late 1940s, in the mid-1950s and then again in the mid-1970s, the famine of the 1990s eclipsed all of these. In order to understand fully how North Korea, a country with a guiding philosophy of self-reliance and planned self-sufficiency, has been reduced to a state of grudgingly relying on international aid to feed itself, it is necessary to understand the history of the North's agricultural system, with its rigid, though comparatively blood-less, process of collectivisation and subjection to the broader principles of the command economy.

Since the establishment of the DPRK, agriculture has taken second place to industrial production in government priorities, reflecting the influence of the USSR rather than China, with Kim Il-sung enthusiastically embracing the theories of the Soviet agronomist Trofim Lysenko.[2] As it did with its industrial economy, Pyongyang adopted a Soviet-style agricultural system. G.A.E. Smith noted that 'the problems of Soviet agriculture are in essence no different from those of Soviet industry'; and the same applies to North Korea.[3] Following the redistribution of all lands formerly owned by tradi-tional Korean landlords (*yangban*) and Japanese colonial interests in 1946, which led to an immediate drop in output, all agriculture was collectivised between late 1954 and August 1958, thereby consolidating the 1946 Land Reform Act, which confiscated the holdings of landowners and distributed them to smallholding farmers and former tenant farmers. Most major landowners were allowed to leave the DPRK to resettle in South Korea or overseas – 5 million accepted the offer.[4]

Although North Korean collectivisation was not overly harsh compared to the more violent dispossession of landlords in the USSR and China, it did contrast sharply with the South's approach to land reform. In the ROK widespread tenancy was replaced with full land ownership by individual farmers, following the passage of a land redistribution law in 1949 that also compensated former landlords.[5] While the DPRK's collectivisation process did not lead to the massive internal struggles seen in similar programmes in other socialist economies, it did set the stage for the eventual collapse of the agricultural system.

Along with collectivisation, a policy of compulsory grain seizures and the eradication of all private trade in food was introduced. However, since their establishment the productivity of these collective farms, considered officially the most advanced form of agricultural production under Juche theory, has been highly erratic. It has been estimated that the 18–20 per cent of North Korea that is arable provides 25 per cent of GNP, despite a lack of modern fertilisers, pesticides, herbicides, other chemical inputs and farm equipment for the highly input-sensitive agricultural system – another legacy of Lysenkoist theory. The peninsula's historical division between the northern industrial area and the southern breadbasket has meant that this ratio of arable to non-arable land in the DPRK has been an inherent disadvantage. The DPRK ranks low internationally in terms of available arable land, which indicates the need to embrace the most advanced forms of agricultural techniques to maximise output and yield. While a low ratio of arable land is problematic, it is clearly not an insurmountable obstacle to food security: countries with comparable ratios have shown this using advanced farming techniques, modern fertilisers, reclaimed land, crop rotation and irrigation.[6]

Indeed, despite this in-built disadvantage, in the 1940s the northern portion of Korea was able to support itself agriculturally. Since the armistice in 1953 food security has been a long-standing problem for the North; food shortages were first reported around the time of mass rural collectivisation in 1954–58. In the 1960s the ideological platform of the 'four modernisations' was applied to agriculture: mechanisation; electrification; irrigation; and use of chemicals. This heavy reliance on technology, chemicals and power was to lead to additional problems as energy and chemical fertilisers became increasingly scarce in the 1980s and 1990s,[7] notwithstanding Kim's declaration in 1961 that the DPRK was self-sufficient in grain. By this point 52 per cent of the labour force was reckoned to be engaged in industrial work.

The DPRK's principal agricultural products are rice, corn, potatoes, soybeans and pulses. The aim of the government, as outlined in Juche, was to achieve self-sufficiency. This led to changes in traditional agricultural production, which would later cause problems, such as the shift away from a number of crops, including millet and potatoes, to increased maize production. This move towards a smaller number of crops increased the reliance on inputs such as fertilisers, herbicides and pesticides, and put the rural economy at greater risk of a total crop failure due to its lack of diversity. However, the continuing food shortages have now made self-sufficiency an unrealisable target and, as we have seen, domestic production is heavily supported by foreign aid.

Currently agriculture in the DPRK remains collectivised (referred to as 'Complete Socialist Co-operatives'), though most farms are smaller than those created in the USSR in the 1930s or the Chinese communes of the 1950s. The process of collectivisation in North Korea was relatively gradual, moving from 'mutual aid teams', where small-scale landholders managed their own land as private property, though they pooled labour, animals and tools, to 'second-stage co-operatives' or 'semi-socialist co-operatives', where all land and equipment was pooled. The final move to full collectivisation was fairly rapid. Those farmers who had gained from the 1946 Land Reform Act found themselves forcibly collectivised into 4,500 co-operative and state farms. Each farm comprises between 80 and 300 households. The brief period of individual landholding before 1958 had stipulated that individual holdings could not exceed 5 *chngbo* in lowland areas, or 20 *chngbo* in mountainous areas.[8] Ultimately this collectivisation aimed to create a proletarianised agricultural workforce with no land ownership ties, strong ideological commitment and without any of the peasant traditions that remained in Russia and China despite their similar policies. North Korea's relative size, and its available arable land, made a greater level of control of the rural population more feasible than in either Russia or China with their more wide-ranging, geographically diverse and remote rural populations.

The new collective farms were based on traditional *ri* or *ni* (village) models. Critics of the system believe that, as well as ultimately reducing output, collectivisation disrupted the traditional kinship system, although of course this was in part its purpose. The government permitted the ownership of small gardens, fruit trees, the small-scale raising of poultry and animals for personal consumption and sale at farmers' markets, as well as limited beekeeping. These private plots, or micro-farms, which can officially be no more than 160 square metres in area, were initially disliked by the government as a diversion. (Stalin had similarly cracked down on private plots.) Collective farm life is naturally seasonal. Typically farmers rise at 5.30 to check the crops, have breakfast at 6.30 before returning to the fields an hour later. The majority of collective farm workers have to participate in a daily 30-minute reading session of the *Rodong Sinmun* newspaper and receive instructions on their daily work. Most rest between noon and 2.00 p.m. and then often work until 8.00 in the evening. They also have regular one-hour so-called 'Life Integration Sessions' in the evenings, although, as in the cities, these Party-related activities have become less conspicuous in recent years, with many people skipping attendance to tend their private plots or search for additional food. Life can be equally hard for rural children: many now have to walk for an hour to get to school.

The farm's work is organised along the principle of the Taean Work System, an industrial management system introduced in 1961 by Kim while on a visit to the Taean Electrical Appliance Plant. Under the Taean System higher-level functionaries assist lower-level functionaries and workers in a 'spirit of close consultation and cameraderie'. Any challenge to the Taean or to collectivisation principles is rarely tolerated; indeed, when former guerrilla general Kim Kwang-yop suggested a new system of small-unit management in the countryside to prevent the collective farms becoming too unwieldy he was ousted from power. Even when the USSR undertook relatively radical agricultural reforms in 1965 that included a guaranteed wage for rural workers and raised investment in farm machinery, Pyongyang resisted any shift from the Taean system. In the USSR the reforms failed to stem the flow of labour away from the rural areas to the cities or lift the general apathy of farm workers. In the DPRK internal migration is more strictly controlled and the limited land mass makes social control in the countryside less problematic for Pyongyang than it was for Moscow.

Food shortages reappeared in the early 1970s, further indicating that the entire economy was stumbling. This was despite the fact that during this period the role of fertilisers in agriculture had been increased to what many foreign agronomists considered excessive levels. This led to stored-up problems for the agricultural economy when, after the collapse of the USSR, fertiliser, pesticide and herbicide imports largely disappeared. Though by this time their untrammelled usage had caused major damage to the soil and exacerbated water pollution, withdrawing their use virtually overnight led to reports of fields of weeds and stunted crops.

In the 1970s the government's response to falling output was to reinforce the central planning system further, which ultimately accentuated the problem. This reinforcement was accompanied by a major social and political campaign designed to reinforce the ideological commitment of farm workers to increase production. This did little to help; indeed it further exacerbated the problem as the new rural education curriculum eroded traditional knowledge of farming and left farm workers with no scope to institute policies to improve crop yields.[9] Later, during the famine, this loss of traditional knowledge was to add to the rapid collapse of the rural population's coping mechanisms and survival strategies.

This agricultural industrialisation process reached its peak at the same time as Pyongyang was admitting that industrial productivity was starting to decline. In 1976 the 'Nature Remaking Programme' introduced rigid regulations on farming, stipulating field sizes, planting standards, increased crop density and crop rotation, continuing to reflect Lysenkoist thinking which had by now been discredited in the USSR. The programme was continually bolstered and occasionally re-emphasised in modified forms up until the late 1990s, with the intention of further cementing political control in rural areas by breaking remaining links between farming communities and the land they once owned or had rented for generations.

This intensified politicisation and reinforcement of the command economy has also contributed to falling yields, a growing reliance on a dwindling supply of inputs, which domestic industry is now incapable of supplying, and ultimately the famine. The measures have also add to the environmental problems of soil erosion, contamination, silting and flooding. The primacy of political decision-making over farmers' knowledge has led to a further erosion in productivity. Kim himself, not known for his intimate knowledge of agricultural techniques, regularly interfered directly in the agricultural economy. For instance, he ordered the cultivation of corn on steep hillsides.

The result was that soil was washed away during heavy rains, destroying crops and further silting rivers. The political dimension of agricultural policy is enshrined in Kim's *Chongsan-ri* methods of farming, which were supposedly based on a collective farm near Pyongyang, though in fact they seemed to reinforce the ideological component of farming techniques developed from Soviet practice, approved in 1964 by the KWP Central Committee, and therefore not easily subject to change.

The loss of Soviet subsidies combined with the failing national economy further depleted energy resources; agricultural production continued to fall in the late 1980s and early 1990s as burning wood became more common than coal and imports of fertilisers and other chemical inputs disappeared. Food shortages became more severe in 1990 and 1991, affecting the PDS ration. Production declined annually until 2001, when it began to rise due to an abatement of natural disasters and the implementation of various programmes designed to raise yields – largely instituted by the UNDP Agricultural Recovery and Environment Plan (AREP). AREP has instituted a number of agricultural reforms including double cropping, crop diversification, a greater concentration on potatoes and better use of advanced fertilisers. Despite this rise in production a serious food deficit persists, particularly of cereals; and Pyongyang continues to oppose the wider use of techniques not originally part of the *Chongsan-ri* system, such as double cropping. Double cropping is a prime example of the adverse effects of the DPRK's isolation. While it was originally used with only limited success, and rejected during the early *Chongsan-ri* period, crop strain and genetic engineering developments have rendered the technique more applicable to the DPRK.[10] Again, politics was dictating a disastrous agricultural policy and preventing rapid improvements in yield. This is despite the fact that where NGOs have been able to force the introduction of double cropping – for example, growing winter barley on land that is subsequently used for rice cultivation – it has been successful. Here the UNDP, with the support of reformist elements in Pyongyang, had persuaded Kim Jong-il to accept double cropping even though it lay outside the Juche theory of agriculture. Kim later claimed the idea for himself and incorporated it into his 1998 'New Theory of Agriculture' policy.

'Slow Motion Famine'[11]

Famine is nothing new in Korea. Famine followed the invasion of the Japanese feudal lord Hideyoshi Toyotomi in the 1590s as marauding armies confiscated food. In the seventeenth century, during the Yi dynasty, famines regularly occurred following severe droughts, and they reappeared again in the mid-

eighteenth century. Flooding caused famine in the early nineteenth century
and led to peasant rebellions. During the Japanese occupation (1910–45)
confiscation of food by the Japanese army led to severe shortages. Even in
good years the northeast of the country has always been perilously close to
shortage due to the lack of arable land and low yields.

The famine of the 1990s has become the international symbol of North
Korea's economic collapse and represents a problem of national security for
the government. It had been signposted since the mid-1970s when economic
decline began: diplomats reported concerns then that food production was
only sufficient for 25 daily rations a month. In the early 1990s rations started
to fall again as shortages mounted and the PDS began visibly to fail. This
was tacitly admitted by the government with its 'Eat Two Meals a Day'
campaign in 1992 and its appeal to the WFP in 1991 – an appeal overruled
by Kim Il-sung, who, though rarely leaving Pyongyang, virtually blind and
in ailing health, still maintained that the economic system was working. A
UN survey at the time concluded that malnutrition and stunted growth in
children were apparent.[12]

The state first officially admitted that food shortages had deteriorated
into famine in 1994, when in certain parts of the country, particularly the
northeast, all levels of society showed signs of severe malnourishment. Reports appeared of rising seed prices and failure in seed allocation, indicating
that farmers were eating their available resources rather than saving seed
for the next season's planting. South Korean President Kim Young-sam
offered some unconditional aid, Pyongyang, however, appealed only to Japan
for subsidised rice, claiming it should be donated as part of a reparations
package to compensate for the colonial period. North Korea did also look
to import additional food; supplies eventually came from the ROK and
Japan on credit. For a brief period in the early 1990s China became the
main supplier of imported food, though in mid-decade reduced the supply
severely as the North Koreans continued to accept food while denouncing
Beijing's abandonment of the socialist cause. Alienating the Chinese at a
crucial moment hastened the descent into famine.

Pyongyang managed both to alienate Beijing and to play politics with the
ROK and Japan. Initially South Korean aid was not accepted, as the ROK
was officially an enemy, whereas Japanese aid could be interpreted domestically as reparations and thus recycled as a political victory for Pyongyang.
Ultimately the situation dictated that Pyongyang had no choice but to accept
food aid from both Japan and the ROK, though the state media only ever
mentioned the former.

Several major NGOs had been liaising with the government since the
1980s, notably the United Nations Development Programme (UNDP),

which opened the first NGO resident office in the DPRK in 1980, and the WFP, which opened a Pyongyang office in 1996, as well as a host of others. However, Pyongyang had no real experience of working with NGOs and, to be fair, at the time most NGOs had no staff with experience of the DPRK's political system or much understanding of what had produced a situation where people were starving. Indeed many NGOs' initial assessments, clouded by government control of access, concluded that famine was not present in the country.

This lack of experience on both sides meant that initial relations between the NGOs and Pyongyang were problematic. The government was suspicious of any major involvement, while the NGOs naturally sought the usual monitoring, verification and evaluation of the aid they were supplying. Some NGOs found the intransigent attitude of the government and the obstacles placed in their path too much and withdrew from the DPRK. As the shortages continued and the famine worsened so Pyongyang managed to build an uneasy but functioning relationship with the NGOs, which has remained, as well as with national donors including the US, the EU, Japan and South Korea. Additionally China has supplied aid, including oil and approximately 1 million tonnes of grain annually. Nevertheless, according to the US Institute of Peace, even by July 2002 some 43 provinces of North Korea, accounting for 18 per cent of the population, still remained inaccessible to NGOs. Most NGOs report that raising money for North Korea has been extremely difficult and is not getting any easier.

The 1994 aid was merely a stopgap, as flooding returned in summer 1995, destroying a further 330,000 hectares of arable land and leading to the loss of nearly 2 million tonnes of grain (approximately half the annual harvest). It also destroyed 3 million tonnes of emergency grain reserves held by the state. Food confiscations by the state and worsened flooding due to desperate fire-field (or brush burning) agriculture on hills and mountainsides exacerbated the crisis further. Though many believed that North Korea exaggerated the devastation caused by the flooding, it was politically useful. Pyongyang was able to justify its 1995 appeal to the international community for assistance in coping with a natural disaster rather than the effects of government policy. Further, though less severe, flooding in 1996 again allowed Pyongyang to continue to argue that the system was not at fault.[13] As the shortages worsened so famine set in for a growing proportion of the population, along with the health problems and social breakdown that accompany famine everywhere.

Although accurate figures on total agricultural output are impossible to verify, the consensus seems to be that in recent years annual North Korean grain production has been less than 4 million tonnes per annum. Almost a decade after Pyongyang asked international agencies to help North Korea and Kim Jong-il reportedly described the situation in the country as 'anarchy' in internal KWP documents, the assistance being delivered is still described as 'emergency' aid. To date aid from the US, the largest single donor (followed by the the EU, ROK, Russia and Italy), has been in excess of 1.8 million tonnes, around US$591 million. Where many NGOs originally operated from a non-resident base, many are now based in-country. However, Pyongyang continues to hamper life for the donors. Back in 2000 massive shipments of food aid from the ROK were greeted by *Rodong Sinmun* editorials stating that 'The imperialists' aid is a tool of aggression ... a dangerous toxin which brings about poverty, famine and death, not prosperity.'[14] Pyongyang was able, at least internally, to represent aid as a form of tribute to the country rather than as desperately needed supplies, and presented it as a 'privilege' for NGOs to be allowed to supply aid to starving communities.

In 2003 the DPRK entered the ninth consecutive winter of severe food shortages, with the WFP feeding an average of 5.4 million people every month, one in five of the population, though down from 6.5 million the previous year. However, following some improvements since the worst of the famine, aid agencies are now concentrating aid to children under 17, while adults increasingly have to rely on the PDS, private plots and farmers' markets. Notwithstanding the continuing burden, donor fatigue continues to be a problem, with the UN stating in December 2003 that the current level of aid was just 62 per cent of the total requested, which translates into just 10 per cent of the level donated in 2000.[15] Winter, the 'lean season', is when domestic supplies run out, privately hoarded food expires and aid becomes essential to survival. As the crisis has deepened so the available aid has had to be extended from just food. For instance, aid has increasingly been di-verted to help provide power for hospitals unable to undertake even routine operations.[16] Additionally NGOs have had to provide basic equipment such as shovels and hoes as well as boots and gloves, and also initiate energy-providing projects such as the Nautilus Institute's wind-turbine generating project in Unha-ri and the solar ovens supplied by the Rotary Club.[17]

This struggle to provide aid reflects ongoing government interference and donor fatigue, despite the fact that a third wave of NGOs, mostly South Korean, set up operations in the country following the June 2000 Inter-Korean Summit. Many have encountered even more obstacles to distribut-ing aid effectively, and as the political situation has deteriorated so public attitudes to aid have hardened in Seoul. The ROK government-run Korea Information Service published a poll in May 2003 indicating that 88.5 per cent of the country's population backed linking aid to the nuclear issue.[18] Nevertheless, there has been some easing of restrictions by the government since 2001, with NGO representatives able to drive their own vehicles within Pyongyang and move around the country a little more freely, after some hard-fought battles between government officials and NGO staff.

In the meantime the agricultural collapse has continued, with domestic animal numbers declining due to lack of fodder, a growing scarcity of farm machinery and fuel, decreased seed availability and crop failures due to lack of fertilisers and other inputs.

Attempts to Resolve the Agricultural Crisis

Prior to calling in the international aid agencies, Pyongyang did attempt to resolve the food shortage crisis in the early 1990s through a combination of traditional Maoist-style mobilisation campaigns and a policy of effectively turning a blind eye to many of those adopting more drastic coping mechanisms by operating outside the official agricultural system. The government did attempt to buy food on credit but the DPRK's poor credit history did not encourage sellers. Some purchases were secured, though this just meant additional bad debt to grain and rice suppliers, including the US food giant Cargill, who reportedly agreed to barter 4,000 tonnes of North Korean zinc for 20,000 tonnes of wheat.[19] It was politically necessary for Pyongyang to try to resolve the crisis itself as it realised that to admit the extent of the famine, even in the coded political terminology it eventually employed ('natural disaster ... the turn from socialism of former allies ... imperialist sanctions'), was effectively to concede that its economic system had failed. That could also be interpreted as a sign of military weakness and of pending social and political collapse.

The reality in the late 1990s was that the DPRK's agricultural economy had been adversely affected by a number of factors including seven or eight years of drought, crop infestation, shortages of fertilisers (down from 217,000 tonnes in 1995 to 81,000 in 1997, with a demand for 350,000[20]) herbicides and pesticides, and of course the scarcity of fuel to operate agricultural machinery and to produce inputs domestically. Additionally, continued large-scale spending on armaments had meant a lack of investment in industry and agriculture, while the secrecy surrounding the military led to a poor rate of technology transfer between military and civilian industries.

Additionally, the outdated farming techniques employed on most farms, the lack of machinery or modern fertilisers and a shortage of suitable transportation to get food from field to market has led to incredible levels of waste. Official figures on waste in the North Korean agricultural sector are not available. However, data from the USSR, which organised its agricultural production along similarly collectivised lines, may indicate the scale. In the USSR in the 1980s between 25 and 30 per cent of all produce grown by collective farms was wasted, including 40 per cent of all potatoes harvested (but not including those left to rot in the fields due to inefficiency and a lack of necessary infrastructure such as farm to market roads). The FAO/WFP have estimated that North Korean losses between harvest and market were some 15 per cent in 1998 and rising, while others have estimated losses at in excess of 30 per cent. In comparison the Netherlands lost 1 per cent of its harvested potato crop in the 1980s.[21]

Although climatic conditions play a role, famines are largely the result of failed economic and agricultural policies. This was certainly the case in the DPRK. The agricultural economy spiralled downwards following decades of badly managed and politically driven agricultural policy. When adverse climatic conditions worsened this trend, the effects were greater because the economy was unable to cope with natural disaster; the ravages of flooding forced starving people to clear trees for emergency fire-field agriculture, trees that had hitherto acted as natural flood breaks. Pyongyang claimed the famine was largely due to natural disaster; it has never admitted that its Juche-driven collectivised agricultural policy was the major cause. That the DPRK's response to the famine has been largely political is no surprise. Yet it has meant that NGO efforts to help the country recover have been consistently hampered, and that efforts by Pyongyang to improve the situation for its people have been driven by their primary concerns of regime survival and maintaining 'face'. This is despite NGO insistence that the agricultural sector must change its mode of operation if it is to hope to provide a sustainable food economy for the country.

Political answers to agricultural inadequacies are not uncommon in planned economies. In the USSR a regular event was the mass mobilisation of soldiers, and often students, to help first plant and then gather the harvest, though much remained left in fields or warehouses to rot due to the poor internal transportation infrastructure. Similarly a large part of the army's time in North Korea is spent supplementing the shortcomings of the agrarian workforce at harvest time and this has reportedly increased since 1997. However, while it is possible to mobilise additional labour to the fields at crucial times, including students, Youth League members, soldiers and underemployed industrial workers, in the DPRK it is impossible to mobilise additional trucks and fuel to match the intensified efforts of the workers. This largely cancels out the effect of the additional manpower. It just changes the point at which the food rots and is wasted.

The partial and limited informal privatisation, in the form of private plots and use of common land, has led to reported low-level subversion of the collective farm system. As in other countries that have experimented with collective farming, such as China and the USSR, there were few built-in incentives to raise production apart from coercion and ideology. In many areas of the countryside, especially as production fell and food shortages grew, rural workers took to developing additional private (and illegal) plots of land on what was formerly common land that had not been cultivated. They began to cultivate this land for private use. The government and the senior management of the collective farms in large part turned a blind eye to this practice as the expanded plots yielded vegetables and other foods that initially lessened the effects of the food shortages and provided a coping mechanism for rural people in the face of famine.

The cultivation of private plots grew in the late 1980s and early 1990s, producing two effects. First, rural workers remained as idle as possible on the collective farms in order to conserve energy to devote to their private plots; and second, the use of formerly uncultivated land meant that during periods of heavy rain many mountainsides experienced landslides as a result of overintensive farming, compounding the frequent natural disasters. This pattern was replicated in the coastal areas, where illegal night-time fishing supplements rations and illegal bartering takes place between communities on the Korean/Chinese border areas. Fishing has become less rewarding as inland waters have been progressively fished out and fleets are unable to secure the necessary fuel to reach deeper waters. As in other declining socialist command economies, the North has also seen the phenomenon of workers stealing large amounts of materials from their jobs in order to work on them at home for private gain or simply to sell them.

While agricultural workers were increasingly concentrating on providing for themselves through their private plots, either by consuming the produce or selling it at farmers' markets, the government exhorted them to work harder to raise production through mass mobilisation campaigns, while seizing greater quantities of grain from the farms to meet shortages throughout the country, though without increasing the rural workers' rations. In 1998 Pyongyang launched a 'New Chollima', campaign 'turning impossibility into possibility and working miracles in the present difficult situation'.[22] The result was further private hoarding and a greater concentration on private plots to supplement the deficits in the PDS. As farm equipment has increasingly became redundant through a lack of spare parts and fuel, so the government has shifted additional agricultural tasks back to human beings. Travelling through the rural areas of North Korea it is striking just how few agricultural machines are employed and how many people appear to be walking great distances or hitching lifts on overburdened trucks.

Whereas the mass mobilisation campaigns were largely ineffective, private plots have helped people survive. One reason for the apparent lack of enthusiasm for the mobilisation campaigns is the fact that since the late 1990s Pyongyang has prioritised the distribution of scarce food resources to the army (a continuing point of contention with many aid donors) and key industrial workers, such as coal miners. The remainder enters the PDS in the urban areas, primarily Pyongyang. Hence the agricultural population has suffered disproportionately during the shortages. This contrasts with the situation in other countries, where food distribution is not so centrally controlled; there rural populations have been able to survive despite falling yields. This unequal distribution to the army and key industrial workers has further encouraged the use of private plots. Under the PDS farmers receive rations during harvest based on work performance. The state deducts expenses for farm supplies, equipment, seeds, fertilisers and pesticides, irrigation and various other fees. After all these deductions farmers' rations differ little from those of ordinary workers and fall below those of key industrial workers and the army.

In the early 1990s the government was so concerned at the rise in the cultivation of private plots and individuals bartering that it considered measures to curb their growth, while at the same time being forced to recognise the fact that the plots were keeping many rural communities alive. Despite this equivocal attitude, special camps and prisons were established to contain those caught foraging for food. By the late 1990s, as we have seen, reform-minded elements in Pyongyang were out of increasing desperation gradually introducing innovations such as double cropping and farmers' markets, hoping that such mild reforms could be introduced during a time of emergency and then, once the situation eased, extended to more broad-based structural reform.

Pyongyang notably never moved to introduce a system similar to China's Household Production Responsibility System (HPRS), which was responsible in large part for boosting reform and production levels in rural China. The HPRS provided opportunities for households to make their own economic decisions, including allocating production inputs and retaining surplus output after fulfilling government quotas. HPRS replaced the commune system that had been established in 1958. Initially, HPRS was a system of contracting specific jobs or responsibilities to commune households in poor areas. It was designed to increase incentives for households to raise output and income by linking farm returns directly to production. Because of its initial success with cotton producers, the system was extended to oilseeds and grains. It also spread from poor to wealthier areas and from inland to coastal regions, with local adoption often preceding official sanction at the national level.

By the end of 1984, 95 per cent of rural households were under this system. For Pyongyang at present this is a step too far in formalising reform in the countryside.

Dying in Silence

The famine first appeared in the mountainous northeastern regions in 1993–94, where industry is scarce and arable land in short supply. Though Pyongyang blames climatic conditions, the initial reports of famine predated the 1995 flooding. It was in this region that reports surfaced of people surviving on 'substitute foods' such as grass, rice roots, acorns, seaweed noodles, berries, tree bark and soups made with wild plants and weeds (and sometimes being poisoned by them). The government later encouraged this trend, even offering recipes and guides to what was edible in an attempt to cut the number of reported poisonings and digestive ailments. In the coastal areas illegal harvesting of fish, crab, shrimp and squid occurred either for food or as barter for corn.

There were also reports of increased underground bartering of possessions, such as sewing machines, winter blankets and bicycles, as well as family heirlooms, for food while homelessness in these regions rose, indicating the increasingly desperate situation and the collapse in people's coping mechanisms. Domesticated animals became increasingly uncommon – rural communities were eating their stocks of farm animals rather than letting them die from lack of fodder. From the northeast the famine spread to the more fertile western plains, and shortages started to hit Pyongyang. In 2003 many people were still surviving on just nine ounces of rations a day, provided by foods with poor nutritional benefit such as corn stalk cakes – according to the WFP, less than half the recommended minimum daily intake.[23]

Despite Pyongyang's attempt to keep the famine secret, by the mid- to late 1990s those visitors and NGO workers with access to the DPRK's interior outside the major cities were reporting the appearance of large numbers of hastily built mass graves, as well as incidents of food riots in Hamhung and Sinuiju, while roaming gangs of malnourished and abandoned or orphaned children had become a major problem, even reaching into the cities and bringing the reality of famine to Pyongyang. Human rights campaigners have asserted that many of these children, some as young as 8 or 9, were put to work on construction projects such as the 42-kilometre, ten-lane, Youth Hero Highway that runs from Nampo to Pyongyang. Public executions were reported for crimes, seemingly of desperation, ranging from 'banditry' to 'stealing rice from a train'.[24] The need to institutionalise large numbers of children became a further drain on the state's woefully inadequate

welfare services, which already had 760,000 children in nurseries dependent on aid. Naturally the groups initially worst affected were the young,
the elderly, recent mothers, pregnant women and the disabled. Visitors to
the countryside, even in government-escorted groups, also reported signs of
malnutrition; these included general emaciation, facial swelling (oedema),
tuberculosis, blotchiness of the skin, eye infections and hair discoloura-
tion caused by protein deficiencies. Hospitals reported widespread cases of
respiratory disease, and liver and kidney disorders, as well as diarrhoea
among babies and small children. North Korea's Ministry of Foreign Affairs
has admitted that the famine has reduced the average North Korean's life
expectancy from 66.8 years in 1993 to 60.4 years in 2001.[25]

Reports citing evidence of cannibalism in the North have, not surprisingly, caught international media attention.[26] These allegations, originally
voiced by the North Korean Refugees Assistance Fund (NKRAF), were taken
seriously enough for the UN World Food Programme to request access to
several farmers' markets where it had been reported that human meat was
being sold as 'special meat'. Pyongyang turned down the requests, citing
'security reasons' and stated that the penalty for cannibalism was death. The
government is concerned by these allegations, as it realizes that they are also
circulating in the North, causing discontent and obvious concern.

Estimating just how many people have died is difficult, not least because
of Pyongyang's efforts to hide the facts. During the famine of the late 1990s
estimates ranged from betwen 220,000 and 600,000 to as high as 3.5 million.
Pyongyang's own estimate, made in 1999, is 220,000, or 1 per cent of the pre-
famine population.[27] In certain particularly badly afflicted provinces, largely
in the northeast, such as Hamgyong, thought to be the worst affected region
(and, by coincidence, where many of North Korea's senior leadership come
from), the death rate may have been as high as 12 per cent of the population.
Clearly, by the late 1990s social order had started to severely break down
in the remoter provinces, with reports of attacks on people rumoured to be
hoarding food, rising suicide rates, growth in human trafficking (with women
sold either into the Asian sex industry or as wives to Chinese farmers), and
abandoned villages where people had moved en masse across the border to
China. Diplomats believe that at least 100,000 DPRK citizens, and perhaps
as many as 300,000, are living in northeastern China having fled the famine.
The state responded to this breakdown where it could, measures including
tighter border controls, severer punishment for murderers and the formation
of camps for the internally displaced (known as *kochibis* – 'wandering swal-
lows') who had left their villages in an attempt to escape the famine.[28]

Food aid levels to the DPRK have continued to fluctuate over the years,
affected by both global demand and, as we have seen, by the political climate

between Pyongyang and donor countries. Japan provided 500,000 tonnes of food aid in 2001, but (following North Korea's admission of kidnapping Japanese citizens) sent no official aid in 2002. Aid from America was cut from 340,000 tonnes in 2001 to 40,000 tonnes in the first half of 2003 as relations deteriorated.

The extent of the food deficit in North Korea is still unknown. NGO statistics are necessarily incomplete, as they are based on access; while North Korean statistics are certainly not reliable. WFP/FAO estimates indicate that the food deficit was approximately 50 per cent of total food requirements. Andrew Natsios, a former aid worker in North Korea, notes that this shortfall is greater than that which caused the 1985 Ethiopian famine, which led to over a million deaths.[29]

Solving the Shortages

WFP/FAO surveys have consistently come to the conclusion that, despite the AREP-inspired changes in the agricultural system, North Korea will continue to be reliant on aid until its economy can recover sufficiently to earn the necessary revenues to pay for food imports, domestic animals, additional fertilisers and farm machinery. This is an almost impossible task for a country with little prospect of rapidly increasing its foreign earnings and that still does not have access to international lending agencies or significant financial aid from major economies such as Japan, South Korea, the US or China.

There has been a degree of internal reform of the agricultural system more recently, in response to government concerns about regime survival should full-blown famine return. For instance, farmers can now sell a larger share of their output in free, or farmers', markets, and in some cases organise themselves as family units rather than collectives – a tentative admission that the collective farm system is failing. One sign of this failure is that collective farms have sought to harvest ever earlier as their rations have run low or in expectation that supplies will run low; smaller units, however, appear to be coping better.

Pyongyang's only solution to the crisis was to ignore private production and bartering outside the plan. This accentuated the greater access to food on the part of the elite, those in positions of power in the rural areas and those with foreign currency or something tangible to barter. As seen in Chapter 4, this informal allocation process that has increasingly usurped the PDS has further hastened the breakdown of the command economy and the collectivised rural economy, questioning their theoretical rationale. Alongside this is the problem that the state's control of much aid disbursement often unmonitored by NGOs has undoubtedly led to a degree of profiteering by individuals, invariably linked to the elite, who have become rich. They could form the core of a potential oligarch system, as seen in the former USSR. It has also been noted by many former NGO workers and observers that the state's high level of control over distribution of aid, where and to whom it is allocated, means that aid has effectively become part of the state's apparatus of control and coercion of the population.[30]

The situation at present means shortages will persist. Although improved climatic conditions have made the threat of famine less immediate, extreme shortages remain and extend across the country, even affecting Pyongyang, where residents have reportedly been regularly travelling into the surrounding countryside in search of food; reports of hungry soldiers crossing the border into China in search of food have also appeared increasingly in the Chinese press. Thanks to more favourable weather conditions, donor aid and price-reform incentives for farmers to produce rice, the agricultural economy recorded 4.2 per cent growth in 2001, and 6.8 per cent in 2002.

Aid supplies alone will not solve the North Korean food crisis. Food security is only possible through a combination of rejecting collectivisation, employing new agricultural methods, securing the necessary inputs, and building reserves of hard currency to purchase food and inputs from abroad in times of shortage. The distribution of aid through the PDS continues to favour the political elite and the military, exposing much of the population to reduced rations and to the vicissitudes of the nascent market in the form of farmers' markets. From the perspective of political change, it can be argued that the long-term effect of aid is to provide sufficient resources to ensure regime survival without forcing economic reform. As the supplies of humanitarian food aid have been increasingly incorporated into the government's PDS, so an equilibrium has been achieved that perpetuates the KWP-led party-state. With government control of most food distribution still in place, it is impossible to ascertain how much is diverted to the elite for profiteering, government hoarding or military use.

The End of the Arduous March

A quip that has circulated in Beijing's economic policy circles for many years is appropriate to the DPRK too: there are two ways for the regime to die – one is to reform itself, the other is not to reform. This clearly voices the belief that the regime must enact more serious economic reform but that change will ultimately spill over to the whole of society and the political system. Deng Xiaoping once remarked that the test of socialism was whether or not it produced economic progress. So far in North Korea the KWP has failed Deng's test.

As we have seen, despite some economic reform the North Korean economy remains largely a tool of ideology; the millstone of Juche weighs down the regime, eroding the industrial base and perpetuating the population's impoverishment. The economy has been, and remains, a tool of regime survival for a leadership that has proved incapable of adapting to a post-Cold War world without its major sponsors. Clearly the development of the economy has not lived up to its description in Article 34 of the DPRK Constitution: 'The State shall formulate unified and detailed plans and guarantee a high rate of production growth and a balanced development of the national economy.' To date, Pyongyang, rather than renounce the command economy, has sought instead to find scapegoats for its failings. At present all the principal means of production remain state-owned, through state-run enterprises or collective farms with all prices, wages, trade permits, budget allocations and the banking sector under total government control. Over 90 per cent of GDP is generated by state-owned firms or agricultural collectives and only 3 per cent by private enterprises.[31]

What is known, notwithstanding the paucity of official statistics, is that GNP, though rising by an estimated 1.3–1.5 per cent in 2002–03, has declined by over 55 per cent since the demise of the USSR (it was a meagre US$23 billion in 1990, going down to US$22 billion in 1995 and US$15.7 billion in 2001), and that since the collapse of Comecon in 1991 exports had plunged by over 70 per cent by 2000, while foreign debt is probably around 95 per cent, if not actually in excess, of total GNP. Foreign trade accounts for approximately US$2.2 billion, less than 1 per cent of the foreign trade of the ROK, while the trade deficit is at a record high of around US$1 billion. One key area of foreign trade that has suffered is with Japan: DPRK exports were down more than 30 per cent in 2003 over 2002, while imports from Japan slumped by approximately 20 per cent.[32] Inter-Korean trade is growing, however, and depending on how the statistics are calculated, the ROK is now arguably the DPRK's biggest export market.

The energy crisis, the lack of spare parts to repair broken-down and outdated machinery, persistent long-term mismanagement and the vagaries of central planning have combined to reduce output of the non-military industrial economy to below 25 per cent (perhaps even as low as 10–15 per cent). Industrial production reportedly expanded by 3.5 per cent in 2001 but then contracted again by 2 per cent in 2002, while the health-care system and the PDS were all but totally eradicated during the decade of famine and shortages. This picture does not reveal the worsening collapse in some key sectors of the economy. Despite the claims of Finance Minister Mun Il-bong that the manufacturing sector expanded by 12 per cent in 2002, it appears that heavy industry, the very sector most emphasised under central planning, contracted by 4.2 per cent, more than eradicating any productivity gains seen in 2001, even though light industry appears to have seen a 2.7 per cent growth in 2002. Industrial production, including mining and manufacturing, accounts for approximately 58 per cent of total GDP (compared to nearly 85 per cent in the ROK). Reports indicate that the only factories working at anything close to full capacity are those engaged in military-related production; defence spending absorbs 33 per cent of total GDP, compared to just 2.8 per cent in the ROK.[33] Average per capita income is approximately US$757, while that in the ROK is US$9,628, higher by a factor of 12.7, according to the ROK's National Statistical Office calculations.[34]

Energy remains a major problem. Measures to develop hydroelectric and alternative energy sources have largely stalled, except in the case of some small-scale projects. The regime is aware of the havoc inadequate power supplies are causing in Pyongyang, in industry generally, and in the inability of ports like Nampo to unload aid when there is insufficient power for the dockside crane.[35] Despite repeated reports of power station construction – in 2003 North Phyongan province announced it was building sixty power stations; others are scheduled in Wonsan, Kumyagang, Orangchon and Taechon, among other places – the source of financing for these projects remains unclear, their progress secret, and completion at best several years away, if ever.[36]

The government claims its nuclear programme will help solve the crisis and has set a target for nuclear-generated electricity of 32 per cent of total capacity by 2020. However, this includes capacity that would be derived from the planned KEDO reactors that were part of the 1994 Agreed Framework and that have yet to materialise. If KEDO's two light water reactors, each with a 2,000 MW capacity, were added to the planned 5 MW Yongbyon plant (reportedly not yet connected to the national grid) and the 20 MW Taechon plant, this would still not account for anything close to 32 per cent of output. It is therefore assumed that construction of additional nuclear plants is planned, though where the funding will come from is unknown. In 2002 North Korea managed to produce 7,300 MW of electricity, with over 50 per cent derived from hydroelectric projects. This is equivalent to roughly 20 per cent of the ROK's generating capacity. In 2003 total energy output is thought to have risen due to the reopening of mines, with coal production reportedly rising 3 per cent over 2002, and hydropower (due to increased rainfall), which saw increased budgets of 30 per cent and 12.8 per cent respectively, year-on-year. However, output fell short of making up for the losses from the suspended US oil deliveries, and Pyongyang was forced to spend its dwindling currency reserves on additional imports of electricity from China – between January and October 2003 imports of electricity from the PRC leapt fifty-seven-fold to 10.03 million kilowatt hours (kWh) compared to 8.84 million kWh for the whole of 2002. Additionally Pyongyang was forced to sell some of its precious electricity capacity to raise finance, around 31 million kWh, again worsening the power situation overall in the country.[37]

Agriculture remains highly problematic, though it still accounts for over 30 per cent of GDP (compared to 4.6 per cent in the ROK), with input shortfalls meaning that many farming provinces have reported the infestation of rice water, amd the incidence of maize weevils and other pests surging. Ryanggang and North Hamgyong provinces experienced a substantially reduced output of maize and rice for 2003 due to heavy rainfall during July and August.[38] Despite half a century of collectivising and industrialising agriculture, as well as proletarianising the rural workforce, it appears that the steep decline in the industrial sector means that agriculture still remains a major component of the North's economy despite the dictates and intents of the command economy to prioritise heavy industry.

The growth of the unofficial economy has offset the decline temporarily in some areas, though, as previously indicated, it will ultimately hasten the decline of the overall command economy. The unofficial economy's major unknown quantities are the revenues earned from the DPRK's arms trade and military transfers, the unofficial cross-border trade with China, the outright illegal activities sponsored by the government, and remittances from abroad. However, with the exception of remittances, it is assumed that most of this income flows to the government directly and then to the nuclear and defence industries, or out of the country to the DPRK's overseas network of shell companies and banks and is therefore not used to support the country's crumbling infrastructure.

The perceived growth of light industry does offer the very distant prospect of North Korea repeating China's reform process and following Beijing's expansion of light industrial and consumer goods production to offset the continued decline in SOE profitability. For instance, trade in consumer goods between North Korea and Japan has grown with Japan's new recession-era chains of low-cost discount stores selling DPRK-assembled products.[39] However, Juche remains wedded to the primacy of heavy industry; hence sparse government revenues are continuing to be used to prop up that sector rather than support the further expansion of light industry. With no substantial levels of FDI or local entrepreneurship, such as China was able to tap into, this possible solution will probably be lost to the rigidity of political-economic theory. Additionally, the shortages in essential consumer goods, such as shoes, winter clothing and warm bedding, have yet to be addressed. Despite expanded production, manufactured goods (excluding arms) are still falling as a percentage of total exports, while textile exports have almost ceased (the Japanese market disappeared in the wake of the furore over the nuclear programme and the kidnapping revelations) and many other international markets remain closed to North Korean goods, primarily America.[40]

A study of Pyongyang's recent trade statistics indicates that, despite the continuing after-effects of famine, agriculture is growing as a share of total GDP, indicating an increasingly deindustrialised command economy. As Jamie Miyazaki has suggested, 'North Korea's economy today more closely resembles a retarded version of post-Soviet Moldova than the 1970s China embarking on economic liberalisation.'[41] Despite the mild growth in some areas of the economy, overall it is now 32 per cent smaller than its peak year, 1990. It must also be understood that the famine was a serious indictment of the regime's policies. Famines in industrial economies, even command economies, are rare. In recent decades famine has generally been more associated with non-industrialised, poverty-stricken countries such as Bangladesh, Ethiopia, Somalia; according to Amartya Sen and Jean Drèze, no famine has occurred in a democratic country.[42] Arguably the famines that have occurred in socialist planned economies have been the consequence of political decisions rather than basic agricultural or climatic reasons. The famines in the Ukraine in the 1930s were the result of Stalin's agricultural collectivisation and war on the kulaks; the Chinese famines were a result of Mao's political war on the peasantry in the late 1950s; the famine in Cambodia in the 1970s was a direct result of the political aims of the Khmer Rouge.[43] Distribution of land rights appears to have a major impact in preventing famine, as has been seen in countries such as the ROK, Taiwan and Japan: with individual land rights have come higher productivity, cultivation and yields, as well as the retention of surpluses against the risk of climatic disaster; excessive political campaigns in the countryside and collectivisation, on the other hand, can lead to and exacerbate a state of famine.

One further indication that the economy and government finances have deteriorated to the point of collapse in the DPRK has been that, despite the reinstatement of the military-first line, repeated attempts at securing arms purchases from countries such as Russia, China and India on credit have largely proved unsuccessful. This indicates that Pyongyang's foreign currency and gold reserves have been depleted despite efforts at renewed economic reform. Lacking the ability to pay, North Korea has had to resort to bartering nuclear technology for arms in some cases, selling its own domestically developed missiles and mineral resources, the latter being needed by the domestic economy too.

Hwang Jang-yop, Pyongyang's highest level defector, told the ROK in 1996 that the only way to defeat the North was to blockade the country (excepting certain food supplies), while for peaceful reunification to occur 'the gap between the North and South must be widened like the sky and the earth.'[44] This indeed appears to be happening if Park Suhk-sam, chief economist with the North Korea Economic Studies Division of the Bank of Korea in Seoul, is to be believed: 'The [DPRK] economy is showing clear signs of stagnating again.'[45]

Kim was aware that any reform initiative would be limited by the sclerotic nature of North Korean politics and that it would be a long time before the DPRK was able to feed itself. Though limited economic reforms were announced, the regime knew the existing level of aid must continue, and if possible increase, in order for the economy, and hence the regime, to remain afloat. Thus, faced with the real possibility of renewed famine, Kim launched a diplomatic charm offensive in an attempt to show a willingness to reform and to normalise relations with neighbouring countries. Following this renewed engagement, Kim initiated economic reforms.

6

The Start of a Sort of Reform:
Change and Regime Survival

Open Windows Attract Flies

By 2002 the economic situation in North Korea had become dire: there were food shortages, industry was grinding to a halt, aid donations were falling due to the political impasse and donor fatigue. Pyongyang has always resisted reform. When Deng Xiaoping told Kim Il-sung that China's reforms were a window to the West, Kim replied 'When you open a window flies come in.' Nevertheless, in July 2002, with collapse seemingly imminent, Pyongyang announced a series of economic reforms that at first appeared to represent a possible way to resuscitate the economy. Following the formal announcement, Pyongyang embarked on a political and diplomatic process that would be ongoing during the reforms' implementation. It included a one-day summit between Kim and Japanese prime minister Junichiro Koizumi; engagement with Russia; and renewed contact with the Americans, by way of assistant secretary of state for East Asian and Pacific affairs James Kelly's visit to Pyongyang in October 2002.

The period between late June and October 2002, when Pyongyang admitted to its continuing nuclear weapons programme, saw a brief attempt by the North Koreans to push a twin policy of political engagement and economic reform. Although this ultimately proved a failure, what initially appeared to be a shift of emphasis in foreign relations and international diplomacy, and acknowledgement of the failure of the command economy, did indicate a new sense of urgency in the North Korean capital.

Kim's diplomatic charm offensive, referred to by one Japanese newspaper as an 'environmental improvement', began with a sealed train trip to Russia, which caused chaos on the country's rail system and produced only the most perfunctory acknowledgements. Clearly there was to be neither a resumption of the once close relationship nor more aid from Moscow.

The second stage in the charm offensive was the Kim–Koizumi summit, which largely failed, in the wake of Kim's surprise announcement that the DPRK, as long suspected, had been behind the kidnapping of Japanese citizens. This wrongfooted the negotiations from the start and sabotaged Kim's agenda. Koizumi, for his part, hoped to be seen as leading a process of engagement with Pyongyang and raising Japan's regional profile; instead he ended up with additional domestic problems. For Kim the point of the summit had been to gain aid. In this he failed. Pyongyang's renewed diplomatic offensive had been mishandled.

Perestroika à la Pyongyang

The benefits to Pyongyang of pushing ahead with economic reform should have been obvious by the end of September 2002, notwithstanding the theoretical precept within Juche that reform after the revolution somehow implied criticism of the revolution itself. This was the first real reform to touch upon the domestic economy. Previous reforms involved economic relations with the outside world, such as joint venture laws and foreign investment regulations.

However, the economic reform process – described as 'perestroika à la Pyongyang' or 'reform by stealth'[1] – was disjointed. This comes as no surprise if we accept North Korean defector Hwang Jang-yop's view that Kim considers the party and military his own possessions and doesn't care about the economy. The initial economic reforms were extremely partial and can be described as at best failures and at worst as the cause of further economic deterioration. The Sinuiju experiment was completely delinked from any other economic activity in the country. Nevertheless, a process had begun, one described by the North Korean press as 'policies of love and trust', and it was without precedent in the DPRK. It is therefore necessary to examine the tentative reform process in more detail to try and predict Pyongyang's possible future direction and available options. There was, as usual, no awareness that an announcement was imminent. When it had been made, some commentators, such as *The Economist*, seemed hopeful; others, however, such as the *Far Eastern Economic Review*, were more suspicious.[2]

Those seeking to do business in the DPRK were, not surprisingly, the most fulsome in their praise of the reforms, as they had long been waiting for a chink of light that might indicate to interested multinationals the possibility that North Korea might open up to them. This was, after all, one of the main reasons for the reforms. Pyongyang was balancing the fact that it needed to continue to secure aid in order to support the system with the imperative to survive in a world that was, in the leadership's view, increasingly hostile. Yet the regime knew that the securing of aid, and the outcome of any future nuclear crisis, which Pyongyang was in a position to know might be pending, would be more successful if the government could show some tangible intention of reforming the economy. What exactly were the economists of Pyongyang proposing?

Wages and Pricing Reforms

The North Koreans themselves undoubtedly saw the 2002 wages and pricing reforms as a major change of direction and as a significant monetisation of the economy. Initially the measures were referred to as the 'improvement of economic management'. Later, however, KCNA used the term 'economic reform'.[3] In 2001 the way had been paved ideologically for some sort of systemic reform. *Rodong Sinmun* had published an article by Kim that declared: 'Things are not what they used to be in the 1960s. So no one should follow the way people used to do things in the past.... We should make constant efforts to renew the landscape to replace the one which was formed in the past, to meet the requirements of a new era.' The process of instituting reform within the KWP involved a process of preparation, discussion and formulation to ensure that Kim had the necessary constituencies on board supporting the reforms. North Korea's constitution had already been modified in 1998 to place greater stress on the related issues of 'costs, prices and profits'.[4]

Nevertheless, the price reforms of 1 July 2002 were still largely unexpected. The retail prices of basic goods were increased, sometimes dramatically. For example, the price of rice rose by 55,000 per cent – effectively ending state subsidy of the key staple. Corn prices rose by 5,000 per cent, electricity prices by 143 per cent, public transportation costs by 2,000 per cent, while wages rose by 1,818 per cent on average. As government-set wage rates no longer guaranteed the ability to acquire basic goods following price rises, it became clear that state rationing, through the PDS public distribution system, was increasingly failing to reflect the actual worth of basic goods and consequently was undermining the basic functions of money. Accompanying wages reform differentiated between those earning an ordinary income and those awarded special wages pegged approximately three times higher. The latter rate was set at NKW 6,000 per month while the average wage was raised from NKW110 to NKW2,000 (approximately US$22).[5]

The price reforms clearly provided a real incentive for producers to increase their output of rice. The price of rice was now comparable to international levels and the economy became somewhat monetised, though at various rates, as the widely varying percentage increases showed. Though monetisation was presented as a way to rejuvenate the economy and improve living conditions, the new system actually further impoverished citizens while benefiting the government in direct financial terms, for with the consumer subsidy gone Pyongyang now made a profit on all rice sold to the public, with the procurement price for farmers rising only 5,000 per cent while the retail price rose 55,000 per cent. The large cost to the state of the rice subsidy disappeared overnight. Meanwhile for consumers the price of a kilogram of rice rose from NKW0.1 to NKW40, while a kilo of pork rose to NKW170, up from NKW8 before the reforms. Hence the subsidy to consumers was effectively terminated, and the government now made a profit on all rice sold. It was not a magnanimous way to treat an undernourished population, but it certainly helped patch up the government's parlous finances, as vast amounts had been spent on rice subsidies.

One immediate effect was a form of economic shock therapy: the devaluing of the NKW against the US$ by between 6,500 and 7,000 per cent. Yet the adjustments to wages, to stimulate additional monetisation, were also a revision of traditional political thinking. Historically wages were fixed (except for the elite) in the spirit of socialist levelling rather than as a motivational tool. Despite some small-scale attempts at introducing bonuses and a few other financial incentives to higher-level SOE managers, motivation largely depended on political tactics such as inculcating the Chollima concept, Speed Battles and other mass motivational campaigns. By this point in the DPRK's economic cycle it was clear that such forms of economic compulsion were no longer sufficient and increasingly begrudged as people enthusiastically embraced their private plots, cultivating them intensively, rather than expending surplus energy on any new Chollima campaign. Yet, despite the fact that private plots are considerably more productive than the collective farms the government has refused to sanction their expansion. SOE managers were urged to manage better, although the systemic reasons why they don't have been left untackled.

Jettisoning the Ration

The partial ending of the PDS went hand in hand with the price reforms, meaning that for the first time many people were now dependent on a form of market economy for an increasing array of goods. North Korea had introduced its food rationing system in May 1952 in accordance with the 'State Food Ration Rules'.[6] The government banned all grain sales and individual commercial transactions in 1957 and thereafter all foodstuffs including meat and fish had been strictly rationed, the only alternative being the fledgling farmers' markets (*jangmadang*) or home-grown produce. The rationing system was justified politically by Pyongyang as designed to guarantee equal distribution of grain, of which there were by the 1960s already signs of shortages, to ensure that minimum levels of need were satisfied. This is still a problem, as rice, the preferred grain, has been increasingly substituted with less popular corn or barley. Of course, rationing of food also functioned as an instrument of social control and labour force mobilisation through the promise of additional rations for achieving state mandated targets. Pyongyang has spoken of its view of socialist distribution in a period of 'new circumstances and conditions'. Officially labour is the 'only yardstick in distributing products'.[7] While the rhetoric is socialist and egalitarian, since the inception of rationing a hierarchy had operated, with military personnel and cadres entitled to larger rations. In part the PDS has survived and been accepted because citizens see sense in rationing given their experience of 'free' markets. When goods sell for more than ten times the state price it is perceived as speculation, which arouses public anger. Severe shortages invariably produce speculation; hence rationing is seen by many as an equitable way to share hardship and as a buffer against all-out scarcity.

The PDS, like North Korea's collectivised agricultural system, was virtually a copy of the Soviet blueprint, with prices traditionally acting as little more than a form of accounting. Overseen by the Food Administration Ministry (FAM), it was designed to provide the basic needs of people, known as PDS dependants and numbering approximately 15.5 million, and then channel additional amounts to select social groups – cadres, military, the elite – and potentially to those sectors of society deemed either temporarily valuable or most likely to challenge the party-state, such as industrial workers, miners, and so on. This ultimately led to the creation of twelve hierarchical ranks, later reduced during the famine to just three. Cadres and the military hierarchy were able to increase their rations through connections; farmers were able to increase their share through private plots and better access to the source of supply. Consequently these two groups are underrepresented in the refugee flow as being the least likely to suffer from famine and also the least likely to leave, due to considerations of perceived political privilege and informal land rights.

The system functioned through the issuing of ration coupons distributed by cashiers at the workplace twice a month; most rural workers, approximately 6.7 million people, received rations during harvest distribution in

November and December. Each county and city district, and many larger institutions, established a central warehouse that delivered food to PDS distribution centres at community (*ri* and *dong*) levels. For the rural population the allocation in the late 1980s was 219 kg per person, or 600 grams per person per day, considered roughly equivalent to the urban PDS ration. Produce left over after the rural disbursement was sold to the government at set prices. According to the Consolidated Appeals Process document, know as CAP2004, issued by the UN Office for the Coordination of Humanitarian Affairs (OCHA) in 2003, children in some regions began receiving lower rations and the monthly average ration was reduced to 250–380 grams per adult per day. The 2003 WFP/FAO Crop and Food Supply Assessment (CFSAM) noted that following the reforms 50 per cent of PDS-dependent households have been unable to cover their daily calorie requirements, with a consequently declining protein intake.[8] The situation is even worse for rural dwellers outside the PDS, where rations have reportedly fallen to even lower levels.

The government attempted to anticipate the ways people might find to circumvent the rationing system. For instance, the authorities required travellers to produce coupons (*yanggwon*) when they bought food. *Yanggwon* were then exchanged for regular ration coupons to prevent repeat use. Rations, particularly of food, have fluctuated since the first shortages in the early 1970s. In 1973 monthly rations were reduced by four days' worth of portions under the stated government pretext of stockpiling wartime supplies.

As the famine became worse and shortages more severe the PDS began falling apart. This was despite the fact that all food aid coming into the DPRK was channelled into the PDS by government order as a means of controlling distribution. In some regions, daily rations were reduced to 350 grams and in some of the worst hit regions were reportedly stopped completely, leaving people reliant solely on aid. As well as lowering the volume of the ration the government has also altered the ratio of rice to cereal both across the board and by region and social status. The ratio until the early 1990s was reportedly 6:4 in Pyongyang, and 3:7 in other regions. It has also been reported that over the last decade the ration has been lowered further to 1:9 or even to no rice at all.[9] Along with the major food rations for meat, fish and cereals North Koreans received side-dish coupons allowing them to purchase items such as soy sauce, soybean paste, cooking oil and eggs, based on family size. Outside the allotted ration small quantities of meat can be purchased on national holidays. In general, meat and fish have been luxury foodstuffs for two decades now.

Ration coupons were also issued for non-food goods. For example, for electrical appliances workers were issued with 'purchase tickets' at the workplace. The allocation was limited, as were supplies of appliances. However, it has been easier to circumvent the non-food item rationing system by using reserves of foreign currency to purchase products at foreign currency stores. The few people who work, visit or study abroad have been able to import appliances (subject to customs duties). Alternatively goods can be bought clandestinely at village fairs where hoarded, second-hand or smuggled goods are available.

Ration coupons remain an integral part of the system of food distribution and allocation despite claims that they had been eradicated. Monthly ration cards are still issued. Their continued existence at least prevents hoarding and speculation by wealthier households able to buy up unused cards for cash. The level of government-organised hoarding is hard to estimate and food may well be stockpiled either by farmers waiting for better prices or by the government attempting to smooth the flow of distribution. This is despite the fact that the government has outlawed hoarding under penalty of execution for farmers withholding grain from the PDS. However, as all households receive the same allowance and are not allowed to exceed it, any speculative hoarding activity necessarily takes place outside the official PDS. In the absence of marketisation, hoarding strategies will continue. A trial system, based upon China's agricultural reforms, that allows farmers to keep an agreed portion of their product for use or sale was tested in Hanbuk province in 2001, but not rolled out across the country.

Although the increase in the procurement price for grain was presented to the public and the world as a reform, it can be seen as an attempt by Pyongyang actually to bolster and protect the command economy in the countryside. As procurement prices had fallen to derisory levels, so farmers had increasingly turned to their private plots as well as to the illegal production of grain liquor; some, through desperation, actively subverted the plan by switching away from unprofitable grain production to alternative crops such as tobacco. The result was that the gap between market and plan prices has been closed somewhat, allowing for continued production and enough grain to maintain the PDS. However, rather than marking acknowledgement of the inefficiencies and contradictions of central planning, rationing and state purchasing reforms have, like the expanding role of farmers' markets, been perceived as a measure taken in the face of a collapsing system.

The Role of Farmers' Markets

As with production outside the plan, the existence of farmers' markets as an alternative distribution network alongside the PDS unbalances the plan: the larger state agricultural sector suffers further reduction in productivity.

Some commentators have gone so far as to claim that most food in North Korea, outside of aid, is now passing through the markets rather than the PDS, despite the fact that technically farmers are not allowed to sell their surplus staple food to anyone but the government procurement agency.[10]

Farmers' markets, more often than not small-scale trading posts, have existed since the 1940s, although until relatively recently their existence was largely hidden as they exposed flaws in the planned economy, notwith-standing semi-official sanction since around 1970. Even though Kim Jong-il initially cracked down on the markets, branding them 'unsocialist', creating 'egoism' and typical of the sorts of theoretical cracks that had appeared in the Eastern bloc, the number of markets, as well as more ad hoc roadside stalls or stalls in schoolyards or vacant lots, grew in the late 1990s as the famine and shortages worsened, the official rural distribution network broke down and additional rural dwellers developed private plots as an alternative source of nourishment and income. Additionally, the government introduced taxes on goods sold at the markets, partially co-opting them. The roadside and ad hoc stalls still appear today, often comprising little more than a few women selling fruit and vegetables, or perhaps cigarettes, biscuits and snacks.

The government realised that it had come increasingly to rely on these markets as supplementing the low level of productivity in the state agri-cultural sector and reflecting its inability to distribute effectively. However, the farmers' markets in their illegal phase, though supplementing the rations system, were a form of economic activity largely outside state control. By May 2003, though, the government was referring to them as simply 'markets' (or 'district markets'), indicating that the scope of what they sold could be increased from private plot produce such as vegetables, potatoes and green maize to include appliances and 'interior decorating materials', and that 'approved businessmen' would be allowed to operate in them. This followed the massive NKW devaluation of 2002, the outlawing of the possession of US dollars, the abolition of the quasi-hard Blue Won currency (North Korean Foreign Exchange Certificates), and the substantial narrowing of the price gap between government procurement and retail prices, which effectively meant that the reforms had both increased the incentive to farmers to sell to the state and partially restored the government's grip on the economy. For those budding entrepreneurs able to secure supplies of non-food items for sale in the markets, the profits may be quite good if buyers can be found. Reportedly second-hand computers available in China for US$400 can be resold in North Korea for over US$1,000.[11]

Consequently, when *KCNA* announced in June 2003, after the reforms affecting the pricing and rationing system had largely been jettisoned, that the State Planning Committee had decided that farmers' markets would start selling a variety of consumer goods supposedly 'in accordance with the actual demand of the socialist society', it was in a climate that had already eroded the market's importance outside the system. The markets remain largely under government control, with upper price limits set by administrative units (though bartering is reportedly common). Rather nebulous and unspecified was the proviso that prices would be allowed to fluctuate 'in accordance with the balance of demand and supply', though not to exceed set limits. In one sense this further legitimation of the markets was an attempt to bring back within the system an element of economic activity that had been slipping out of the government's control. Since their emergence the markets had become increasingly undifferentiated from the black market, with consumer goods (often smuggled in from China) appearing for sale alongside food. As other goods, such as domestically manufactured appliances, were highly rationed, their appearance in the markets could only be due to either opportunist worker theft or more organised 'redistribution' by SOEs' management and county administrators. In this sense the extension of the role of the markets merely formalised this de facto unofficial extension of their role.

In other transitional command economies farmers' markets have been important transitional tools responsible for introducing more realistic pricing mechanisms as well as filling gaps in the state rationing system. In both China and Gorbachev-era Russia these markets and their development were crucial. However, the reforms in both of these countries were more extensive and far-reaching in their aims than those in North Korea. In the USSR Gorbachev was able to tolerate the extension of farmers' markets[12] as necessary even though among many sections of the population they were seen as the breeding ground for profiteers and a new level of exploitation, while others saw them as evidence of inherent nascent capitalism. Indeed in Russia they invariably became home to the resurgent organised crime that perestroika in part unleashed. In China the markets were generally welcomed by the rural population, who were able to raise their incomes, and occurred at a time of far wider economic reform and of rising wages and disposable income in the urban areas. This ability of Chinese farmers to sell their own produce outside the state system also occurred at a time when the government was guaranteeing staple food prices and restraining inflation. The newly wealthy private entrepreneurs emerged as Deng Xiaoping had predicted in the 1980s when he advised society to 'let a small group grow rich first'. This small group was largely responsible for China's fourfold increase in per capita income in the first decade of reform. In North Korea's case the price reforms and the farmers' markets are essentially the only reforms. Furthermore, the emergence of an entrepreneurial class with new-found wealth remains an unacceptable notion, being perceived as a threat to the regime.

The government was obviously not ignorant of the fact that the markets, even if dealing in goods not strictly meant to be sold there, whether derived from the state system or smuggled in from China, were satisfying people's demands as well as drawing additional currency into circulation by easing shortages in certain key sectors. To this end the markets have been able to increase the circulation of NKW (and also of saved supplies of US$, ROK won, RMB, etc.) while also satisfying pent-up demand for food and consumer goods. In this sense, rather than the more extensive economic reforms of Dengist China or Gorbachev's USSR, Cuba may be the more instructive example regarding the direction, extent and ultimate success or failure of the North Korean reform process.

Cuba had imposed a more obviously Soviet-style economic system in the 1970s, in response to closer Comecon integration, and largely rejected the somewhat alternative 'Maoist-Guevarist' path of the 1966–70 period. By the time of the collapse of the USSR, the rigid command economy in Cuba had brought economic decline and almost total reliance on Moscow.

Cuba launched its *periodo especial en tiempo de paz*, or 'special period in a time of peace', in the wake of the economic crisis that followed the cessation of Soviet aid after the USSR's collapse. Havana asked the Cuban people to endure shortages and upheaval, such as the curtailment of many public transport services, while the economy adjusted to the new reality. Cuba's reforms went further than North Korea's, notably in the extent of foreign investment,[13] the liberalisation of the tourism sector, and, most importantly, the effective legalisation of the US dollar. However, by the time the *periodo especial* was launched the Cuban peso had already fallen substantially from the official parity of peso to dollar, and fuel, transport, energy and food shortages had become chronic. Castro had introduced reform too late: the *balsero* crisis, when tens of thousands of Cubans took to the Florida Straits in anything that floated to escape to the US, was one result.

However, in 1994 Cuba opened *agropecuarios*[14] – fruit, vegetable, lamb and pork markets. These were effectively farmers' markets where agricultural producers who had previously been obliged to sell direct to the government at state-plan-dictated prices could sell a portion of their produce for private gain. Hitherto Cubans had only known woefully understocked state stores or rationing. *Agropecuarios* eased food shortages somewhat, varied the limited Cuban diet, and improved money circulation.

The Cuban reforms also included other elements, such as the introduction of a new category of worker, *cuentapropistas*, or small businesspeople, who were able to be self-employed in occupations such as manicurists, repairers, artisans and entertainers. Additionally, to ease the food shortage further and to increase money circulation, *paladares*, or private restaurants, were allowed to open, and could charge in dollars (although most *paladares* would eventually go out of business due to a combination of bureaucratic rigmarole and the introduction of excessive licensing and tax requirements).

A side-effect of the reforms in Cuba was the creation of a division in society and inequality between those with access to dollars and those reliant on low state salaries. This adversely affected society. Those workers with low-paying jobs but access to foreign currency, such as hotel staff and domestic workers, saw their total earnings rise to over twenty times that of a state-employed engineer or doctor.

In North Korea the equivalent of *cuentapropistas* or *paladares* is considered a step too far. As Marcus Noland of the Institute for International Economics has said, 'These boys [the North Koreans] make Cuba look like something out of Adam Smith.'[15] Nevertheless, those in the DPRK able to charge higher prices in the farmers' markets have the prospect of becoming richer, and thereby causing social divisions and a level of inequality that only exists presently between those with privileges (the elite) and those without (everyone else).

Ultimately the farmers' markets are a stark reminder of the PDS's failure to feed the population adequately, while the state gradually shifts responsibility from the collective to the county level or even to the individual. The markets have seen government attitudes swing from hostility to tolerance to active sponsorship, where stalls are rented to merchants. They have certainly also been a space where corruption and theft have been the source of profit for some, and where others have survived through trading. These markets are novel in the DPRK, even though they formed part of mild reform processes in other socialist command economies, such as Poland and Hungary, in the late 1970s.[16] While the inclusion in the markets of non-food goods has extended their remit and relieved some shortages, it has also shown that North Korea is decidedly less egalitarian than the government claims, with some people clearly able to afford consumer goods while others sell their possessions to buy food to survive.

As the collapse of the PDS had been tacitly admitted in the introduction of reform, so prices have risen and availability become more random while wages have not kept pace for most workers. Ultimately more people are now reliant on an inherently unstable and largely unregulated secondary food distribution system that is subject to abuse by the military, police and senior cadres. The attempt to mix an incentive-driven farmers' market system and a state distribution system has made basic food procurement for ordinary North Koreans more problematic, time consuming and expensive.

Reaching under the Mattress

Kim Jong-il, in the meantime, continued to come up with ideas. Historically, attempts at liberating North Korean citizens from their savings have been limited.[17] However, in late November 2002 the North announced that it was switching from the US dollar to the euro as the North's preferred hard currency.

Currency reforms have been attempted on four occasions in North Korea. The first was in 1947 and the most recent in 1992. The last was designed by the state to collect the large sums of currency believed to have been retained privately, under the mattress, and not in general circulation. Each household was allowed to exchange up to NKW399 into new notes, while the remainder up to NKW30,000 had to be deposited. People were not allowed to change or deposit cash in excess of this. Consequently, those with large sums of cash saw their savings evaporate overnight. There were, reportedly, scenes of people selling cartloads of old currency. Since this time people have tended to keep only an essential sum of NKW, holding their remaining savings in foreign currency. The state has tolerated, or at least turned a blind eye to, a degree of black-market money changing.

To allow the government to tap into these funds all citizens were ordered to exchange any dollars they had for euros. The North flew in the euros, largely from South Korea, to handle the switch. Kim's aim was to flush out the dollars he believed many North Koreans had stashed away, as well as letting the USA know it didn't like the decision to cancel the fuel aid negotiated under the 1994 Agreed Framework in November 2002. This harked back to earlier reforms that aimed at unlocking citizens' savings. These had largely been accumulated due to the shortage of goods to buy in the DPRK along with the absence of a property market or financial investment opportunities. Some argued that North Koreans were simply reacting to the dollar's weakening international standing. Pyongyang also hoped to unleash activity in the economy, but with little for consumers to buy this didn't work. The state rigged the deal to benefit itself. Foreign consulates and NGO offices in North Korea also had to make the switch, and found the exchange rate offered generally unfavourable.

The North's central bank believed that it would flush out 'hundreds of millions of US dollars'. This scale seemed a little high to most observers, although an unquantifiable number of dollars enter the black market via Chinese traders and smugglers as well as in remittances. Park Suhk-sam, of Seoul's Bank of Korea, estimated that there was around US$960 million of foreign currency dormant in the DPRK, approximately 70 per cent of it being in US dollars.[18] Most households, even in the countryside, have traditionally kept some foreign currency for a rainy day. For many years US$ and NKW notes were officially of the same value. In reality, on the black market foreign currency exchanged at fifty to a hundred times its official value.

The reform netted Pyongyang's central bank an undisclosed amount of hard currency. It did little to benefit ordinary people. Any extra NKW they now have is being rapidly eaten up by growing inflation and rising costs. The majority of people in the DPRK are particularly vulnerable to inflation.[19] North Koreans are allowed to exchange their hard currency for local currency but cannot spend the former.

In Cuba the US dollar was effectively decriminalised, and became the de facto national currency. The right to shop at *agropecuarios* or use private tradesmen paying dollars eased some shortages in the economy. Cuba's relationship to the US differs from that of North Korea in that sending dollars to Cuba is less problematic. Be this as it may, the retention of the command economy in tandem with farmers' markets and other small-scale reforms ultimately has done little but point up the contradictions of state planning, and the Cuban economy too has continued to deteriorate overall.[20]

Chinese and Russian Reform Precedents

The model for Kim Jong-il's nascent reform process in the DPRK is undoubtedly China, despite the fact that the country's economic model is more Soviet in conception. Perestroika with no glasnost suits the DPRK best. The CPC has held on to power in China virtually unchallenged since the start of the Dengist reforms. Tiananmen Square in 1989 showed that democratic spirits could rise but also be dealt with. In China the reforms and the economic zones involved massive involvement and support of local people: in Kim's Sinuiju zone (of which more later) the North Korean people were to be virtually excluded.

Throughout the reform process North Korea has remained distrustful of and antagonistic towards potential foreign investors, describing them in such terms as 'impure elements' and 'infiltrators'.[21] The granting of further credits or loans for the purchase of equipment or technology by Western firms or international lenders may well prove pointless. Just as the Western companies that granted credits in the 1970s found themselves with an instant bad debt problem, the same would invariably happen again. The equipment would be too advanced for the crumbling North Korean infrastructure and impossible to integrate cost-effectively, while the lack of a steady flow of credit or foreign currency into the Pyongyang treasury would inevitably mean that the same problems would recur and lack of maintenance would once again render most of the investment wasted.

In China Deng had seen price reform and liberalisation as the key to long-term reform. China's price reforms were essentially about a transfer of decision-making within the SOEs away from the local planning bureau to the manager on the shop floor. Managers were given more control over key issues of SOE operation such as production techniques, output, distribution, investment of profits and bonus payments. These were similar to Soviet Prime Minister Kosygin's 1965 enterprise reforms, themselves based on the University of Kharkov's economist Evsei Liberman, who introduced bonuses for SOE managers and tried to link manufacturers to retailers while stimulating cost–benefit thinking and raising quality. These reforms eventually petered out in the USSR, although they were revived briefly in the 1980s by Gorbachev and his favourite economist Abel Aganbegyan, then at the influential Institute for Economics and Organisation of Industrial Production at Novosibirsk University.

The price reforms in China seemed bold but were in fact inspired by similar projects in other socialist planned economies, most notably Hungary and Yugoslavia, both of which had moved away from the Stalinist model still adhered to in the DPRK. Although inflation had burgeoned in the 1980s in China, this had created problems for the government's finances rather than for consumers, as price controls seemed to artificially restrain retail prices. Deng, clear that price reforms were risky, had made one highly significant move: he forewarned the Chinese public that price reform was imminent. Pyongyang failed to follow this lead in June 2002, presumably seeing it as unwise. Price rises in China were also significantly lower in percentage terms than those in the DPRK in 2002–03: the 1979 Chinese price reforms raised the nominal consumer retail price of rice by 25 per cent; in North Korea the price leapt 55,000 per cent. The announcement in China led to a certain amount of public panic and inevitable hoarding and speculation by people and organisations, including the government, many of whose agencies just went ahead with dropping price controls and started selling goods to the highest bidder. In contrast, price reform in North Korea simply happened overnight and was announced after the fact.

Further Chinese price reforms in 1988 were not wholly successful either and some price controls had to be reintroduced to rebalance the market. The major goods affected by the removal of price controls were staple food items, which meant that many ordinary workers were among the hardest hit. The reforms did have an effect on the high inflation rate, more than halving it in a year. The fact that 1989 was the year China exploded in rebellion is partly explained by the economics of the government in 1988: high inflation, corruption, hoarding and price reform all added to the anti-government environment in Tiananmen Square.

There are other crucial differences between China's and North Korea's reforms. In the aftermath of Tiananmen the Chinese economy was fortunate enough to have a record grain harvest due to good weather conditions.[22] This surplus helped tame inflation and retail prices. It was also the case that despite the setback in the reform process following the 1988 price liberalisations the agricultural sector was the one sector that had undergone real and radical reform. The reforms in the countryside encouraged farmers to plant, the crop level rose and food supplies improved, as did national distribution and the emergence of a more developed retail chain. In contrast North Korea has done little to reform its ailing agricultural sector, which is still inefficient, wasteful and largely unproductive – farmers prefer to expend their energies on the alternative agricultural economy. It is also arguable to what extent reforming the agricultural system in North Korea would yield benefits for a significant percentage of the population. In China (as in Vietnam) approximately 70 per cent of the population was engaged in agricultural work; therefore any reform of procurement pricing that increased farmers' incomes could potentially benefit a large slice of the population. By contrast, in North Korea the agricultural population is only 30–35 per cent of the total.

The other factor was that in China FDI continued flowing, even after Tiananmen Square. The Hong Kong investors, who in the late 1980s were the main source of financial input into China, kept on investing. This largely flowed into southern China, but its influence was felt across the country. The investment in Guangdong province prompted export growth. North Korea, on the other hand, has virtually no FDI and so does not have this income to offset the costs of its reform programme. Additionally, where foreign investment has occurred the government has stipulated that foreign-invested enterprises pay their workforce in hard currency at government-determined wage rates higher than those in China, thereby immediately destroying any competitiveness that North Korea may potentially have had. Most importantly, the growing foreign currency earnings of the Beijing government allowed them to subsidise goods if necessary or increase wages in the state sector to match rising living costs.

While the North Koreans do not have foreign currency reserves to speak of, they are attempting to move a greater amount of NKW into circulation. A budget session of parliament in March 2003 agreed to the issuance of what are termed People's Life Bonds (*Inmin Saenghwal Kongch'ae*), the first bond issue in North Korea's history.[23] As the NKW (like China's RMB) remains non-convertible, any funds raised through bond issues must be used within North Korea. Essentially the bonds are another way of harnessing personal savings and enterprise profits. With no ostensible state debt to be repaid, the profits from the bond issue may help subsidise the payment of wages during the introduction of the new pricing mechanism while dealing with the liquidity in the financial system following the onset of wage and price reform. However, this is a gamble, as it relies on a one-time 'windfall' to the Pyongyang treasury that must cover the period before the new price system is fully functional or SOEs start selling at the new higher prices and generate revenues to pay the higher wages (it has been reported that factories have closed, unable to pay the increase[24]). What the DPRK has not wanted to do is print money and create inflation. In this regard, it appears that the North Koreans have learnt one of the lessons the Chinese had been trying to teach them, and also avoided the mistakes of Russia. Pyongyang rigged the bond repayments in its own favour with a ten-year maturity term and no interest payments. The bonds are being sold across the country through work units and communities; some say that purchasing the bonds is mandatory.[25] Whether their purchase is compulsory or not, they are closer to a lottery than a true bond issue. The emphasis is on blind patriotism rather than sound investment skills, suggesting political duty rather than a financial decision.

The impact of the economic reforms has meant that there is a pressing need to get additional currency into circulation. The notion that this can by achieved by simply printing money brings into the frame the example of Russia after the collapse of the USSR. The overnight collapse of the controlled pricing system and the crash programme of instituting capitalism required the mass printing of rouble notes to stave off economic collapse. The result was impoverishment for many ordinary Russians, the growth of a black market, the US dollar becoming the most trusted currency and people's most prized possession, business bankruptcies across the country and price hikes all round.

However, the Russians had some advantages over the North Koreans. First, it was clear that the international community could not sit back and allow Russia to collapse: it was simply too important geopolitically and was still a highly significant nuclear power if not an economic one. Although few actually want North Korea's economy to collapse, the urgency to prop up Pyongyang is not the same as that of supporting Moscow. Russia was a new ally and the fear of nuclear weapons getting into the wrong hands meant that the degree of international goodwill was considerable.

Additionally, Russia had virtually instant access to the large global lenders including the World Bank, the IMF and the specially established European Bank for Reconstruction and Development (EBRD). Also, Russia was willing to call on foreigners to provide advice and assistance, notwithstanding the history of the Cold War and the tradition of Russian isolationism.

Lastly, it was also the case that despite the decades of Soviet economic planning, waste in the economy and the excessive weight apportioned to the military sector, Russia's industry was in relatively good shape compared to North Korea's. Russia had assets and strong deposits of untapped natural wealth that could be used to jump-start a new free-market system.

Pyongyang's Twilight Economy

Even though there is apparently no official policy of encouraging additional exports, the government routinely urges enterprises to seek export opportunities. There has been a renewed effort to seek overseas markets to generate additional foreign currency revenues. The lack of foreign currency reserves has been a major drain on the economy and has made serious reform impossible. North Korea still has debts outstanding from the 1960s and 1970s, which it largely defaulted on in 1976, long before the severe shortages and famine set in. At present the DPRK is in no financial position to honour these debts and has little political will to do so. This means that the DPRK is unable to access credit from foreign manufacturers. The country's political isolation and attitude of self-reliance, along with the DPRK's lack of creditworthiness, prevent it accessing funds from international lenders. While Pyongyang can feign disregard for the likes of the IMF, the likelihood of large nongovernmental financial institutions investing where the Fund or World Bank – the so-called 'catalyst' lenders – will not invest is virtually non-existent. To make matters worse, NGOs in North Korea are not keen on providing loans in hard currency, which they cannot monitor effectively, and over whose ultimate use they have little influence.

North Korea's government became acutely aware of the need to generate hard currency reserves when the Russians began to demand that goods, aid and military equipment be paid for in hard currency. At present North Korean exports are minimal for a country of its size. Major exports include minerals, metals, agricultural products and low-cost manufactured goods. However, it is not known how far mineral reserves, including gold, have been run down. Meanwhile exploitation of possibly sizeable reserves of oil have been hampered by suspicion and lack of investment. Then there is the question of military products, which do not necessarily show up in official figures but are a viable export category. Earnings from arms sales are of course secret. The ROK estimates that even these exports have collapsed: from around US$250 million a year in the 1980s to perhaps lower than US$50 million by the late 1990s.

In 2001 North Korean exports were just 0.5 per cent of South Korea's total. The collapse of the USSR led to a further overnight decline of 25 per cent. On the other hand, trade with China grew by approximately 17 per cent in the last decade, as the PRC became the DPRK's major export destination.[26] With the industrial decline worsening, the agricultural sector unable to meet even the basic needs of the people, and the current political crisis far from conducive to additional foreign investment, North Korea has had to seek alternative ways to generate hard currency. The methods have included outright illegal activities conducted with government connivance.

The need to earn foreign currency, then, is nothing new. Defectors reported in the 1970s that every district was being required by the government to form 'work companies' that could devise and undertake new businesses specifically aimed at earning foreign currency. These so-called 'dollars for Kim'[27] campaigns have continued ever since. For the most part the businesses involve small 'companies' of less than fifty people operating outside the central plan. Some have been in service sectors such as tourism; others have been agriculturally based, growing high-value crops such as ginseng, peppermint, rare pine mushrooms, herbs for traditional Chinese and Korean medicine and ostrich farming, not to mention the Pyongyang catfish factory, which uses wastewater from the East Pyongyang thermoelectric power plant. These enterprises have duly managed to gain some exports – for example, ginseng and honey are popular in East Asia – though they are hardly major foreign currency earners, and they encounter similar levels of waste and bureaucracy as the SOEs, which eradicate profit margins.

Despite legal changes put in place in 1986 permitting local enterprises to retain between 20 and 50 per cent of their earnings once they have made the required contribution to the government, there is little more incentive for managers and workers in these companies to produce than there is in the SOE or collective farm sector, as all profit is ultimately destined for the government. In 2000 the Bank of Korea calculated that these organisations accounted for no more than 3.6 per cent of total GDP at best. Nevertheless, such businesses are legal and could potentially represent nascent opportunities for entrepreneurs should more realistic economic reforms materialise. Other, more profitable, activities aimed at amassing hard currency are unquestionably not legal. However, so long as the foreign currency is directed to the government, a wide array of illegal currency generation methods are seemingly tolerated by Pyongyang.

Reportedly North Korea's major foreign earners come through the so-called Division 39, an organised network of trading companies designed to procure hard currency through various businesses. Division 39 is by its nature a state secret; consequently, details of the organisation are only derived from high-level defectors, ROK intelligence services and the CIA. Some estimates claim that Division 39 may have earned Pyongyang in excess of US$5 billion, which is purported to be held in bank accounts in Pyongyang, Austria, Macau and Switzerland.[28] The actual uses of this hard currency are unclear, although intelligence sources believe that it has been used to procure equipment and expertise for Pyongyang's nuclear programme and to fund North Korean intelligence operations overseas, as well by Kim to maintain loyalty among senior cadres.

Operations believed to come under Division 39's remit are drug trafficking, money laundering and counterfeiting, especially US$100 bills, apparently considered among the best forgeries in the world. The US reports that these large denomination bills have been intercepted in 'at least nine countries', and that DPRK officials in possession of counterfeit money have been arrested in Macau, Russia and Cambodia. It is also believed that Pyongyang has bought 'state-of-the-art European printing and counterfeit detection equipment with training courses included'.[29]

Japan believes that Pyongyang is involved in drugs cultivation and running (Hamgyong province has been cited as the main area for opium poppy growing, with production at approximately one tonne each of opium and methamphetamine annually as well as substantial amounts of ephedrine) and this has led to the tightening of inspections of boat services between Wonsan and Nigata in Japan. Major destinations for North Korean narcotics are thought to be Russia, South Korea, Japan, Hong Kong and Taiwan. There are also allegations of new heroin smuggling routes into Australia. According to the US State Department's Bureau for International Narcotics and Law Enforcement Affairs, the DPRK has been involved in the drugs trade since 1976, when a DPRK diplomat in Egypt was arrested with 880 lbs of hashish. Since then, there have been at least fifty arrests or drug seizures involving the DPRK in more than twenty countries.[30]

Division 39, according to defectors, was established in the 1970s, at around the same time as the Work Companies, to generate funds for Kim Jong-il. Division 39 retains an arm that involves itself in apparently legitimate businesses through the Daesong Group, which controls the Daesong Bank and the Vienna-based Golden Star Bank (which reportedly has 15 million euros in assets). The Daesong Group routinely denies that it is involved in any illegal activities. However, Japan has blocked certain sales by Japanese companies to Daesong divisions. These have included power control devices. While such devices have a range of uses, in April 2003 after the admitted resumption of North Korea's nuclear programme, the Japanese and South Korean authorities decided that the technology could be used to advance the enrichment of uranium. The Daesong Bank uses a network of shell companies in Macau under the umbrella of the Zokwang Trading Company. In 1994 five Zokwang employees were arrested in Macau trying to pass US$250,000 in counterfeit notes.[31] Estimating Pyongyang's earnings from trafficking and counterfeiting is of course problematic, though reports submitted to the US Congress by the Congressional Research Service in 1999–2000 estimated earnings at approximately US$85 million.

There is one final source of hard currency for Pyongyang: ethnic Koreans resident in Japan. These Koreans remit 'millions of dollars annually' to the DPRK, according to the Japanese authorities, as well as sending aid in the form of clothing, food, fuels and household appliances. Ethnic Koreans living in Japan who remain loyal to the DPRK are invariably members of the *Chongryun*, otherwise known as the *Chosensoren*, the General Association of Korean Residents, many of whom consider themselves to be overseas nationals of North Korea. The *Chosensoren* technically retain a number of seats in the North Korean parliament. The value of remittances from these Koreans living overseas, though once important, has declined as distaste for the regime has grown. Younger generations feel fewer ties to the North and links between the countries have been gradually weakening. Meanwhile Japan's recession has in any case reduced the available amount of disposable income held by Japanese Koreans.

A Fishing Rod of Temptation

The economic reform process is clearly one that Pyongyang began reluctantly, given past statements such as Kim Jong-il's 1998 comment in the *Rodong Sinmun* that 'The market economy is one of the fishing rods of temptation. Hanging from the fishhook are two specious baits called "economic co-operation" and "aid".' Kim's price and PDS reforms can be seen as an attempt to hint at further reforms in order to stave off pressure from foreign governments seeking to paint Pyongyang as totally beyond reform and use this as a pretext to stop aid flows.

Price reform as practised by the Chinese was also likely to have been perceived by Kim and his planners in Pyongyang as a process that almost got out of control. The problems led some Beijing economists to demand more reform. For instance Li Yining, an economist at Beijing University, declared that 'The economic reforms can fail solely due to the price reforms, yet the success of the reform process cannot be determined by price reform alone but primarily by ownership reform.'[32] In other words economists like Li, who were being taken seriously in Beijing, were arguing for a more far-reaching overhaul of the SOE sector, advocating the conversion of SOEs into joint stock or shareholding companies. This appalled the more conservative planners in Beijing at the time. Such calls in the DPRK now would meet the same response in Pyongyang.

What seems likely following Pyongyang's price reforms, and was witnessed in China, is that dual-price systems will lead to a greater incidence of corruption. In the DPRK those with connections are able to appropriate goods at planned economy prices, with difficulty through the PDS and with ease using foreign currency, and resell them at market prices. For a long time the rigidity of the system meant this activity was rare, but as famine, shortages and partial government acceptance of a black market have shaped daily life it is reported to have begun growing. While this 'blind eye' approach may work in the short term, history has shown that in most command economies citizen ignorance means that inflation is rarely blamed; instead cadre corruption is held responsible, which can lead to political resentment, dissent and ultimately agitation against the regime. Indeed, there have been instances of underground political satire reported in North Korea. The regime is called the 'Cadres' Feudal Republic of Korea', referring to corruption, bribery, official abuses of power and embezzlement. Needless to say, Pyongyang rejects this form of commentary.

It is not clear whence within the closed world of the KWP the reform impetus came. It is assumed that Kim Jong-il himself was the instigator of reforms. Yet who played the role of Zhu Rongji? This is an important question, as was demonstrated in China. After Tiananmen and the beginning of the reform process Deng was able to sideline hardliners and move closer to the reformers away from Beijing's harsh glare. China has a history of this: a centuries-old saying in the south has it, 'Heaven is high and the Emperor far away.' Prime among these reformers was the then mayor of Shanghai Zhu Rongji, who was busy reinventing Shanghai by attracting foreign investment and creating a financial and export processing centre in Pudong. It is here that Deng launched his new campaign to restart the reform process. Deng found the reformers in the eastern and southern cities, brought them on board and rounded back on Beijing.

This is a traditional course of action in China and has been used by various political leaders including Mao. However, in the highly centralised environment of North Korea this option is not available. Doubtless Kim himself is one of the major blocks to foreign investment – he is not liked internationally and is not seen as a man you can do business with. Although Deng was in a similar position after Tiananmen, he was able to elevate the likes of Zhu and Jiang to positions of national power and partially sideline the hardliners. Zhu and others thus became the front men internationally for the reform process and were perceived as men you *could* do business with. North Korea has no equivalents.

In terms of political economy the reasoning behind the reform process, its timing and its extent, can be explained in several ways. Certainly it seems that the government realised that the reforms would cause a degree of inflation within the system and that this could potentially kick-start the economy, though why they enacted the reforms in the middle of a fiscal year (which runs from January to December), which was guaranteed to disrupt the process in terms of planning the following year's budget, has never been ascertained. However, this would assume that the economy had a mass of underutilised resources waiting to be activated. Fifty years of command economics has led to a system geared to produce industrial goods for which there is a limited domestic market, and to decades of stagnation and decline; this has also meant that there are few export markets for North Korean goods, which are invariably substandard by international criteria. The economy could switch production to better-quality, more modern products (though Kim Il-sung registered the issue of poor quality as far back as the late 1950s) that could absorb resources, but it can not do so within the current straitjacket of the planned economy and indeed without significant currency reserves for investment and upgrading. Although the regime sought to assuage farmers with raised procurement prices, this has largely failed in its objective. The heavy reliance on expensive inputs, such as fertilisers, itself a relic of the command economy, means that any gains in income are eaten up rapidly in acquiring these inputs on the international market.

The financial reforms appear to have been undertaken to stamp out nascent entrepreneurial activity rather than encourage it. While bartering at markets may be acceptable to ease food shortages, large-scale private economic activity remains anathema to the regime and also tends to show up the inadequacies of the SOEs. When Deng started his reform programme in China, SOEs accounted for 75 per cent of all production; by 1995 they were producing only one-third, with the percentage falling as debts mounted. In this sense, the twin policy of promoting inflation and forcing citizens to turn in their US dollars for euros can be seen as a measure to ease speculation and profiteering. The issuing of People's Life Bonds, like the lotteries that went before, also allowed the state to tap into people's savings while giving little in return, as the bonds had a ten-year maturity with the principal repaid in instalments after year five without interest. Some economists have estimated that the bonds may have accounted for as much as 10 per cent of total GNP in 2003.[33]

The economic reform process in the DPRK must ultimately be seen as one that accentuates politics rather than economics. A primary factor is that the reforms followed the traditional practice of overtly favouring selected political constituencies. The key industrial sectors, the military and the political elites all received the highest pay increases to cushion them from the worst effects of price rises and inflation. Additionally, the regime knows full well that while curtailing supplies of foreign currency among the general population may have the effect of forcing the markets to rely on barter or NKW as the currency of transaction (thus preventing individuals or groups acquiring larger stocks of hard currency with which to speculate), the political elite will retain their privileged access to US dollars through the perks of overseas travel and business connections. This policy ultimately impoverishes the masses further while preserving senior cadre lifestyles. If it is true, as Seoul's Bank of Korea estimates, that there is twice as much hard currency in circulation as NKW and that most of this is under elite control, then politically Kim may have shored up elite support by protecting them from an erosion of purchasing power during the reforms.

The reality of the reform process is that it was undertaken by a small clique of the elite, themselves involved in the planning system, with Kim's blessing; a clique with only a rudimentary grasp of economics and one that was and is accustomed to decision-making based on consensus rather than debate. Raising issues that challenge the consensus have serious ramifications for those stepping outside the circle of agreement: ostracism, loss of privilege and political purging. For the elite, consensus on a bad decision is preferable to a debate that leads to a properly thought out policy. The political system established by Kim Il-sung at the country's inception, bolstered by the dominance of Juche and state planning at the economic level, have ossified political debate to the point where often patently ill-informed decisions are made and adhered to without question.

Additionally, while some systemic adjustments have been made the regime has consistently urged people to work harder in new speed battles or through renewed Chollima-style campaigns. While the reforms were being formalised Pyongyang was still also urging people to support a new revolutionary movement called *Ranam*, named after the apparently miraculous production levels and the 'revolutionary militant spirit' of the workers at the Ranam Coal Mining Machine Complex in the port city of Chongjin. Reform remains primarily a political issue in Pyongyang.

Reform or Die

In 2002, according to Bank of Korea estimates, the DPRK's economy grew by 1.2 per cent, continuing a low-growth but nevertheless positive trend seen since 1999, with its high point of 3.7 per cent in 2001. However, as a major series of reforms the 2002 initiatives have not created the massive growth spurt predicted while they have eroded the average citizen's purchasing power. Some 80 per cent of the average person's income is now devoted to feeding themselves,[34] thereby eating up the wage increases while ignoring their failure as a motivational tool – workers are unlikely to work harder unless their wages can actually buy something. While a low growth rate is evidenced, it is not high enough either to overcome the long-term industrial decline, or to restore the agricultural system to a position whereby it can feed the people or serve as a basis for providing sustainable long-term growth.

In a sense the reforms, if indeed intended as such rather than as a piecemeal effort to protect the last remnants of the command economy and collectivised farming, were back to front. The bond issue came after price reform, the foreign currency switch followed the removal of subsidies, increases in procurement prices came after farmers had started switching crops. In the meantime the command economy continued to use (and waste) labour, energy and raw materials. With prices rising faster than wages, a serious gap emerged. The only way to bridge this gap was with loans, but these were not available while currency reserves remained insignificant. Hence the SOEs remained technically bankrupt and were unable to pay higher utility bills and wages. The result was that, having been encouraged to reform, the SOEs were then brought back under the canopy of the command economy. Indeed their role is being still further protected; for if a real reform process was started that also encouraged private enterprise, the failings of the SOEs would be revealed even more starkly. However, against economic logic, the SOEs remain favoured sons of the state.

It appears that no SOEs were able to go it alone outside the plan. The government, unable simply to declare them bankrupt (not wanting to see unemployment and factory closures) continues to prop them up as best it can. This is similar to the consequences of the 1965 Soviet industrial reforms under Kosygin, where managers were told to prioritise costs and where profits arising from management control over employment, redundancy and wage rates were non-existent. Costs and waste continued to spiral. By contrast, in China the non-performing SOEs have been drip-fed with political loans, underwritten by the state with its massive foreign currency reserves, while the successful part of the Chinese economy continues to draw FDI and hard currency earnings through exports while supplying a greater range of goods to keep money in circulation through growth in consumer spending. North Korea was simply not up to this level. Despite this the DPRK kept up the pretence that there was momentum in the reform process in 2003. In March the DPRK finance minister, Mun Il-bong, addressed the North Korean parliament during the 2003 state budget discussions declaring that, 'In all institutions and enterprises a system of calculation based on money will have to be correctly installed, production and financial accounting systems strengthened, production and management activities carried out thoroughly by calculating the actual profits.' This statement, combined with the price reforms, seemed to acknowledge that Pyongyang accepted that price was a mediator between supply and demand, and that the state should lessen its role in the economy, although financial accounting had already been partially reformed as early as the 1978–84 Second Seven-year Plan in response to the failing economy with the introduction of the Independent Account-ing System, which gave more fiscal responsibility to SOEs at a local level. However, by 2003 the statement was largely meaningless as the reforms had faltered, although the elite could not openly admit this.

There has been some relaxation in the rules governing SOEs, such as the ability to engage more easily in international trade, and managers who have fulfilled their plan quotas can now continue to produce providing they can purchase the necessary inputs from their own revenues. However, it is not clear where these inputs are supposed to come from. Most are in short supply in North Korea and importing them requires currency, which is scarce even for the best-performing DPRK SOEs. This indicates that the plan becomes essentially 'frozen' and a market economy kicks in. Certainly this is the definition many North Korean economists have publicly attempted to give the reforms, claiming that the measures will remove vestiges of the 'Soviet system'. However, military procurement remains a priority, continu-ing to distort the market; and the ability of managers to lay off workers, introduce seasonal working or make other fundamental changes to the labour force structure, let alone any element of worker involvement in manage-ment, is not possible or envisioned. With no real unemployment system, no legal way for firms to declare bankruptcy and no effective banking system it seems that the state will continue to provide subsidies to support ailing SOEs.[35] Consequently any notion that the DPRK has somehow introduced a version of the Chinese system, never mind a more 'marketised' economy, is overly optimistic.

Nevertheless, these reforms were still expected to run alongside the com-mand economy. An article in *Pyongyang Kyongje Yon'gu* (Pyongyang Economic Studies) in February 2002 stated that 'In the socialist society, the domestic market is divided into two: the market based on the socialist economic forms, and the farmers' market.'[36]

By September 2003, following the 2002 economic reforms that initially saw the adjusted exchange rate of the NKW drop from NKW2.12 to NKW150 to the US dollar, the currency had devalued to around NKW900 to the dollar as Pyongyang introduced a floating exchange rate.[37] The second revaluation also indicated that the disparity between the official and the black-market rates for the US dollar was widening. This effectively brought in a form of parity with both the US dollar and the Japanese yen and recognises their increased use in general circulation as hard currencies. This acceptance of varying rates and a subsequent revaluation have a parallel in China: in 1994 Beijing effectively devalued when it abolished its foreign exchange certificate scheme.

The WFP estimated that rice prices rose by a factor of fifty in the period between January and September 2003.[38] Observers noted that the effect of the spiralling inflation was that private activity was increasing but involved the illegal sale of state assets and goods as well as the private bartering of home-produced agricultural produce, such as fruit juice, from private plots. With new requirements for SOEs to be self-financing, factory managers have also started asset stripping and selling machinery, scrap and plant to China for much-needed cash and food, ultimately eroding further productive capacity. Undersupply grew while hunger and shortages were still fuelling demand. Though salaries had generally doubled, as promised, at the start of the reforms this was inadequate to match price rises. The government recognised the growing mismatch in supply and demand and promised to maintain subsidies to the very poor, though NGOs largely believed this to be impossible given the government's strained financial resources. Reports that people were eating grass and tree bark now started to include Pyongyang, where such practices had before been observed only in the countryside. A daily exodus of Pyongyang residents to the countryside in search of food – consequently meaning that they were not being productive in the city – was reported in several sources, indicating that the economic realities were hitting home even in the traditionally privileged capital. This has led to further reports that farmers have been building guard posts and organising watch committees to guard their crops from looters.

The government attempted to continue to provide survival-level disbursements while hoping that the market, in the form of farmers' markets and private plots, could supplement the PDS. Indeed, the PDS did survive, despite the extremely low rations it had been reduced to distributing, which led many NGOs to conclude that the PDS had effectively collapsed. The inclusion of humanitarian food aid shipments in the PDS ration undoubtedly helped raise the levels of food the government was seen to be handing out in recent years. In 2002 agricultural procurement prices were raised to stimulate the amount of food in the PDS, though a further mismatch occurred with PDS prices remaining largely unchanged between July 2002 and October 2003. Meanwhile market prices moved steeply upwards, merely accentuating the different levels of access to food and goods within the system, further fracturing society into a mass of have-nots and an elite of haves. Many observers have concluded that the effects of the reform of the PDS will ultimately be revealed in increased mortality rates among these have-nots. In the absence of a mechanism for periodically adjusting prices, it seems that the mismatch between prices paid to farmers and market prices will continue and could easily become exaggerated again. It has already been seen that grain and rice prices have soared in the markets while remaining more steady in the PDS. Consequently farmers are no more likely to sell to the state now than they were before the initial reform of state procurement prices. Access to grain will remain the preserve of the wealthy, though farmers, if able, may increasingly hoard in the hope of higher prices. For many analysts this lack of a periodic adjustment mechanism indicates that Kim's reforms were aimed primarily at reducing the gap between the black market and government prices, reining in activity outside the official economy and reasserting economic control.

When the government's major strategy for attracting the much-needed inward investment – Sinuiju – ignominiously failed, the government simply jettisoned the notion of reform entirely. One analyst who was initially hopeful for the reforms indicated in May 2003 what the outcome would be if the reforms failed:

> A collapse of the DPRK attempts to reform could create yet another humanitarian catastrophe; it might result in increased and desperate attempts to make money by trading arms, drugs, falsified currency, and so forth. A failure of the proponents of an economic, i.e. civil, attempt to ensure regime security and prosperity might result in effectively strengthening the role of the military in domestic politics and a greater likeliness of an armed conflict in the region.[39]

This sentiment was echoed by the World Bank's Bradley Babson, who stated that 'The reforms are not sufficient to assure a turnaround in North Korea's economic crisis and even add new risks, particularly the risk of inflation.' Babson continued: 'To achieve sustainable economic growth, North Korea will need more policy reform towards a market economy.'[40] For those trying to organise the relief effort on the ground, the reforms also appear to have made life harder for their constituents. Masood Hyder, the UN Humanitarian Coordinator for North Korea, sees the reforms as causing further hardship for at least a million people in failed SOEs and for those whose wages are far from keeping pace with the price of goods. The wage and price reforms were meant to rectify a problem. However, in Hyder's view the additional suffering they are causing is 'more than a temporary blip', while the 2003 WFP/FAO Crop and Food Supply Assessment noted that it was now the urban population and industrial workforce that had become the most vulnerable sectors,[41] and Park Suhk-sam of the Bank of Korea observed that

'The reform programme didn't go smoothly because they lost their bearings from the beginning. It has only worsened the economic situation, imposing a heavy burden on the leadership.'[42]

By mid-2003 it was clear the reforms had failed and any suggestion of 'capitalist creep' was largely cast aside in the face of nuclear standoff. However, as a device to reassert government control of the economy and pricing they had been a success for Kim. The ROK National Intelligence Service indicated that Division 39 was becoming increasingly active and it appeared clear that the military hierarchy had lost its patience with economic reform. Kim's two strategies to resuscitate North Korea – a charm offensive and economic reforms – had both failed: the only option left to the regime was to gain time with the nuclear gambit. The decision by Pyongyang deliberately to leak details of their nuclear programme, and kick-start a process of nuclear brinkmanship with the US, came after the government had decided privately, though not publicly, that the reforms had largely failed.

The nuclear crisis is dealt with in Part III. Before we consider this, we need to look in some depth at the events surrounding the launch of the other major prong of Kim Jong-il's economic reform programme, Sinuiju, as this reveals, even more glaringly than does the detail of the price, wage and rationing reforms, the mindset of Pyongyang. We should bear in mind here these words of a foreign diplomat in North Korea: 'I didn't meet anyone who had even a passing knowledge of market economics: they have no money, no sense of how things work, no legal framework.'[43] Further, a pertinent question is raised by the Sinologist Ross Terrill: 'Where in the world has a Leninist party retained power after the economy ceased to be state directed?'[44]

7

The Reality of Reform:
A Case Study of Sinuiju

Caged Investment

While the reforms to the wages and prices system, the PDS and the financial sector were adjustments to the command economy, modifications that ultimately further revealed the contradictions of the planned economy and aggravated the economic collapse, Sinuiju was different. Sinuiju, the third plank in Pyongyang's economic reform strategy in 2002, was to be a special economic zone. Its creation attracted more headlines than the other economic reforms. The decision to launch the Sinuiju experiment clearly indicated that, with the demise of the USSR, China was now the favoured economic paradigm. The Special Economic Zones (SEZs) of southern China, which, combined with the astute use of FDI, have done so much to power economic growth in the PRC over the last fifteen years, were the model, even though in China they effectively symbolised the ending of the politics of self-reliance. However, Sinuiju was not a straightforward attempt to replicate the Chinese SEZs.

The Sinuiju experiment can be seen as a case study of the North Korean attempt to enact economic reform. As a 'pet project', it involved a personal political risk for Kim Jong-il, though we may never know to what extent his personal position was at stake. Kim was certainly closely identified with the Sinuiju project. Its ultimate collapse and resultant bickering would annoy China. The imprisonment of the project's chief executive must also be seen as Kim's personal failure. It seems unlikely that the entire DPRK leadership could have been in support of Sinuiju, which effectively would have created a capitalist enclave in North Korea and could have been seen as effectively ceding national sovereignty over 132 square kilometres of territory. Certainly it is hard to imagine that the military hierarchy was wholly supportive. That the idea was forced through reflects not just the dominant position of Kim Jong-il but also the distorting effects that Juche and the personality cult continue to exert on the country's development. That such an ill-conceived, badly thought-through and generally botched project could ever have got off the ground is testament to the lack of economic policy skills in the DPRK and the economic culture of a collapsing command economy.

Sinuiju is Announced

The news on 12 September 2002 that the presidium of the DPRK's SPA had issued a decree creating a new Special Administrative Region (SAR) in the decidedly down-at-heel town of Sinuiju on the border with China was not wholly unexpected. Rumours of a plan to establish an SAR had been circulating since 1997. According to some sources, Kim Jong-il actually consulted China's then president, Jiang Zemin, about Sinuiju when he visited Shanghai in 2001. Jiang is thought to have advised Kim against the location, saying that there would be too much competition from the thriving city of Dandong, on the Chinese side of the Yalu river. In June 2001, reports began circulating that 'ideologically suspect' residents of Sinuiju were being expelled, with as many as 30,000 people reportedly being relocated. As if in confirmation, the North Koreans finally decided to go ahead with Sinuiju, a process described by Lim Dong-Won, a special advisor on security to the ROK president, Kim Dae-Jung, as 'a change quite similar to that of the early years of China's reform'.

Sinuiju SAR was to be a closed-off capitalist area within North Korea: using US dollars as its currency; operating its own legislature, courts and police force; issuing its own passports; operating gambling premises; with its own flag; and hopefully benefiting from some inward investment as well as a fifty-year mandate – all in a loose tax environment, though Pyongyang would retain diplomatic and defence functions.[1] According to Pyongyang, the DPRK's cabinet, SPA and other central government agencies would 'not interfere with the Sinuiju SAR project' and the SAR would be entitled to conduct external business under its own mandate. Furthermore Korean, English and Chinese would be the official languages. An estimated 400–500,000 residents of Sinuiju would be forcibly relocated to make way for the SAR (none of whom appeared to know anything about this process when the announcement was made), which would 'flatten' the existing city.

In their place would come 200,000 'young and technically skilled new residents' from other parts of the DPRK and also, perhaps, China (although the Chinese never officially said that they would allow their citizens to work in Sinuiju). The 200,000 North Koreans would, it is thought, be military personnel and all would only get into the SAR following a screening process, with the usual preferences being given to those with no 'negative' past and with experience of working in consumer goods manufacturing. The relocation was set to begin by spring 2003. Other events intervened, however. Nevertheless, the North Koreans retain ambitious plans for Sinuiju including skyscrapers, a four-lane highway, a bridge linking Sinuiju and Dandong, an international convention centre and apartment complexes – all environmentally friendly.[2] DPRK sources talked of Sinuiju looking like Shanghai's Pudong New Area – a tall order for impoverished North Korea.

These plans went much further than most people had expected. After all, the DPRK had experimented with investment zones before, with little success. For a long time foreign interests, and the Chinese in particular, had pressured Pyongyang to loosen the economy and many analysts had cited the early Chinese experiments, with Shenzhen on the Hong Kong border as the model for North Korea to follow. Indeed, something similar had already been tried, although it was less ambitious and decidedly unsuccessful.

The Rajin–Sonbong Free Trade and Economic Zone had opened in 1991 on the DPRK's remote northeastern coast by the Chinese and Russian borders. Rajin–Sonbong was smaller than the planned zone in Sinuiju, at just 700 square kilometres, though it benefited from a potentially strong location close to the United Nations' Tumen River Area Development Programme and close also to North Korea's largest oil refinery. Nevertheless, potential ROK investors mostly thought the location too remote.

North Korea announced aims to attract US$7 billion in investment to Rajin–Sonbong and envisaged it as a major regional container port, tourist destination and hub for various export industries. However, there was little interest, aside from a handful of companies. These included the courier and logistics firm TNT and the Hong Kong-based Emperor Group, which opened a casino, to date the major investment in the zone. Those who visited the zone mostly went away disappointed. The location was not ideal and government interference remained predictably high. Rajin–Sonbong has largely withered on the vine in the last decade. Just how tough conditions were is illustrated by Emperor Group's experience. Emperor launched its casino in 2000 and has invested approximately US$600 million. The Group was forced to build its own water supply system and to generate half of the electricity the casino needed, as the zone's infrastructure was so underdeveloped. Pyongyang was so economically out of touch that when Kim

Jong-il toured Rajin–Sonbong in 1998 he was reportedly appalled to see adverts that were larger than the banners containing Kim Il-sung's image. All the offending billboards were removed and the word 'Free' was deleted from the zone's official title. The zone's director, Kim Jong-u, was duly removed from his post and disappeared, rumoured to have been shot.

Although the zone was effectively de-prioritised as a government initiative in 1998, things have reportedly now improved in Rajin–Sonbong, due largely to the persistence of the few investors; the casino now buys 90 per cent of its power from local utilities.[3] However, Rajin–Sonbong was decidedly not Shenzhen or Hong Kong, and, despite the casino, neither was it a new Macau. Contracting to run a casino business and finding it necessary first to build a power generator is not an ideal situation. Significantly, Sinuiju is similarly bereft of infrastructure. An official at the Dandong Border Economic Merchants Co-operation Bureau confirmed that 'In Sinuiju they hardly have water, electricity or telecommunications, all of that will have to come from here.'[4]

Another experiment with a special zone on a less grand scale than Rajin–Sonbong, and certainly less extensive than what was proposed at Sinuiju, was the Mount Kumgang Tourism Zone (the so-called Diamond Mountains). This industrial park was largely a joint venture involving Pyongyang and South Korea's Hyundai conglomerate. Hyundai was to manage the zone, seek to attract ROK small and medium-sized enterprises (SMEs) and develop tourism aimed at South Korean visitors as its centrepiece attraction. Mount Kumgang was a pet project of Hyundai's founder, Chung Ju-yong, who once walked across the border from the South with 1,501 cows. Chung's son, Chung Mong-hun, continued the relationship with the North, meeting with Kim Jong-il several times. Chung Mong-hun committed suicide in August 2003 after being linked to the secret money transfers to Pyongyang that bought the North's participation in the Inter-Korean Summit in 2000.

Again, as with Rajin–Sonbong, the lack of a viable infrastructure or legal protection put off SMEs, despite some economic cooperation agreements between the ROK and Pyongyang. Mount Kumgang ultimately became a tourist destination rather than an investment zone. In later years the North would use restriction of access as a political football to extract concessions from the ROK. Hyundai, despite technically remaining committed to the project, found it a cost centre rather than a revenue stream.

However, the relationship forged between Hyundai and Pyongyang did lead to discussions on other zones. This was when the idea of Sinuiju first appeared, with the North Koreans keen to locate any new Hyundai-sponsored zone in the city, while the South Korean *chaebol* argued for a location closer to the ROK–DPRK border around Haeju. The compromise location, agreed upon in June 2000, was Kaesong, a city of 400,000 just forty-four miles north of Seoul. However, the project has been problematic despite being close to the border with the South. Lack of infrastructure in the Kaesong Industrial Zone, a rigid legal framework (all printed materials, CDs, photographs and bullets are banned) and the non-appearance of the necessary improved transportation links, as well as a minimum monthly wage of US$50, all initially doomed the project which remains technically operative but with little progress made so far. Nevertheless, a reported 900 ROK companies have expressed interest in the zone, with Hyundai claiming it will invest US$184 million by 2007.[5]

Kim's 2001 trip to Shanghai was a major offensive by the Chinese to encourage the North Koreans to follow the Chinese lead. Kim was given a high-profile tour of Shanghai and local officials made sure he saw lots of streets lined with neon signage and busy shoppers. The Chinese also made sure Kim recognised the benefits of foreign investment with a trip around the city's massive GM plant and an opportunity to measure the success of local technology companies. The message to Kim was clear: follow our example and Pyongyang can start to look like Shanghai. Kim was not necessarily keen for Pyongyang to look like Shanghai, of course, though he couldn't fail to be impressed by what he saw.

The potential problems with Sinuiju are mostly obvious. North Korea badly lacks infrastructure; just how Sinuiju will provide the power, water, gas and other utilities potential investors demand is unclear, as apparently no budget has been dedicated to the projct. The zone would be largely reliant on China for supplies of raw materials.[6] The zone had no import or export tariffs and income tax was set at 14 per cent; yet the SAR was still just an area of land. There were clearly safer places to put money, and investors demanded third-party jurisdiction despite the zone planning to have its own legislature. North Korean law was not deemed suitable for arbitration purposes or for contract law. There were also the unresolved issues of repatriation of profits and access to offshore banking.

The Orchid Grower Comes to Town

Perhaps nothing excited the press and Pyongyang watchers as much as the surprise announcement that Sinuiju would be run by Yang Bin. Most had expected Park Tae-joon, a former ROK general, to get the job. The day Yang Bin was sworn into office by Kim Yong-nam, Kim Jong-il's number two, the world's press started to take an interest in him. To those who had followed business in China over the last decade Yang Bin was well known, and he had both admirers and detractors. But to much of the outside world Yang was unknown.

When Yang took the job he was just 39 years old, though he looked older. What most people who followed China knew was that he was the second richest man in the PRC and the fifteenth richest person outside the US according to a *Forbes* magazine survey.[7] Most people described him as Chinese, which he is ethnically, though he is actually a Dutch citizen. Officially, Yang, born in 1963, came from a poor family in Nanjing, in eastern China's Jiangsu province, and was orphaned when he was 5 years old. In the late 1980s he studied and later taught at a Chinese naval college before moving to Europe to study at Leiden University in the Netherlands. While there he gained Dutch citizenship, claiming political asylum after the 1989 Tiananmen Square demonstrations (though he had no involvement in the protests), and started a successful textile trading business between Europe and China. Yang was married and had two children.

Yang returned to China to become involved in the agricultural technology business. His timing was excellent. The skills he had picked up in the Netherlands observing the Dutch market gardening industry[8] transferred well to China. The booming cities of the Chinese coast were starting to demand flowers and a floristry industry was emerging rapidly. Young urban Chinese were starting to celebrate St Valentine's Day and give flowers at social occasions. Yang tapped into this and profited from the new consumer market, amassing a personal fortune estimated to be in the region of US$900 million, allowing him to enjoy a lavish lifestyle which included 'a Mercedes, Ferrari, two Rolls-Royces and an office modelled on the Royal Palace of the Netherlands'.[9]

The company Yang created with US$20 million start-up capital, Bermuda-registered Euro-Asia Agricultural Holdings, was listed on the Hong Kong Stock Exchange in 2001 and instantly became a favourite with investors looking to invest in China. As a Dutch citizen he was able to register the business as foreign-funded and import equipment duty-free. Euro-Asia specialises in the hydroponic cultivation of *Cymbidium* and *Phalaenopsis*, two species of orchid. The company's facilities include seventeen hectares of greenhouses across seven production bases in Liaoning, Jilin, Hebei and Shandong provinces in northeastern China, near the DPRK border. Yang also had a cooperation agreement with Singapore-listed fruit distributor FHTK Holdings on a US$10 million fruit and vegetable greenhouse in Shandong province and owns a minority stake in a Japanese supermarket chain.

Euro-Asia profited on the HKSE, with Yang's own stakeholding rising as high as HK$2.80 a share in May 2002, nearly double the issue price. This was despite a growing chorus of analysts who pointed out that much of Euro-Asia's profits were being reinvested in a bizarre scheme to build a 400-hectare amusement park in northeastern China based on the theme of the Netherlands and all things Dutch – Holland Village, a US$217 million tourist attraction, property development and agricultural production base on the outskirts of the windswept city of Shenyang, complete with tulips, windmills, gabled roofs and Dutch sculptures as well as a replica of the International Court of Justice and of Amsterdam train station, employing 1,000 people. Yang declared of the Holland Village project, 'I want to leave something for posterity.' However, the project failed to take off, in part because it is a 30-minute drive from Shenyang city centre, and also due to rumours that it had been built on the site of an old graveyard. There was of course the possible reason that nobody but Yang was interested in visiting a replica of the Netherlands in northeast China.

Even those who chose to ignore Yang's theme park project could not ignore the decision in early September 2002 by Hong Kong's Securities and Futures Commission (HKSFC) to halt trading in Euro-Asia shares, which by then had slumped to just HK$0.69. The HKSFC claimed that the share suspension was due to a pending announcement on price-sensitive information, namely the resignation of Chen Jun, Euro-Asia's short-lived chief executive officer.[10] However, Euro-Asia told the Hong Kong press that it hadn't announced the resignation because the board had not yet officially accepted it, and Chen had continued to represent the company in business dealings. One analyst declared, 'There is no big problem in the fundamentals of the company, it's just the fact that there are too many negative rumours on the Chairman and the company.'[11]

Those rumours included one that Yang was being investigated by the Chinese authorities for tax evasion, another that he had misused company assets, and a third that he had used land illegally. Yang denied the allegation of tax evasion though did admit that a routine investigation had been conducted on Euro-Asia's taxes and assets. Still the rumours persisted. The situation continued to attract attention when, in August, Yang reduced his personal stake in Euro-Asia from 72 per cent to 54 per cent through the sale of 300 million shares to two investors for a total of US$49 million.

Despite its floatation and later suspension, Euro-Asia effectively remained Yang's company. Even after the announcement of his new role in North Korea he maintained that he would stay on as chairman, an announcement that did not help Euro-Asia's share price and annoyed many investors. Clearly other senior officials were having problems working with Yang. Notwithstanding early denials, Chen Jun resigned officially in September after only a five-month stint with the company claiming that he lacked the executive power he had required and had never had the authority to mobilize capital or staff in line with the company's business plan.

Chen was apparently concerned with the direction of Euro-Asia under Yang and had advised the company to get out of the cultivation sector and concentrate on preparatory and post-farming work such as processing and packaging. These activities would make use of China's seemingly infinite resource of cheap labour. Chen reportedly believed that by staying in the cultivation business Euro-Asia would have to compete with China's 800 million peasant farmers eventually, something he deemed an insurmountable task. Clearly working with Yang was tough. Executive director Li Gang, who had eight years of horticulture marketing experience, and had worked with Yang since 1998, replaced Chen as CEO.[12]

Greenhouses from Shenyang to Pyongyang

Yang became involved with North Korea in December 2000, when Kim Jong-il reportedly offered him 150 hectares of prime land in front of his father's tomb on the outskirts of Pyongyang 'to show my father's spirit that we have made great advances in agriculture'. Yang had long been based in northeast China's Liaoning province. It was here he had announced that he intended to build 100,000 greenhouses in the DPRK to grow vegetables for sale in Russia and Japan. To many potential investors there was a logic to this. Despite the problems of doing business in the DPRK it was true that North Korea had room for the greenhouses and could locate them near to the Chinese border. Russia and Japan sounded likely potentially good markets given the Russian Far East's intemperate climate and Japan's premium-priced agricultural land that makes vegetable prices among the highest in the world. The greenhouses never appeared. However, Yang's link to Pyongyang remained active. Indeed in late 2002 there were strong rumours that he had fled to North Korea to avoid the Chinese tax authorities.

This was not the first doubt over Yang's character. Yang had become recognised as a consummate insider with strong ties to the leadership of the local authorities in Shenyang, including the Mayor of Dalian and senior officials including the provincial governor (whom he had known since childhood). (This sort of relationship raised some eyebrows in 1999 when Shenyang's mayor was arrested for corruption and US$6 million worth of gold bars were found in his house.) Yang was also well travelled and had acted as an unofficial representative of Shenyang in Japan, South Korea and Australia. The *Far Eastern Economic Review* had already reported the story of Yang's close relationship with Liaoning's governor, Bo Xilai, a man tipped to be a future leader of China. The *FEER* story suggested that Yang had received state bank loans for his private business ventures.[13] This news came at a time when private businesses across China were finding it increasingly difficult to secure state financing. This story was followed by another – that Yang's new theme park was being expanded. Joe Zhang, an analyst at UBS Warburg in Hong Kong, questioned Euro-Asia's finances, pointing out that the company had claimed a turnover significantly higher than that of its major competitor Yinghao Technology. It was also noted that Yang had once been a substantial shareholder in Yinghao. Additionally, visitors to Euro-Asia's headquarters had noted a certificate granting Yang honorary citizenship of Shenyang displayed in a glass case and signed by the city's ex-mayor Mu Suixin, a man who been handed a suspended death sentence for corruption following a scandal linking organised criminals to top officials in northeast China. Another picture showed Yang standing alongside vice-premier Li Lanqing, demonstrating Yang's connections all the way to the top in Beijing.

All of this rather took the gloss off Yang's reputation. Yang had been a poster boy for returning overseas Chinese entrepreneurs and had been used by Beijing as an example of how China's business environment had changed sufficiently to allow overseas Chinese to return and invest in China. Yang's subsequent fall from grace embarrassed Beijing and placed him distinctly out of favour. This process coincided with then premier Zhu Rongji's announcement that China's new rich must be brought to heel and pay their taxes. The spotlight fell even more sharply on Yang, who was one of the richest.

Then came the announcement from Pyongyang of Yang's appointment as Sinuiju's chief executive. To suggest that surprise was the major reaction would be an understatement. Those who knew of Yang's business past were amazed. Others, including most of the Korean and non-Chinese press, were nonplussed, not knowing who Yang was. Though he may have forged strong links to the Pyongyang government Yang was a capitalist entrepreneur and a foreigner and did not even speak Korean. Many were surprised to see Yang pictured in the press lighting the cigarette of North Korean vice-minister for the economy and deputy premier Cho Chang-dok at an official dinner in Pyongyang, and displaying a Kim Il-sung badge. A more casual picture appeared of Yang in Pyongyang in informal clothing under the twin portraits of the Great and the Dear Leaders and still sporting his Kim Il-sung official badge, just above the more famous Lacoste alligator logo on his shirt.

The Chinese media were largely silent on the appointment, reflecting Yang's growing problems with the authorities. The *Financial Times* claimed that China's Propaganda Department had issued an internal circular in June 2002 forbidding media coverage of Yang and his business dealings. The FT cited one source, a Chinese journalist, as saying, 'We have written a long story on the North Korean zone and Yang but we are not allowed to publish it.' Another source stated, 'We don't know how much of our reservation about Yang Bin to communicate to our North Korean friends, it is delicate.'[14] But if China was between a rock and a hard place, then it was one partly of its own making: after all, it was Beijing and the Chinese media that were largely responsible for Yang's profile and reputation before the rumours and the problems started to become public.

To all intents and purposes, despite the growing storm around him Yang appeared intent to follow through on the Sinuiju project and refused to step down as chairman of Euro-Asia (though he indicated that he might do so in the future), making the project seem like an adjunct to the company's other business concerns. He intimated that his major appointments in Sinuiju would be mostly foreigners, including a European judge and with the possibility of an American becoming police chief. He was also looking to attract talent from China. The whole experiment in extraterroriality got off to a bad start when, on 30 September 2002, the South Korean newspaper *Joongnag Ilbo* reported that the DPRK Consulate General in Shenyang had rejected visa applications by a group of ROK journalists. The reason given by the DPRK authorities was that 'South Koreans are not foreigners.' Their visa applications were sponsored by Euro-Asia. A group of Japanese journalists applying for visas were also rejected.[15] Yang was later quoted as saying that he 'deeply apologised that the visa-free entry failed to materialize'.

Given Yang's increasingly tarnished reputation in China and the failure to announce any investment, Sinuiju increasingly appeared doomed, not least because no budget for the project had been announced. Sinuiju would have been a hard sell even without Yang's failing reputation and seeming Chinese indifference to the project. Many diplomats and Korea analysts asked why a business would choose to invest a significant amount of money in Sinuiju when there were plenty of established, and more predictable, investment opportunities in China's SEZs, and even in more fragile Asian markets such as Vietnam, Myanmar or Cambodia. Sinuiju was most often described as 'dilapidated', with little industry save for a few-run down chemical, metal and food processing factories. Yang gave himself ten years to turn it into a thriving economic zone focused on processing, high-tech, finance, tourism and trade.

Yang was always inconsistent on the subject of why he was chosen to run Sinuiju. He claimed he was selected for three reasons: first, because he had contributed to North Korean agriculture; second, because he was Chinese; and third, because he had Dutch citizenship. However, so far as anyone knows, Yang's announced investment in the DPRK, the 100,000 greenhouses, have failed to materialise, so his contribution to North Korean agriculture is questionable. The second and third reasons revealed Yang's continuing schizophrenia over his nationality, touting both his 'Chineseness' and his 'Dutchness' as reasons for his appointment. This argument worked well for Yang in the 1990s in China but by this point the Chinese had soured on this pitch though it still appeared to have some appeal in Pyongyang. There was also the question of just how much of his time Yang would devote to Sinuiju given that he seemed intent on retaining the helm at Euro-Asia. One Hong Kong-based analyst stated that, 'We don't know whether Yang will have enough time to devote to Euro-Asia' despite Yang's assertion that his role as Sinuiju CEO would have 'little impact on its [Euro-Asia's] daily operation.'[16]

What Kind of Zone Was Sinuiju To Be?

There is little doubt that the model for Sinuiju was Shenzhen and the other Chinese SEZs around southern China, as we have seen. Yang Bin may have talked of Sinuiju being comparable to Hong Kong but the grounds for that comparison are hard to see. There are possible advantages to the location: if it is ever completed, the Kwongui railway line will run the 486 kilometres between Seoul and Sinuiju, connecting with the Chinese rail network at Dandong. The city also lies at the end of the road from Pusan, through Seoul and Kaesong.

However, there are important differences between the Chinese zones and Sinuiju. Primary among these is the fact that Beijing never gave up control of the SEZs, though it did allow them a freer reign. Pyongyang, by contrast, appeared to be simply taking a town and giving it to a foreigner. Simply put, Shenzhen and Sinuiju are not the same. Furthermore the Chinese eventually used their SEZs as stepping stones – to encourage investment across the country, first along the coast, then inland through policies such as the 'Go West' programme. North Korea in all its attempted zones sought to corral any investment within the borders of the zone and actively prevent investment from occurring outside these designated areas. The wealth and investment, as well as the possible 'spiritual pollution', was to be contained and not allowed to spread randomly throughout the country.

The Chinese government opened the initial four SEZs in 1980, three of which were in Guangdong province with easy access to Hong Kong's markets, capital and manufacturers looking for cheap land and low-cost labour. This influx of investment worked and Guangdong advanced economically at a furious rate. By 1986 Guangdong was China's largest exporting province, surpassing even Shanghai. By the early 1990s Guangdong accounted for 40 per cent of all China's exports. Sinuiju does not have these benefits, unless Japanese and South Korean capital and investment can be attracted. Neither does it have the massive hinterland to serve it, nor the improved port facilities that Guangdong cities such as Shenzhen, Zhuhai and Shekou have. As Hu Angang, an economist at Beijing's Tsinghua University, declared, 'North Korea may not be ready for opening up its interior.'[17]

Guangdong was also where the Shenzhen Stock Exchange was located. There is no prospect of a bourse in the DPRK. There is also no proposal by Pyongyang to integrate Sinuiju into the wider economy and social system. The absence of local entrepreneurs means that Sinuiju loses the competitive advantage that China's SEZs had of being talent magnets for China's new entrepreneurial class. Deng was able, during his infamous Southern Tour of 1992,[18] to declare that 'SEZs are socialist, not capitalist' and that 'foreign funded enterprises ... are good for socialism', adding that 'the Chinese, having more than once missed the opportunity to modernise, must not fail again.' In contrast Pyongyang simply sought to create a capitalist zone it hoped would generate revenues and raise North Korea's economic profile, while treating the place as a leper colony and putting a wall around it to control access. Reform was something Deng wanted to filter through society; to Kim reforms are a virus that threatens to infect his people. With Kim so keen to keep Sinuiju at arm's length from the rest of the DPRK this raises the question of just who would invest there.

Joint ventures and FDI in North Korea have to date been few and far between and usually small scale. Yang commented that he expected the Chinese to get involved in Sinuiju. And it is true that there is growing Chinese investment in North Korea. Take, for example, the case of Chinese Panda Electronics. In May 2002 Panda launched the Morning-Panda Joint Venture Computer Company between Panda and the DPRK's Daedonggang Computer Corporation with the objective of manufacturing computers for local distribution. However, the level of actual Chinese FDI in the DPRK remains small scale.

Several analysts have seen in Sinuiju another take on Pyongyang's developed aid economy. The lack of facilities or budget for Sinuiju revealed that there was a tendency to expect investors to sort out the problems them-selves. At any rate, by Chinese standards Sinuiju was small scale. Dandong on the Chinese side of the border is seen as being relatively underdeveloped by Chinese standards, yet it is still far larger than Sinuiju at 14,950 square kilometres and with a population of 2.4 million people. Dandong is also intended to be part of the Europe–Asia Railway system linking Japan, Seoul, Beijing and Moscow eventually. It has substantial reserves of timber, mag-nesium and water as well as a surrounding agricultural hinterland. The city has built up strong industries in textiles, electronics and chemicals. Dandong is also a growing point of trade between the ROK and China, a trade that amounted to US$31.4 billion in 2001, 6 per cent of all China's overseas trade.[19] Shenzhen is even more of a contrast to Sinuiju. Its GNP increased 49-fold between 1980 and 1990, when the zone was first established.

The Departure of the Orchid Grower

Then, after the flurry of activity and his becoming international news, Yang was gone. His high profile in Pyongyang hadn't gone unnoticed in China. His appointment coincided with a crackdown on tax avoidance in China. Yang was aware that he was coming under the spotlight, as were others. Yang Rong, the head of Brilliance Automotive, fled to the US, complaining that he was being 'persecuted' by Chinese officials and fearing he would be detained.[20]

Tax avoidance was a major issue in the Chinese media following the 29th Session of the Standing Committee of the Ninth National People's Congress in Beijing, when Wang Chunzheng, the vice-minister of the State Development Planning Commission, told delegates that 'The government will spare no effort to enhance the supervision of tax collection.' Tax collection in China had become a major problem that threatened the government's spending commitments and raised the threat of social disorder. The tax avoidance problem became public when it was revealed that none of the 200 wealthiest people in China (as identified by *Forbes*) paid any income tax. The burden had fallen on the increasingly hard-pressed urban middle classes. The campaign gathered steam throughout 2002 with uncollected taxes from businesses alone reckoned to be in excess of US$3.7 billion per annum, according to the State Administration of Taxation.

Rumours about Yang and tax were nothing new. However, after his appointment by Pyongyang, Beijing demanded he pay his overdue bills. The tax authorities in Shenyang issued a notice to Yang and Euro-Asia, demanding payment. This was the first time Beijing officially confirmed that Yang had failed to pay taxes, a charge that was added to others concerning illegal land use.[21]

In October 2002 Yang was detained by Shenyang police on suspicion of tax evasion. He was about to leave Shenyang for Sinuiju when the police arrived at five in the morning to stop him crossing the border to the DPRK. Yang's bank accounts were frozen. Initially officials at Euro-Asia denied Yang's detainment, claiming that as he was a Dutch citizen the police would have had to go through diplomatic channels. However, the charges were not light. China's securities regulator, the China Securities Regulation Commission (CSRC), later said that investigations by the tax bureau had concluded that US$24 million was missing from Euro-Asia and that US$400,000 had been stolen; in addition US$1 million in back taxes were owed. It was later revealed that Euro-Asia owed Germany's Hamburgische Landesbank and Chiyu Banking Corporation, a unit of the Bank of China, a further US$7.7 million.

The North Koreans reacted in support of Yang, and Hong Kong's *Ming Pao Daily News* reported that the DPRK had dispatched vice-minister-level officials to Beijing to find out what was going on. This report was confirmed by *KCNA*, which reported that Yang Hyoung-seop, the vice-chairman of the DPRK People's Commissariat and Pyongyang's number four, was to lead representatives to China on 15 October to ask questions, albeit in a 'friendly' manner. However, other sources reported a different story, which was that Beijing had asked for Yang to be dismissed as the head of Sinuiju, and that in return China would support Pyongyang's plans. Pyongyang could then move ahead with Sinuiju under a new chief executive and Beijing could deal with Yang ahead of its politically sensitive 16th Communist Party Congress that was to deal with changes relating to China's leadership succession.

Clearly the Chinese were not prepared to allow Sinuiju to damage investment in Dandong, whatever it might mean for Sino–DPRK relations. If China's main economic reasoning in the last two decades has been to attract FDI to raise living standards and fund reform, then Beijing was highly unlikely simply to allow Pyongyang to mimic the tactic. In November 2002 it was announced that Cai Zhefu, the CPC general secretary of Dandong had concluded an agreement with South Korea's Commercial Minister, Shin Kook-hwan, to establish a joint Sino–ROK industrial complex in Dandong. The Chinese were clearly seeking to anticipate Sinuiju.

Despite this, Beijing sought to assure the DPRK government that it supported its overall economic reform effort. When the Chinese met with a DPRK delegation in mid-October, after Yang's arrest and at the start of the nuclear crisis, the North Koreans were entertained by the same high-level Beijing officials as was traditional. At the meeting vice-president (and Jiang Zemin's eventual successor) Hu Jintao and National People's Congress chairman Li Peng reportedly told the North Koreans that Chinese support for their reforms was still forthcoming despite the Yang Bin issue.

Yang remained confined to his luxury villa in Holland Village with a police guard while Euro-Asia security guards restricted access to Yang's other house in Horangchun. Yang claimed to CNN that he was not permitted to talk to the press about the case directly and could only use the telephone under supervision. Clearly the senior management at Euro-Asia were feeling the strain. On 6 October the company's vice-chairman and CFO Yan Chuang resigned, followed by non-executive director Wong Hon Sum. In the meantime the announcement of the South Korean investment in Dandong struck many businesspeople as real and tangible and, with support from the Chinese and ROK authorities, something that would happen, compared to Sinuiju with Pyongyang backtracking and its chief executive now under arrest in China.

Yang's woes with the Hong Kong regulators went from bad to worse, with Euro-Asia being twice suspended from trading. The Hong Kong press reported that he was suspected of falsifying accounts to obtain a Hong Kong listing. It appeared that the HKSFC had been tipped off by China's securities regulators, who asserted that Euro-Asia had exaggerated its sales 21-fold between 1998 and 2001. In other words, Euro-Asia's reported US$254 million in sales in this period were far in excess of the US$12.2 million in revenue estimated by China's tax authorities. The term 'fabrication' was reportedly used in the letter. Euro-Asia's stock price plummeted further (it had by now fallen by 79 per cent in 2002 alone). It was clear that the Chinese were making sure that Yang's arrest was justified to the financial community.

Yang had clearly become an embarrassment to Beijing. The authorities were in a quandary as to whether or not he should be put on trial. A trial seemed in keeping with his alleged crimes and the ongoing crackdown against tax evasion. However, Beijing had other considerations, including not wanting to see awkward questions raised about Yang's links to the Party and provincial officials, trying to limit press speculation, and maintaining good relations with the DPRK ahead of a visit to China by Kim Jong-il. The Chinese would have preferred the Yang issue simply to go away. In Pyongyang, meanwhile, the realisation that they had backed the wrong horse was sinking in.

By the time Pyongyang's nuclear secrets went public it seemed clear that Yang would be punished. Mark Clifford, *Business Week*'s Asia correspondent, told CNN at the time:

> I don't think Yang Bin's future is very good. At the very least he's going to pay a lot of money in back taxes. His company looks like it's, if not ruined, at least on the edge of collapse. Its shares are down 80 to 90% from their peak earlier this year. He's no longer China's second richest man, as he's been billed. I think he'll be lucky to stay out of jail.

Clifford was correct: Yang received a sentence of eighteen years in prison along with a fine of US$1 million from the Liaoning court. His subsequent appeal was rejected.

Sinuiju's Confusing Message

Sinuiju ultimately sent out a highly confusing message. Pyongyang had intended to show that it was serious about economic reform after the changes to the PDS, wages and prices earlier in 2002. Sinuiju was Pyongyang's version of opening up to the world and inviting in FDI. However, unlike China, which had gone through the same process, the DPRK was not willing for any investment to alter the overall system. China had realised that changes would happen and had pursued a slow opening up, one that led to the country's accession to the WTO and numerous other concrete changes in the country from the introduction of a consumer society, the Internet, through to greater opportunities for PRC citizens. Kim is not prepared to accept this scale of change, even though in China it does not appear to have affected the Party's grip on power and hegemony.

Sinuiju also showed how out of touch Pyongyang was with concepts of international business and economics. The North Koreans had earlier made economic decisions that any student of economics would have known would lead to rampant inflation, though the country's economists were surprised. Now they had taken a piece of land with no utilities, few transport links, no skilled workforce and expected foreign investors to flock to it. It didn't happen and they couldn't work out why.

The Sinuiju experiment can be viewed in two lights. Either it was an act of desperation by Kim Jong-il to generate much-needed revenues for the country. If successful then Sinuiju could be rolled out in a similar form on the model of the initial SEZs in China, which were the testing ground for Deng's economic reforms. However, it is more likely that Kim saw Sinuiju as a way to generate hard currency. His decision to cede, in effect, national sovereignty over a substantial area of North Korean real estate to someone else, necessarily a non-national, was to try out reform without the risk: if it failed, the central leadership, and Kim himself, could avoid blame. That few North Koreans even knew what was happening was a bonus.

There were no real plans for Sinuiju beyond some artists' impressions. There was no budget, no infrastructure. *South China Morning Post* journalist Mark O'Neill, who accompanied Yang's team to Sinuiju, maintains that Yang personally could not have explained exactly how Sinuiju would work for investors; he did not possess that foresight. Rather, he assumed that the investment coming in from, say, a hotel group, a casino or a factory would serve to create development, investment funds and growth.[22]

There was another important aspect to Sinuiju that many overlooked at the time. Certainly to SOE and other enterprise managers across North

Korea the new rules and commitment to reform that Sinuiju seemingly represented sent a signal that the leadership supported a wider economic reform process. For those in the state bureaucracy and industry keen to reform, a major problem has been that in the restrictive world of North Korea it is impossible for anyone to go beyond the parameters set by the state. Sinuiju indicated to some reform-minded North Koreans that exploring new economic and industrial organisational concepts may be permissible. However, the divorce between Sinuiju and the government meant that reformers had to choose either to be inside the zone or operate outside. They consequently kept their heads down.

As Sinuiju collapsed as an ideal and Yang languished in prison, Kim Jong-il abandoned any further serious attempt at political reform. Instead the nuclear crisis reared its head, with a distinct shift away from the North Korean 'charm offensive' of 2002, and the country plunged back into isolation and assumed a largely uncompromising negotiating stance. The failure of the economic reforms coupled with the demise of Sinuiju can be seen as a double blow for Kim. The return of harsh rhetoric since October 2002 may be evidence that, having pushed the reforms against the advice of some elements within North Korea, notably the military hierarchy, Kim is now in the process of appeasing these elements with a 'return to normal' policy that takes North Korea back to its more familiar Spartan-style permanent war atmosphere.

PART III

Diplomacy and the Military: Foreign Relations, Nuclear Crisis and Self-Defence

8

Don't Poke the Snake:
US–DPRK Relations

The year 2002 proved a challenge to those committed to understanding Kim Jong-il. Following the admission that the DPRK had been kidnapping Japanese citizens and resultant diplomatic flurry in Pyongyang, and then the announcement of economic reforms, including the largely unexpected plans for Sinuiju, the statement on 17 October 2002 that North Korea had continued its nuclear weapons programme despite repeated claims to the contrary caused many jaws to drop. To understand the American reaction to the announcement from Pyongyang it is necessary to look at the history of US–DPRK relations.

The Eternal Afterthought

American relations with the DPRK have been largely conducted in a Cold War atmosphere. The US and the USSR fought one of their many ideological battles on the Korean peninsula, while Japan and China looked after their own security interests. The American and Soviet roles in the Korean War have been well documented and need no further detail here.[1] However, that war, despite the involvement of many countries and parties, ultimately ended in a conflict between the US and China: at the 1953 armistice the US wanted to see an anti-communist and relatively capitalistic Korea below the 38th parallel, while the USSR wanted a communist, centrally planned satellite above it. Both got more or less what they wanted. In the South the Americans were prepared to accept a certain level of state economic intervention, protectionism and cartelism, as well as patently undemocratic governments, as long as the ROK remained within an anti-communist framework. In the North, Kim Il-sung had to accept that the Soviets would initially dictate economic policy as the price for being the USSR's chief client state in East Asia to counteract the American presence in Japan. While Kim came increasingly to dominate the Northern political scene, Syngman Rhee, an English-speaking ardent anti-communist who had a Ph.D. from Princeton, was the first US-supported leader of the South.

Even before the Korean War American soldiers wanted little to do with Korea. Most analysts in the US would probably agree that, for America, Korea is in the wrong place geographically, and at the end of the Second World War was neither large nor powerful enough to move high up the American agenda. As the former *Washington Post* journalist Don Oberdorfer wrote, 'Korea's fate was often to be an afterthought, subordinated to the more immediate or compelling requirements of larger powers, rather than a subject of full consideration in its own right.'[2] Little has changed in the intervening years since the Korean War, and the refrain of GIs posted to post-war US-occupied Japan with the possibility of transfer to Korea that the things to fear most were 'diarrhea, gonorrhea, and Ko-rea' remains popular. However, South Korea was seen as a necessary bulwark against communism and so the US was willing to deal with despots such as Syngman Rhee and commit large amounts of military manpower and financial aid to the penin-sula. As well as the troops stationed in Korea, between 1953 and 1961 South Korea received approximately US$2 billion in aid from the US, around 10 per cent of total GNP.

Throughout the 1960s North Korea stayed resolutely off the American agenda as events such as the Cuban missile crisis in 1962 absorbed the White House and the US public alike (the DPRK condemned the US, sup-ported Castro and stayed silent on Soviet capitulation). Korea remained an 'afterthought'. However, America's ever-closer relationship with Seoul and continued involvement in Japan did have the effect of forcing Pyongyang to broker a rapprochement with Moscow after the problems of the Sino–Soviet dispute and Khrushchev's de-Stalinization campaign. The growing US mili-tary presence in the ROK, along with America's growing involvement in Vietnam, led Pyongyang to establish a closer relationship with Brezhnev's USSR after the fall of Khrushchev. Tensions became heightened in 1968 following the seizure by the North Koreans of the USS *Pueblo* and the at-tempted assassination of President Park Chung-hee in Seoul, which many in America saw as timed to coincide with American preoccupations over the Tet Offensive in Vietnam – all of which contributed to Lyndon Johnson leaving the White House. This was followed swiftly by the North Korean interception of the US EC-121 spyplane.[3]

Nixon as Catalyst

After the stand-off following the Korean War, while the US and the USSR eyed each other warily around the world and the two Koreas began their economic race to see which system would triumph, little direct intervention was made by the US in Korean affairs despite the continuing American military presence in the South. The US guaranteed South Korea's security, tolerating a military regime that was blatantly abusing human rights but remained fervently anti-communist. With US involvement in Vietnam in full swing this was an accommodation America was ready to make. Korea remained largely an 'afterthought'. However, American actions would have consequences for the peninsula, even if unintended. In this sense President Nixon became a catalyst for both greater contact between China and North Korea and in terms of a major breakthrough in relations between North and South Korea.

Nixon's visit to China in February 1972 was an event of world historical importance, profoundly changing global geopolitics, radically affecting relationships in the Communist bloc, as well as signalling a change in Washington's Cold War tactics. Nixon's triangular diplomacy of engaging both Moscow and Beijing had a major effect on North Korea too. Nixon and Kissinger had not intended this; indeed, in his talks with Mao and Zhou Enlai, Nixon was seeking to end hostilities between the PRC and the US and to turn China into a diplomatic bulwark against the USSR.[4] Korea was again an afterthought. (A footnote to the Nixon visit to Beijing is the fact that in July 1971, when Kissinger secretly visited Beijing to prepare for the president's trip, Kim was also in the Chinese capital on one of his regular and often unannounced visits to consult with the leaders of the Chinese Communist Party.[5])

The talks between Nixon and Mao had two ramifications for Kim. First, he concluded that Beijing had effectively betrayed the common struggle against US imperialism and that the DPRK would now be facing the might of US forces in Asia alone. Second, he decided that communication with South Korea was now called for as the situation had shifted beneath his feet and beyond his control – though Kim publicly derided Nixon for having 'capitulated' and effectively conceded American defeat globally. Following the Second Plenum of the Fifth Central Committee meeting of the KWP in April 1971 it appears that engagement with the South in light of changed Sino–US relations was decided upon. An immediate benefit for Kim was that the Chinese, keen to assuage any anger felt by their allies after the Nixon visit, launched a new economic and military aid package for North Korea, the first for fifteen years. Thus in 1972, the year the historic North–South

Communiqué was signed by Pyongyang and Seoul, the DPRK received tanks and Chinese-made versions of the Soviet MiG-19 fighter.

Despite having influenced events on the peninsula and largely forced Kim's hand in opening the way to talks with the South, Nixon had not intended this directly and the peninsula remained, at best, a secondary consideration in American thinking. Nixon had withdrawn the US Seventh Infantry Division of 20,000 men in 1971, against strong objections from the ROK president, General Park. Fearing an escalation of US troop withdrawals and the new warmth in Sino–US relations, Park introduced his repressive *Yushin* (revitalising reform) measures, including martial law; they would last until 1979. His argument was bolstered by the decline in the US Military Assistance Program, which fell from US$300 million in 1974 to zero by 1978. Fears of American withdrawal helped guarantee Park's continued military regime, without American interference. Following Park's attempted assassination by a disgruntled Japanese Korean on 15 August 1974, Korean Independence Day (from Japan), an attack which left Park's wife dead, America again had nothing of substance to say, despite the dangerous breach that had opened up in ROK–Japan relations, as the US was embroiled in Watergate, the subsequent resignation of Nixon and the appointment of President Ford.

Ford, Carter and Kim

The suggestion that US Forces in South Korea (USFK) should again be scaled back after the cuts following the introduction of the 'Nixon Doctrine'[6] in 1969 was made by the Carter administration and its assessment of post-Vietnam American foreign and military policy. Carter had included full withdrawal of US troops from Korea in his 1975 election manifesto, which attracted voters in a political climate shaped by the fall of Saigon, an active anti-war movement, the degraded reputation of the military in public opinion along with a general questioning of America's imperial role around the world. South Korea had been worried about American intentions on the peninsula after Nixon's resignation in 1974. Ford had given Park an assurance that the US would not completely withdraw, though did not rule out partial withdrawals. Park saw that Ford was unlikely to be around for long, as he was facing increasingly serious opposition from the Democrats. He responded to the uncertain situation by upping the ROK's defence expenditure; by the time Carter occupied the White House the South was outpacing the North's military expenditure by a factor of nearly two to one.

All this was played out against the backdrop of heightened tensions along the demilitarised zone (DMZ), which followed the death of two American officers after a confrontation between US/ROK troops and DPRK soldiers arguing about the cutting down of a poplar tree in the Joint Security Area (JSA) in August 1976.[7] Ford was busy fighting the election against Carter, so Kissinger was left to coordinate foreign policy. Despite Kissinger's apparent wish to respond with force, the final decision was that the war alert status would be raised, F-4 and F1-11 fighters would deploy to South Korea, B-52 bombers would start 'practice' runs closer to North Korean airspace, and the aircraft carrier USS *Midway* would sail from Japanese into Korean waters. Ford ultimately decided that military reprisal was too likely to lead to war. Certainly the North Koreans went on full war alert, with precautionary blackouts in Pyongyang. Soon after this the Americans moved back into the JSA and cut down the poplar tree, backed by the US Air Force and the threat of the USS *Midway*. A back-up plan, which would effectively have constituted the start of World War III, was to hand if the US and ROK tree cutters were attacked. Kim made no move against the felling of the poplar. Indeed shortly after the troublesome tree had been removed, Kim finally agreed to the American proposal that the JSA be formally divided to prevent clashes between US/ROK and DPRK personnel.

The ultimate upshot of the tree-felling incident was that the US and the DPRK came closer to war than at any point since the 1953 armistice. One outcome may well have been that, had war broken out on the peninsula and been seen to be in retaliation for the killing of US personnel, then Ford may well have been elected president. However, war did not break out, Ford lost and Carter entered the White House with relations between Washington and Seoul at a new low point.

Carter, true to his manifesto, announced plans for a gradual but complete withdrawal of US ground forces from Korea while also seeking a thaw in US–DPRK relations, which did nothing to resuscitate relations with Seoul. Though Carter was later to renege on his pledge to withdraw troops, initially White House discussions were solely around the issue of how best to complete the withdrawal. This downsizing and intended eventual ending of the American commitment was matched by the stated intention of the commander of USFK, Lieutenant General James F. Hollingsworth,[8] to turn the ROK army from a defensive into an offensive force with artillery deployed closer to the DMZ to support this new forward defence posture. Carter, along with Zbigniew Brzezinski, his national security adviser, Cyrus Vance, his secretary of state, and Harold Brown, his secretary of defense, fought consistently for two years to fulfil Carter's commitment to withdraw troops from the peninsula.

Increasingly Carter became aware that his plans for complete withdrawal from the peninsula had worried other American allies in East Asia. Tokyo was concerned about the implications for its own security while Seoul felt increasingly unable to control its own destiny in the face of a president apparently committed to full rollback. Additionally, the Carter administration never, as it had promised Seoul it would, briefed either Beijing or Moscow about its plans in Korea. Clearly Carter, a committed democrat and advocate of human rights, while disliking the Pyongyang regime, was also ill at ease with the leadership in Seoul and its human rights abuses.[9] By March 1976 Park knew where he stood when Carter told him that he intended to withdraw all US military personnel while supporting a strengthening of the ROK army as per Hollingsworth's plan.

With America still in the bloody process of extracting itself from Vietnam and trying to learn the lessons of that conflict, Kim had apparently been keen to consider a strike against the South, though neither China nor the USSR supported such action. A confrontation with America over Korea was not something over which either Mao or Brezhnev was prepared to go to war. However, the continuing US/ROK joint manoeuvres, 'Team Spirit', were seen by Pyongyang as tantamount to a preparation for a joint US–ROK invasion of the DPRK.

Carter's campaign insistence on Korea troop withdrawals had revealed the deep policy differences within the US government and military hierarchy. Carter had pushed for the implementation of his exit plan but had met resistance from the military high command and, in particular, the US Command in Korea. Carter had a timetable involving 6,000 troops being pulled out in 1978 and another 9,000 by 1980; simultaneously American nuclear weapons in the ROK were to be gradually removed and US$1.9 billion provided to Seoul in military aid.

Clearly Carter's timing was bad and his gradualist plan was blocked by a Congress that distrusted Park's regime and its human rights abuses and yet was concerned at the spate of events that preoccupied America – DPRK spying in the ROK, the tree-felling incident and the loss of an American helicopter over the DMZ;[10] followed by the fall of the Shah of Iran in April 1979, and the Soviet involvement in Afghanistan from December 1979, not to mention the assassination of the ROK's President Park in Seoul.[11] These events did not, to the minds of many in Congress, suggest it was a good time to scale down the military presence despite the recent experience of Vietnam. Carter had been effectively isolated and felt himself outmanoeuvred by the Washington establishment and forced to renege on campaign pledges.

It seemed that one of the only supporters of Carter's pledged withdrawal of troops was Kim, who since Carter had taken office had toned down his anti-US rhetoric. When Carter began to backtrack, Kim was quick to point out that he was jettisoning campaign pledges. Meanwhile Carter's resolve was further undermined by CIA claims that they had previously underestimated the North's military capabilities and that it would take a greater effort than originally envisaged to bring the ROK up to parity and guarantee its security. Consequently, in 1978, large-scale military exercises ('Team Spirit'[12]), involving over 200,000 US and ROK troops, were held, alarming Pyongyang, which already felt vulnerable following the signing of the Sino–Japanese Friendship Treaty the same year. In 1979, the Carter administration ceased its programme of troop withdrawal in reaction to North Korea's upgrading of its army and the discovery of DPRK-built infiltration tunnels under the DMZ. Hollingsworth's forward defence strategy, 'Team Spirit' and the tunnels under the DMZ led to a serious escalation of the arms build-up on the peninsula.

Carter, despite the collapse of his plans, still sought ways to engage the DPRK, though these sometimes revealed his weak understanding of the situation on the peninsula. In January 1979, with Park distrusting him and Kim alienated and aware of the imminent normalisation of Sino–US relations, Carter suggested brokering a meeting, similar to his 1978 Camp David summit with Israel and Egypt, between Park and Kim at Panmunjom. This showed how out of touch Carter was with the peninsula's realpolitik. Still, Carter was emboldened by his recent Camp David success and also with the establishment of full diplomatic relations with Beijing in January 1979.[13] The reality of the situation was finally driven home to Carter when he visited Seoul to meet Park in June 1979, a meeting that went badly with Park insisting the US could not withdraw without seriously destabilising the peninsula and Carter urging the ROK to upgrade militarily and improve its human rights record. When Carter got back to Washington, Brzezinski announced to the press that the troop withdrawals were suspended till 1981 (the date of an anticipated Carter second term) pending the ROK achieving military parity with the DPRK. Throughout the Carter presidency only 3,000 troops had been brought home; 37,000 remained on the peninsula along with a reduced deployment of 250 nuclear missiles. While little had changed, the illusion of a possible pull-out by the Americans remained with the creation of the US–ROK Combined Forces Command, headed by General John Wickham, which would provide continued American military leadership in the event of troop withdrawal.

In October 1979 Park, seriously undermined internally following the disputes with Carter, was assassinated by the director of the Korean Central Intelligence Agency (KCIA), Kim Jae-kyu. An emergency cabinet meeting appointed the prime minister, Choi Kyu-ha, as acting president, the USFK moved to a higher alert level, anticipating an invasion from the North.

President Carter sought to use the death of Park to encourage democracy and human rights in South Korea. However, what should have been clear to American policy makers was that the ROK was no longer a supplicant but an increasingly strong economic power in its own right, despite the negative effects of the fluctuations in world oil prices after the Iranian revolution, a resultant spate of business failures and continuing labour troubles. The government continued to crack down on pro-democracy protestors and political groups. Park's *Yushin* doctrine remained in effect. On 12 December 1979 the successful so-called '12/12' military coup led by the defence security commander, Chun Doo-hwan,[14] occurred, further indicating that although America was the guarantor of the ROK's security it had little influence in domestic politics. The Americans were left watching impotently, despite their military presence and the Combined Forces Command, while events on the peninsula took place and were largely settled before the Americans knew they were happening.

Chun was immediately unpopular with the Americans, who saw him as unscrupulous and unreliable though politically adept and shrewd. America worried about the signals being sent to the North by the coup, but Chun and his advisers felt that there was no imminent danger of a clash. Chun correctly anticipated that ultimately the US would support his government, partly because it was a fait accompli and partly because at the time American concerns were centred on the Tehran hostage crisis. Carter was clearly not pleased with the events of 12 December but for domestic political reasons had to focus elsewhere.

In 1980 renewed protests by pro-democracy advocates occurred across the ROK. The US urged a cautious approach on the part of Kyu-ha Choi and his government, but Chun, now KCIA acting director, told the Americans that he believed the North was fostering the agitation, although the Americans saw no evidence of this. Nevertheless, it was used as a pretext for Seoul to start moving against the demonstrators, in particular the 'Three Kims', including Kim Dae-jung again,[15] and declaring martial law. The result was effectively a military takeover of the government, sparking further protests in Kwangju, the provincial capital of Cholla and Kim Dae-jung's hometown. The repression of the dissent in Kwangju, led by ROK special forces, was severe. With 30,000 protestors on the streets of the city, the term 'insurrection' was increasingly being used to describe events. Nonetheless Carter decided that the situation should be resolved by the Koreans; meanwhile support for the government should remain, with the usual codas about moving towards democracy. The Korean-led solution to Kwangju, on 27 May 1980, left at least forty people dead. Nevertheless it did lead to a growing distaste among the people for government by generals as well as prompting an outburst of anti-Americanism among students and the population of Cholla, who had seen the US stand by as troops retook Kwangju. Within weeks the events were known universally as the 'Kwangju Massacre' and assumed to have occurred with American complicity. By the end of August, Chun Doo-hwan had moved into the Blue House following the resignation of Choi Kyu-ha and Chun's endorsement by the ROK military command. Carter remained cool towards the new administration, instigating an arm's length strategy of engagement, while Chun sought to defuse the tension after Kwangju and legitimate his regime by launching an anti-corruption drive throughout government. However, in 1982 Chun's regime was indelibly tainted by a major loan scandal when a relative of the president was found to have earned US$300 million pedalling access to the Blue House, the president's official residence.

Chun then cleverly used the issue of Kim Dae-jung to maintain relations with Washington. Kim had become a cause célèbre in American political circles. Carter sent emissaries to try to secure the commutation of Kim's death sentence. They were unsuccessful. What eventually saved Kim's life was Carter losing the presidential election. Chun rightly saw a more pro-ROK president in Reagan and stalled the commutation until Reagan was in the White House, then agreed to it in return for an official visit to Washington.

The Reagan and Bush Years

Chun used his key pawn, Kim Dae-jung, well, and got his official visit to the White House in February 1981, the month of Reagan's inauguration. Reagan was more inclined to back Chun than Carter had been, and recommitted the US military to the ROK. He was also more overtly hostile towards global communism, pursuing what Alexandre Mansourov of the Asia-Pacific Center for Security Studies has called a policy of 'strategic benign neglect and back-breaking arms race' whereby the White House sought to isolate the USSR following its invasion of Afghanistan, force Moscow into bankruptcy in an escalating arms race and bring down the Soviet party-state.[16] Reagan and his secretary of state, Alexander Haig, fully realised that Chun's Washington visit would go a long way to normalising what was by now a long strained relationship between the US and Seoul. Reagan announced a policy of no troop withdrawals and indeed bolstered the force to 43,000 personnel while agreeing to sell South Korea F-16 warplanes, a deal Carter had blocked. While the new relationship was good for Chun, his seeming embrace by Washington stirred additional anti-American opinion among those in South

Korea who saw the US as complicit in the Kwangju Massacre and 12/12. For the incoming Reagan team Korea was a way to build support among the US military leadership, sell some armaments and position Washington against Pyongyang as part of larger plans to combat communism and the USSR. Again, in terms of US policy Korea had been largely an afterthought. It was also the case that Kim now found that his high level of military spending was wasted as he was effectively trying to match US military spending as more arms and weapons technology was transferred to Seoul from America. This placed additional strains on the DPRK's economy and played a major role in shifting Pyongyang's thoughts towards the nuclear option. North Korea, like China, saw Reagan as a leader who would not easily back down, and certainly no Carter.

As Reagan ratcheted up his campaign against the USSR, Korea came centre stage again with the shooting down of Korean Airlines flight 007 in September 1983. The Soviets eventually admitted to the shooting (radio communication from the Soviet fighter pilot had anyway been captured by Japanese intelligence, proving it), claiming that the commercial jet had entered Soviet airspace on a US intelligence mission with its South Korean ally. US–Soviet relations effectively collapsed in the wake of KAL 007 and the announcement of America's plans for missile deployment in Europe. There was also a serious decline in USSR–ROK relations, which had been slowly, and largely secretly, improving. KAL 007 was followed in October by a bombing in Rangoon that killed four members of the ROK cabinet, two presidential advisers and the ROK ambassador to Burma. Chun, due to his late arrival, survived.

The immediate fallout from the Rangoon bomb was the end of relations between Burma and Pyongyang, a short-lived alliance. Pyongyang denied blame but few accepted this. As Kim Jong-il was thought to be head of North Korea's clandestine operations, many assumed the assassination attempt had official sanction at the highest level. The two episodes, KAL 007 and Rangoon, led to a heightening of the US military presence in Korea and additional reinforcements along the DMZ. It appeared likely that DPRK attempts to kill Chun were not directed so much at him but at creating another, and larger, Kwangju-type incident. Reagan visited Seoul, after Tokyo, in November 1983 and praised Chun's restraint in the face of KAL 007 and Rangoon.

Kim did not appear to think that these events would stop some form of re-engagement with the US. He also hoped to compete militarily with the US and ROK forces again. After Reagan had released the F-16s to Seoul, Moscow decided to resume armament shipments to the DPRK – MiG-25 fighters, SAM-3 surface-to-air missiles and SCUDs – while Kim allowed

Soviet jets back into DPRK airspace and Russian warships to visit North Korean ports.

Following the new ROK leader Roh Tae-woo's engagement with Pyongyang, Nordpolitik, in 1988 Reagan thawed in his approach to Pyongyang, publicly approving the policy during a visit to Seoul in October. However, Kim was still wary of Reagan, following the US bombing of Tripoli in Libya in 1986. Engagement with the North increased, however, and American diplomats, previously told to discuss only 'non-substantive' issues with DPRK officials, were now encouraged to build stronger connections as a prelude to the possibility of more substantive talks and contact between Washington and Pyongyang. Subsequently thirty-four meetings took place between the North and the US between December 1988 and September 1993.

By the late 1980s America started to feel that the threat of war on the peninsula was subsiding once again, and when George Bush assumed office in 1989 North Korea was not uppermost in the new administration's mind. Bush, the former CIA chief and ambassador to China, was patrician and traditional where Reagan had been overtly political and showman-like. Bush spent his presidency embroiled in the first Iraq war after Saddam Hussein invaded Kuwait, and consequently had little time for North Korea and other foreign-policy issues outside the Middle East.

State Department and CIA analysts declared that South Korea would be more militarily advanced than the DPRK by the mid-1990s and able to handle any attack emanating from the North without large-scale support from American forces. These forecasts were based partly upon former President Park's aim to have deployable nuclear weapons by 1981 at the earliest and definitely by 1985. Park had decided that the lesson of Vietnam was that American military might was not unassailable and that he would be better positioned as a close friend rather than a client state of the US. Ultimately the assassination of Park and American pressure effectively ended the programme, which the US opposed. Nevertheless, its existence was sufficient to spur Pyongyang to announce the creation of its own nuclear weapons programme – one that did not stop when Park was shot in 1979.

By 1990 the belief that the threat of war had receded was gone and the fact of North Korea's nuclear programme, its state of development and ultimate date of deployment were major issues for Washington. Consequently the US and South Korea held consultative talks on launching a major non-proliferation campaign aimed at the DPRK that would involve the Russians and Chinese.

Pyongyang's decision to start a nuclear programme came at a time when the so-called 'second nuclear age' was under way and countries did not need to develop their own nuclear technology but could effectively buy it 'off the shelf'. Defence analysts point out that in this period at least a dozen countries were offering on the market fuel rods for uranium enrichment plants.[17] This allowed for greatly speeded up nuclear programmes in the late 1980s and early 1990s.

In February 1990 the US defense secretary, Dick Cheney, announced that 5,000 American soldiers would be withdrawn from South Korea in line with CIA estimates of ROK military self-sufficiency. Additionally, undersecretary of defence Paul Wolfowitz stated that by the mid-1990s the US would cede command of the ROK–US Combined Command of forces in South Korea to the ROK military at the same time as the number of US soldiers was reduced. Implicit in this thinking was the notion that missiles make forward bases more vulnerable. The North's ballistic missiles, possible nuclear weapons and WMDs all raised the stakes for any US intervention strategy, and the anti-proliferation pressure mounted from 1991 with the development of the so-called 'carrot and stick' strategy of engagement and aid in return for the curtailment of Pyongyang's nuclear programme. The collapse of the USSR spurred the nuclear downsizing lobby in Washington and by December 1991 the US had removed all its nuclear warheads from ROK soil, although Seoul stayed under the wider US nuclear umbrella.

The annual 'Team Spirit' joint operations between the ROK and the US military reflected American government opinion in 1990 that the future scenario on the peninsula was that ROK forces would act primarily in a defensive role against any attack from the North while USFK would concentrate on attacking the enemy's front line and rear to disrupt supply lines. During the 1990s the plans of Cheney and Wolfowitz were put into action as Washington urged the ROK to take more responsibility for frontal assaults and spend more resources on air force training. The US was keen for Seoul to pick up more of the bill for the defence of the South and fortification of the DMZ while also extending its military alliances more broadly regionally through the building of alliances with other countries, especially Japan. The ROK did go some way towards complying with this request, as witnessed by the ROK navy's participation in the RIMPAC 90 military exercises.[18]

America was also becoming increasingly aware that since the late 1980s anti-Americanism had become a potent political force in the newly democratic South Korea. By the 1990s two-thirds of South Korea's population had been born after the Korean War. For many of these younger Koreans their experience was not one of US support in wartime but rather of US support for the successive military regimes from Rhee to Park to Chun.

By the early 1990s North Korea was faced with a significantly altered global reality and 44,500 US troops on the peninsula. The collapse of the

USSR had a catastrophic effect on the DPRK's economy. Pyongyang's erstwhile allies in Moscow and Beijing had now forged strong partnerships with Seoul, while both Japan's and South Korea's economies were forging ahead as the North's went into reverse. The North felt isolated and deserted. It was in this atmosphere of alienation that the DPRK announced its intention of withdrawing from the Nuclear Non-Proliferation Treaty (NPT) in 1993, as it had nothing to lose, and concentrate on developing its own nuclear deterrent. In 1992 it had gone so far as to allow IAEA inspections. This concession from the North paved the way for a US–DPRK nuclear weapons conference.

The American reaction to the North's nuclear programme, the extent and success of which was far from clear, was extreme belligerence. The Clinton administration criticised Pyongyang (this time backed by Boris Yeltsin in Moscow), and transferred Patriot missiles to Seoul, indicating the perceived threat of attack from the North. This late realisation of the North's potential nuclear capabilities reflected a general American lack of awareness of the extent of nuclear proliferation worldwide. By the mid- to late 1990s it was clear that if pre-emptive strikes were going to be made on countries with nuclear weapons programmes, then missiles were going to have be targeted at a growing range of countries.

America also had to deal with the claim made by General Park before his assassination that South Korea was developing nuclear weapons, a major part of the reasoning behind the North's nuclear programme. The December 1991 Joint Declaration on the Denuclearisation of the Korean Peninsula obliged the South and North not to 'test, manufacture, produce, receive, possess, store, deploy or use nuclear weapons', as well as committing both countries 'not to possess nuclear reprocessing and uranium enrichment facilities'. This had stopped any further development of the ROK nuclear programme and also saw the Americans offer in June 1991 to start a denuclearisation process on the peninsula. By September this seemed likely to happen, with Pyongyang praising the White House's weapons reduction plans. However, the plan was interrupted when the world's focus shifted to the Iraqi invasion of Kuwait. Nevertheless a series of meetings between the DPRK and the US at the UN starting in January 1991 resulted in the DPRK eventually ratifying its safeguards agreement with the IAEA in April and allowing the IAEA, in the person of Hans Blix, to restart inspections. Blix arrived in Pyongyang in May 1992 to begin an official inspection of the Yongbyon reactor. His view was that the reactor was primitive and below CIA assessment levels. The North Koreans were reportedly shocked at the thoroughness and expertise of the inspectors. The 1992 'Team Spirit' exercise was cancelled and it appeared that tensions has eased palpably on the pensinsula.

New Potential: Clinton Engages

During the Clinton administration America effectively gave up the military option against Pyongyang and settled for a strategy of engagement. This engagement process, culminating in Secretary of State Madeleine Albright's visit to Pyongyang, was a 'carrot and stick' approach of selective negotiation, engagement, concession and sanctions. Throughout Clinton's presidency the CIA grew increasingly alarmed at Pyongyang's potential nuclear capacity and at the conflicts between the IAEA and the DPRK over the scope of the inspections, though Clinton's policy largely remained one of providing aid in return for concessions while Pyongyang sought to extract aid in return for concessions. This duly politicised the aid situation, mixing famine relief with politics and diplomacy. North Korea was to call for international aid in 1996, for help to overcome the famine that was by now common knowledge.

In 1993, the CIA concluded that in the late 1980s 'North Korea ... had produced enough plutonium for at least one, and possibly two, nuclear weapons.' This judgement was reaffirmed in all declassified intelligence assessments through the latter half of the 1990s, up to mid-2001.[19] However, these were not definitive statements but 'assessments'. CIA assessments changed emphasis around the end of 2001, when a declassified version of a National Intelligence Estimate (NIE) claimed that North Korea had indeed produced one nuclear weapon, and possibly two. By November 2002, the CIA was adamant that the DPRK had used plutonium to make one or two weapons, or, as undersecretary of defense Walter Slocombe more graphically expressed it, 'North Korea could be turning out plutonium like sausages'. It was around such assessments that the Clinton administration built its North Korea policy. Before Clinton the assessments had been of possible nuclear weapons; by Clinton it appeared that North Korea had probably joined the club of nuclear powers. By 2003, with Clinton gone and George W. Bush in the White House, the CIA shifted its assessment back to 'probable'.

Sanctions do not seem to represent a viable option for the US in its bid to bring the DPRK to heel. To be effective they require the invoking of UN Charter articles 41 and 42.[20] Such a move would undoubtedly be vetoed by China and not popular with many other nations after the acrimonious debates over sanctions against Iraq. It is also the case that North Korea may not be guilty of anything, having officially withdrawn from the IAEA and the NPT. Besides, the effectiveness of sanctions is questionable, and would achieve little but further impoverishment of the North Korean people. From a regional strategy viewpoint full sanctions against the DPRK would potentially cause ruptures with America's allies – the ROK and Japan are also opposed. Seoul sees sanctions as likely only to deepen the suffering of the North Korean people without threatening a regime that has already survived famine and industrial collapse; indeed such a move would provide the leadership with another argument to galvanise support and present itself as embattled by imperialist forces.

When Clinton arrived in Washington in January 1993, he did not in effect have a North Korea policy: it certainly hadn't been a campaign issue and he was eager not to repeat the mistakes of George Bush and become embroiled in foreign-policy issues. However, the North was alarmed by the resumption of the 'Team Spirit' exercises in 1993 that featured 50,000 US troops, 70,000 ROK troops and the USS *Independence.*

Clinton's campaign slogan, 'It's the Economy, Stupid', reiterated his desire to concentrate on a domestic agenda and appeal to the American electorate's traditional distaste for messy situations in faraway countries they had little understanding of. Once elected, Clinton was immediately faced with the likelihood of the DPRK's pulling out of the NPT in the face of renewed 'Team Spirit' manoeuvres and pressure from the IAEA inspections. The North initiated some talks with the US that averted a withdrawal from the NPT but did not resolve the crisis over the inspections. Pyongyang was still jittery, even more so following Clinton's visit to the DMZ in July. However, the North was still seeking concessions and raised the issue of the possible supply of two light-water reactors to generate much-needed electricity in return for a security guarantee. The US was broadly supportive of this new realpolitik from Pyongyang, though Seoul expressed concern at the growth of direct US–DPRK talks and the ROK's apparent marginalisation.

The carrot-and-stick approach continued with Clinton using as an unlikely envoy the Evangelist preacher Billy Graham, who told Kim in Pyongyang, where bizarrely he was permitted to hold a 'crusade', that Clinton would talk in return for an ending of the nuclear programme. The stick remained, with talk of deployment of Patriot missiles to the ROK (which did arrive in April 1994, along with a squadron of Apache helicopters) and more 'Team Spirit' exercises. However, tensions between Pyongyang and the IAEA continued with Blix pushing for more inspections and Pyongyang seeking to maintain 'face' and not appear to be bullied.

Clinton's desire to remain distanced from foreign policy convinced him to use ex-President Carter as his proxy in negotiations with Pyongyang; Carter was seen by Kim as someone who had tried to promote peace when in power. Clinton's only alternative to engagement was a pre-emptive strike. Clinton requested, in spring 1994, a detailed plan for an air attack on the DPRK's major nuclear facilities designed to entomb the plutonium in the reactor and destroy the reprocessing facility. However, senior US officials believed the attack would trigger full-scale war between the US and DPRK. In that light, engagement was the option taken, though the risk of war remained high with Congress urging that more reinforcements be sent to Korea while Seoul called up reserves for temporary drill. Proliferation was now a major issue for the administration following the Joint Chiefs of Staff's 1994 National Military Strategy that identified weapons proliferation and WMDs as the top threat globally. During 1993 and 1994 major policy speeches by Clinton, national security adviser Anthony Lake and secretary of defense Les Aspin all focused on issues of proliferation.

Kim was willing to accept Carter in his role as head of the Carter Center[21] knowing that, as an envoy of the White House, Carter could make promises of assistance in return for concessions, which was more than the IAEA was able to do, as well as bolster the regime's legitimacy. To Kim's thinking the continued IAEA demands for inspections were one-sided and offered North Korea nothing in return. Carter could offer aid, as well as encouraging both Japan and South Korea also to provide aid to the DPRK, which was in the middle of cholera and tuberculosis epidemics. Additionally, Kim had seen Clinton grant China 'Most Favoured Nation' trade status in May 1994 without any preconditions on human rights, which had forged stronger links between Beijing and Washington.

The outcome of the Carter visit was the 1994 Agreed Framework, with Kim agreeing to freeze his nuclear programme in return for American support in the form of two 'proliferation resistant' light-water reactors to develop the North's much-needed civilian power generation programme. It appeared that the policy of engagement had succeeded. Additionally, with a deal in place, some distance had been travelled in shoring up the fraying relationship with Seoul that Clinton's engagement policy had caused. The South Koreans had been feeling vulnerable and insisted on a tougher approach to Pyongyang, with President Kim Young-sam making unprecedented attacks on the US position before the agreement and urging a more independent ROK policy on dealing with the North.

History intervened again immediately after the 1994 Accords were agreed. On the day set for discussion of their implementation, 8 July 1994, Kim Il-sung died. The implementation talks were postponed while North Korea went into a period of mourning and Kim Jong-il secured power. While the death of Kim and the elevation of Kim Jong-il did not effectively interrupt the talks, as Kim Jong-il naturally adhered to the agreements his father had reached with Carter, America was faced with problems in the ROK. While the ROK had not involved itself overtly in the Carter–Kim negotiations, the death of Kim Il-sung caused tensions to mount as Seoul banned any grieving in the ROK for Kim's death, Christian groups demonstrated at the DMZ with government permission, and the Seoul press reported the release of documents in Moscow that claimed the North had started the Korean War. Additionally, riots broke out between police and students at Seoul National University, with the students protesting the presence of US troops as a block to reunification.

Despite these setbacks Clinton pushed forward with engagement and was also keen to see a similar deal to the Agreed Framework covering the North's missiles. This desire to trade security for concessions led to the May 1999 visit to Pyongyang by former secretary of defense William J. Perry, initially Clinton's presidential envoy and policy co-ordinator for North Korea. This was followed by a visit by a senior DPRK military official, Vice-Marshal Jo Myung-rok, to the White House in October 2000, and finally by the visit of Albright to Pyongyang later that same month. Only at the last minute did Clinton finally discount a personal visit to Pyongyang.

This flurry of engagement by the Clinton administration was partly made possible by the election of Kim Dae-jung in Seoul and his June 2000 visit to Pyongyang for the first-ever South–North summit as part of his 'Sunshine Policy' of engagement, as well as by the worsening domestic situation in the DPRK, which had become a major humanitarian crisis.

The 1994 Agreed Framework

The Agreed Framework was finally signed by the DPRK's first vice-minister of foreign affairs, Kang Sok-ju, and the US ambassador-at-large, Robert Gallucci, in October 1994 following nearly three months of talks in Geneva. The deal was that the US would arrange, through the Korean Energy Development Organisation (KEDO), the construction of the two 1,000 MW LWRs in North Korea to be completed by 2003. These would replace outdated Soviet-designed graphite-moderated reactors.[22] Additionally the US agreed to supply half a million tonnes of heavy fuel annually until 2003 (then around 15 per cent of North Korea's annual consumption), sufficient to replace the energy lost by the decommissioning of the Soviet reactors. It would also withdraw the threat of pre-emptive military action and begin a process of trade and diplomatic relations. The North Korean side of the deal required Pyongyang to dismantle the Soviet reactors, dispose of the nuclear fuel rods, remain in the NPT and allow the IAEA back to conduct inspections.

The US was pleased with the agreement, especially as South Korea and Japan were to pay 70 per cent and 20 per cent, respectively, of the US$4.5 billion cost of the new LWRs. KEDO was established to do the actual construction and installation. Washington signed the agreements but incurred few costs and little responsibility for actually building the reactors, while achieving its objective of seemingly preventing the construction of a 50 MW reactor at Yongbyon and a 200 MW reactor at Taechon, which combined were expected to yield approximately 275 kilograms of weapons-grade plutonium annually. KEDO and the DPRK signed a contract for the LWRs in December 1995.

KEDO has since become a political football, with the Japanese suspending funds as the political winds changed between Tokyo and Pyongyang. America, too, has been haphazard in its support of the Agreed Framework and KEDO. Indeed, with renewed troop commitments in the ROK, it appeared that the US was betting on total economic collapse in the DPRK, based on the State Department's analysis of the North's economy post-USSR and the expected demise of the regime before final implementation was due. (The Americans had compelling evidence to support their collapse theory. The DPRK's trade volume had slumped to US$2.6 billion in 1991 from US$4.6 billion in 1990 following the USSR's collapse, and analysts could see no scenario whereby the economy would resurge.) Promised oil supplies have been erratic, with the White House blaming blocking processes in Congress, while food aid has been delivered but in amounts that only ensured basic survival but were not sufficient to end the famine. While Tokyo and Washington played politics in 1997, Seoul found itself racked by the Asian financial crisis and backed out of its promised payments to KEDO, while America refused to make up the shortfall. Nuclear brinksmanship by Pyongyang had worked initially to achieve the Agreed Framework, which most people agreed was in the DPRK's favour. Such brinksmanship could not be repeated to enforce the deal without the DPRK restarting its nuclear programme.

Many American politicians responded to the North's brinksmanship enthusiastically, one even claiming that the DPRK could hit Seattle with a nuclear weapon; while the CIA under George Tenet was starting to see North Korea as a major threat. Yet, as the CIA looked towards military action against Pyongyang, events again intervened and Yugoslavia became the major focus of US foreign policy.

In the DPRK the Agreed Framework was initially seen as forcing the US to be Pyongyang's virtually exclusive nuclear interlocutor and tacit guarantor of sovereignty and security. Whatever the omissions and oversights of the Agreed Framework, and US capitulations or lack of seriousness, it defined US–DPRK relations for the remainder of the Clinton administration. The deal may have averted the potential disaster of a pre-emptive strike, but it did Clinton little good domestically. It was not a subject of major public interest. However, it did stir Republican opposition, which became increasingly vehement after the Republicans won control of Congress in the 1994 mid-term elections, while also being unpopular in Seoul. Both the Republicans and Seoul saw Clinton's strategy as one of Pyongyang leading and Washington following. Still, Clinton guided the deal through with some sweeteners that assuaged the domestic audience, including negotiations regarding US soldiers still missing in action in Korea. This was a far cry from the aspirations of the Clinton team in 1994 that had hoped the Agreed Framework would see the DPRK follow a similar path to that taken by East Germany. They even went so far as to date the final implosion of North Korea as 2003.

The US was provided with another chance to become involved in the peninsula with the election of Kim Dae-jung in 1998 in the wake of the Asian financial crisis. Kim's 'Sunshine Policy' opened new opportunities for engagement, which culminated in Albright's October 2000 visit to Pyongyang when her delegation spent more than twelve hours with Kim Jong-il over two days, half of that time in negotiations and the other half at dinners and ceremonial functions. The Americans were also involved in two rounds of four-party talks – between the DPRK, ROK, China and America – in 1998 and 1999. However, it still appeared to conservatives in the US as if America was being led by the nose and blackmailed by Pyongyang. Conservatives fought back, passing as part of the fiscal year 1999 the Omnibus Appropriations Act, mandating 'a full and complete interagency review of US policy towards North Korea', which also stated that 'Not later than 1 January 1999 the President shall name a "North Korea Policy Coordinator".' William Perry was subsequently appointed to that position.[23]

In December 1998, when the US asked to inspect a nuclear site at Kumch'ang-ri, it was only allowed to do so after a substantial additional donation of food aid.[24] To conservatives this clearly indicated that the administration was 'buying off' Pyongyang. Following a test missile firing by Pyongyang in August 1998, a further test launch was cancelled after the US agreed to lift certain trade restrictions. Then, in May 1999, when Perry visited Pyongyang, he broached a range of proposals designed to address North Korean nuclear activities outside the scope of the Agreed Framework and to prevent further ballistic missile development. Five months later Pyongyang agreed to a moratorium on further long-range missile tests providing the US–DPRK missile negotiations continued. In return the US announced a partial lifting of economic sanctions while Pyongyang made some concessions such as allowing foreign (and ROK) commercial airlines to overfly DPRK airspace. Perry furthered the policy of concessions in October 1999 when he argued for a 'comprehensive and integrated approach' to the DPRK to achieve a complete and verifiable cessation of testing, production and deployment of missiles exceeding the parameters of the Missile Technology Control Regime (MTCR), as well as the complete cessation of exports of missiles and all equipment and technology associated with them. The US in return would 'normalise' relations with the DPRK and further ease sanctions.

While the US had clearly benefited in its relationship with the DPRK through Seoul's inauguration of the 'Sunshine Policy', it was at this point that Clinton made the decision to engage Pyongyang seriously again, a process that included support from Seoul for the US–DPRK bilateral accords and then, in June 2000, the additional relaxation of trade sanctions against the North, in return for the DPRK reaffirming its moratorium on missile tests. However, Washington's acquiescence in providing aid for concessions in the past had left Pyongyang with a taste for this additional source of income. In a fifth round of missile talks, in Kuala Lumpur, Pyongyang demanded US$1 billion in annual compensation in return for halting missile exports. Seeking to exploit the Clinton administration's past willingness to do deals, Kim Jong-il sought even more from the US, suggesting to Russian president Putin that Pyongyang would stop its missile tests in exchange for the US agreeing to launch North Korean satellites.

The engagement process did not stop, and culminated in Albright's trip to Pyongyang. It appears that Kim Jong-il had decided the US would go to extreme lengths to secure a deal on Pyongyang's missiles and that Clinton would sign this directly with him. The North Koreans sent a letter from Kim inviting Clinton to Pyongyang, and when Albright was there she was told that the DPRK would stop further testing of the Taepodong 1 missile and negotiate an immediate freeze on long-range missile testing, as well as cease missile exports if the US provided sufficient aid. Pushing the Americans further than they had before, it was clear that the regime aimed at survival at US expense. Clinton, approaching the end of his term of office, refused Pyongyang's offer.

Nevertheless Albright's Pyongyang trip reflected the seriousness of Washington's engagement process, as well as the fact that the Clinton team in 1999 was no longer convinced that the DPRK was in terminal crisis. In 1993 Perry had declared that the DPRK was on the brink of collapse. By 1999, having visited Pyongyang, he acknowledged that 'the regime is very much in control and it would be imprudent on our part to assume that this regime is going to collapse.'[25] Faced with this reassessment by senior administration personnel and already suspicious that the North was continuing its nuclear programme in contravention of the Agreed Framework – and that Kim was probably keen for the White House to know this, as frustration at the slow process of the delivery of the two promised LWRs by KEDO was annoying Pyongyang – Clinton maintained his engagement policy. In 2001 the lack of any progress on the LWRs was leading *KCNA* to declare KEDO 'meaningless'. The new strategy from Pyongyang was the claiming of compensation for the delays while continuing its nuclear programme. Before the issue could reach a head, Clinton exited the White House and Bush moved in.

Bush II: Dialogue or War?

The US conservatives' argument that in Clinton's policy Pyongyang led and Washington followed was broadly supported by the new Bush team, which had Donald Rumsfeld and Condoleezza Rice, two Cold War hawks who had worked for the first President Bush, Colin Powell and Dick Cheney all in crucial positions. The Bush team believed that Pyongyang was in breach of the Agreed Framework. Its stated aim of pursuing national missile defence to protect the US against potential 'rogue states' of course required the existence of such states.[26] North Korea was a prime candidate, as its missile programme was potentially more advanced than that of Iran or Iraq.

Additionally, it was far from clear that the seemingly good working relationship between Clinton and Kim Dae-jung would continue under Bush. Secretary of State Colin Powell did offer a broad endorsement of the 'Sunshine Policy' but also expressed concerns. Kim Dae-jung received an audience with Bush in Washington in March 2001. Powell stated that the administration planned broadly to continue Clinton's engagement policy. However, Bush himself, in talks with the South Korean leader, was more hawkish. The mood then changed swiftly: Powell effectively retracted his remarks, Kim Dae-jung took offence at Bush's stand, and the North declared itself ready for either dialogue or war. From the start the tensions between the Bush White House and Pyongyang adversely affected Kim Dae-jung's 'Sunshine Policy', both hardening the North Korean attitude and encouraging the Seoul opposition to think that they would receive a warmer welcome in Washington now that the atmosphere of appeasement under Clinton was seemingly over.

The Bush administration policy review on North Korea came to the conclusion that from now on Washington should lead and Pyongyang follow. If the North could demonstrate a continued commitment to the Agreed Framework then talks and aid would continue but there would be no new initiatives from Washington and no endless negotiations, which the Bush team identified as the hallmark of the Clinton policy. The ball was in Pyongyang's court.

Kim Jong-il was reluctant to break completely with the Americans. He informed visiting EU and Russian delegations in Pyongyang that he would maintain the moratorium on missile testing until 2003. The subsequent 11 September 2001 events hardened Washington's stance towards rogue states and yet pushed the North Korean issue down the agenda. Bush's now infamous January 2002 State of the Union address, including North Korea as part of the 'Axis of Evil' (even though it had signed several international anti-terrorist protocols), changed the nature of US–DPRK relations completely. Despite these threatening noises the Bush team in fact shared the view (and hope) of Perry in 1993 that the DPRK would collapse internally, with defense secretary Donald Rumsfeld telling the US–Korean Business Council in 2003 that he was confident that the country would 'eventually collapse and join the ranks of democratic societies'.[27] The 'Axis of Evil' speech was not an all-out declaration of war on the three nations mentioned (the others being Iran and Iraq). Nevertheless Bush did state that 'We will not wait on events while dangers gather.'

The Bush administration's heightened interest in WMDs and reference to 'new methods of deterrence'[28] also indicated that the US no longer felt bound by the Agreed Framework. A December 2002 addendum to Bush's national security strategy stated this clearly: 'The US ... reserves the right to respond with overwhelming force – including resort to all our options – to the use of WMD against the US, our forces abroad, and our allies.' Bush clearly saw no point in further engagement. The 'Axis of Evil' speech and the rejection of the DPRK as an interlocutor were seen as not just threats in Pyongyang but as a sign of America's diminished view of the DPRK's global status, something that enraged the North Koreans. This, to them, was an insult as well as a threat.

Prior to the admission by Pyongyang that it was continuing its nuclear weapons programme there was some limited contact between the US and the DPRK. In July 2002, Powell met briefly at an APEC meeting in Brunei with the DPRK's minister of foreign affairs, Paik Nam-sun, and in August the US special envoy to North Korea and American representative to KEDO, Charles Pritchard, visited Kumho, the proposed site of the LWR project. Pritchard was the highest ranking US official to visit the DPRK since Albright. However, in October 2002 the visit of the assistant secretary of state for East Asian and Pacific affairs, James Kelly, to Pyongyang led to the admission that the programme would continue and the effective public ending of the Agreed Framework – and to the onset of the nuclear crisis.

A Useful Whipping Boy

Former *Washington Post* journalist Chalmers Johnson has claimed that,

> Even though it remains a small, failed communist regime whose people are starving and have no petroleum, North Korea is a useful whipping boy for any number of interests in Washington. If the military needs a post-Cold War opponent to justify its existence, North Korea is less risky than China.[29]

Certainly the talk over the last few years of 'rogue states', with accusations flying around Congress that one or another politician is 'soft' on Pyongyang, in the same way people were accused of being 'soft' on communism for seeking engagement with Moscow, has become common. Those companies with large contracts derived from the Theatre Missile Defence (TMD) programme and other military contracts benefit from the heightened tensions.

However, while the rhetoric against North Korea has been maintained in the American media, and responded to in kind by Pyongyang, it is the case that despite its occasional convenience as a whipping boy, Korea, North and South, remains an afterthought in American foreign policy. Korea was an afterthought in 1945 when the US had intricate plans for the occupation and administration of Japan and no plans whatsoever for Korea. Since then it has largely reacted to events rather than anticipated them, while dealing with the conflicting and hasty positions of the military establishment and the State Department. Successive presidents have known that Korea is not worth many votes in the American heartland.

This tendency by America to react to events has been exploited to the full by Kim Jong-il. The Agreed Framework was a reaction by the US to the DPRK's nuclear programme, and subsequently Kim's hints about his nuclear programme have forced the US to react again. Kim is clear that this is the only way to engage the Americans. In August 2000, after Kim's breakthrough 'Sunshine Summit' with Kim Dae-Jung, he met with a delegation of South Korean media executives in Pyongyang. Reportedly Choe Hak-rae, then publisher of *Hankyoreh Shinmun*, a newspaper sympathetic to North Korea, asked Kim why Pyongyang was spending its scarce resources on ballistic missiles instead of education or in other civilian areas that would directly benefit the DPRK's population. Kim's reply was that 'The missiles cannot reach the US and if I launch them, the US would fire back thousands of missiles and we would not survive. I know that very well. But I have to let them know I have missiles. I am making them because only then will the US talk to me.'[30]

9

Nuclear Ambitions Revealed:
Bluster, Brinkmanship or Battle?

Whispered Admissions in Pyongyang

The delayed visit of America's assistant secretary of state for East Asian and Pacific affairs, James Kelly, to Pyongyang in October 2002[1] was the first prolonged, high-level dialogue between the DPRK and the Bush administration. It was greeted in North Korea by the screening of a five-minute commentary on DPRK TV titled 'US Warmonger's Curse Distorting the Reality'. The delay in Kelly's visit was seen as an expression of US anger at Prime Minister Koizumi's apparent upstaging of America at his summit with Kim earlier in the year. The delay would undercut any engagement process between Japan and the DPRK that might limit America's role in East Asia.

Kelly's visit was planned as a major event. Allegedly a Pyongyang official, the deputy director general of the Foreign Ministry's American Affairs Bureau and chief North Korea delegate, Li Gun, had mentioned the weapons programme to a US delegate Donald Keyser, US deputy assistant secretary of state. Li was also reported to have said that Pyongyang was prepared to manufacture more weapons, or export them, depending on the US response. After reviewing CIA intelligence data and weighing US policy options, Bush had despatched Kelly to Pyongyang where he informed DPRK officials of the CIA's findings, apparently including bills of sale and other evidence of commercial transactions as proof that the DPRK was attempting to produce enriched uranium at a supposedly closed nuclear facility. However, the CIA did not provide proof to substantiate these claims. Kelly indicated that his intelligence introduced a 'precondition' to any furtherance of US–DPRK relations: Pyongyang would have to verifiably dismantle its covert nuclear programme prior to the US considering a resumption of high-level exchanges. According to State Department officials, the DPRK first denied the allegations; then, in a subsequent meeting, the first vice-minister of foreign affairs, Kang Sok-ju, admitted the existence of a covert weapons programme, while asserting a sovereign right to develop nuclear weapons and 'more powerful things as well', which was taken by the Americans to mean WMDs.[2] This effectively and publicly terminated the 1994 Agreed Framework in America's eyes as well as raising the spectre of what had been seen as one of the Bush administration's three priority threats, namely al-Qaeda, WMD and nuclear weapons proliferation, and China's growing military strength.[3]

By the end of the 1990s it had become clear to Pyongyang that the US was not going to live up to its side of the Agreed Framework without some form of coercion. In Pyongyang's view the lack of progress with the promised LWRs and the continuing downward spiral of the economy indicated that another strategy was called for to restart talks, force America to honour its commitments and reassert the DPRK's international position. Simultaneously Japan, mired in recession, was using KEDO as a political bargaining tool, while South Korea was unwilling to honour its financial commitments to the project. Pyongyang saw no other way to enforce the agreement except to restart its nuclear programme and continue to develop medium-range missiles with potentially long-range upgrade capabilities. This it did, exporting missiles to countries such as Iran (which it had started doing during the Iran–Iraq War, 1980–88) for hard currency and to supplement the oil supplies America had promised in 1994 but only falteringly delivered. America was angry at this weapons trading but North Korea has defended it vociferously with statements such as that from the North Korean diplomat Kim Ming-ho, who summed up Pyongyang's position on the issue thus:

> The US is the world's largest seller of weaponry. It earns thousands of times more money selling guns, warships, and fighter planes than we do. We are called an evil nation, we are subjected to international trade boycotts, for doing the same thing America always does.[4]

Some saw the announcement as just another example of Pyongyang's diplomatic brinksmanship. However, many believed that the aim of the announcement was to force engagement with the US – what Leon V. Sigal, director of the Northeast Asia Co-operative Security Project called 'A Bombshell That's Actually an Olive Branch'.[5] Certainly this was the majority South Korean viewpoint. Yim Sung-joon, Kim Dae-jung's senior secretary for national security, believed Pyongyang was 'looking for a window of opportunity' for re-engagement rather than playing nuclear brinksmanship. The

DPRK seemed to support this view when it suggested everything should be put on the table for discussion.

All the major powers affected by the announcement sought to emphasise that they wanted talks not confrontation. White House spokesman Scott McClellan stated that the Bush administration was 'seeking a peaceful resolution', though Bush viewed the North's admission as 'troubling, sobering news'. In Beijing, Chinese Foreign Ministry spokeswoman Zhang Quiyue stated that 'We hold that the nuclear issue in the DPRK should be solved though peaceful means, through dialogue and consultation.' Koizumi's spokesman told the press that talks aimed at 'turning the relationship between America and North Korea from one of enmity to co-operation will benefit Japan'. (The North Koreans retorted: 'Japan has the effrontery to intervene in the nuclear matter and complicate the issue. It is none of their business.') Russia's news agency was more forthright, stating that it believed America had leaked the DPRK admission in order to put pressure on the imminent North–South talks.[6]

One question loomed in the background: was it true? Most of the media didn't raise this question, even though it seemed plausible that the admission was made simply to force the US to engage. After all, the news came at the end of Kelly's visit, which had not delivered as much as Kim had hoped for, so it was possible that the whole thing was cooked up for political reasons. Kim was hoping for unilateral US–DPRK talks while Kelly stuck to Washington's policy of insisting on a multilateral format. Ultimately it can be argued that it didn't matter much whether the programme existed or not, what its level of development was, or whether Kim could ever use his nuclear weapons should he get a button to push. Just saying he had contravened the Agreed Framework did the trick. Engagement was forced. In the view of most of the international community, though, Pyongyang was solely at fault.

Kim's timing couldn't have been better in many ways. The only other stories dominating the news globally were the continuing debates in the US about the attack on Iraq and forcing 'regime change' in Baghdad, and the Bali bombing in Indonesia. One of the questions that many supposed Kim wanted an answer to was being asked in American newspapers and political talk shows such as NBC's *Meet the Press*: if regime change was a legitimate policy in Iraq, another member of Bush's 'Axis of Evil', then why not Pyongyang? The majority answer, for a variety of reasons, was that Iraq was apparently different. Kim, watching the broadcasts, surfing the web and reading the American press, would have got the message that to Washington at least, Baghdad and Pyongyang were different entities and that America had different resolution strategies for each. White House spokesman Scott

McClellan told reporters, 'Iraq is an aggressive regime run by a "homicidal dictator" who threatens his neighbours. These are different regions, different.'[7] Kim's admission that he had a nuclear programme was not wanted in Washington. It threatened to divert attention from America's identified number one target after Osama bin Laden: Saddam Hussein, still then in power in Baghdad. Kim threw a spanner into the works of the American press machine – what the writer and commentator Gore Vidal has called America's 'Enemy of the Month Club'.[8] After the fall of the Taliban in Kabul, when Bob Woodward of the *Washington Post* interviewed the president, Bush, declaring that he loathed Kim, conceded that North Korea had massive military might that directly threatened the ROK.[9]

Most Americans had never even heard of Kim Jong-il. Until the crisis broke North Korea was rarely reported in America's popular media. Even the satellite imagery of the North's labour camps and the shooting spree by a US postal worker outside the UN building in New York in protest against North Korea in October 2002 was little reported in America,[10] any more than were the cases of North Korean refugees in the US. Most Americans also have little knowledge of American involvement in North Korea since 1953. The Americans had no alternative but to try to sideline Pyongyang through engagement. This was not to become an issue with the American voting public; Kim would be quietly engaged and dealt with while the major focus, Iraq, was pursued.

It should be noted that the DPRK offered the US 'constructive talks' on the nuclear issue if America stopped using what Pyongyang called 'threatening' language towards the North. This was as Chinese President Jiang Zemin was heading to America for four days of talks with Bush, at which nuclear proliferation on the Korean peninsula was at the top of the agenda. Jiang was then to move on to Mexico for an Asia Pacific Economic Conference (APEC) meeting, at which Pyongyang's nuclear revelations would also be high on the agenda. Kim had successfully, though informally, co-opted Jiang as his emissary, knowing that the Chinese leader would urge Bush to engage the DPRK.

Beijing's Facilitating Role

News from the meeting was not to be the fillip to renewed engagement that Kim sought, as Jiang saw the issue as one that could potentially bind the US and China closer rather than divide them. Jiang and Bush agreed to shake their heads in despair at Kim and officially parted better friends than before. Pyongyang would not be allowed to interfere with foreign investment into

China. The same day that Jiang flew to the US, North and South Korea met in Pyongyang. Kim Jong-nan, DPRK vice minister of foreign affairs, said he wanted dialogue; yet again an inter-Korean meeting was dominated by Pyongyang's indirect messages to Washington. As it turned out, the North's admission that it had an enrichment programme fitted relatively well with the new foreign-policy line emitting from Beijing. By the time of Jiang's visit to Bush and of the APEC leaders' conference, a more moderate, engaged Chinese foreign policy was in force. Largely missed by the world's press was that China had begun to introduce new rules to control the export of missile technology and dual-use biological and chemical agents, and to tighten military export regulations – all long-time thorns in the side of US–PRC relations.

China has increasingly embraced rather than shunned multilateral organisations and become active in a range of bodies from the WTO and APEC to regional alliances on its western borders (the so-called 'Shanghai Five' of China, Tajikistan, Russia, Kazakhstan and Kyrgyzstan, and latterly Uzbekistan) and has enjoyed better relations with old adversaries such as India. The upsurge of foreign investment into China has meant that Beijing has had to accept a greater level of integration into the world economy. As John Pomfret wrote in the *Washington Post*, 'The new buzzword from senior PRC diplomats and scholars, repeated in several interviews, is that "time is on China's side".'[11] Additionally, since the Sixteenth Party Congress in Beijing in November 2002, it was becoming increasingly apparent that the senior leadership was dividing responsibilities to reflect China's new engagement strategy. Jiang Zemin would remain as elder statesman and handle international issues; Hu Jintao and Wen Jiabao, the new Chinese premier, were to concentrate more on domestic issues such as justice in China, income gaps, worker and peasant unrest and unemployment. This division was effectively ratified in March 2003 when Hu and Wen assumed the positions of president and premier, respectively.

The Chinese were presented with additional leverage during the Jiang visit to Washington. What was initially intended as a farewell from Bush to Jiang before the latter's semi-retirement became a chance for Jiang to show that China could do its bit to calm and mediate in international disputes, in this case facilitating between Washington and Pyongyang in a round of regional shuttle diplomacy. One senior White House official told the American media: 'The Chinese have influence. We think it's important that they use it.'[12] Jiang used the trip to show himself as a mediating statesman, declaring that the PRC and the US should step up cooperation to prevent the spread of WMDs and maintain peace on the Korean peninsula. By the time of Jiang and Bush's third summit in October 2002 the US administration appeared to have done a virtual 360-degree turn on its original harsher China policy, voiced after coming to office. During Jiang's visit, Bush's national security adviser, Condoleezza Rice, commented that her view of the PRC–US relationship was 'quite favourable', a far cry from the 'strategic competitor' strategy Bush's team first adopted towards China.

Enrichment Brinksmanship

The North's strategy in coming clean on its nuclear transgressions has been described as 'enrichment brinksmanship'.[13] It certainly seemed to indicate a DPRK assessment of Western, Japanese and South Korean weakness. The argument by those who saw the North's admission as a form of 'blackmail' realised that America's 'national security establishment was occupied with a possible war against Iraq and has shown a marked inability to multitask'.[14] But this inability to handle multiple problems also affected US–PRC relations and strengthen Jiang's position. Below the surface Washington was still concerned about China's growing military and economic strength. It had after all been the Bush team that approved the new US–China Security Review Commission (UCSRC) and a new Congressional–Executive Commission on China; it was a team with close links to many of the well-funded and increasingly assertive right-wing Washington think-tanks. At a deeper policy level there was certainly to be no return to the so-called 'Panda hugger' days of Clinton's administration. In the last months of Clinton's second term the Classified Intelligence Review Panel, created at the direction of the Senate Select Committee on Intelligence and known as the Tilleli Commission, (after John Tilleli, the former commander of US forces in Korea who headed it) was given the remit to assess the depth and quality of CIA intelligence on China. The result was a bigger China budget for the CIA.[15]

Throughout this process of trying to engage the US and to further Chinese policy aims, Jiang had to maintain a balance between bolstering Beijing's growing role in defusing the crisis and maintaining Kim in power. Beijing's worry has naturally been that any implosion would send millions of desperate North Koreans across the border into China; furthermore, there was concern that American troops stationed in the ROK would move up to China's border with Korea if the North collapsed. The growing refugee crisis only diminished Pyongyang's increasingly negative standing in Beijing. *Time Magazine* claimed that China's vice foreign minister, Wang Yi, had submitted a memorandum to the Beijing politburo describing the DPRK's behaviour over the nuclear issue as 'diplomatic adventurism' and that a conversation had taken place within the Central Committee that raised the option of cutting food aid to Pyongyang and opening the border to refugees.

Jiang's strong card in the negotiations concerning Pyongyang is that no Iraq-style sanctions regime could be remotely successful without Chinese cooperation. The 500-mile-long Chinese border is undoubtedly the most porous of the DPRK's borders and China is still the North's main aid donor – it supplies over 70 per cent of all fuel oil now the Americans have stopped their supply. China's Yanbian University has predicted that China will remain the major donor of food for the rest of the decade.

China has no interest in Pyongyang continuing its nuclear programme, which could persuade Japan to break out from its traditional non-nuclear stance. Therefore China's actions have been limited to cracking down on the flow of refugees, rounding up those living illegally in the border area and stepping up security around embassies in Beijing.

The flood of refugees into China is, of course, a problem for Pyongyang. Although *The Economist* reported in December 2002 that there were signs that treatment of returned refugees was becoming less harsh, it noted that 'The lucky ones are kept in detention for a few days or weeks before being released, a process that can be expedited with bribes of money or food. But KWP members and people in politically sensitive jobs can still expect far worse treatment.'[16] Some have suggested that Beijing has asked Pyongyang to limit the harshness of its treatment of returned refugees to relieve the pressure on China not to return them. The result of the policy is hard to predict. While an awareness in North Korea that the Chinese are tightening the border area may discourage defectors, the knowledge that an unsuccessful escape attempt will not be punished so severely may encourage more to try.

Jiang has used the nuclear crisis to improve relations with Moscow. When Putin visited Beijing in December 2002 he and Jiang issued a joint statement backing America's plans to persuade the DPRK to abandon its nuclear programme. This reflects the joint belief in Moscow and Beijing that nuclear proliferation in North Korea is no longer something that threatens just Western interests in Asia but also their own as neighbours of the DPRK. A nuclear arms race in Asia would be of little benefit to China or Russia.

Certainly any Chinese compliance with an international sanctions package against Pyongyang would be a symbol of Beijing's advancing new foreign-policy agenda and the ending of what Hugo Restall, in the *Asian Wall Street Journal*, described as Beijing's traditional foreign policy based on 'European rules of statecraft adopted with the 1684 Peace of Westphalia. Accordingly China claimed to place respect for sovereignty and non-interference in other countries' affairs above all other goals.'[17]

The threat of economic collapse that sanctions could entail is a real one to the North, and the question of how much pain Pyongyang can take is debatable. One theory is that sanctions would worsen the food supply situation to such a point that even senior cadres would experience shortages – potentially leading to growing disaffection with the Party, and Kim Jong-il's leadership, and possibly even regime change from within. Yet this is far from guaranteed. What is certain is that full sanctions would be regarded as an act of war by Pyongyang. There is also the question of just how exactly, beyond ending food and exports, you isolate a regime that seems often to wish to isolate itself.

This self-isolation process appeared to be deepening further in 2003 as Pyongyang retreated from diplomatic engagement and economic reform and reaffirmed and accentuated a military-first line that appeared designed to harden attitudes across the board. This line replaced economic reform as the primary ideological thrust of Pyongyang.

10

Something Different Emerges: 'Military First'

North Korea's Third Estate

It seems clear that Pyongyang decided in March 2003 that the economic reform process had largely failed, despite *KCNA* hailing 2003 in its annual New Year message as 'The Year of Brave Offensive and Ambitious Reform'. Pyongyang tinkered with its exchange rates and claimed to be continuing with meaningful reform though any further moves away from the command economy were apparently being politically resisted or at least on hold.

On 21 March 2003, *Rodong Sinmun*, the KWP's primary domestic mouthpiece, published a special article entitled 'Military-First Ideology is an Ever-Victorious, Invincible Banner for Our Era's Cause of Independence'. This was a firm indication that policy had shifted from economic reform and diplomatic engagement to a reassertion of the military-first (*songun*) line. The diplomatic charm offensive had failed to yield a normalisation of relations with Japan. Meanwhile relations with Russia remained cold and China was applying direct pressure on Pyongyang, thereby changing the dynamic of the long-standing relationship between the two erstwhile allies. The nascent economic reform process in the DPRK had been too little, too late to turn the economy around in the time Pyongyang demanded, and had instead led to inflation, further impoverishment, a surge in corruption, embarrassment at senior levels over the debacle at Sinuiju, and also possibly a renewed rift between Kim and the military top brass. In 2003 North Korea resorted to the tried and tested strategy of accentuating military-first and *songun* thought.

There were other reasons for the shift, notably the onset of the nuclear crisis and a general escalation of tension. The US redeployed twenty-four long-range bombers (twelve B-52s and twelve B-1s) to the Western Pacific following the interception of an American surveillance aircraft over the Sea of Japan in international airspace by four DPRK MiG jet fighters. While ramping up militarily the White House gave the ROK pledges that it would not stage a surprise attack against the DPRK, but the fear remained.[1] Pyongyang was also concerned about the recently initiated joint military manoeuvres, similar to the annual 'Team Spirit' operations that had been a persistent North Korean complaint. These involved over 200,000 troops and included USFK, the USS *Carl Vinson*, US reinforcements from overseas and the ROK army in what was termed the 'Foal Eagle' drill, while another joint US–ROK exercise dubbed 'Reception, Staging, Onward Movement and Integration' (RSOI), occurred between 19 and 26 March. Following 'Foal Eagle' the US announced that it was leaving a number of B-2 stealth bombers and F-117 radar-evading jets in the region.[2] The DPRK responded by ending tours to Mount Kumgang and declaring a maritime exclusion zone off its coast in the Sea of Japan, and subsequently test-firing a cruise missile. With relations between Washington and Pyongyang deteriorating, tensions rising again along the DMZ, the ROK publicly launching its first officially admitted radar-evading warship – the *Moonmu the Great* – and with the war in Iraq under way and Baghdad about to fall to American forces, Kim himself maintained a low profile. He was not seen in public between 12 February and 11 April, even missing a parliamentary session.[3] Kim eventually reappeared to visit an air force base, hours after the fall of Baghdad.

The military-first line has always been a major theoretical pillar of the regime and Juche, establishing the military as the DPRK's effective third estate. It is attributed officially to Kim Jong-il, though derives from Kim Il-sung's 'Four Great Military Lines'; namely, arm the populace; fortify the country; make each soldier a cadre; and modernise the military. Kim Jong-il extended this policy in 1999 with the formalisation of military-first, aimed at creating a strong nation state in both military and economic terms (*Kangsong Taeguk*), and thereafter promoting the *songun* line.

Military-first has bolstered Kim's succession. It provides what many in the DPRK hierarchy believe is the only conceivable means by which the regime can survive and achieve what it perceives will be its ultimate security: a fiercely defensive posture to outside forces. Several well-informed commentators, including Hwang Jang-yop, believe that the escalation in importance of the military-first line was originally conceived as part of the compromise between the military leadership and Kim Jong-il after Kim Il-sung's death, where the army hierarchy grudgingly accepted his ascendance to power in return for a greater role in the power structure and in policy-making. Since around 1980 no senior military figure has been elevated to the Politburo; this was the period when a new generation of professional army leaders began to replace the ageing former guerrillas with whom Kim Il-sung had risen to power. Kim Jong-il immediately started promoting senior military figures up the political hierarchy. Typical of those who have remained at the top of the elite is Kim Il-chol (1934–), vice-chairman of the NDC and minister of the People's Armed Forces, who is reportedly a confidant of Kim Jong-il and the first individual from the navy to become the nation's top defence planner. Kim Il-chol is from the elite, with a Soviet education, and is best known as the commander who captured the USS *Pueblo*. The new balance of power between the military and Kim has remained in place, though was severely tested during the 2002 economic reforms, in particular the Sinuiju project.

The Korean People's Army (KPA) continues to grow in terms of firepower. Pyongyang believes that its existence has been one of the regime's most effective tools of leverage in international negotiations to date. 'Military-first' provides a *raison d'être* for the large standing army that masks unemployment, acts as the country's major domestic purchaser and maintains the KWP's power base.

'Military-first' 'calls for giving priority to military issues over everything, and it is a line, strategy and tactics of putting the army before the working class'. This is clearly a fundamental reworking of classic Marxist–Leninist thinking whereby the KPA is positioned as 'the most pivotal group' in society. Officially the ideology declares that 'the gun barrel should be placed over the hammer and sickle'. Therefore from the start of the regime the KPA has been the basis of North Korea's revolutionary strategy.

The March 2003 editorial in *Rodong Sinmun* restated that military-first is derived directly from Juche and links the ideology to both the North's permanent war footing and its attempts at economic reconstruction by declaring that 'The army is held to be decisive in achieving and protecting sovereignty, in economic construction.' The reassertion of military-first clearly indicated that the country was retreating from reform and engagement, though the question was whether the ideological line would be taken to its natural conclusion and be used as a pretext for obtaining deliverable nuclear weapons. Although this was the firmest indication that military-first was once again the primary theoretical line, this had been strongly hinted at in the *KCNA* annual New Year Message of January 2003, when Pyongyang vowed to increase its military strength and described 2002 as a year of 'hard struggle', urging people to keep themselves ready for their fight against 'invasion to the last … under the banner of army first'.[4]

'Fighting Invasion to the Last'

Military-First involves isolation from international norms, advocating that without a strong military the country will be 'swallowed by outside forces'. The reinforcement of military-first was continued in *Rodong Sinmun* editorials and other DPRK newspapers throughout the latter half of 2003.[5] Though military-first envisaged the linkage between a strong economy and a strong military, even in North Korea this combination was clearly not believable in a period of continued economic collapse. This led to a certain reformulation of the ideology to embrace the idea that military power and its extension would form the basis for economic growth through providing a necessarily peaceful climate within which reconstruction could occur. Pyongyang often cited the example of China, which it believed had only been able to start its reform process once it became a nuclear power and had attained rapprochement with the Americans. Hence, interference in the DPRK's self-defence in the form of threatening postures from other countries was necessarily impeding the reform process. Translated into the ongoing situation, the official position was that continued US military threats were designed to prevent economic recovery, promote collapse, and were therefore an attack on the nation as a whole and, through this prism, could be interpreted as acts of war.

For anyone believing that the economic reform process had not ceased and that the command economy was still being reformed the *Rodong Sinmun* editorial statement that the military–industrial complex, and especially heavy industry, were still primary, and that a self-sufficient national defence industry would lead to the rejuvenation of both civilian industry and agriculture, should have confirmed that the command economy remained firmly in place.[6]

Without doubt the US was now the main focus of North Korean attention. American policy towards the DPRK, at least as interpreted by Pyongyang, was the legitimacy needed to reassert military-first and a more hard-line stance. *Rodong Sinmun*, and the KWP that controls its editorials, clearly believed that the DPRK's military might was what was forcing the US to hesitate and not opt for pre-emptive action. This rhetoric was occurring against the build-up towards Operation Iraqi Freedom and the continuing military operations in Afghanistan and much talk of regime change and its potential uses and justifications.

Key now to the DPRK's military might was the issue of nuclear weapons. On 6 April 2003, *KCNA* published a statement that implied that the North needed 'ultra-modern weapons' to resist American aggression. This was interpreted by many as meaning the nuclear option was now core to military-first.

The second Iraq War and the ousting of Saddam in April 2003 led to further declarations of the new theoretical primacy of military-first. The head of North Korea's SPA, Kim Young-nam, stated in a speech to a meeting with South Korean representatives at a joint Liberation Day event in Pyongyang in August 2003, after Saddam had gone and American troops had occupied Baghdad, that 'The Iraq war proved we were right and justifiable in building a strong war deterrent while tightening our belts for so long.'[7]

North Korea's Armed Forces: An Unknown Quantity

Shortly after the inconclusive first round of six-way talks in Beijing in late August 2003, the DPRK celebrated its fifty-fifth anniversary in September. It celebrated in more style than it had for several years. The continuing economic collapse had humbled the regime somewhat, which also realised that the traditional annual military parade did not endear them to either foreign governments or NGOs (or NGO supporters, who increasingly blanched at giving funds to a regime so blatantly showing off its expensive military hardware). Hence Pyongyang's downplaying of the annual military parade for a few years. In 2003 with military-first back in the ideological ascendant, parades were back in vogue. It was at this time, immediately after the Beijing talks, that Kim was unanimously re-elected chairman of the National Defence Commission (NDC) during a regular session of the rubber-stamping SPA.

The 9 September 2003 military parade was expected to feature approximately 20,000 troops, 150 tanks and other military vehicles with a total of 50,000 participants passing through Pyongyang's mammoth Kim Il-sung Square. While the DPRK's ambassador to Russia, Pak Ui-chun, spoke at a reception in Moscow accusing the US of still trying to disarm North Korea and threatening pre-emptive nuclear strikes, true to form Kim did the opposite of what had been expected. The parade featured a much-downscaled military presence with soldiers and rifles but few military vehicles and not the unveiling of a new ballistic missile that many analysts had been expecting. The dwindling list of foreign dignitaries willing to attend North Korean military parades was also short. The Russian president's Far East representative, Konstantin Pulikovsky, attended and met with Kim. However, the Chinese chose to send only Chen Haosu, president of the rather inconsequential Chinese People's Association for Friendship with Foreign Countries.[8] As is usual, Kim himself did not speak but rather let the chief of the KPA General Staff, Kim Yong-chun, speak for him, arguing that Pyongyang's development of nuclear weapons was warranted by the security threat posed by the US in the region. His comments were dismissed in Washington as rhetoric meant to bolster North Korea's negotiating position ahead of the then expected next round of six-way talks.

The parade once again raised the issue of the strength of the KPA. North Korea is the world's most militarised regime; it is also, according to Donald Gregg, former CIA Seoul station chief in the 1970s and later American ambassador to the ROK, 'the longest running intelligence failure in the world'. The KPA is undoubtedly large in terms of the percentage of the total population engaged in military-related activities, but to what extent had the regime been able to protect it from the economic collapse, shortages and hunger affecting the rest of the country?

The KPA has traditionally received priority in supplies, resources and rations to maintain its loyalty as well as its fighting strength. However, by autumn 2003 the number of reports indicating heightened malnourishment and disaffection in the KPA were growing. Perhaps nothing indicated this better than reports that the KPA had reduced its minimum height require-ment to 4 ft 11 in (1 metre 25), the shortest in the world. Reports from visitors to North Korea indicated a noticeable growth in the shabbiness of military uniforms among the lower ranks, poor levels of hygiene, signs of malnourishment, stunted growth and the appearance of physical weakness – all signs that have been reported since the mid-1990s as the famine reached even the military. Additionally reports emitting from China indicated that there was a growing problem along the Sino–DPRK border, with hungry and disaffected troops crossing into China and raiding remote farmhouses and even urban banks. In addition to intelligence that conventional military supplies were dwindling, news reports that the DPRK was trying to source military hardware on credit terms from countries such as India, Russia and China became commonplace, though few countries were now willing to deal with Pyongyang given its lack of creditworthiness.

The Sword of the Revolution

Founded in 1948, the KPA maintains a force of between 1 and 1.2 million soldiers (compared with the ROK's 650,000–700,000 – a figure that has remained fairly stable since the mid-1950s), with another 300,000 assorted military non-combat personnel and 550,000 reserves. The total number of citizens under arms is possibly as high as 4 million if the Militia of Worker-Peasant Red Guards (*Nonong Chogwidae*), Red Guard Youth (*Pulgun Chongnyon Kunwidae*) and College Training Units are included. Most of the population undergoes some form of fairly regular military-style training. However, many of these soldiers are largely engaged in construction or agricultural work, a process that started in 1969 when Kim Il-sung realised that acute manpower shortages were threatening economic growth.

What is certain is that the KPA remains one of the largest standing armies in Asia, after China and Indonesia, and the fifth largest in the world, with in the region of a million personnel (the world's third largest ground force) organised into 32 active infantry divisions; 40,000–60,000 in the navy, which has submarines and patrol craft; and an estimated 70,000–92,000 in the air force, which also provides anti-aircraft defence. The army has approximately 5,000 tanks, 2,000 armoured personnel carriers, 2,400 multiple rocket launchers and 13,000 artillery pieces. About 70 per cent of the army is deployed south of Pyongyang, though North Korea's current military orientation is primarily defensive, not pre-emptive. It is estimated that between 60,000 and 100,000 personnel are designated as Special Forces; these have been used repeatedly for operations in the DMZ, border incursions and clandestine overseas missions. Additionally, there are some 115,000 paramilitary forces under the Ministry of Public Security (MPS), including border guards at the DMZ.

The army has been bolstered by military hardware from the USSR, China and other sources, although the CIA notes that many lower ranks are equipped with weaponry of 1950s/1960s vintage, while much of the North's formidable artillery is of World War II and Korean War issue, including 1970s vintage tanks.[9] The Korean People's Air Force (KPAF) maintains a fleet of 1,700 aircraft, and the Korean People's Navy (KPN) more than 800 ships, though the battle readiness of these resources is disputable.[10]

According to intelligence reports, the DPRK has a large stockpile of chemical and biological agents, including 'several hundred' SCUD B and C missiles deployed at various locations.[11] It has approximately 30 Nodong 1 and 2 missiles with a range of up to 1,300 kilometres (that is, able to reach Japan). In recent years the emphasis has been on missile build-up. Fighter jets are expensive, extremely fuel-hungry and require highly trained pilots, unlike missiles, which are equally, if not more, effective and feared. North Korean pilots are thought to only fly 20 per cent of the time that their ROK and US equivalents spend in the air. It is also the case that in the current climate acquiring fighter jets, spare parts and fuel are problematic. As fuel shortages have worsened, so the annual KPA military exercises have been scaled back by as much as 50 per cent.

The armed forces are all ultimately under the control of Kim, who holds the posts of Supreme Commander of the Army and Chairman of the NDC.[12] Party influence within the military is high and several committees exist to direct military policy, including the KWP Military Affairs Committee and the NDC. The large army is a major consumer of resources and finance as well as the major purchaser from many SOEs. Conscription involves three years of army service and four years for the KPN and KPAF; military service is between 10 and 13 years for men and between 7 and 10 years for women. All soldiers serve in the reserves up to the age of 40.

There is little doubt that, notwithstanding the growth of the army, the move to gain nuclear weapons has also been seen as a way of reducing North Korea's reliance on a large standing army. However, this army has been essential in spearheading various economic stimulus measures, providing manpower during harvest season and speed battles. For the reasons examined in previous chapters, the collapse had reached such a point that the traditional tactic of mass mobilisation was rendered useless and the army had to be incorporated into the economic plan.

This incorporation has continued and been extended in an attempt to overcome the energy shortages. The army is the major construction workforce for the building of new power plants and has also became more closely involved in agricultural work. Although there are precedents for the military being used as surplus labour, their involvement became more concerted in the 1990s, when they were closely involved in major construction projects including the Anbyon Youth Power Station and the Kaechon-Lake Thaesong waterway. In addition they built a large number of fish farms and poultry factories. Along with this they maintained their presence working in the fields and providing regular logistical and transport services to industry.

The KPA thus remains an integral force in society and one in which virtually every family has serving members. Armed Forces Day has been a national holiday since 1996. Alongside Kim himself, the military is the living role model for society and a defender of the Party's position as the leading social organisation.

The military is closely monitored: soldiers, even senior commanders, live highly regimented and carefully observed lives with regular checks for political allegiance. KPA members generally have little contact with foreigners and rarely form part of official delegations overseas; in compensation, military officers receive privileges in terms of food and consumer goods. This reflects the political leadership's recognition that the KPA is a force for social stability, economic control and, possibly, change. This quid pro quo of allegiance in exchange for access to food, goods and services goes a long way towards building strong loyalty in the KPA officer corps along with the generally heightened sense of nationalism in the DPRK. A KPA career remains a fast-track into the KWP ranks and eventually cadre status, with all that entails in terms of additional privileges and access. Despite this, as we have seen, conditions for the ranks have been deteriorating since the 1990s and now involve extended periods of non-military physical labour on reduced rations. Discontent may well have grown, but effective action against the regime is only imaginable among the highest elite of the KPA where military authority meets political power.

Universal military service provides a further means of population control. A great deal of time is spent inculcating Juche and patriotic values. The armed forces are also a way to mask unemployment and underemployment. On the other hand, the removal of large numbers of men and women from the labour force at a key age has added to the economic downturn. The emphasis on military service rather than on the acquisition of skills of more direct use to the economy has retarded the knowledge level of the labour force for decades.

With national defence and warfare becoming ever more technology-based, so large standing armies have become tactically less important. North Korea, however, due to its economic pauperisation, has been unable to match the ROK or America in defence spending. Under the North Korean system a large standing army is more affordable than acquiring military technology. The US has estimated that, although the North could not win an all-out war against the ROK, it does have superiority in terms of short-range ballistic missiles, artillery and special forces.[13] Maintaining a large conventional army is nevertheless extremely costly for Pyongyang. The country has few financial reserves to draw on to maintain a lengthy conflict – unlike, for instance, Saddam Hussein's Iraq, which was able to count on oil revenues. In 1989, the first year after the Iran–Iraq War, Baghdad earned US$13 billion from oil sales, not that different from North Korea's entire GNP.

The major exception has been nuclear weapons: Pyongyang has long seen the ability to use weapons of mass destruction as a bargaining chip to secure aid, international recognition and negotiating power, ultimately ensuring the regime's survival.

The Nuclear Bargaining Chip

The North Koreans have undoubtedly understood the seriousness of the nuclear threat better than most countries. The possibility of a nuclear strike against the country has been a constant since its establishment. In July 1950, at the start of the Korean War, President Truman authorised ten nuclear-configured B-29 bombers to be deployed within striking range of the North. Truman declared that the US would take 'whatever steps are necessary' to prevent the triumph of Northern forces and Chinese intervention on the peninsula and admitted that the use of nuclear weapons was under 'active consideration'. In the winter of 1950 General Macarthur actually sought permission to drop 'between thirty and fifty atomic bombs', which would have laid a belt of radioactivity across the peninsula. These threats had also been directed at the Chinese and Soviets to discourage their involvement in the war.

When Eisenhower was elected president in 1952, partly on a mandate to end the war in Korea, he continued with the nuclear rhetoric through 1953, arguing to the National Security Council that nuclear brinksmanship was a cheaper way to end the war than conventional forces. Through conversations with Nehru in India, US secretary of state John Foster Dulles let the powers involved on the peninsula know that America was still considering the nuclear option. He knew the message would be relayed to Beijing that the talks in Panmunjom had to succeed or the White House might exercise its nuclear capabilities. After the signing of the 1953 armistice Eisenhower and Dulles both claimed that the nuclear bluff, their ultimate bargaining chip, had played a major part in forcing a truce. Kim Il-sung, operating under the shadow of the threat from first Truman and then Eisenhower, could hardly have failed to learn the lessons of nuclear brinksmanship.

Virtually as soon as the war ended Kim ordered work to start on a nuclear weapons programme. Pyongyang identified the lack of a nuclear deterrent as its major weakness against a renewed US attack. This lack of an equivalent retaliatory device has dominated North Korean military thinking ever since. In this sense the desire for the bomb was defensive rather than offensive and designed to ensure regime survival at a time when the US was antagonistic towards Pyongyang and the ROK increasingly came under the US nuclear umbrella. These fears only increased further with landmark events such as the 1972 Nixon rapprochement with China, the admission by General Park in Seoul that the ROK had had a nuclear weapons programme since the 1970s, and the collapse of the USSR in 1991. Allies with a nuclear capability were becoming ever more distant; threats ever closer.

As early as 1958 the US-led UN Command in Korea announced that it was introducing nuclear weapons to South Korea in response to violations of the armistice agreement by Pyongyang. The build-up was rapid: in 1959 the US moved Matador Cruise missiles with a range of 1,100 kilometres to South Korea; in 1961 they introduced the Mace 1,800-kilometre range missile; and in the late 1960s both Atomic Demolitions Munitions (essentially nuclear landmines) and nuclear-tipped Nike Hercules anti-aircraft missiles were based in the ROK.[14] In 1963 Kim declared 'We have to fortify our entire country. By doing so, we can defeat those who have atomic weapons even though we do not possess them ourselves.'[15] Combined with the Juche concept of *chawi* (self-defence), the non-dependence on other countries armed forces, Kim felt compelled to seek the bomb. Nuclear weapons, in

Pyongyang's eyes, offered a way to secure the regime, protecting it against being outspent by the ROK's US-backed conventional forces and providing diplomatic leverage in a hostile Cold War world. By 1972 the US had 763 nuclear warheads stationed in the ROK facing north.

When the US eventually withdrew its nuclear weapons from ROK soil, the South remained firmly under the US nuclear umbrella. Even without nuclear weapons on-site the Americans have a large array of sophisticated weaponry currently in the ROK, including plans to deploy 19-tonne Stryker armoured vehicles, Joint Direct Attack Munitions ('smart bombs'), new Shadow-200 unmanned surveillance planes and GBU-28s or 'bunker busters'. From 2005, B/A-22 Raptor fighters will be stationed in Guam.[16] This is in addition to 37,000 troops on the peninsula (along with 4,000 US military contractors and 11,500 dependents) and 47,000 stationed in Japan.

Since the late 1940s the North had been marginally involved in the Soviet nuclear programme, with the USSR seeking uranium-bearing mozanite sand for Moscow's scientists. In the mid-1950s the USSR agreed to help Pyongyang with nuclear research, training 250 DPRK technicians at its Dubna United Institute of Nuclear Research in Moscow. Other physicists were recruited in the DPRK, including a number who had been educated in Japan before the liberation and some who defected from the ROK after Syngman Rhee's purge of leftist professors at Seoul National University. The nuclear facility at Yong-byon (80 kilometres north of Pyongyang), which attracted so much interest in 2002, was originally established in 1964 by the combined efforts of Soviet scientists, North Korea's Academy of Science and Kimchaek University. Additionally in the 1960s the North discovered itself to be fortuitously blessed with large deposits, perhaps as much as 4 million tonnes, of uranium, which it could sell to Moscow. It now has uranium mining, milling and fabrication facilities, allowing for the possibility of an HEU (highly enriched uranium) programme. In 1965 the North received a 2–4 MW research reactor from the Soviets, utilising enriched uranium. This was installed at Yongbyon and began operation in 1967, with the North successfully re-engineering much of the equipment they needed from Soviet designs. Yongbyon became a re-stricted area as scientists sought to expand the capacity of the Soviet reactor. Reports of the early days of the North's nuclear programme are sketchy at best, although defectors have reported many deaths from radiation sickness among the physicists who worked at Yongbyon.[17]

While the Russians supplied the basic tools and much of the know-how for the North's nuclear programme, Kim also appealed for cooperation with Beijing. In 1975 he asked Premier Zhou Enlai to include the DPRK within China's expanding nuclear umbrella to counter the position of the ROK under the US umbrella. Beijing did not agree. Neverthless in the late 1970s it did offer training to North Korean nuclear technicians at China's Lop Nur Nuclear Weapons Test Base.

The nuclear programme, though highly classified, was not a total secret. The DPRK joined the IAEA in 1974 and in 1977 signed the 'Type 66' agreement allowing for IAEA inspections of Yongbyon, which effectively complied with the NPT, though Pyongyang did not formally sign up until 1985. By the mid-1970s the North was seeking to acquire larger reactors from Moscow to complement the existing one at Yongbyon. The Soviets eventually did supply a larger, graphite, reactor in the early 1980s, which was installed at Yongbyon. This raised American fears at the apparent advances Pyongyang's nuclear programme was making, with Yongbyon now a major facility and not connected to the domestic electricity grid. The second reactor was also significantly different from the one delivered in the 1960s. The new reactor, re-engineered from older British and French designs for gas-graphite, air-cooled, uranium-powered models, had the capability to produce plutonium. Both India and Israel had already used similar reactors to produce plutonium for their nuclear programmes.

By the mid-1980s concerns were raised when a smokestack appeared at Yongbyon. The CIA noted steam being vented from the cooling tower and other indications that nuclear reactions were being undertaken, while additional power was due to be supplied to the facility from the new 760 MW Taechon Hydroelectric Plant near Yongbyon. The North attempted to obtain two further 440 MW reactors from the USSR, although by this time Gorbachev was insisting on hard currency payment and the North simply could not afford them. When Soviet foreign minister Eduard Shevardnadze visited Pyongyang in 1990 to inform Pyongyang that Moscow was normalising relations with Seoul, Kim, seeing that the Soviets were not going to change their mind, reiterated his call that North Korea must now take concrete steps to ensure its own nuclear protection. At the same time China expressed concern at Pyongyang's nuclear programme being increasingly militarily orientated and withdrew all technical support and halted nuclear-related technology transfers. The loss of Soviet and Chinese patronage, and the USSR's complete collapse in 1991, led the North to start the process of scouring the world for parts and technology using funds from Division 39 and bartering nuclear know-how for resources with nations such as Pakistan, as well as using its access to the useful and informative IAEA archives in Vienna.

By the late 1980s, intelligence services, as well as the Japanese and South Korean press, were increasingly reporting that the North's programme had advanced to the stage of being capable of reprocessing plutonium into weapons-grade material and that this could potentially be done at one or more of an identified 8,000 underground sites. With the North's apparently abundant natural resources of uranium the only explanation for such reprocessing would have been as part of a nuclear weapons programme. A further alarm sounded in 1989 with the release of intelligence identifying a high-explosive test site at Yongbyon, at which 'scores' of tests had been reportedly conducted.[18] Yongbyon was now believed to be developing a third reactor reliant on natural uranium and ending its reliance on foreign fuel sources. The projected third reactor, like the first two at Yongbyon, did not appear to be connected to the national grid.

By the start of the 1990s – with the USSR gone, China maintaining distance and the experience of Iraq (itself thought to be close to detonating a nuclear device at the time) in the 1991 Persian Gulf War – Pyongyang was more determined than ever to provide its own nuclear deterrent. The issue was increasingly whether or not Pyongyang could deliver nuclear weapons if it developed them. The North had started investigating the procurement of ballistic missiles in the 1970s, trying unsuccessfully to purchase SCUDs from the Soviets and then reverse-engineering the USSR's FROG rockets. Some cooperation with China took place in developing the DF-16 missile, with an estimated range of 370 miles and a payload of 2,200 lbs. However, this programme led nowhere, as the Chinese cancelled it, though not before the North had gained access to the basic technology.

In the 1980s the North did manage to acquire some SCUD B missiles from Egypt, which Pyongyang reverse-engineered with help from Iran. This was further developed into the SCUD C with a 310-mile range and 1,760 lb payload. The North started manufacturing these on a larger scale in the 1990s. The SCUD C design, with the ability to carry a heavier payload and travel a longer range, eventually metamorphosed into the Nodong missile.

After achieving a ballistic missile capability, the North turned its attention to long-range missiles, developing the Taepodong 1 with an 850–1,240 mile range, and possibly capable of up to 3,500 miles. Reportedly the DPRK has approximately a hundred of these missiles sited across the country, including in underground sites on the border with China. This raised concerns in the US as, if true, it gave the North the capacity to reach Alaska or Hawaii. The developments in delivery technology in turn helped to stimulate American engagement, with Clinton realising that a pre-emptive strike was not possible. Such concerns informed the 1994 Agreed Framework.

The Porcupine Strategy

Rumours persist in Pyongyang-watching circles that the military hierarchy, as far back as the 1980s, opposed Kim Jong-il's succession to the leadership. Kim, though, was able to outmanoeuvre the generals at the time of Kim

Il-sung's death, controlling key appointments, limiting military access to decision-making and convincing the army that at a time of national crisis Confucian continuity was essential to maintain security. It is also believed that there was a further estrangement between Kim and the military from the late 1990s until recently – over the extent of the famine, the industrial collapse, the involvement of foreign aid workers in the DPRK and the 2002 economic reforms. Kim has no official military training or combat experience. However, he has maintained a front of unity with the military high command, remains technically the supreme general of the armed forces (as chairman of the NDC) and has declared 'my power comes from the military'.[19] The result, as USAID's Andrew Natsios states, is that

> prior to the crisis of the 1990s, the famine, the collapse of services, and the rise in the human misery index have meant a substantial decline in public support even among party cadres for Kim and his government, which now more than ever relies on the state security apparatus and military to maintain control.[20]

It is also clear that the continuation of the military-first line is a self-defeating tactic unless it can extract concessions from the US and other regional powers, such as additional aid and investment, through nuclear brinksmanship. With a declining GDP the DPRK cannot possibly hope to win a conventional arms race. Neverthless the country can deter attack by building itself into an 'impregnable fortress' and further discourage any would-be onslaught with its 'porcupine strategy'. It may be able to counter any form of overt regime change strategy, like that undertaken by the US in Iraq, but can only secure the borders of a crumbling state at best.

The continuation of military-first ensures that an additional percentage of GDP will be spent on the military, on armaments production and procurement, while scarce resources and inputs are diverted to the KPA. Since 1962 the DPRK has followed the policy of 'equal emphasis', linking high economic growth rates to equally high levels of armaments production, a policy that has led to military spending absorbing as much as 30 per cent of GNP (compared to 2.8–3 per cent in the ROK), some 15 per cent of all budgeted expenditure.[21] However, with the collapse of the economy this large percentage is nevertheless lower than the expenditure of neighbouring countries – the DPRK's US$2 billion budget compares to the ROK's US$12.5 billion and Japan's US$44.5 billion; thus the North spends approximately US$20 a year on each soldier.[22]

Although this expenditure is relatively low, it is adding to the economic decline and undermining any notion of reform or a move away from the command economy, which remains militaristic in many of its basic characteristics. Military-first is gambling on the successful outcome of the nuclear brinksmanship policy, otherwise it will drag the political and economic system ever downwards. Yet it is difficult to see how Pyongyang can discontinue its high expenditure given the financial capabilities of other countries. Japan is increasing military spending to approximately US$50 billion a year, though much of that money covers the costs of the 40,000 US troops stationed in Japan. American military spending is now around US$400 billion annually, with US$11 billion set aside to bolster America's military presence on the peninsula between 2003 and 2006.[23] In late 2003 ROK President Roh Moo-hyun announced a surge in defence spending with an 8.1 per cent increase in the military budget for the 2004 fiscal year alone, as part of a ten-year strategy to bolster Seoul's ability to defend itself. The Bush administration has refused to rule out a pre-emptive strike in the North, while the Pentagon's Operational Plan 5030 is designed to use allied troop operations to diminish North Korean resources, wear down their military and promote a coup attempt.

Perhaps the most searing indictment of the military-first policy is that, according to the Seoul government, a reduction of just 5 per cent in the DPRK's defence budget could resolve the North's food crisis.

PART IV

Change, Collapse and Reunification

One Korea:
The Dream of Reunification

Is Reunification Inevitable?

Drive out of Pyongyang on the Reunification Expressway that slices through the mountains via Kaesong towards the border with South Korea and, after the usual security formalities, you travel down a single-lane road, past tank traps and fields of landmines dotted with observation posts, an occasional soldier and flying cranes, towards the DMZ at Panmunjom – which President Bill Clinton described in 1993 as the 'scariest place on earth'. The DMZ is a 2.5 mile-wide, 156 mile-long strip of landmine-laden land separating the two Koreas. Along the road to what is often termed the last border of the Cold War you pass a single hoarding: a picture of a giant index finger with the words 'One Korea' painted below it. At Panmunjom you look past, first, the lines of KPA border guards in their strangely dated uniforms, and then the lines of the South Korean border guards accompanied by the odd American GI. Behind them is South Korea.

Despite the tenseness of the border the overriding theme that is emphasised by the guards is reunification – the ultimate goal of the two Koreas, the historical destiny of the Korean people, something that Kim Jong-il desires resolutely, we are told. But, despite the propaganda, 'One Korea' has become a somewhat hollow and trite slogan. In the 1970s the Australians attempted to mediate talks between the two Koreas and were rebuffed by the North Koreans. Pakistan's Prime Minister Bhutto offered to mediate but was also rejected.[1] The non-aligned Algerians attempted to broker talks too but were equally shut out by Pyongyang. Gorbachev proposed a meeting in Krasnoyarsk in 1988 with both Koreas; this did nothing but antagonise Pyongyang, which accused the USSR of capitulating to the South by recognising it as a legitimate nation. All this time the Neutral Nations Supervisory Commission (NNSC),[2] formed after the Korean War, continued to provide some sort of talking shop. However, most of the NNSC's efforts have been blocked by arguments about what is proper for the international community to become involved in and what should be the sole preserve of the Korean people.

After more than half a century of separation the two Koreas seem further apart now than ever, despite the millions of divided families, and the common language and culture. Many observers of ROK society believe that unification is not high on the agenda of a new generation of South Koreans more concerned with their careers and the state of the economy than historical destiny, while the regime in Pyongyang cannot credibly believe that Korea will be united by Seoul's sudden realisation that progress from military regime to economically successful democracy has been misguided and that it should instead embrace Juche. Since 1953 any perceived gain in influence by the North has been seen as a loss for the South, and vice versa, meaning that a delicate balance has had to be maintained and only when both sides were able plausibly to claim a diplomatic victory has any tangible movement occurred.

A Brief History of Korean Unification

The history of Korean unification falls essentially into four phases of concerted talks. These have been relatively short, and punctuated by periods of confrontation and insults: 1972–73; 1984–85; 1990–91; and the current period since the North–South Summit in 2002. Although rafts of communiqués, agreements and treaties have been signed, implementation has remained elusive. Who exactly should be regarded as legitimate parties to talks has long been an issue of disagreement through bilateral, three-way and, more recently, six-way talks on reunification. The ROK has always sought to manage its negotiating strategy with regard to its allies in the US and in the region; the DPRK's strategy has largely reflected its own domestic situation based on the belief that foreign policy is essentially an extension of domestic policy.

After the separation of the two Koreas in 1945 and the formalisation of the division in 1948 the atmosphere has been one of classic Cold War hostility. Prior to the outbreak of the Korean War the North naturally moved closer to the USSR, while the South feared a communist takeover and took appropriate measures as it saw fit to safeguard itself. Of course the war was, in many ways, a massive attempt to unify the country by force – one that claimed as many as 3 million lives, and reflected Kim Il-sung's belief that the reunification problem was to be viewed primarily in military terms. However, this involved the necessary cancelling out of one or the other side's ideology.

Kim Il-sung had always yearned for reunification, albeit under a socialist system. Documents made available after the fall of the USSR revealed an imploring communiqué from Kim to Stalin in 1950 requesting Stalin's permission to invade the South[3] with Kim writing,

> Lately I do not sleep at night, thinking about how to resolve the question of the unification of the whole country. If the matter of the liberation of the people of the southern portion of Korea and the unification of the country is drawn out, then I can lose the trust of the people of Korea.[4]

Stalin vacillated for some time, though Mao, looking to build a revolutionary foreign policy, told him 'We should help little Kim.'[5] Ultimately Kim did not need the trust of the Korean people, or even of the Northern portion, but just the support of the Kremlin and Beijing to maintain him in power.

From the 1953 armistice to the early 1970s the two Koreas eyed each other warily across the 38th parallel and got on with the job of reconstruction and economic growth on their opposite tacks. Kim never made reunification the subject of a major address between 1953 and 1964, uttering only routine phrases and saying nothing of substance, wishing to concentrate on economic and military rebuilding and also aware of the USSR's stated 'two Koreas' position. Syngman Rhee wanted unification but was an ardent anticommunist. In the early 1960s the North could have supposed that some sort of upheaval in the South would bring reunification after the 4–19 (19 April 1960) student riots forced Rhee out of office. The subsequent interim government in Seoul collapsed in May 1961 in the coup that brought General Park to power with the US not intervening in events. President Johnson courted Park, after which Park sent 50,000 ROK troops to Vietnam annually between October 1965 and March 1973. Park also forged better relations with the Japanese, signing a normalisation treaty in 1965 that was accompanied by a US$500 million grant from Tokyo. From 1967 Pyongyang pursued a policy of attempting to foment revolution in the South through the creation of the ill-fated Revolutionary Party for Reunification (RPR), which attacked the South's 'military fascist leaders' and which culminated in the botched assassination of Park in 1968.[6]

The secret visit of Henry Kissinger to Beijing in 1971 to pave the way for Nixon's visit was a catalyst for North–South relations, an unintended side dish to the main course of Sino–American engagement. As we have seen,

Kim, who was in Beijing during the visit, saw rapprochement between China and America as a cause for insecurity and greater DPRK vulnerability to American military might. Although the Chinese attempted to assuage Kim's fears through an economic and military pact in late 1971, the watershed Nixon–Mao meeting convinced Kim to take matters into his own hands.

In August 1971, now aware of the change in Sino–US relations, Kim made a characteristically unannounced declaration at a Pyongyang mass rally that he was ready to 'establish contact at any time with all political parties including the ruling Democratic Republican Party (DRP), and all social organisations and individual personages in South Korea'. This was a complete volte-face for Kim, who only months before had reiterated that the DRP would have to be ousted from power before any DPRK–ROK contact could occur. While it appears that few in the North were prepared for Kim's public U-turn on negotiations, in Seoul nobody, including Park, was told of Nixon's plans to visit Beijing. Again, as so often in American strategy, Korea had been an afterthought.

Both Park and Kim were aware of the stated American position, declared in mid-1969 in the Nixon doctrine, that Asians would have to be more prepared to provide for their own security. Clearly, to Seoul at least, the US was preparing to disengage after what by then was the clear, though largely still unacknowledged, disaster in Vietnam. By 1972 and Nixon's Beijing trip, his doctrine was being acted on – Washington withdrew 20,000 of the 62,000 US troops stationed in South Korea and also began the long-drawn-out and painful withdrawal from Vietnam. The accumulated evidence of the US withdrawal from the fight against communism in Indochina, rapprochement with Beijing, and the downsizing of troop commitments all indicated to Park that the US would not rush to his defence in the case of another attack from the North. Park was left to ask in Seoul 'How long can we trust the US?' Despite Park's concern being relayed to Washington, in the wake of the breakthrough in China, Korea was now still decidedly low on Nixon's agenda. Park increasingly began to look to engagement with the North as a way to protect himself and the ROK, to make unilateral actions that might anger the Americans but would ensure his own regime's survival. These led to the development of what one analyst at the time described as an 'Israeli Complex' in Seoul.

A Flurry of Engagement

With both sides feeling somewhat betrayed and neglected by their allies, Park agreed to a meeting through the proxy of the Red Cross.[7] The negotiations were drawn out and tense, and yet the decision was made to scale up the level of meetings. Thus, in March 1972, erstwhile South Korean Red Cross delegate and deputy director of the KCIA's International Affairs Bureau, Chong Hong-jin, visited Pyongyang in the first of what were to be many secret visits by KCIA personnel. Senior North Koreans would also visit Seoul. By April 1972 a direct telephone hot line had been established between the KCIA in Seoul and Pyongyang to facilitate all this traffic. The KWP Central Committee issued a statement endorsing these contacts, noting 'the changing domestic and foreign political situation'. By visiting Beijing Nixon had unwittingly provoked a flurry of engagement on the peninsula. Eventually the contact between the two sides reached the highest level: KCIA head and former chief of staff to President Park, Lee Hu-rak, met Kim face to face in Pyongyang.

The meeting, apparently full of the usual pleasantries, was not officially reported.[8] The record kept by the South Korean delegation noted that Kim apologised for the attempted assassination of Park in 1968, claiming that he had no knowledge of it, which is hard to believe. A purge of the military hierarchy did then follow, though it is unclear if the two events were linked. The meeting in Pyongyang was followed by a visit to Seoul by DPRK deputy premier Park Sung-chul, who met personally with Park.

The result of this flurry of engagement was the South–North Joint Communiqué of 4 July 1972.[9] The Communiqué came at a time when détente was in fashion globally and some form of mutually assured re-unification appeared possible as the two Koreas were relatively close in terms of economic development following the destruction of the Korean War. The Communiqué, which also led to the establishment of the South–North Coordinating Committee (SNCC), stated three principles: (1) that reunification should be an issue for both Koreas and not come about through outside imposition or interference; (2) that it should be achieved through peaceful means; and (3) that it should be achieved in a way that transcended differences in ideas, ideologies and systems. There was also a pledge to end 'slandering' and take measures to stop military incidents along the DMZ.

The Communiqué was viewed as a breakthrough by both Koreas, but for different reasons. Kim believed that it went some way towards driving a wedge between the ROK, the US and Japan, while Park saw it as de-escalating tensions at a time when he was concerned about the strength of the KPA. Neither Park nor Kim had much interest in actual reunification. Park believed that if he could defuse the threat from the North then he could concentrate on building the ROK into an economic power, while Kim had no desire to reunite with the South unless it was under a Juche system. However, globally the Communiqué was seen as good news, a major breakthrough and a reduction in tension, as well as the possible harbinger of a more permanent peace and eventual reunification.

At the end of 1972 it was clear that Park did not believe the threat from the North had receded. He introduced the concept of *Yushin*, which led to the arrest of opposition political leaders, the disbanding of the National Assembly and the throwing out of the constitution. It would stay in place until 1979. Clearly Park, despite some limited US pressure to democratise, was determined to stay in power for the next twelve years. He had realised that the US would do little to stop him or even censure him. Less than a month before, Ferdinand Marcos had consolidated power in the Philippines in similar fashion and Washington had done nothing. America was in an election cycle and had little time for foreign affairs.

The 1972 Communiqué and the exchanges between North and South, though they raised expectations among many South Koreans that reunification might be imminent, only revealed the two starkly different societies that had emerged since 1953. South Koreans went to Pyongyang and met what they described as 'programmed dolls', saw artificially stocked shops and buildings brightly lit that were normally dark. The North Koreans who went south were similarly treated to illusion, though now it was dancing girls that embarrassed the delegation while Seoul office buildings also left their lights on all night. The story is told that while the DPRK delegation was due to drive on the expressway from Seoul to Pusan, people were told to drive around aimlessly to create the impression of heavy traffic. By and large neither side was fooled by such PR tricks. What didn't occur was any serious political dialogue; instead the two sides berated each other.

Kim used the imposition of *Yushin* in the ROK to suspend the political talks and exchanges. Meanwhile Park, unsure about American intentions during the Ford–Carter period, boosted ROK military spending, which increased from US$411 million to US$719 million between 1971 and 1975, averaging 4.5 per cent of GNP, though this was pushed up by the ROK's commitments in fighting alongside America in Vietnam until 1973. Park doubled defence expenditure in 1976, and did so again in 1979, despite the twin adverse effects of the oil crisis and domestic recession limiting GDP growth. Although the ROK was still devoting a smaller percentage of total GDP to defence spending than the DPRK, it started to outpace the North in terms of total expenditure by the mid-1970s, and by 1979 was spending approximately double the amount Pyongyang was on defence. Most of this military spending went on American-made armaments. In Pyongyang Kim believed that this rise in military spending and the growth of the ROK's GDP were temporary aberrations and would be revealed as a bubble economy.

Kim cited the repression of the Korean people as his reason for ending contact. The truth was that the exchanges had caused unease in Pyongyang, with the developmental gap between the Koreas becoming glaringly obvious to many who had not previously been aware of the North's decline and the surge of the South. Meanwhile America's failure to condemn Park for either the Communiqué or *Yushin* revealed that Kim's strategy of driving a wedge between the ROK and the US had failed. Park tried to resuscitate the Communiqué but failed. The SNCC collapsed amid military skirmishes along the DMZ. Despite the collapse, both leaders had benefited from the talks. Park had been able to impose *Yushin*, extend his rule and eliminate much of the opposition without US interference. Kim had been able to show that he could engage Seoul. This led to a number of benefits, including a flood of new diplomatic missions to Pyongyang and a recognised observer mission at the UN. Perhaps the biggest benefit to Kim was that the seeming rapprochement brought the first contacts with the US since 1953. By the end of 1972 Park had been unanimously elected to a further six-year term; Kim, for his part, had introduced a new constitution that further enshrined Juche as the national creed and cemented his position as Great Leader (*Suryong*).

Stalemates, Assassination and Entrenchment

It was ultimately domestic politics that ended Park's rule. In 1979, as student and worker protests continued, the head of the KCIA, Kim Jae-kyu, shot Park dead over dinner, claiming that it was a move to 'end repression of the people'. The engagement process held despite the ensuing political turbulence in Seoul and the increasing realisation that the North was starting to lose the economic growth race. Arguably the time was propitious for a renewed invasion before the economic gap opened too wide.

The North did not take the opportunity, however, though it is widely believed that Kim, aware of Park's nuclear programme, which had been started in the early 1970s, considered restarting the war while the Americans were overstretched in Vietnam. Despite Kim's apparent keenness, neither the Chinese nor the Soviets would back him and, despite Juche's doctrine of military self-reliance, he did not feel strong enough to go it alone against the ROK.

For the North Koreans the breakthroughs in the 1970s had come partly out of the political situation in the ROK. Political leaders like Syngman Rhee and Park had been despotic rulers, though solidly anti-communist. Decisions regarding contact with Pyongyang were taken by the president and his KCIA advisers without too much concern for public opinion. Indeed those who offered differing strategies for engaging the DPRK, such as Kim Dae-jung, were dealt with harshly.

By 1974 the Communiqué was effectively dead, following the discovery by ROK soldiers of underground tunnels from the North running under the DMZ, and a series of armed skirmishes along the border. The tunnels indicated long-term planning by the KPA to infiltrate the South, and effectively broke one of the terms of the Communiqué. Militarisation was stepped up in both North and South as tensions rose. The atmosphere further deteriorated in August 1976 when the increasingly frequent shoving matches between ROK/USFK and DPRK soldiers on the DMZ escalated with the tree-cutting dispute and the first fatalities in the JSA since the armistice.

As the rhetoric between the US and the DPRK intensified following the killings, so the ROK appeared left on the sidelines, adding fuel to the argument that the US completely controlled the ROK military. With the arrival of Carter in Washington, Kim saw a possible way to engage the US. Immediately after Carter's election Kim started sending him letters (via third parties in Pakistan, Gabon, Yugoslavia and Romania) requesting direct contact, while DPRK foreign minister Ho Dam simultaneously appealed to Carter's secretary of state, Cyrus Vance. Carter's response was to seem interested and lift some restrictions on travel to the North but he insisted on Seoul's participation in any talks. However, as Carter lost the battle for troop withdrawal so Kim accused him of being a 'con-man' and reneging on campaign pledges. With the Carter opportunity seemingly gone, Kim moved decidedly away from the more engaging rhetoric of the 1972 Communiqué and towards more traditional ground.

During a visit to Pyongyang by GDR leader Erich Honecker in 1977 Kim outlined his new strategic direction: to complete the socialist organisation of the DPRK; to support and encourage revolutionary struggle in the ROK; and to further develop solidarity among the 'international revolutionary forces'. In short Kim was aiming to secure the DPRK, isolate Park and precipitate his overthrow in a way that would turn the South Korean people against the US military presence and restart the stalled 1972 dialogue.

Renewed Engagement and Terrorism

In effect, the 1980s can be seen to have begun with the 1979 assassination of Park. Kim's response to the killing was merely to reiterate that Park was a 'traitor' to the Korean people and watch what transpired to fill the growing political vacuum in the ROK.

In May 1980 dissident leader Kim Dae-jung was arrested again, this time by the government of President Choi and Chun Doo-hwan on charges of 'favouring North Korea' and being an instigator of the Kwangju rebellion (even though he was in prison throughout the events) when he proposed a federal system for a reunified Korea. Kwangju was a turning point, with agitation against the military government continuing for two years. This seminal moment in Korean history is seen as the catalyst that propelled a wider movement to end the successive military regimes and install democracy in South Korea. Significantly, the American command in the country remained silent during the events, believing that stability was paramount in the face of the North Korean threat. A proposal from Chun that Kim and he meet to establish a climate of mutual trust was swiftly rejected by Kim following Kwangju.

North Korea clearly thought that a larger Kwangju-type incident could precipitate a revolution in the ROK. This was the thinking supposedly behind the 1983 assassination attempt on Chun in Rangoon. Certainly any engagement between the two Koreas was off the agenda, with Chun even considering retaliatory bombing of the DPRK, though ultimately he did not respond with force. In part this was due to the fact that Pyongyang was once again appearing to soften its stance on talks with the ROK, even while arranging the assassination of members of the ROK cabinet. Pyongyang, via Beijing, agreed to three-way talks between the DPRK, ROK and US – with Seoul as a full participant.

This agreement to talk was a watershed. Pyongyang had accepted Seoul as a legitimate party in any talks, as well as ending its long-term insistence that Seoul was merely a tool of US imperialism and that all negotiations on the future of the peninsula be between Pyongyang and Washington. This time Beijing helped broker talks, another major change. In 1983 Deng Xiaoping agreed to help foster talks, even though reportedly angry with Pyongyang over the Rangoon bombing fiasco, and had raised the new proposals from Pyongyang with Reagan's defense secretary, Caspar Weinberger, adding the warning that if the South attacked the North, China would inevitably find itself involved in any renewed conflict. The twin strategy of renewed engagement and assassination emanating from Pyongyang revealed how little the North Koreans still understood the concept of 'linkage', any more than it did the need to pursue twin policies of concessions and no concessions. What bizarre conjunction of tactics allowed you to agree to meet up with people you had just attempted to blow up?

While in Seoul in November 1983, Reagan personally endorsed three-way talks. This went against Alexander Haig's stated position in 1981 that the Reagan administration would not accept such a format. Then the US again changed its mind and called for ROK–DPRK bilateral negotiations first. If these led nowhere, then four-way talks, to include the Chinese, should be the route forward. This plan from Washington was strange, as the Americans appeared not to realize that, along with the DPRK's rejection of Chinese participation, the USSR was adamantly against any direct participation by Beijing in events that could affect the peninsula's future. Whether anyone actually wanted dialogue is unclear. Pyongyang was always keen to advance peace proposals to force America's hand and get them to declare openly that they did not wish for reunification, while the ROK saw the proposals as a way to stall US military aid to the South. The US, seemingly not overly keen to talk to anyone, managed to upset the USSR, their allies in the ROK and China. When Chinese Premier Zhao Ziyang visited Washington in January 1984 he hand-delivered a letter from Kim to Reagan proposing tripartite DPRK–ROK–US talks on reunification. The letter was made public in Pyongyang on the same day; it was made clear that the ROK would attend the talks 'on an equal footing'. However, the proposal also contained the precondition that the US withdraw all troops from the peninsula. This killed the offer in Washington and Seoul. Kim must have realised that this would be the response. He was probably probing for weaknesses in the US–ROK relationship, as Adrian Buzo has noted.[10]

Floods, Decline and Economic Talks

Major flooding in the ROK in September 1984 opened the door to a bizarre turn of events when Pyongyang offered relief assistance, which Seoul accepted. However, relations quickly iced over again following a firefight at Panmunjom in November. This event, coming at a time when the North's economy was clearly in freefall, did at least lead to a round of North–South economic talks – thirteen in all – and in September 1985 a series of family reunions; this was the most active engagement since the 1972–73 round. The talks yielded little, though they did result in a degree of ROK access to DRPK raw materials (by 1990 the ROK was running a significant trade deficit with the DPRK of approximately US$110 million). The family reunions, for their part, did indicate a softening of attitudes.

What was unknown until the 1990s was that while these talks had been occurring, secret higher-level meetings had also been taking place between Kim and emissaries from Chun Doo-hwan that promised a possible North–South summit. At the time, North Korea was still issuing statements eschewing further contact with the South. Again Pyongyang was using a strategy of concession and no concession while simultaneously a new direct line was being established between the Korean capitals. Delegates from both sides met secretly on forty-two occasions between 1985 and 1991 at Panmunjom, in the ROK, DPRK and in Singapore. In 1985 Kim even sent a personal letter to Chun – whom he had tried to kill two years earlier – urging continuation of the talks. At the Fifth KWP Congress he once again raised his idea of a confederal republic, premissed on US troop withdrawal. Despite this intervention, the talks once again stalled as the DPRK demanded the cancellation of the 'Team Spirit' joint ROK–US military operations in 1986. Chun refused this demand and the talks collapsed over details. These 'Team Spirit' operations were the most extensive to date, and duly led to a ratcheting up of the military alert levels north of the border. Kim ruled out any further discussions between the Koreas. Chun took comfort in the fact that, following the recession of the early 1980s, the appreciation of the yen and growing US demand meant that South Korean exports were booming again, approaching US$60 billion per year, and filling his treasury. Meanwhile the obvious disintegration of the North's economy was becoming increasingly apparent.

Democracy Flourishes, the North Feels Isolated

The growing prosperity of the ROK was eventually Chun's downfall, as an expanding, educated middle class increasingly rejected non-democratic rule. The 'June Resistance' finally brought democracy to the ROK in December 1987, with the election of Roh Tae-woo,[11] riding the wave of falling dictatorships worldwide, followed in December 1992 with the popular election of Kim Young-sam as the first civilian head of state since 1961. This development became a factor in dealings with the North. Roh, and then Kim Young-sam, posssessed a legitimacy in their dealings with both the South Korean public and the international community that no unelected leader had previously enjoyed.

The pro-democracy movement of the late 1980s saw the highest levels of political mobilisation witnessed in Asia in modern times. The Seoul Olympics in 1988 were another catalyst for political change, and national pride, in the South when the country was thrust into the international limelight. The US did not interfere in the political protests except to discourage the use of force against pro-democracy protestors. The agitation by students, backed by a growing segment of the middle class, eventually secured a victory for democracy. Significantly, though, the protesters were often as anti-American as they were pro-democratic and noticeably less receptive to the political tactic of raising the spectre of invasion by the North.

Following the advent of democracy, with elections impending and the success of the Olympics anticipated, the North responded with the bombing of the KAL 858 airliner in November 1987, thought to have been designed to scare away teams from the Seoul Games.[12] Clearly the loss of Soviet and Chinese patronage – Gorbachev opened negotiations with Seoul in the late 1980s, before the USSR collapsed, agreeing diplomatic relations in September 1990 and also securing US$2.3 billion in loans and trade credits from the ROK; China followed in 1992 – also impacted on Pyongyang's view of unification. The balance of allies was flowing to Seoul and away from Pyongyang, as Roh and Gorbachev met three times in one year and Yeltsin visited Seoul in November 1992. To add insult to injury the North saw other erstwhile allies, including the Hungarians, also establishing relations with Seoul. Hungary was a particular slight as Kim Jong-il's half-brother, Kim Pyong-il, had just been installed as ambassador in Budapest.

Kim's last gambit to restore the balance in Pyongyang's favour was to try and open dialogue with Japan. Just weeks after Gorbachev and Roh met to agree diplomatic recognition, the vice-president of Japan's Liberal Democratic Party (LDP), Shin Kanemaru, led a joint LDP–Socialist Party delegation to Pyongyang. The trip was Kanemaru's own initiative and opposed by the Foreign Affairs Ministry in Tokyo. The meeting ended up a mess of misunderstood messages. Pyongyang interpreted the visit as a signal of official recognition and engagement; Seoul saw the visit as an attempt to undermine the new Moscow–Seoul friendship. The trip was actually none of these things; rather, it was little more than another scam by a terminally corrupt Japanese politician who believed that if he could resolve the historic argument over reparations to the North for Japan's colonial occupation (Kanemaru reportedly suggested US$8 billion; the US suggested the figure should be closer to US$12 billion) then Japan would be favoured in any reconstruction of the DPRK, while Kanemaru would profit from the implicit graft. Japan's Foreign Affairs Ministry deemed the meeting unofficial. In 1993 Kanemaru was arrested on bribery and corruption charges; he died shortly afterwards. Little further contact took place between the DPRK and Tokyo until the Kim–Koizumi one-day summit of 2002.

The advent of participatory democracy in the ROK did not fundamentally change Pyongyang's perceptions of the South as much as Seoul's new recognition internationally did. South Korea remained in the eyes of Pyongyang, and many others, justifiably, as a 'client' state of the US.[13] However, it did mean that Pyongyang would inevitably have to speak to the people of South Korea in a way it hadn't done before. One example of this was the ending of the North's long-standing opposition to both Koreas joining the UN as separate entities, which they did in 1991.

Nordpolitik, Unification and Eastern Bloc Collapse

As reform swept Eastern Europe, and both the USSR and China appeared to be further reforming, Roh announced his new pragmatic Six Point Declaration policy of cross-recognition and engagement – Nordpolitik[14] – in July 1988 and in September 1989 proposed the Korean National Unity Unification Formula. Re-engagement of the North had been a key part of Roh's manifesto and included a confederate republic concept similar to that put forward by Kim Dae-jung (for which he was arrested), and by Kim Il-sung, although the latter's proposal had been ignored as it required US troop withdrawal. The Americans were consulted, and prior to its release passed Roh's six-point plan to the Chinese and Russians, with whom it met general approval.

Reagan largely welcomed Nordpolitik and thawed somewhat in his approach to Pyongyang; there were thirty-four meetings between the North and the US in the years 1988 to 1993. By this time, with economic collapse under way, the North was arguably more concerned with regime survival than with reunification. There was also an attempt at inter-parliamentary talks, but these stalled, with the ROK proposing delegations of twenty each from the Supreme People's Assembly and the National Assembly, and the DPRK insisting on a joint meeting of both full houses – which favoured the North with 655 SPA members to the National Assembly's 299. Once again the 'Team Spirit' exercises in 1989 led to the cessation of all initiatives.

Following the apparent ending of diplomatic iciness between the ROK and the socialist bloc after the Seoul Olympics and the collapse of initiatives in 1989, there was little discernible progress between the two governments. Nevertheless, further private initiatives did occur, most notably a visit by Hyundai's founder, Chung Ju-yong, to sign an agreement on the development of tourism around the Mount Kumgang area, and his 'cattle diplomacy' when he accompanied 501 cows across the border to the North.[15] Further expected cross-border family reunions floundered in the face of the North's strange insistence that it be allowed to stage socialist realist 'Cultural Revolution' style anti-ROK revolutionary operas in Seoul. These operas, common cultural events in the North, were unlikely to achieve anything in Seoul except attract a crowd of curious spectators and annoy the government.

As the ever-problematic 'Team Spirit' exercises came around again in 1990, another initiative proposing talks fell apart, while the Mount Kumgang–Hyundai initiative stalled and the ROK military discovered more Northern tunnels under the DMZ. However, a breakthrough of sorts occurred in July when a new round of talks was announced, with DPRK approval; these in part represented Pyongyang's rather panicked response to the ongoing collapse of the Eastern Bloc. For Pyongyang the collapse in 1989 of Ceausescu's

Romania was a pointer, as the much trumpeted independence of Romania from Moscow rather dented the North's claim that the collapse of the Eastern bloc was due solely to those countries' overreliance on Moscow.

Prime ministerial talks were held in Seoul in September 1990. Yet again progress stalled around demands that 'Team Spirit' be suspended, plans for separate UN membership cancelled, and over the arrest and imprisonment in Seoul of Southerners for illegally visiting the DPRK.[16] Ultimately the two sides restated their respective positions yet again. Yet further talks took place in Pyongyang in October and in Seoul in December. By February 1991 the talks were suspended by the DPRK in response to the now annual stumbling block of the 'Team Spirit' exercises.

With the collapse of the USSR, Pyongyang made a more concerted effort at negotiation. Initially North Korea offered support to the communist hard-liners who staged the August coup in Moscow against Gorbachev, although this was of little help as the coup collapsed. A rash of accords were signed indicating some progress: these included the Agreement on Reconciliation, Non-Aggression and Exchanges and Co-operation (the 'Basic Agreement') and the Joint Declaration of the Denuclearisation of the Korean Peninsula, both in December 1991. These two documents became active at the start of the sixth round of high-level talks that began in February 1992, after the ROK finally suspended the troublesome 'Team Spirit' exercises. The former agreement was something of a breakthrough as it enshrined the principle of mutual recognition of each other's system; while the latter agreement, on nuclearisation, was signed at a time when the South suspected the North of being close to developing nuclear weapons and when Roh announced that the South had no such capability and that no US nuclear weapons remained on ROK soil. Although this earned some concessions from the North, the two could not reach agreement on mutual inspection procedures; hence none of the all-important confidence-building measures (CBMs) could be found. The inspections issue became linked to the continuance of further cultural and family exchanges, and by September the two sides were deadlocked once again. In 1992 the ROK and the US resumed 'Team Spirit'. This led to the resumption of an official war alert in Pyongyang and to probably the lowest point in the North–South dialogue for a decade.

A New Geopolitical Reality

From the end of the Cold War in the late 1980s through the emergence of democracy in South Korea, Pyongyang was faced with new realities, which it did not like but had to deal with: the collapse of the DPRK's support network in the socialist bloc and the rapidly rising economic power of the ROK. In the space of fifteen years North Korea had gone from being economically ahead of a military regime in the South to facing an emergent economic power with a vibrant democracy. The DPRK had slumped into global isolation, industrial collapse and famine. Additionally, as the military spending gap moved increasingly in Seoul's favour, Pyongyang was left trying to secure deals with Indian, Russian, Chinese and other arms manufacturers based on credit to maintain some sort of parity.

During the 1990s relations between the Koreas remained relatively tense, with the now ascendant ROK more interested in consolidating its own economic growth than engaging the South. As the North's economic collapse deepened, and became more obvious as the international aid agencies were finally called in to try to deal with the open state of famine, the ROK spent money on the North to try to prop it up. If the DPRK collapsed then the ROK's fragile economic growth and democracy would also be threatened. The general thinking was that Seoul was just not in a position yet to absorb the North. The government had watched the cost and process of the West German absorption of the GDR. While the historical inevitability of the reunification of Germany struck a chord in Seoul, many feared the costs. The likelihood of multiparty talks appeared slim, with the DPRK negotiating with the Americans separately over their nuclear programme while the US concentrated on securing the Agreed Framework and Russia had little role left in the region after the collapse of the Soviet Union. While the multiparty talks envisaged previously were the so-called 2 + 4 scenario, involving along with the ROK and DPRK the US, Japan, China and the USSR, Russia's reduced circumstances now led people to talk of just 2 + 3½.

What the ROK could do was help the North through aid, investment and developments that stemmed from the 1994 Agreed Framework, notably the KEDO organisation. One outcome of the 1994 Carter visit to Pyongyang was that Kim agreed to meet with Kim Young-sam. Seoul accepted the invitation brokered through Carter, expecting a debate on the merits of the North Korean leader's confederate model, which amounted to a 'one country two systems' solution, and on those of their own more gradualist reunification programme. The first ever South–North Summit was scheduled for summer 1994. However, just two weeks before the meeting Kim Il-sung died, and Kim Jong-il ascended to the primary position in Pyongyang.

Kim Il-sung's reunification proposals were never taken seriously, even if they were meant to be, and he was never anything but generally reviled by the South Korean public. Following Kim's death reunification took second place to the reality of famine and shipments of aid from the ROK. In the South Kim Young-sam, who had taken office in February 1993, ordered the arrest of former presidents Chun and Roh on charges of abuse of power. In 1996, they were sentenced to death.

Limited inter-Korean talks were conducted in June 1995. They yielded little but did see the Seoul government agree to provide 150,000 tonnes of food aid to the North, as well as a 'donation' of US$232 million through the government's North–South Cooperation Fund. Kim Young-sam began to ease restrictions on the involvement of South Korean aid groups in the North in the wake of the disastrous floods in 1995 and tolerated the formation of the Pan-Religious Order Promotion Committee to Help Our North Korean Brothers, which had been established by six leading religious groups in the South. In January 1996 another organisation, the Korean Sharing Movement (KSM), was established to help deal with flood relief in the North. This was part of a generally greater engagement of ordinary ROK citizens in the plight of the North. The restrictions on ROK citizens becoming active in projects aimed at helping the North had been gradually, though not totally, rescinded since 1995. Fundraising for aid was increasingly successful, with organisations such as the YMCA, the Korean Federation of Trade Unions and the Korean Federation of Farmers making donations. In all, over US$4.5 million was raised outside of official government channels. Kim Young-sam had to tolerate this, but he tried to insist that all relief efforts be channelled through the Red Cross. However, much of the aid from the ROK was in fact positive and included urgently required fertilisers and pesticides. At the same time there was increasing cross-border business contact, which was often low key, but sometimes high profile, such as Hyundai's activities. By 2001 over 300 ROK companies had some form of contract in place with a DPRK partner, usually to supply materials and pay for finished products in US dollars.

Terminal Decline in Pyongyang, Financial Crisis in Seoul

In 1997, Kim Jong-il, after a protracted period of mourning, announced, that he would continue his father's policies towards reunification. However, the DPRK had changed, as became evident in February 1997 with the defection of Hwang Jang-yop, the so-called architect of Juche and mentor to Kim Jong-il, to the ROK. Hwang identified the growing role of the military hierarchy in the DPRK, the resurgence of martial values and the possibility that this power and theoretical shift could lead to war. Hwang argued that the 'North was fifty years behind the South' and that the ROK should provide the DPRK with food and nothing else. Hwang also argued against any further four-way talks, as these were only being used by Pyongyang to further regime survival.

This concern over the possible costs and consequences to the ROK of reunification was heightened after the Asian financial crisis of 1997 and 1998. The period between 1960 and 1997 had been one of largely sustained economic growth following Seoul's imitation of Japan's rapid post-war growth strategy. As well as rising incomes, the ROK had managed to reduce its birth rate by 3 per cent over the 35-year period – a demographic transition in one generation. It was selling over a million cars a year domestically and nearly 2 million computers. The country's financial system had begun to mature, with credit a commonplace way of fuelling growth in consumer demand. The average household size had been brought down to three from four in just a decade and an estimated 28 per cent of the population was middle class. However, this rapid growth had also stored up a series of systemic problems. A financial crisis ensued, brought about largely by a depreciating currency and problems of weak corporate governance and lending.

In August 1997 the severity of the crisis hit home when Seoul announced emergency measures to prevent bad loans from collapsing the banking system. By November Seoul was forced to ask the IMF for US$20 billion in loans, which were eventually granted and subsequently raised to US$57 billion. Figures released by the Central Bank of Korea in March 1998 indicated that soaring inflation and record unemployment meant the ROK was headed for a major recession. Mounting unemployment and wage reductions led to a collapse in domestic demand, further weakening the economy. The Seoul stock market also underwent a series of downward jolts presaged by unemployment, the threat of labour unrest and the general regional economic crisis.

Kim Dae-jung and the Sunshine Policy

In December 1997 one-time dissident Kim Dae-jung was elected president of the ROK at the age of 72, with 40.3 per cent of the votes. He launched the 'Sunshine Policy' in early 1998. Kim, the eighth president of the ROK, was the first example of a transition of power from the ruling to the opposition party in the country's history. After formally taking office Kim held summit meetings with the leaders of Japan, China and Russia and subsequently met with Clinton and European leaders, all in the cause of promoting his 'Sunshine Policy'.

Kim's Sunshine Policy had three guiding principles: (1) no toleration of armed provocation of any kind; (2) no unification by absorption (i.e. no German-style process); and (3) the active promotion of inter-Korean reconciliation and co-operation, starting first with those areas of mutual interest on which both parties can most readily agree. The Sunshine Policy effectively enshrined the general consensus that any reunification process would have to be more gradual than that which had occurred in Germany. It would have to be peaceful, without the burden falling on the ROK. There needed to develop a greater understanding between the two Koreas over issues such as military integration, social differences and property claims. Meanwhile it was hoped that some sort of economic recovery in the North would make any future reunification less painful, socially disruptive and affordable.

The Sunshine Policy raised expectations to the highest level since the 1972 North–South Communiqué. South Koreans felt that progress was being made with family reunions and flows of aid from South to North and took comfort from the North–South summit in June 2000. The North, for its part, saw the Sunshine Policy as a way to guarantee aid that could prop up the regime, as well as paving the way for Pyongyang's upcoming charm offensive. This strategy worked for Pyongyang in the form of the four-party talks that occurred between the DPRK, ROK, China and the US in 1998 and 1999. From an economic recovery standpoint the Sunshine Policy also offered hope, in that Kim Dae-jung stated that he wished to see aid from the South to the North extended beyond food to grants that supported the DPRK's substandard 'social infrastructure', which could potentially relieve further the burden on government spending.

The major event of the Sunshine period was Kim Dae-jung's historic visit to Pyongyang in June 2000 for the North–South Summit. Kim Jong-il even appeared on the tarmac at Pyongyang's Sunan International Airport to greet the South Korean president, which raised Southerners' hopes of some sort of breakthrough. Polls in Seoul found that the expectation by ordinary people of an imminent invasion by the North had fallen from 40 per cent to 10 per cent.

South Korea was one of the first nations to bounce back from the Asian financial crisis; the North, on the other hand, carried on its slow decline during the entire period. However, the economic landscape had changed, and some of these changes affected the South's approach to the issue of unification. A less secure workforce was more concerned about career and standard of living, and preventing a repeat of the crisis, than it was in reunification – a process likely to precipitate a tough period of adjustment for both Koreas, in which the South would have to make sacrifices to drag the North into a modern economy.

Despite an initial groundswell of support, Kim Dae-jung found it more difficult to run a democracy than he had imagined. Additionally, traditional Korean politics intervened alongside continued problems with the North. Kim lacked a majority in the National Assembly and his initially popular

Sunshine Policy was not enough to secure his coalition a majority in parliamentary elections. Economically, the fallout from the Asian financial crisis proved harder to deal with than expected. Kim's government spent billions trying to deal with the accumulated bad debts of the *chaebol*, but, facing internal opposition from the organised labour movement, did not implement many of the tough measures needed to restructure them fully.

Ultimately the failure to deliver on the Sunshine Policy led, in part, to Kim Dae-jung's downfall, as disillusion set in among the population, despite his being awarded the Nobel Peace Prize. Other North-related issues, such as Kim's admission in February 2003 that in 2000 the KCIA had made, through a subsidiary of Hyundai, substantial cash payments (as much as US$500 million) to the DPRK in exchange for the invitation to visit Pyongyang, caused trouble. However, Kim's policy also suffered from internal opposition and the new atmosphere that affected US–DPRK relations when Bush came to power in 2001. It is also the case that Kim handled the media poorly. The Sunshine Policy seemed like the president's personal triumph rather than the nation's. Consequently, when the policy went sour Kim was the only one to blame. The initial agreements negotiated between the ROK and DPRK targeting social programmes and infrastructure development mostly failed without firm financing and cost sharing agreements being finalised. The North–South relationship came to be seen, in the public's eyes, as too one-sided, with the ROK conceding and Pyongyang remaining inflexible. Optimism had been high, along with expectations, and ultimately Kim Dae-jung was left relying on a gesture from Kim Jong-il to save his initiative. Domestic political problems mounted as the public lost faith in the Sunshine Policy, ultimately unseating Kim.

Sunshine Departs

Kim Dae-jung's government and his Sunshine Policy eventually fell due to growing allegations of corruption. The last year of Kim's presidency was dogged with charges involving his sons and his wife's nephew. The Millennium Democratic Party (MDP) suffered losses in the August 2002 by-elections and Kim eventually resigned from the MDP. The June 2002 ROK–DPRK naval skirmishes that occurred along the disputed sea demarcation line between the two countries and saw several sailors killed, as well as the onset of a renewed nuclear crisis, caused an increasing number of voters to reject Kim's policies.

The election of MDP candidate Roh Moo-hyun in December 2002 appeared initially to presage another rift in US–ROK relations following his anti-American sentiments expressed during the campaign. This was the second time the ROK's conservative-leaning elite had lost an election. The US had preferred the Grand National Party's (GNP) candidate, Lee Hoe-chang, who appeared closer to the Bush administration and the policy of 'tailored containment'. Anti-American sentiment grew stronger after the June 2002 killing of two 14-year-old Korean girls by a US armoured vehicle. Public demands for an open trial and changes to the legal status of US forces on ROK soil became major election issues. The Americans handled the PR situation badly, with the military command and the US embassy seen to value the soldiers' lives above those of the girls. Anger rose when the soldiers were acquitted and sent home.

Roh suddenly found that the fact that he had never visited the US was a bonus. Although much of his campaign focused on the need to reform the *chaebols*, he also campaigned for some form of détente and cooperation with Pyongyang, even in excess of the Sunshine Policy, arguing that dialogue and persuasion were the way to get Pyongyang to disarm. Roh's supposed anti-Americanism did not last after the election and he immediately sought to repair and strengthen bilateral relations, notably being photographed in military fatigues with US and ROK forces. The North Korean reaction to Roh's election was swift. They tested a surface-to-ship missile the day before his inauguration and restarted the Yongbyon reactor two days later.

Roh's policy of 'Peace and Prosperity' backed multilateral talks and quickly started to promote trilateral cooperation with Tokyo and Washington. However, just how far Roh can go in promoting dialogue with Pyongyang on a multilateral basis without alienating his own constituency will be down to the so-called Generation 386 – those South Koreans born in the 1960s and now in their late thirties and forties, who are thought to be most opposed to the traditional form of elite politics in South Korea. Roh symbolised the shifting of power to this younger generation, also called Generation 2030, and away from the so-called Generation 4050. Voters under 40 reportedly see engagement with Pyongyang as the only sensible way forward.

The German Example

German reunification is often cited as the potential blueprint for the reunification of Korea. However, the 1997 Asian crisis only reaffirmed the fears in South Korea over reunification that had been growing since German reunification in 1990. To many in Seoul, West Germany had been in much better economic shape and more developed institutionally and politically to cope with reunification than the ROK was.

While Seoul has studied the German example closely, the DPRK's interest in Germany goes back even further. Former GDR leader Erich Honecker was one of Kim Il-sung's closest foreign friends and the two discussed their respective divided countries on a number of occasions. Clearly there are parallels between the GDR and the DPRK: divided countries with the socialist portion losing out economically to the capitalist side; heavily militarised borders; the involvement of the US and USSR on opposing sides of the border; the socialist portion less populous than its capitalist opposite.

Despite the obvious differences, Germany does seem to provide the best case study for any reunification scenario in Korea. While the FDR followed a path of free-market capitalism backed by the largesse of the Marshall Plan, the GDR instituted the Soviet-style command economy and, though aided by the USSR, did not receive the level of subsidy the US was able to offer the FDR. The Berlin Wall became a permanent symbol of the division, much as the DMZ has on the Korean peninsula. Despite their shared heritage and language, West Germans often knew little of ordinary life in the GDR and the citizens of East Germany likewise had no insight into life in the FDR. Cultural and artistic exchanges were few, contact between citizens was limited, broadcasts were blocked, travel was discouraged. Similarly, not many Seoul residents have been to Pyongyang; few North Koreans have visited the ROK. When the Wall fell in 1989, the reaction of many Easterners entering West Germany was one of obvious shock, so total had the blackout been across the border for fifty years. It is safe to assume that most North Koreans arriving in Seoul would be even more amazed by what they saw, given that the lack of information and contact between the two Koreas is even more total than that which existed in the divided Germany.

Although direct contact was limited, West Germans could at least see GDR athletes performing at the Olympics; mail was exchanged between separated families; and there was passage of refugees from East to West. Between the two Koreas, the separation over the last fifty-five years has been virtually total. That families had no knowledge of their Northern or Southern relations was evident in the emotion displayed during the family reunions in the early days of the Sunshine Policy. For most South Koreans their Northern relatives simply disappeared in 1953 and were never heard of again. Additionally, North Korea has no previous experience of any form of social and political system except highly centralised Confucian authority and colonialism. East Germany, of course, had known forms of federalism and democracy.

Although the East German economy stagnated under the command economy, there can be no comparison with the scale of the current North Korean collapse. Shortages were common, but in essence the GDR provided a sustainable standing of living to its residents and developed strong industries in mineral extraction, steel and manufacturing. While the country suffered from the inherent flaws of state planning, it remained an active Comecon member and even managed to be an active exporter of products such as rolled steel and cars.

By the time the Wall fell and the two Germanys reunited, the citizens of the GDR had become acutely aware of their economic pauperism and were increasingly eager for reunification on the terms of a market economy. By the late 1980s any notions of the superiority of the GDR's command economy had been shattered and a growing segment of opinion was in favour of being absorbed into the FDR's free-market system while aware that they would for some time be poor cousins to their Western relatives.

The reunification of Germany became an issue for all of Europe and many other nations, not least the Americans. While the former West Germany was to shoulder the major burden of reunification, there were also massive influxes of cash, aid and advice from international organisations and NGOs to support the effort. The World Bank, the IMF and the specially created European Bank of Reconstruction and Development (EBRD)[17] all became involved. During the period immediately prior to reunification the cost to the former West Germany of absorbing the East was estimated to be DM2–2.5 trillion, while to raise the East to the level of the FDR at the time of reunification was later estimated to require a growth rate of at least 13 per cent. At the time of unification it was estimated that to bring the two Germanys to a position of equality would require real growth rates of 16 per cent per annum in the Eastern portion of the country.[18]

Most Koreans who favour some sort of reunification along German lines – the 'soft landing' approach as opposed to military conflict – concede that the process must be more gradual than that which occurred between the GDR and FDR. Certainly the estimated costs alarm many South Koreans – perhaps as high as US$1 trillion by some estimates.[19]

Additionally, as Park Young-kyu has pointed out, geography will play a part. Half a century of division has led not just to different levels of development but to different rail gauges, electricity grids, cabling systems, and so on. The costs of upgrading infrastructure, including road networks, ports and telecommunications, will be very considerable. Social welfare benefits, far higher in the DPRK than in the former GDR, are another factor.[20] Then there is the question of the DPRK's outstanding debts to Western nations, the former USSR and Japan, which would require either cancellation or their discounted purchase on the international market by South Korea to offset the DPRK's lack of creditworthiness – which would be a costly exercise.

More than a decade after German reunification, problems remain in the country. Although great strides have been made to integrate the East German economy, unemployment is more persistent in the East, as is the pace of deindustrialisation. Fostering an environment conducive to entre-preneurship and new business creation has been problematic. The costs of unification pushed the German economy into the red, as it sought to spend its way out of recession and combat rising inflation in the East. Many of the industries of the East have simply not been able to modernize and compete globally – for instance, East Germany's once proud steel and shipbuilding industries have largely collapsed (indeed much of this business has moved to South Korea).

While living standards have continued to lag behind those of the Western regions, the East has also seen social strife in the form of greater dis-illusionment among youth, and an increase in organised crime, drug taking and suicides. Most alarming, perhaps, has been the resurgence of German nationalism in the East with the reappearance of the neo-Nazi move-ment. There also remains some grassroots support for the old Communist Party. Indeed, the initial sense of 'Germanness' that greeted reunification evaporated relatively quickly as social confusion grew. Knowledge of such experiences causes deep unease in the ROK about just how soft a 'soft landing' would be.

A Less Paranoid Peninsula?

The issue of reunification has been turned on its head by the economic col-lapse of North Korea. Up until the mid-1970s, when the Northern economy was growing faster than in the South, reunification seemed feasible to Pyongyang. It seemed possible to win over a Southern population witness-ing slower growth, lower per capita standards and a military government answering to American command. However, by the 1980s and then after the USSR's collapse the North became unattractive to citizens of an economi-cally powerful ROK. This was itself a shock to the North Koreans, who by and large had believed in state planning and Juche, and increasingly lacked the answers as to why their country was lagging behind and collapsing. This situation was all the more confusing considering that Juche teaching includes a substantial component of Confucianism, which decreed that power should reside with those who govern well and act in a morally superior fashion. Had they not done this? Had Kim not shown the way? As the USSR and the Eastern bloc fell away, as the non-aligned movement fell into inaction, and as China largely ignored North Korea, it must have been perplexing to Juche/Confucian thinking.

The North Koreans also had to deal with the fact of the phenomenal success of South Korea: it had become one of the world's fastest growing and largest economic powers while managing a transition to democracy. Indeed the South was a case study and role model for many developing countries globally, not just the North. The official North Korean answer is that South Korea's growth has come with American aid and massive investment.[21]

The starting point of any reunification of the Korean people must depend on the will of the people involved, although it seems unavoidable that a unified peninsula will look a lot more like South Korea than North. Many in Seoul remain concerned that reunification could have negative implications for the real wages of Southern workers and that the North could drag down the South economically. Others see the infusion of North Korea's younger population as a way to avoid the coming demographic problem in the South – an ageing population, 2 per cent unemployment and over 250,000 foreign workers required already. The North may be able to provide much-needed labour, not just for the reconstruction there but also for low-wage jobs in the South. It could be a new base for locating the manufacture of products such as domestic appliances, work that is now being transferred to China and Southeast Asia.

The American journalist T.R. Reid, commenting on Korea, asked 'How long can an entire country stay angry?'[22] There is still no no rush in the ROK towards reunification. The thinking remains that it is better to wait, and for the North to recover economically. The DPRK has often accused the US of preferring a divided Korea to perpetuate its military presence in the region and influence on Japan. As Brad Glosserman, director of research at the Honolulu-based think-tank Pacific Forum CSIS, warned in 2003, South Koreans should be careful if what they wish for is US withdrawal and dis-engagement from the South's future whilst being unwilling to deal with the problem of reunification with the North.[23] There remains little enthusiasm for reunification in Beijing; Washington remains essentially disengaged from the debate. At the end of the day the simple truth is that no reunification scenario envisages the continuance in power of the KWP or Kim Jong-il. As long as Kim and the KWP are in power, North Korea must remain independent and the peninsula divided.

12

How Will the Story End?

The Predicted Collapse

Predictions of North Korea's collapse have been many and frequent. Most have been fuelled by an ideological dislike of Pyongyang, though also largely hopeful of a 'soft landing'. It is anyone's guess, however, whether the demise of North Korea will be peaceful or violent, gradual or immediate. It should be recalled that predictions of the collapse of the Soviet Union and Eastern Europe were often based more on hope than on reality, and analysts failed to predict the actual nature of the downfall. Many have predicted the collapse of China, but the government remains firmly in control.

Following the USSR's demise, the collapse of the regimes in Eastern Europe, and the end of subsidies, predictions of the DPRK's end grew more confident as the economy slumped, the trade volume halved overnight and the energy crisis became acute. With the collapse in 1989 of the two most isolated regimes of Eastern Europe, Albania and Romania, the DPRK's implosion seemed even more likely. The cases of Albania and Romania provided observers of North Korea with a plausible model, one the Clinton administration certainly came to believe after the 1994 Agreed Framework. Both Albania and Romania were reclusive regimes that deviated from standard Soviet Marxism–Leninism. Neither had engaged in any significant form of reform. Both had strong personality cults; had experienced prolonged periods of industrial, agricultural and financial decline; and had comparatively low levels of engagement with the West. Albania was also a country that pursued a form of military-first policy, with large amounts of expenditure directed to the army which was broad-based and appeared to be in a permanent state of war readiness. Albania and Romania maintained strong police states and monitoring of their citizens' activities. Romania suffered a severe debt crisis engendered by extensive borrowing from the West. Ceausescu was overthrown and executed in December 1989. The Albanian government fell in 1990. Other friendly governments, such as the GDR, collapsed.[1] Yet North Korea has remained to confound the critics. Since the break-up of the Eastern bloc the DPRK has redoubled its efforts to avoid 'contamination' by capitalism. Meanwhile it has accepted massive doses of aid in the form of food, fuel and other essentials, which have allowed the regime to survive.

North Korea is a nation of proud and yet increasingly desperate people that has found itself brought to the point of economic destitution. As Chalmers Johnson has noted, 'The northern leadership still could not help noting that the endgame of the Cold War was particularly dangerous for players on the communist side.'[2] Many had talked of the end of the DPRK when Kim Il-sung finally died, much as commentators today predict Cuban socialism will collapse with Castro's death. Although the regime did not end with Kim's death, many nevertheless predict this outcome when Kim Jong-il is removed or dies. Those who advocate active regime-change strategies certainly believe that removing the head will free the body to reform itself. Yet this may well underestimate the depth to which the party has rooted itself and based its survival on more than simply the supreme leader. The party elite, the military hierarchy, the security services and other pillars of society all have an interest in survival that could transcend their need of Kim Jong-il, or Juche theory.

In considering the possible ways that change may come to the DPRK, several scenarios present themselves, over and above regime change imposed from outside or total economic implosion.

The Mass Exodus Strategy

One defector from the DPRK joked with this author that the last person to leave North Korea need not switch off the lights, as there will inevitably be a power cut. The scenario of mass defection is, however, a real one. According to the ROK's Unification Ministry, in 2002 a total of 1,141 DPRK citizens defected to the ROK, up from 583 in 2001, 312 in 2000 and 148 in 1999.

Some activists, such as the human rights campaigner Norbert Vollertsen,[3] have advocated a policy of urging all North Koreans to walk over the border to China in similar fashion to the mass exoduses from East Germany. The Chinese, not surprisingly, disapprove of this mass defection. (For the East

Germans, of course, crossing the Berlin Wall involved simply moving from one area of Germany to another.) The movement of a large contingent of PLA troops, and the installation of high-voltage fences, to reinforce the border areas between China and the DPRK in September 2003, following a spate of cross-border crimes by North Koreans, confirms that this is the case. Additionally, following a lull in repatriations, Beijing began sending back a hundred or so DPRK defectors weekly from detention centres in China. Mass migration across the DMZ between the two Koreas is not seriously contemplated.

In late 2002 and through 2003 it was reported that rates of defection to China had slowed overall, notwithstanding high-profile defections through the occupation of foreign embassies and consulates in Beijing, Shanghai and Shenyang. The reasons for this decrease are multiple. The work of the NGOs and better climatic conditions have meant that the famine has receded in some parts of North Korea. Economic reforms have increasingly legitimated the black market allowing for greater purchasing of goods and a slight monetisation of the economy. The hardening of government attitudes towards the families of those leaving may also be a factor. However, such benefits are unquantifiable and likely to be only temporary. Despite the additional security on the PRC border there are reports of people paying up to US$3,000 to be smuggled out via lower-profile routes such as through Mongolia or Vietnam.[4] The low-intensity steady exodus is likely to continue.

Being a healthy person able to walk over the border is one thing; losing contact with family and friends who will be punished and then placed out of reach or imprisoned is quite another. The recent relative easing of border restrictions contrasts with the late 1990s, when China reportedly rounded up refugees for repatriation back to the DPRK, and North Korean border guards were given orders to shoot to kill anyone trying to cross into China.[5]

While campaigners against Pyongyang, such as Vollertsen and some members of the US Congress, argue that mass defections will bring the regime down, there is also the view that a more porous border could be used by the regime to stimulate the nascent market in the DPRK, ease shortages and bring additional hard currency into the country. This scenario would require Pyongyang effectively to turn a blind eye to regular crisscrossing of the border. A similar situation has been used in other countries to alleviate shortages and mismatches in the market. For instance, thousands of so-called 'ants' regularly move between the Ukraine, the Russian enclave of Kaliningrad and Poland carrying alcohol, cigarettes and other goods. Although this vibrant trade in black-market goods has deprived Warsaw of tax revenues, it has provided a survival mechanism against total pauperisation for many Russians and Ukrainians. The scenario whereby North Korean citizen-entrepreneurs could cross into China or Russia, to buy goods and return to the DPRK to sell them at farmers' markets, could ease some shortages and free up reserves of local and hard currency in the DPRK while stimulating a little business in China's hard-pressed northeast or Russia's poverty-stricken far eastern extremes.

In 2003 the mass exodus strategy was gaining support from certain members of the US Congress. Their logic is relatively simple: if the US and other countries were openly to accept North Korean defectors, then this would encourage more. This strategy requires the support of China, the major point of transit, which already has an estimated 100,000–300,000 refugees living illegally in its northeastern region. The move to spur greater defections was advanced by Senator Sam Brownback (Republican, Kansas), chair of the Senate Foreign Relations Asia Subcommittee, who championed a revision in US immigration law that formerly made it difficult for DPRK refugees to gain legal status in the US. Previously, American law considered any North Korean refugee to be effectively a South Korean citizen. Brownback's efforts were supported by a coalition of thirty-five, mainly conservative, religious groups in the US who have formed the North Korea Freedom Coalition to lobby for easier access for DPRK refugees to America. Michael Horowitz, one of the organisers of the coalition, has stated that the group 'seeks the implosion of the regime without a shot being fired'.[6]

The senators' mass resettlement programme is problematic in a number of ways, however. Not the least of these is how unpopular it might be with many voters, and with others such as the new Department of Homeland Security, who see parallels with previous mass exoduses from Cuba and Vietnam. Kim Jong-il could, as Castro did, offload his criminals, sick, insane and destitute as well as a sprinkling of agents. However, the crucial factor is the Chinese attitude to such a programme of exodus. China retains a treaty with the DPRK, requiring defectors and refugees apprehended in China to be sent back to North Korea. The ability of North Koreans to get into third-country embassies in China has allowed Beijing effectively to save face and get out of this clause, but it remains problematic. China has no wish to become a transit country in the way that Hungary did for East Germans or Hong Kong did for Vietnam's Boat People, problems that took decades to resolve and added to social strains in the host countries. Additionally, many North Koreans wish to stay in China, largely around the ethnic-Korean region of Jilin province, rather than move on to the US or South Korea.

Whether or not China likes the continued flow of refugees, it seems likely that it will continue. In the eventuality that renewed crop failure should coincide with further economic collapse, causing famine to return, then this trickle may well turn into a flood.

Blowing Down a Paper Tiger

It is clear that any mass exodus from the DPRK will be largely driven by hunger and desperation. Should this occur we will have the answer to one of the most vexing questions regarding North Korea: what percentage of the population actually believes in Juche? In the words of Pyongyang-watcher Aidan Foster-Carter, 'Is North Korea George Orwell's *1984*, or is it Aldous Huxley's *Brave New World*?'[7]

The experience of the last fifteen years, the collapse of the USSR and the Eastern bloc, provides some guidance. Although these regimes were perceived as repressive, there appears to have been more political space for dissent than there is in North Korea today. The USSR had a tradition of intellectual dissent with its refuseniks and samizdat, a movement that snowballed during glasnost and the Afghan intervention, when public disaffection became increasingly vocal. From the mid-1970s onwards, cynicism became increasingly commonplace across the USSR and Eastern Europe. After the collapse of the European socialist bloc it became clear through the testimonies of numerous former apparatchiks that Orwell's concept of 'doublethink' in *1984* was extremely close to the mark in describing the mindset that existed in the bloc's nomenklatura elite.

However, while it is possible to comprehend elite doublethink and the willingness to accept the discrepancy between actual living conditions and the propaganda, on the grounds that there is something to gain from preservation of the status quo, these comprise at most 5 per cent of the North Korean population.[8] For the country to suffer mass exodus this doublethink would have to extend to a much more significant proportion of the population. Even as the rate of defections from the DPRK has grown (the ROK embassy in Beijing was closed in autumn 2003 due to the number of refugees turning up seeking asylum), the numbers of people fleeing North Korea remains low compared to the scale of those leaving the USSR and the countries of the Eastern bloc. It can be argued that the need for the KWP and the media in North Korea constantly to launch Juche reinforcement campaigns is itself a sign that the regime is concerned about social dissent and disillusionment. Clearly the 'spontaneous' demonstrations against US imperialism are not entirely voluntary.

However, it does appear from defector testimonies that there is a strong attachment to socialist principles and nationalism on the part of many who manage to leave. This was also true of Soviet and Eastern European defectors and of many overseas Chinese too, however politically incorrect it may be for them to voice these beliefs in their new host societies. Nevertheless, a survey of refugees found that 20 per cent blamed the famine on climatic conditions, while 45 per cent blamed the government, Kim Jong-il and the bureaucracy for the lack of political and economic reform.[9] The stark evidence of economic collapse around the time of the succession from Kim Il-sung to Kim Jong-il is clearly a connection many ordinary North Koreans appear to have made.

Belief in traditional land rights and ownership patterns seems to have been retained regardless of collectivisation. Although the imperative of hunger is a complicating factor, rural dwellers appear to have worked more conscientiously and with more dedication on their private plots than on the collective farms, indicating that the impulse to care for one's self and family still takes precedence over serving the 'national family under Kim Jong-il'.

The major difference between the USSR, the Eastern bloc and North Korea is that restriction of access to news and information about the outside world − potential 'spiritual pollution' − has been far more successful in the DPRK than in any other communist country. Comparisons between life in the DPRK and outside are rarely made, there are few ways for citizens to evaluate rumours of life abroad, and for the majority of the population there is no widely understood social system outside North Korea to contrast with their own existence. As Oh and Hassig put it, 'If the North Korean people do not believe what they are told, they have nothing else to believe.'[10]

Thus the potential for political debate or alternative conceptualisations is limited under the present regime. Nevertheless, political debate emerged vigorously and quickly in the former USSR and Eastern Europe. Revolutions and political change invariably involve a failing on the part of the ruling party to govern effectively and for the population to cease to believe in them and to seek alternatives. While the KWP's inadequacies are legion, the search for alternatives is problematic. Other states have managed to survive these issues, not least China, which emerged from the disasters of the Great Leap Forward and the Cultural Revolution, through Tiananmen Square to some form of economic liberalisation and global engagement. In China the Party delivered an improvement in living standards for a sizeable proportion of the population and liberalised society to a degree. It was able to maintain the line that success was due to Party policy and that without the Party the country would be vulnerable to Soviet-style collapse, Islamic fundamentalism, flooding and SARS. Reform in North Korea is presented by the party-state as designed to improve the gains of the revolution, not to overturn them as happened in the USSR and Eastern Europe.

If belief in Juche has faltered at all, it did so with Kim Il-sung's death. Kim was undoubtedly revered and respected by the majority of North Koreans; most of the tearful outpourings witnessed at his death were genuine. It is questionable, though, whether this reverence has been wholeheartedly transferred to Kim Jong-il. Defector testimonies invariably retain an admiration for the Great Leader and an undisguised loathing of the Dear Leader. Kim Jong-il lacks the credentials to be Father of the Nation that Kim Il-sung posssessed, despite all the Confucian notions regarding father–son relations. Kim Il-sung died before the worst effects of the planned economy had made themselves felt in the famine. This is now perceived to be Kim Jong-il's legacy, despite the fact that the groundwork for the failings was in place when he was just a teenager. Andrew Natsios recalls a conversation with Doug Coutts, a WFP director in Pyongyang in 1998, where Coutts argued that the role of the NGOs as aid donors in the country was a visible manifestation of the failings of Juche.[11] It should have been evident to North Koreans, not least the elite, that their Juche-inspired economic and agricultural policies had consistently failed them.

Despite the constant exhortations to advance the cause of socialism and Juche, the proclamations that the economy is about to turn the corner to prosperity and that the DPRK is perceived as a great nation internationally, the reality is that most people in North Korea are concentrating on survival. Indeed, many defectors note that with famine and shortages rampant the harsh struggle of daily life means that there is simply no energy left for organised dissent. That an increasing number are seeing their survival in terms of exiting the country is apparent from defector numbers. For each person who defects, many more must be planning and weighing up their options. The question is, when will the trickle become a flood, in the way that it did through the Berlin Wall, or across the Florida Straits? These episodes, though, were arguably less political than opportunist. The Wall was falling, so people walked through it; Havana appeared to make no moves to prevent people leaving Cuba, so they did. A mass exodus and a rejection of Juche may occur if Pyongyang decides it no longer cares, or if it prefers to let any potential dissenters go rather than risk an organised internal opposition. At present, with internal dissent seemingly non-existent, this last scenario seems unlikely. Those who go are more likely to be driven by extreme desperation than by politics. This lack of obvious opportunity may also reveal that the average North Korean has largely retreated into his or her own private space, working just to get by, and politically uninterested due to the lack of options or the means to realize them. If this is the case, then a mass exodus is less likely. However, as the events of the late 1980s and 1990s in the USSR and Eastern Europe showed, change can come surprisingly rapidly.

For those who remain, the question of their level of belief in the system persists. No North Korean has known political freedom: the half-century of the DPRK were preceded by periods of war and Japanese colonialism. Also Korea's traditional Confucianism confirms the notion of people having a proper station in life and submitting to the will of superiors. Such notions have been woven into Juche and exist in an atmosphere where political debate is presently impossible.

Should the party-state collapse, any new ruling elite will surely propose a fresh doctrine in the interests of the nation (or the newly unified portion of the nation). In this scenario it is likely that Juche will be thrown out in order to 'save' the North in the same fashion that Marxism–Leninism was discarded to save Russia, and that Confucian notions of monarchy were rejected to save China in 1911. The fact remains, though, that while in other repressive socialist societies there were possible alternatives to communism, such as the Catholic Church and Solidarity in Poland, North Korea apparently lacks a rallying focus other than opposition to a failed regime. This may be enough, as largely it was in the USSR. The same equation exists in China, where no other tradition except heavy-handed authoritarianism exists.

Military Takeover

For a country with a military-first policy and a massive standing army, the possibilities of government takeover by the military – in effect, an internal regime change – must be considered highly probable. Though Kim Jong-il may technically be leader of the military, he is not essentially *of* the military, not having been a serving officer and lacking combat experience, while the government, though neither elected nor democratic, remains technically civilian. Kim Il-sung could legitimately claim a military heritage as a guerrilla leader. For Kim Jong-il this claim is harder, and his expanding role as Supreme Commander may be increasingly questioned among the military hierarchy.

Regime change by the military has long been considered a possibility. The paucity of information emerging from North Korea and the secrecy that surrounds the political and military elite make verification of any antagonisms between Kim and the military difficult. In the late 1980s when the ageing Kim Il-sung announced that the succession would go to Kim Jong-il there was apparently resistance to the idea from some in the military hierarchy. The dispute was seemingly resolved, though, as the USSR's collapse and the ailing economy at home, and then the onset of famine, required a show of unity among the leadership to maintain political legitimacy and ensure the regime's survival in a suddenly much changed world.

Nevertheless, rumours of attempted military coups, and subsequent crackdowns, have emerged over the years. The 1950s and 1960s saw show trials of senior military personnel, when Kim Il-sung purged political rivals. In the late 1960s Chinese Red Guards claimed that Kim had been arrested by KPA generals. A further purge of the military hierarchy reportedly followed. And around 1970 senior KPA commanders were again purged for opposing Kim's 'people's military strategy'. There have long been rumours of a coup attempt in 1992 by Soviet-trained KPA officers, and of a planned coup by army units in the famine-stricken northeast in 1995. In 1998 a shoot-out between police and soldiers, which led to a curfew in Pyongyang, was taken to have been a direct challenge to Kim Jong-il's rule.[12]

The KPA, like many armies in Asia, has its origins in anti-colonial struggle. There is a tendency for the military leadership to become politicised, as they necessarily become involved in nation-building. This has been as true in South Korea, with its legacy of military leaders, and in Indonesia, the Philippines, Taiwan and Thailand, as it has in North Korea. Perhaps the major difference between the situation in North Korea and that in China and other Asian countries is that, due to the rigidity of the Pyongyang regime, the military has not had the opportunity to become involved in business activities to the same extent.

However, this can make events such as the establishment of foreign NGO operations, economic reforms and the de facto secession of territory that was the Sinuiju project all the more important to the military; in such cases the army identifies itself closely with the fate of the nation. In a country where nationalism and national survival are basic tenets of the party-state's legitimacy, issues of nation, independence and the respect of the international community assume particular importance. If Kim is seen to be seriously threatening such important principles, the risk of a military coup is heightened. Furthermore, should the rhetoric about military-first and the primary position of the army in national life turn out to be meaningless, and if due to economic collapse the military finds itself starved of resources and its soldiers hungry and demotivated, then the risk is again heightened that the military could step in to settle matters in its own favour.[13]

As economic collapse and shortages have wreaked their damage, so the military has assumed increasing importance in the struggle for regime survival, even though its influence on policy remains nominally under the direct control of Kim and the KWP. The military in many ways guarantees the nation, and the KWP's survival, by remaining strong during a time of national crisis. It even enhances its strength through the acquisition of missiles, nuclear capability and WMDs, which link the rest of the region and the US to the survival of the regime. At the same time, much of the declining economic activity is either in the service of or supported by the military in terms of manpower, construction capacity, transport and logistics.

Further collapse carries the very real risk that the situation will become irretrievable. The military may decide that its role is to safeguard the nation and push Kim Jong-il aside. Older military leaders may well feel that the politicians have consistently undervalued them, notwithstanding the military-first rhetoric. Politically motivated covert military operations have often seemingly bypassed the KPA command structure. Commando operations against South Korea, the Special Forces mission to assassinate ROK leaders in Seoul in 1968, and in Myanmar in 1983, are cases in point. Following such operations the North Korean armed forces have been placed on alert. Many analysts conclude that the military hierarchy had simply not been informed of these potentially regime-threatening operations, any one of which could have resulted in war.

While some argue that the internal situation and Kim's alienation of the military hierarchy through projects such as Sinuiju or by attracting international ire will cause the military to revolt, others disagree. Hwang Jang-yop believes that Kim's control of the military hierarchy currently remains secure, but that as the structure begins 'trembling' through continued shortages and lack of resources, lower ranks in the military could rise up. At the point when ordinary soldiers cease to have confidence in the leadership, then the whole military-led structure could collapse.[14]

In a military coup scenario it is envisaged that Kim could go but the KWP remain in control, though without the *Suryong*. This would mean the continuation of one-party rule. There would be no elections, political pluralism or free press. Thus the military may turn against Kim but the army's hyper-nationalism would ensure that it sought to preserve the DPRK's existence. The question though is, should they take power, would they be able to present solutions to the economic malaise?

Will the Next Kim Step Forward?

Another possibility is that change in the elite will come with a member of the ruling clique deciding that the Dear Leader should step down. As the Sinologist Ross Terrill has noted, 'In truth, legitimacy and succession must always be time bombs in a dictatorship.'[15] Although relationships within the Pyongyang elite are beyond scrutiny, it is clear that Kim Jong-il has been grooming his sons for possible leadership positions and eventual succession. It is obviously the case that with another Kim family member at the helm continuity would be achieved. It is reckoned, however, that Kim III would be kept under closer control by the elite and the military hierarchy in terms of policy.

For many years the likely candidate seemed to be Kim Jong-nam, Kim Jong-il's eldest son (now about 32), however his 2001 arrest in Japan with a substantial quantity of dollars and a fake Dominican passport severely eroded his credibility. Many now believe that the successor will be Kim's other acknowledged son, Kim Jong-chul (now around 22), who has so far avoided scandal and works within the regime.

Since August 2002 there has been a campaign in the DPRK to elevate the position of Koh Young-hee, Kim Jong-chul's mother; this has been accompanied by a study, 'The Respected Mother is the Most Faithful and Loyal Subject to the Dear Leader Comrade Supreme Commander'. The former ROK unification minister Kang In-duk has stated that 'It's the first material verifying that the military has decided upon Kim's heir apparent.' Ku Bon-tae, a former unification policy director at Seoul's Ministry of Unification comments:

> Through the material the armed forces declare an end to an eight-year-long power struggle involving the dynastic heirs, waged since the death of Kim Il-sung. The military leadership that has upheld Kim Jong-chul as heir apparent has apparently defeated the KWP executives who pushed Kim Jong-nam as heir apparent.[16]

Whatever the truth regarding Kim Jong-chul, the ongoing speculation indicates that the military values the role of balance, continuity and precedent in the leadership.

Although the relationship between either of the Kim sons and the military hierarchy is unknown, it is probable that any military decision to remove Kim Jong-il would involve replacing him with one of his sons or another relative. For many years it was rumoured that the army favoured Kim Jong-il's half-brother, Kim Pyong-il, who as well as supposedly closely resembling Kim Il-sung has been an ambassador to various East European countries, speaks English fluently and spent time in the military.

In the event that Kim Jong-il is deposed, the international community may believe that a sea change has taken place. A new Kim, for example, may be willing to sacrifice nuclear weapons while instituting broader economic reforms in return for aid, loans and recognition. Internally a new Kim would maintain the Mandate of Heaven and ensure some form of continuity domestically that would reduce the possibility of internal dissent against the regime. However, this scenario would also involve the supply of long-term aid as clearly any meaningful economic restructuring will require a lengthy period of perilous perestroika, as seen in China and Russia.

Many in the elite are increasingly internationalist in outlook and have a greater understanding of both the image of the DPRK in the world and the havoc wreaked upon the country by KWP rule. This group could, in the current climate of collapse, move from a politics-first to an economics-first viewpoint. This elite includes people who have knowledge of South Korean society, are aware of China's reforms and have access to the foreign press and publications through the *Chamgo Tongsin* (Reference News), a government publication for the elite that collates international news. However, the leadership is wary of this elite's privileged access, and consequently surveillance of them is even more rigorous than that of the masses.

It is known that Kim fears plots against him. Such fears have been around since Kim Il-sung's time, after President Park's assassination brought home the reality of political assassination on the peninsula. In an interview with the South Korean news agency Yonhap, Lee Young-kook, one of Kim's former bodyguards who later defected, claimed that Kim fears a Ceausescu-type situation and is increasingly concerned about his personal safety. Kim is accompanied by a team of bodyguards at all times, who are reportedly never from the same family and are not allowed to contact relatives during their service. Kim's car is always accompanied by four other identical sedans in the same motorcade, making it difficult for anyone to attempt an assassination.[17]

Any new Kim would obviously need support among the DPRK's elite. This would mean building alliances within the military hierarchy. More importantly it would entail gaining support among the state security apparatus, which is closely identified with the current leadership and arguably has the most to lose from any regime change. In many totalitarian countries it has been the security services that have held out longest in attempting to prop up a failed regime.[18]

It is possible that the risks of a coup failing may be too great for the elite. It is more likely that those sections of the elite that are now disillusioned and realise the extent of the country's isolation are starting to feather their own nests and prepare their exit strategies. This process appears to have started already, signs of which are the growth and extension of the black market, and the selling of assets, including machinery and scrap, by some SOEs, largely to Chinese interests, though it is not clear what is happening to the proceeds of these sales. Likewise, it is unclear who benefits from the illegal funds that continue to be generated by Division 39.

There is a tradition of rivalry for the leader's job despite the Confucian rules. Kim Jong-il was by no means the favoured candidate of all in the DPRK elite. Despite being the eldest son, he initially faced competition from his stepbrother Kim Pyong-il, and his uncle Kim Yong-ju. Any Kim III would be obliged to create a new personality cult to fill the vacuum; such a cult having been a central pillar of the regime from its foundation. The transition may be far from smooth, with no clear front-runner.

The Poisoned Carrot

Much has been written about the relationship between aid donations and political policy. Certainly during the Clinton administration the US used aid in an attempt to leverage concessions from Pyongyang, the so-called 'food for talks' or 'carrot and stick' strategy. Marcus Noland gives nine examples between 1995 and 2000 of America extracting concessions in return for continued aid. Andrew Natsios of USAID has provided a recent example: in 2003 America promised to provide 40,000 tonnes of grain to the DPRK in return for talks on the nuclear issue.[19]

The Japanese and the South Koreans have both used aid in the past (including under-the-table payments) to try to stimulate diplomatic dialogue with Pyongyang, and continue to do so. Beijing reportedly switched off oil supplies from China to Pyongyang in an attempt to force multilateral six-way talks on the nuclear issue. These were eventually held in Beijing in 2003. Japan ceased aid in 2002 after the Kim–Koizumi summit and the revelations of North Korean kidnapping of Japanese citizens that outraged Japanese public opinion.

It is possible that as the economic situation worsens and the possibility of famine returns, elements within the DPRK leadership either supporting Kim Jong-il or seeking to replace him could be brought in to discuss the nuclear issue seriously and to enact meaningful economic reforms through the leverage that aid donations provide. On the other hand, Hwang Jang-yop has argued that foreign aid helps Kim retain the loyalty of the military and the elite and this is why he is so concerned about successfully bargaining his nuclear capability for continued aid.

In Pyongyang, the linking of aid to reform is seen as effectively imposing sanctions on the DPRK. The head of the North's Flood Damage Rehabilitation Committee, Yun Su-chang, has declared that using aid to extract concessions is a flagrant violation of humanitarian principles. However, few countries take advice on humanitarian principles from Pyongyang. As the largest donor, the US would be accused of imposing sanctions to strangle the regime, a strategy that the Pentagon has dubbed 'Cuba lite' a lesser version of the US blockade imposed on Cuba during the 1962 missile crisis. Pyongyang has repeatedly stated that economic sanctions would equal war. In 2002, *KCNA* denounced the seizure of a shipload of DPRK-made SCUD missiles bound for Yemen, calling it

> part of the US-tailored containment strategy against the DPRK. The strategy means total economic sanctions aimed at isolating and stifling the DPRK. Sanctions mean a war and the war knows no mercy. The US should opt for

dialogue with the DPRK, not for war, clearly aware that it will have to pay a very high price for such reckless acts.[20]

Although rigorously imposed sanctions in the form of a blockade have not occurred, many in the American administration have been critical of aid donations. These include US secretary of defense Donald Rumsfeld, who suggested that money and goods sent by Japan, the ROK and the PRC were helping to sustain the DPRK's dictatorship.[21] To be effective, though, sanctions, or the use of aid to force change, would have to involve China.

One option is for the US to help the DPRK with it energy crisis. James Kelly suggested this in January 2003 as a possible way out of the impasse between the two sides. Under the 1994 Agreed Framework the US is supposed to ship to the North 500,000 tonnes of fuel oil annually. However, this arrangement was halted in late 2002 as the nuclear crisis escalated, with the result that the North's energy shortage has deepened further. The DPRK has subsequently become increasingly reliant on Chinese oil. In 2002 alone China shipped 472,167 tonnes of crude oil to the DPRK, and the figure is growing annually. Trade between China and the DPRK works both ways: North Korea's trade with China rose 16 per cent in the first six months of 2003 to US$378 million. DPRK exports to China have increased 4 per cent year on year to US$108 million, while imports from the PRC have grown by 22 per cent to US$270 million.[22]

It seems unlikely that a direct deal involving aid in return for change will occur. However, more than one analyst has suggested that there may be forces within the regime, increasingly antagonistic to Kim and believing that his strategy will lead only to collapse, who might seek to oust him. It is more likely that continued aid will serve as a form of containment to prevent total collapse and the threat that poses to East Asia. Washington is left with the prospect of financially supporting a regime it clearly finds repugnant – something it probably would not consider doing if North Korea had only limited military reach. For NGOs the fear is that the humanitarian effort will be linked to some form of military action – what novelist Julian Barnes has called 'the humanitarian attack on Pyongyang'.[23]

Certainly North Korea, particularly the army, remains wary of the destabilising effect of aid and its ability to introduce new ideas into the country. The need to appeal to the international community has long been an uncomfortable truth, given the stated superiority of Juche, and has represented a loss of face for Pyongyang. Consequently the party-state has operated a double-edged policy, described by L. Gordon Flake in his study of the experience of American NGOs in the DPRK as 'reaching out with an open hand, while wrapping itself up to protect its people from external influence', which for Pyongyang means interfering NGO workers and journalists.[24] Although the North has talked of aid as a 'poisoned carrot', it has nevertheless created a significant link between the North and South. According to Chung Ok-nim, an adviser to the Seoul government, 'From 1995 until 2001, assistance to the North totalled more than US$1.6 billion. Of that amount US$591.96 million was donated by South Korea – US$430.05 million from the government and US$161.91 from NGOs.'[25]

Aid, however, can be destabilising. It can raise political consciousness by challenging government-generated stereotypes of Western nations, and can undermine support for the government by starkly revealing its inability to provide for the people. Aid is leverage, notwithstanding the North Korean disdain for it. Though the government may object to aid and its suppliers, it is now an integral part of the economy and vital to the regime's survival. Aid may well be the rest of the world's key bargaining chip with Pyongyang.

The End Remains Elusive

Consider the following statement:

> Not only did the movement fail to achieve the exhilarating aims it had set itself, but the entire economy was plunged into chaos when the construction effort met paralysis and breakdown. Natural catastrophes followed, to complete the disaster. The population, already exhausted by the frenzied and fruitless efforts enforced upon it, began to experience the miseries of famine. The credit and prestige that the party had gained suffered irreparable damage, and the regime's authority was directly threatened by the discontent and despair of the masses.[26]

This could be North Korea today, though it actually describes the Great Leap Forward in China, in the words of Sinologist Simon Leys. Eventually in China, it will be recalled, Mao reasserted his authority through the Cultural Revolution, an even more disastrous policy for the people.

One of the main reasons the DPRK continues to survive, despite economic collapse and famine, is that the US has not taken concerted action against it. There have been warnings and low-level boycotts, but nothing that compares to the US boycott against Cuba. Unlike Cuba, which is a constant political topic in the US, North Korea has remained stubbornly off the mainstream political agenda, despite the efforts of some congressman and the DPRK's inclusion in Bush's infamous 'Axis of Evil' speech. North Korea has simply not managed to excite US public opinion the way that Iraq, and to a lesser extent Iran, have. And there are no major lobby groups to push the issue. Korea is, to quote Don Oberdorfer, an 'afterthought' for US foreign policy.

13

Conclusion:
The World's Most Dangerous Tripwire

Survival and Change

The DPRK is clearly an anachronism in the modern world, adhering rigidly to principles that its former allies have either jettisoned or sought to reform. The continued espousal of Marxist–Leninist economic philosophy in a world where the USSR and the Eastern bloc have ceased to exist and China has moved towards a marketised system leaves North Korea in a small coterie of economies. As Joe Studwell has commented, 'The only countries other than China which officially subscribed to Marxist–Leninist economic theory by 1992 were Cuba, Vietnam and North Korea. It was not an enviable club of which to be a member.'[1] *The Economist* cover of June 2000 featuring a picture of Kim Jong-il with the caption 'Greetings Earthlings'[2] summed up most people's attitude towards the DPRK and the way it engages the international community.

The command economy has collapsed in terms of output, though the continuing dominance of Juche and *songun* thinking prevents the government admitting it. Aid is providing a drip-feed to the regime. Maintaining this flow of aid has become an integral part of the DPRK's economy and food supply, much as the economic involvement of the military and prison labour reinforce what is left of the command system. Nuclear weapons are developed as a bargaining chip, a way for Pyongyang to gain a seat at the table and force engagement. The continued existence of the KWP party-state is at stake. As Hwang Jang-yop has observed 'Given the choice between regime survival and national prosperity, it's pretty clear which he [Kim Jong-il] would prefer.'

North Korea has been in economic decline since the mid-1970s, during which time it has become increasingly inward looking and has practised an often bizarre version of international diplomacy. The result has been Pyongyang's version of the Needham Paradox.[3] British Sinologist Joseph Needham noted the paradox that, while imperial China had many talented people and was advanced in science, the country declined around the middle of the last millennium. According to Needham, the primary reason for China's decline was that the country suppressed technicians, economic change and the merchant class, who all posed a threat to the emperor. Similarly, since the mid-1970s the DPRK has suppressed innovation, to preserve a political system with no significant entrepreneurial or business class. Consequently technology adoption, legal reform, a modern financial and accounting system, industrial management techniques and world trade have all largely passed North Korea by.

Despite shortages, famine, low industrial and agricultural production, the lack of consumer goods and inflation, a sizeable opposition advocating social and political reform is yet to emerge. Conditions should be ripe for such a movement, despite the state's heavy repression. While in other countries political dissatisfaction combined with nationalism and growing cynicism channelled itself into new movements, such as Poland's Solidarity, in the DPRK no such movement has emerged and instead alienation manifests itself in the form of low productivity, worker alienation, desperate migration strategies and reliance on survival mechanisms such as private plots and the black market. North Korea has not been without dissent, both overt – food riots in Hamhung and Sinuiju, prison riots, suspected coup attempts in 1970, 1992, 1995 and 1998 – and covert – including political satire and listening to short-wave radio – though this has tended to be driven underground or easily contained by security forces. No overt protest has been known to have effected any change other than an increase in repression, executions and the imposition of martial law.

It has been argued that the lack of a revolutionary tradition on the Korean peninsula has meant that North Korean citizens are somehow more passive than people in other countries and also that the effectiveness of the state's security apparatus is more pronounced. Both these aspects are true, though in the past Koreans both sides of the border have shown themselves willing to protest, fight and revolt against what they consider to be wrong. It is also a fact that security forces can only operate with a degree of compliance from the mass of the population. When such compliance ends, the state invariably crumbles rapidly, as has happened even in countries with relatively repressive regimes, such as Albania or Romania, where eventually the people decided that the emperor did indeed have no clothes. Nevertheless, North Koreans so far appear to have preferred to adapt to the prevailing conditions, even though their severity would indicate the likelihood of widespread protest.

The answer to the passivity of the masses appears to lie in the DPRK's history, commitment to self-reliance and refusal to buckle under Soviet or Chinese attempts to dominate the peninsula. The creation of the DPRK from the ashes of the Korean War, and with seemingly hostile forces positioned south of the 38th parallel, led to the extension of the guerrilla tradition to a form of warrior communism. The act of rebuilding the country, its economic base, agricultural capacity and social system, was itself an act of defiance and a formidable declaration of independence. From the start the population was asked to sacrifice economic growth and access to services and goods in the name of national independence and self-reliance. Industrialisation and collectivisation were both political and economic goals. Seen through the prism of the potentially fratricidal Sino–Soviet dispute, with enemies at the gate in the ROK and the Cold War atmosphere, together with the Confucian heritage of the peninsula and its traditional isolation, the fact that ordinary people sacrificed rather than protested becomes understandable, whatever the failings of the country's leaders. The history and tradition of the peninsula have been about balancing the demands of powerful neighbours with the need to assert independence. During China's Sui dynasty, Emperor Yang Di described the Koreans as 'little freaks' (*xiao chou*) and 'vicious' when they failed to defer sufficiently and pay tribute to his court.

The real tipping point for the DPRK may occur if famine returns. Releasing pent-up demand through the informal economy of farmers' markets, private plots and the black market may ensure the system's survival but it would be placed under immense strain. Any political and economic retrenchment to more direct social control and a clampdown on the emergent informal economy would deprive a vast number of people of their fragile support networks, forcing them to look to other alternatives to ensure survival. Similarly, the growth of an economy that increasingly demanded bribes or the use of foreign currency to function would polarise society still further. The accelerating growth of asset stripping, bribery and the black market appear to be a consequence of the recent reforms. If they are allowed to continue unchecked, a more obvious society of haves and have nots will be created, with an unbridgeable access gap. This could lead to the rise of that particularly unpleasant class of corrupt entrepreneurs that has been seen in other countries – such as the Russian 'biznessmen' or Mobuto's crony *grand legumes* (big vegetables), who pillage the nation's resources to amass personal fortunes then leave the country. Reports of bribery are on the increase from housing allocation to being allowed across the border into China. As Peter Hayes, director of the Nautilus Institute, has observed, 'These guys [North

Korean officials] want to become billionaires selling real estate in the DMZ. They don't want a war."[4] In consequence the privileged status of the elite is likely to be laid bare as opportunities for profiteering become pronounced. Already North Korea is far from being a socialist economic system. The government is abandoning a greater percentage of the population to their own resources and forcing them to turn to the hidden and informal market economy to survive. The rule of law is absent and increasingly only money, access and power count.

Yet such developments may not in themselves force change. Countries from Colombia to Zaire have managed to continue functioning with endemic corruption, asset stripping and economic anarchy as the norm. However, the final consequence will be that the NKW will become increasingly worthless. With most ordinary people unable to gain access to alternative currencies, support networks will be further eroded for many. Meanwhile the elite will maintain access to their own survival system, which encompasses the PDS. This will continue to award them above-average rations; allow them access to foreign business and investment contacts, with which they can extort bribes and raise foreign currency; maintain their senior management positions in SOEs, allowing them to asset-strip; and foreign travel that allows them to acquire goods and currency overseas as well as move their assets out of the country. With remittances from Japan and the ROK falling, and aid levels declining, the support network for ordinary people has already been stretched to breaking point.

In a country that has already suffered a devastating and prolonged famine, many of the options that could be used have already been used up: many families have already sold their valuables and heirlooms, cultivated their private plots to the maximum, cleared most available common land for additional production, and increasingly sold off movable assets such as plant, minerals and timber for cash and food.

Other factors may lead to further impoverishment, revealing the system's profound inadequacies. As the years pass so the generational link between town and country erode, with fewer urban people able to call on friends and family in the countryside to help them with food supplies. Clampdowns along the border with China will also adversely affect the inflow of black-market goods, further reducing the availability of consumer goods, clothing and food, as well as opportunities for people to earn hard currency.

Unlike the experiences of the USSR and Eastern Europe, a major factor preventing change in the DPRK is the lack of an alternative rallying point. The sort of debate and democratic heritage that East Germans had known before 1945 do not exist in North Korea, where the heritage is of feudalism and colonialism. Similarly the Church plays effectively no role despite a tradition of Christianity. The KWP's erasing of the North's religious past has been almost total, thereby excluding the renewal of allegiances such as was seen in Poland with the Catholic Church, Russia with the Orthodox Church, and the former Soviet Central Asian Republics with Islam. A nominally oppositionist intelligentsia does not exist within the country comparable to the rallying point provided by figures such as Vaclav Havel in Czechoslovakia or by the influential refugee communities of the Soviet and Eastern European diaspora. Most intellectuals left in the early days of the DPRK and institutions such as the Kim Il-sung University have no tradition of independent thinking.

The party-state in the DPRK has effectively used a sense of hyper-traditionalism and nationalism to portray all dissent as anti-government. This has been a historical constant in the DPRK from the purging of the pro-Moscow and pro-Beijing factions after the country's foundation, through the mistreatment and marginalisation of the Japanese Koreans, to the rigid socio-political classification system that pervades life from cradle to grave and condemns anti-party individuals and groups to discrimination and preju-dice. As refugee testimonies have shown time and again, although there may be dislike of Kim Jong-il, feelings of nationalism invariably remain strong in most people, even though the social classification system is considered unfair as movement between classes is impossible. The fact is that the country still considers itself at war, while rhetoric against the South and the US permeates life, and the heavy emphasis on the Japanese colonial and militarist period maintains a Spartan nationalism of epic proportions, constantly reinforcing the fierce national pride and theatrical victimhood of a country portraying itself as contained, threatened and avenging former national humiliation. The theoretical linking of the party-state to the entire nation's fate makes this nationalism a powerful tool of social manipulation and control. The Party's control of history acts as a principal source of legitimacy for the regime. The shared mythology, reinforced from school age and constantly referred to, eventually becomes part of an individual's consciousness.

The primacy of the armed forces has been a guiding philosophy of the regime from the start; the guerrilla tradition that liberated, defended and established the country has continued to loom large over the national culture. North Korean propaganda constantly refers to external threats; this bolsters the patriotic nationalism, which in turn reinforces the regime. Nuclear weap-ons, WMDs and CBWs are the culmination of this – a 'deterrent' against attack and annihilation; symbols of independence, modernity and success that physically demonstrate the primacy of the military-first line. The links between the military and the wider economy are fundamental. Army generals control many economic concerns; soldiers labour in the fields, mines and on construction sites; for many SOEs the military is their largest, and often only, customer. For the politically ambitious the military is the fast track into the party and state apparatus. Divorcing these two entities after so long is problematic: the dividing line between the military and civilian is blurred.

Lastly, there is the legacy of fifty-five years of a closed society. Unable to see, hear or communicate with the outside world, North Koreans have arrived in the twenty-first century with considerably lower expectations than their peers in Russia, China or Eastern Europe. As people have come increasingly to depend on themselves, their families or their immediate community, so organising or mobilising any significant group is problematic. Families tend their private plots together for their own benefit, people hunt for supplies at the farmers' markets alone, and farm communities guard their own crops against theft from outsiders. Stratification is growing, as are alienation and individual survival strategies as people, particularly the rural and more remote populations, learned in the 1990s that the state could not save them from famine and starvation.

Others have become even more alienated, as is evidenced in the reports of high rates of suicide, stress-related illness, and alcoholism – what Norbert Vollertsen has called the 'burnout syndrome'. We have seen this descent into alienation before. Hillel Ticktin noted that during the particularly stagnant period of Andropov's USSR in the 1980s

> a sclerotic state was unable to adequately feed or clothe its people, life expectancy was falling along with the rouble and tinkerings with the economic system produced little except further impoverishment while the country was caught in the vicious cycle of an arms race with the US. One of the side effects of this degenerating society were rising rates of alcoholism, drug taking and hooliganism.[5]

While recent history may seem to offer strong grounds for rebellion and desire for change, it is not prime organisational territory for nascent opposition groups. As USAID's Andrew Natsios has observed, 'The unwritten and unspoken contract prior to the famine was that the people surrendered their freedom in exchange for which the state agreed to care for them, heavily tempered by political loyalty, from cradle to grave.'[6] This deal has now largely fallen apart. Pyongyang did not keep its side of the bargain.

Risks, Possibilities and Stagnation

In 2003 Kim Jong-il celebrated his sixty-first birthday with the usual display on state television of fireworks and images of an adoring citizenry. Fifty years after the death of Stalin, a form of Stalinism continues to exist in the upper half of the Korean peninsula. The economy is down but not out, thanks to aid supplies and the people's seeming acceptance of their reduced circumstances. The military, though perhaps also now suffering from short-ages and deprivation, was still able to lob a missile into the Sea of Japan on the day South Korea's newly elected president was taking his official oath and being sworn in.

Today, the people of North Korea are among the most desperately poor, hungry and economically deprived on earth. There is a serious danger that the entire society could collapse. If this happens then the consequences for the entire peninsula will be devastating, both for North Korea's impoverished citizens and for South Korea, which would be left to pick up the pieces. The current vogue for 'regime change', first strikes and active anti-proliferation measures featuring 'boots on the ground' strategies would do little other than kill North Koreans and create a humanitarian, financial and political crisis for East Asia – all the sooner as South Korea nurses a fragile economic recovery, Japan remains mired in recession, and China needs all its considerable resources to overcome the hurdles thrown up by its continuing reform.

The relationship and interaction between the DPRK and the US will continue to be crucial. American policy towards the peninsula has almost always been one of reaction and not anticipation, of last-minute compromise between the military and State Department, and rarely subject to deeper consideration. As John Swenson-Wright has noted, the White House still lacks a clear strategy for dealing with Pyongyang.[7] America now finds itself on the horns of a dilemma and at a time of growing involvement globally. American sabre-rattling may have the effect of mobilising support for the regime at home, and give it a legitimacy it may have been losing. Containing North Korea militarily is costly. In 1999 the US Senate voted 97–3 to build a 'national missile defence', essentially against China and North Korea, with Clinton permitting US$10.6 billion to be spent on the system over the next five years. Since 1994 US analysts have spoken of a 'red line', or the trigger-point beyond which the US feels it will have no alternative but to exercise some form of military action against Pyongyang.

Military action against Pyongyang would result in a disaster whatever way it was planned or executed. With Seoul just thirty-seven miles south of the DMZ, it makes no military sense. The South Korean capital city of 10 million people lies within the range of the DPRK's formidable batteries of artillery and missiles. North Korean jets can reach the city within several minutes of takeoff. North Korea certainly has the ability to inflict massive damage on the ROK in any military conflict, but it also knows it would be destroyed if it attacked. The North's porcupine strategy, or Masada complex, is designed to ensure that in any conflict a US victory would be at the highest human cost possible and thus politically unacceptable in Washington. According to Pentagon estimates, a conflict on the peninsula would lead to 52,000 American and 490,000 South Korean casualties within the first ninety days. Former CIA chief James Woolsey has argued that 4,000 daily air strikes over a period of thirty to sixty days would be required to demolish North Korea's nuclear programme as the US believes it exists, and to blunt its capacity to retaliate. Additionally, the Pentagon's public war plan for Korea estimates that the DPRK has 12,000 artillery pieces, including 500 long-range weapons, located largely in close proximity to the DMZ in deep mountain bunkers. This artillery is thought to be capable of firing 'several thousand' shells per hour towards South Korea. Even with improvements in intelligence, weapons technology and missile accuracy, not to mention the Bush administration's declared willingness to use nuclear weapons, any strike is seen as a risky and potentially disastrous operation both militarily and politically.

Engagement, however, carries its own risks. Wendy Sherman, an adviser to Madeleine Albright and a special adviser to Clinton on North Korea, described the dilemma well:

> I have no illusions about Kim ... he is a leader who has left his people with no freedom, no choices, no food, no future. People are executed. There are labor camps. But the decision we have to make is whether to try to deal with him to open the country so that the people of North Korea do have freedom, do have choices, do have food. Do I think it would be preferable to not deal with him? Yes, but the consequences are horrible, so you have to deal with him.[8]

The North Korean leadership is increasingly divorced from reality. Lack of knowledge filtering up to the leadership leads at best to mistakes, and at worst to outright stupidity. Flunkeyism (*sadaejuui*) is identified as the opposite of Juche and is theoretically objected to. However, the reality of the situation in Pyongyang is that by the late 1970s Kim Il-sung was surrounded by a politburo of largely aged, poorly educated, ex-guerrilla generals who showed blind obedience rather than offering advice and alternatives. Kim Jong-il may have seen many of the older generation pass away, he has cultivated an elite that has little interest in letting him know the reality. Kim Jong-il is not the crazy and irrational dictator much of the tabloid press seeks to portray him as; nor is he necessarily the 'the hawk of hawks',[9] yet he may not have a truly rounded grasp of the situation. As one journalist noted, 'The real issue isn't whether Kim is crazy enough to amass a nuclear arsenal but whether he is crazy enough to dispossess himself of his one bargaining chip.'[10]

Time is running out for North Korea. Another crop failure could occur at any time, aid is dwindling, allies are virtually non-existent. Pyongyang lacks the assets that China had when it began its reform process. China had no shortages and was not obliged to rely on foreign aid. It had a wealth of domestic entrepreneurial traditions and resources, as well as the invaluable 'bamboo network' of overseas Chinese capital, know-how and contacts. The DPRK's economic reforms of 2002 did not show us how socialism with North Korean characteristics would look; they simply showed how a government had panicked in the face of a collapsing economy.

Which economics textbooks Kim Jong-il and his planners read we can never know, but it is plausible to suggest that the Chinese economist Chen Yun numbers among them. Chen was an advocate of Soviet-style planning in China in the 1970s, but in the early 1980s moved towards a more modified version of the USSR's blueprint – what Chen called a birdcage economy, where the bird is the economy, the cage is the central plan and the size of the cage is the market:

> One cannot hold a bird tightly in one's hand without killing it. It must be allowed to fly, but only within its cage. Without its cage, it would fly away and become lost. Of course, the cage must be of appropriate dimensions.... That is to say, one may readjust the size of the cage ... but regulation of economic activity by the market must not entail abandonment of the orientation provided by the plan.[11]

This notion seems to be where the economic planners and ideologues of Pyongyang have been heading, with cages like Sinuiju, Rajin-Sonbong, and adjustments to the state pricing mechanism and other limited economic reforms. Chen, like his latter-day colleagues in Pyongyang, retained his faith in the plan and in the subordination of agriculture to industry. He, like Pyongyang, believed that central allocation was preferable to the market as it allowed for control and the eradication of market inefficiencies as well as supplying full employment. Chen's arguments for a slightly modified Soviet system in China didn't win out. Deng Xiaoping, Hu Yaobang and Zhao Ziyang were looking not to Moscow but to Hungary and Yugoslavia, which seemed to offer less rigid forms of socialist economics. Deng, Hu and Zhao also made a simple comparison and asked, who fared better economically? Was it market-driven South Korea, or plan-driven North Korea? Was it market-driven West Germany or plan-driven East Germany? Eventually they looked at economies such as Singapore, Taiwan, South Korea and, of course, the Asian economic giant, Japan.

It is clear that Kim Jong-il knows he needs to do something about his shredded economy. Yet he is not ready to admit, as Deng did in 1984, that 'a little capitalism isn't necessarily harmful'. He is not ready because meaningful steps towards the market require decentralisation and the granting of greater personal freedom. As Philip Bowring has observed, 'the North wants change without regime change.'[12] While the command economy remains dominant, the overall trend, despite possible blips, will be downwards. The official New Year Message from Pyongyang in 2003 stated that the DPRK flag 'is adorned with great victories and no defeats'. This may be the case militarily. The real defeat, though, for the party-state in North Korea, has been the economy.

POSTSCRIPT

Decline, Deadlock and Hope

The Great Game of Show and Tell

The propaganda chiefs in Pyongyang have consistently and repeatedly argued that sanctions against North Korea are tantamount to a declaration of war. They would – for an effective, truly all-encompassing sanctions package supported wholeheartedly by South Korea, China and Russia as well as the USA and the EU is the one thing that could mean the final death of the regime. The DPRK leadership's endgame of regime survival would have failed. However, the world needs to be absolutely clear that the human misery and death, the scale of the resultant humanitarian catastrophe, would be colossal. Most importantly, sanctions would politically isolate any caucus pushing for economic reform that exists in Pyongyang and slam the door firmly shut on change – and room for meaningful change and economic reform does still exist.

The North remains in a parlous state economically – its 2006 national budget was just US$2.9 billion, with an estimated 16 per cent of the total being spent on the country's military (a growth in official military spending of 3.5 per cent over 2005). Of course, officially the North Koreans have claimed that their economy continues to grow – 1.8 per cent in 2003, 2.2 per cent in 2004 and 3.5 per cent in 2005 'officially' – though if changes in consumer prices are taken into account (and notwithstanding the suspect nature of any economic statistics released by Pyongyang), the economy has continued to contract.

While overall the North Korean economy has continued to shrink it should be noted that between the failed economic reforms of 2002 and today North Korea has managed to boost light industrial production and successfully launch the Kaesong Industrial Zone – the most substantial and tangible product of the Sunshine Policy begun under President Kim Dae-jung. When the first edition of this book was published Kaesong was just getting started and it was too early to tell what its future would be. The Zone is a joint development project between Pyongyang and Seoul in the border town of Kaesong, just north of the DMZ. It has not all been plain sailing – the Southern partners, mostly manufacturers, have had to ensure the power supply to the Zone as well as the telecommunications connections. However, it has started producing light industrial goods for sale in the South, and for export – goods made in Kaesong now account for over 20 per cent of the North's exports to the South, according to the Korea International Trade Association and the ROK's Unification Ministry. The North is now exporting approximately US$1 billion worth of goods to the South and exports from North to South are growing at around 32 per cent year on year, mostly due to the growing output from Kaesong. More importantly Kaesong is a symbol for the nascent pro-reform caucus in Pyongyang – it may not work perfectly, but it does earn the North money and shows that investment can be managed and contained while still delivering some benefits.

Even a small growth in the output of light industrial products in the DPRK is not to be overlooked, especially given the chronic power shortages, widespread lack of spare parts for machinery and scant availability of raw materials and necessary inputs. In China such basic products as cigarette lighters occasionally now feature 'Made in the DPRK' stickers; similarly, basic products, such as household ceramics, T-shirts, small electronic appliances made in the DPRK have appeared in recessionary Japan's ultra-discount stores. These are basic, easily assembled and replicated products maybe, but they are exactly the kind of productive start that launched the propulsion of global manufacturing powerhouses in China such as Shenzhen or Wenzhou nearly twenty years ago. From small acorns grow large oaks, as well as major manufacturing corporations, budding entrepreneurs who become wealthy owners of listed companies and, most importantly, workers with a little more money in their pockets ready to become consumers and perhaps entrepreneurs themselves to further propel the economy.

Despite this, waiting for the economic collapse of the DPRK has been popular in Washington but has not so far been a particularly fruitful activity. In 1994, at the time of the Agreed Framework between Washington and Pyongyang, the US State Department advised President Clinton that the DPRK's economy would collapse in a matter of years. Again in 1997, the CIA convened a group of government and outside experts, who concluded, in an assessment that only became declassified in 2006, that political implosion stemming from irreversible economic degradation seemed the most plausible endgame for North Korea. This too has not come to pass a decade later.

However, though industrial production has picked up slightly, the 'second apocalypse' of a complete collapse of the North's agricultural economy and a cessation of humanitarian food aid flows, as suggested by Andrew Natsios, the former administrator of USAID, is now closer than previously. The continued felling of timber on hillsides, mostly for sale to China, has meant that the negative effects of the floods that hit North Korea after heavy rainfall in the summer of 2006 were exacerbated by the reduction in natural flood breaks. The desperation of rural dwellers and the reclaiming of hillsides for common land and private farming, to try and add extra food to the meagre rations doled out by the state, was both inevitable and contributory to the problem and continued a process begun long before. Short-termism, such as felling trees and asset-stripping scrap metal, copper wire and lead from factories for sale across the border in China, is a necessary way of life now and a common personal survival strategy.

Were Pyongyang's Reformers Undermined?

Among all the press speculation and expert opinion in the weeks following 9 October 2006 and Pyongyang's decision to conduct a nuclear test, one analysis was largely missing: that the test was one of two distinctly different possible options for the North and that they decided to go ahead with detonation after one of those options was seemingly denied them.

Since the effective retreat from the partial economic reforms of June 2002 the notion of reform has not totally disappeared in the DPRK. However, it has been on the back burner, indicating that those advocating reforms were weakened politically. Though we have no way of conclusively knowing, many suggest that Kim Jong-il, along with some of the newer generation of more technocratic senior cadres close to him, have continued exploring possible roads to reform. Kim has returned to China several times to see examples of reforming industries; he has backed the Kaesong project; and he has personally supported the new Sino-North Korean manufacturing joint ventures that have been appearing in the last few years. Other initiatives indicate that the reform impetus is still alive and includes:

• Reviving the stalled Sinuiju Economic Zone plan, with Chinese support, and also involving investors from Hong Kong, Macao and Taiwan. It has been suggested that mainland Chinese investors could benefit from a preferential tariff policy.

- Chinese investment in the upgrading of Rajin Port on the DPRK's north-east coast through investment from the north-east Chinese border town of Hunchun in Jilin Province. The plan involves building a free-trade road and port zone in Rajin and would include a 'free market zone' in Hunchun City – the so-called Hunchun Border Economic Cooperation Zone. The original impetus for the Hunchun–Rajin connection was that Rajin could feasibly supply the landlocked Chinese provinces of Jilin and Heilongjiang with an eastern seaport, consequently reducing congestion at the massive Dalian Port in Liaoning province while also cutting journey times to the Korean eastern seaboard, Japan and the west coast of North America. However, the port facilities at Rajin remain in dire need of upgrading, electricity is in short supply, equipment is antiquated and road infrastructure is extremely poor.
- The involvement of China's Ministry of Railways in upgrading the North's decrepit rail system, along with China's major railway carriage and engine manufacturers, mostly based in the city of Changchun in China's north-eastern Jilin province.
- Joint Sino-North Korean explorations for oil and gas reserves off the North's western coast. This would allow the Chinese to extend their exploration and drilling down from the Bohai Gulf to the waters off the DPRK's coastline.
- The reclamation and restarting of the DPRK's coal mines through new regulations adopted by the DPRK Cabinet on developing and operating small and medium-sized coal mines. The new regulation allows institutions, companies and organisations to procure coal through their own mining operations, while paving the way for potentially increasing coal production for domestic use and export.
- A venture between North Korea's Ministry of Power and Coal Industries (MPCI) and the Chinese energy ministry to construct jointly two hydroelectric power plants on the Yalu river at the North Korean border town of Manpo and China's Jian City. The two plants could potentially jointly generate 42,000 kilowatts of energy. China wishes to develop a diversified power grid based on hydro as well as more traditional methods of generation and nuclear power to reduce the country's reliance on oil, while the DPRK is seeking to utilise its natural landscape and climate to generate hydroelectric power.
- An extension of the growing number of Sino-North Korean joint venture factories. These already number over 250 and include textiles and garment assembly as well as electronics and food packaging. Chinese entrepreneurs have also started to become involved in retailing and services in North Korea, including acquiring Pyongyang's largest department store.

However, during 2006 two things happened. First, from February, the North's international banking facilities came under pressure, with accounts frozen in various locations, from Macau, where the North's accounts with Banco Delta Asia were frozen by Macau's Monetary Authority, to China, where the state-controlled People's Bank of China froze the North's accounts reportedly containing millions of dollars. The North's ability to move money around and finance trade was severely hampered. The country was left with only minor accounts, in countries such as Mongolia and Vietnam. According to US authorities, freezing the North's bank accounts was essential to pressure the regime and to prevent the North taking part in nefarious activities. However, the freezings also prevent the North from purchasing imports, spare parts, much-needed pharmaceuticals and a whole host of other products, while also preventing them from effectively underwriting trade deals or contracts.

Second, at the Free Trade Agreement (FTA) negotiations between Seoul and Washington that began in February 2006 Kaesong-made goods were ruled off the agenda by the US negotiators. Seoul was disappointed and had hoped Kaesong-made goods would be included, though, as the USA is the largest foreign investor in South Korea and a major purchaser of ROK exports, Seoul's trade negotiators were limited in the pressure they could apply. For the cautious reformers in the DPRK watching the US–ROK FTA negotiations the acceptance of Kaesong goods would have represented a potential shaft of light that would have allowed them to argue for more such projects and present economic reform as something to be embraced and not feared. Washington's rejection of Kaesong-made goods from the US–ROK FTA ended that hope and weakened the reform element in Pyongyang – ironically the very element Washington publicly claims to wish to support.

To the pro-reform caucus in the DPRK it appeared that the door had effectively been slammed on the North's ability to finance trade and underwrite deals following the bank account freezes, while potential exports, and the foreign currency earnings they could bring, which could have encouraged the growth and proliferation of Kaesong and Kaesong-like zones, had been stymied. Washington's 'double whammy' of cutting off access to cash and to the earning of cash was disastrous. The end result may well have been that the reform-minded caucus in the North's governing clique was undermined, severely weakened and forced into retreat politically. Amidst a mood set by shrinking options, Pyongyang reverted to the old strategy of nuclear brinkmanship and bargaining by plutonium refining.

Searching for Chrysanthemums

The pro-reform element in Pyongyang, which may well include Kim Jong-il, is known unofficially as the Chrysanthemum Group. They are thought to have strong ties to leading economists and politicians in Beijing and to follow the Chinese economic reforms closely. At the same time, leading economists in Beijing believe that the Chinese economic reform model is a blueprint with a certain universality that can be applied to the DPRK, to help improve conditions in the North and ensure longer-term stability on China's north-eastern border.

What does this Chrysanthemum Group want? As a confirmed nuclear power the North hopes that America will accept the legitimacy of the regime, not purely as a political end but rather for what that acceptance could bring. If a renewed round of economic reforms are to be successful, fresh thinking and access to institutional support will be required, which only a greater level of formal legitimacy and recognition could bring North Korea.

Primary among such developments would be the ability to raise loans and funding from the World Bank, the IMF and the Asian Development Bank – institutions that are currently not open to the North on account of its pariah status. However, the North has looked at the development of China, and to a lesser extent the ASEAN member countries, and understands that lending for infrastructure projects and other forms of technical assistance from these institutions is crucial. The North realises that there are political strings attached to World Bank and other loans but also notes the Bank's significant presence in other one-party states, such as China and Vietnam. The North is also aware that unless it can reach the point where the 'catalyst' lenders invest, then it has no chance of securing investment from non-governmental banks and thereby ending the sanctions regime that prevents American companies investing in the DPRK. The DPRK believes that were these sanctions lifted, the investment floodgates would open – involving not just US investors but those from the EU, Japan and around Asia.

Furthermore, dealing with organisations such as the World Bank is something that the reformist tendency in Pyongyang feels can be achieved. The North has shown a strong preference for government-to-government deals, such as those with the Chinese energy ministry or the railways ministry or the South Korean government around Kaesong, and also now has over a decade of experience of working with NGOs since the famine of the mid-1990s. These experiences, as problematic and troubled as they have often been, have yielded better results than Pyongyang's experiences with private investors and businesses, which have largely ended in stalled negotiations, mutual recrimination and abject failure for both sides.

The second major lesson of the failed reforms of 2002–03 was that a boost in manufacturing capacity and exports needs to occur to underpin and finance domestic price reforms and to boost both revenues for SOEs and workers' incomes in a climate of rising consumer prices. The ability to export, and to earn hard currency from these exports, then becomes crucial. In light of this the future of the Kaesong project, despite the refusal of Washington to accept Kaesong-made goods as part of its FTA with Seoul and the general collapse of the Sunshine Policy since the nuclear test, becomes critical.

For the reformers, looking at the Chinese experience, Kaesong is so far a mixed result. On the one hand it has shown that North Korean workers can, with investment (in the case of Kaesong wholly from the ROK), manufacture goods of exportable quality across a range of product sectors. However, on the other hand, Kaesong has shown the limits of the DPRK's approach to joint ventures to date. As we have shown in the chapters on the North's previous economic reforms, without the sort of closer involvement in the manufacturing process between local SOEs and foreign investors that was seen in China's early economic zones the North can only remain a provider of cheap labour to outsiders and not enjoy the benefits of technology transfer, training and observing best practice. The ideas floated in 2006 regarding the economic zone at Sinuiju have tended towards a more 'Chinese style' of economic zone, where North Korean companies would become more actively involved with foreign investors and so benefit from technology transfer and the earnings potential of the products produced rather than serving simply as hired help, which is essentially the situation at Kaesong now. The realisation that the Kaesong model is a starting point rather than an end in itself has now seemingly sunk in, with significant ramifications for the design of any future economic reform package.

Needless to say, the ability to export requires access to the international banking system, and therefore it is not surprising that the North has set the unfreezing of its overseas bank accounts as the determining factor as to whether the Six Party Talks continue or not.

The bringing in of 'catalyst' loans, along with the start of more targeted foreign investment, supported by aid, both financial and intellectual, from China, would allow Pyongyang's reformers to turn once again to the domestic economic situation, this time with a greater financial cushion and consequently more breathing space than was the case in 2002–03.

However, we should not underestimate the problems that stand in the way of a renewed and extended reform process. Primary among these problems is the lack of real reform in the agricultural sector, which leaves the North still far short of any notion of independent food security. In the agricultural sector Pyongyang has remained by and large rigid ideologically, proclaiming successful harvests that do not translate into more food for the people while still, in 2005 and 2006, mobilising urban workers to leave their offices and factories to work on collective farms bringing in the harvest for a number of weeks at a time. As shown in Chapter 5, this mass mobilisation and 'sending down' to the countryside remains more useful as a tool of political indoctrination and reinforcement than as a farming policy.

Additionally, there has been little movement on cross-border transport links, and the long-heralded rail link between the two Koreas remains, as of early 2007, politically stalled. The reconnection of the cross-DMZ line was agreed as part of the Sunshine Policy, the line was reconnected in 2003, tests were scheduled several times in 2006. However, Pyongyang cancelled the test runs a day before the highly symbolic event, saying that conducting them without resolving military tensions was 'as silly as planting beans in a minefield'. The line, which could both improve access to the Kaesong Zone and allow for an unbroken rail link between Seoul through to Russia, China and on to Central Asia and Europe (the so-called 'Iron Silk Road'), remains closed, meaning that Kaesong's growth is limited and North Korea cannot use the Iron Silk Road either to export or to earn transit fees from the line.

Crucially, there has been no further reform of the North's SOEs, and there can be no successful reform of domestic prices without ownership reform. At the very least the best performing SOEs need to be set free to develop export markets, new products and reinvest any profits in upgrading their manufacturing capacity to compete.

Renewed Deadlock

Following the October 2006 nuclear test by Pyongyang it appeared that relations between the North and the rest of the world retrenched into deadlock. The American government by and large wrung its hands in frustration and seemed to suggest that somehow this was a policy failure for Beijing rather than for Washington.

However, what 9 October showed more clearly than had been realised by many before was the differing views on North Korea and the possible roads to a solution. At the same time Beijing's importance in the process of resolving the issue of the nuclearisation of the Korean peninsula became clearer – if for no other reason than that by the time of the nuclear test some 90 per cent of the DPRK's daily oil supply and 50 per cent of its food imports were coming from China. In effect, the lights have remained on and people have been fed in North Korea thanks to China. This role as being the major donor of food and energy, as well as being the North's largest export market and the major foreign investor through a raft of joint-venture manufacturing operations and the activities of Chinese businessmen in the North, has given the Chinese a distinctly different interpretation of the situation than that held in Washington.

There is little doubt that China was irritated by the October 2006 nuclear test – Beijing was reportedly only given twenty minutes' warning and felt that the test undermined Beijing's concerted efforts to keep the Six Party Talks in motion. Beijing lost face and was angry. However, China fears instability on its borders and so has not been keen to impose strict sanctions on the DPRK. In one sense this reluctance reflects the old and long-standing ties between the two countries; in another sense it reveals a certain realpolitik at work in the Chinese capital, as observed by Professor Yan Xuetong of Beijing's Tsinghua University, who believes that a strict sanctions package could simply provoke an embattled North into conducting more tests in order to perfect its nuclear deterrent. The third point of view heard regularly in Beijing is the major point of difference between China and the USA and can be summed up thus:

- the North's economy is in poor shape but is not about to collapse;
- Kim Jong-il is firmly in political control and is rational and pragmatic;
- Pyongyang is willing to trade its nuclear weapons for security guarantees and economic assistance.

Increasingly Chinese analysts have dismissed many of the American concerns regarding the North. Beijing's analysts see it as highly unlikely that Kim will, as Washington fears, sell nuclear technology to terrorist organisations. There is no evidence that this has happened in the past and, given the North's continuing preference for government-to-government deals rather than with either private companies or independent groups, seems unlikely in the future too. Simply put, the notion that Pyongyang is refining plutonium to sell to terrorists is a baseless accusation and serves only to stymie the Six Party Talks process.

Signs of a Roadmap

In the run-up to the North 's nuclear test and immediately afterwards, Washington continued publicly to rule out serious negotiations with Pyongyang. Rather, it called for sanctions – in some cases, bizarre sanctions such as those on luxury goods, which would deny the North access to items such as Segways, lead crystal ornaments, silk scarves and rare stamps. What was not seen or suggested were the sort of negotiating tools that Washington had previously embraced in a range of other international crises, from the Middle East to the Balkans to Africa – namely some sort of roadmap and a series of confidence-building measures (CBMs) that would allow for a staged process of denuclearisation with mutually reinforcing steps to satisfy both sides. Washington's strategy initially remained one of all or nothing – the North had to decommission before any meaningful talks could start. Even the North's opening suggestion of more constructive talks in return for unfreezing Pyongyang's overseas bank accounts was rejected by Washington, despite Beijing's suggestion that the unfreezing could be partial, staged and monitored to show good faith.

This lack of a roadmap or any CBMs from the American side was perplexing to the Chinese who saw Kim's desire for nuclear weapons as a way to bolster the DPRK's international status. Chinese analysts were infuriated by the DPRK's cold shouldering of Beijing but understood this approach – after all, hadn't nuclear weapons played a part in changing the relationship between India and China from one of mutual distrust and tension to one of greater cooperation and friendly competition? Isn't Israel less vulnerable to attack through its possession of the bomb? Chinese analysts think so. However, they also argue that while Kim was seeking security and recognition, he was also aware, as a member of the pro-reform Chrysanthemum Group, that his domestic economy was fragile and unsustainable over the long term. Therefore his nuclear weapons were tradable commodities if the price paid helps shore up the domestic economy, thus preserving Kim's regime and control. Nuclear weapons could, argued the Chinese, be bargained away to ensure regime survival.

The Chinese analysts and others also pointed to a growing list of global issues where the use of roadmaps and CBMs from Washington had led to denuclearisation, reductions in tension and normalisation of relations – South Africa in the early 1990s, Libya in 2003 and the normalisation in relations between the USA and Vietnam that followed a Washington-proposed roadmap in 1991. However, notwithstanding these examples Washington had refused to propose a roadmap with a timeline that would test North Korean intentions more forcefully and answer the question of whether Kim was willing to trade or not.

Then the constantly moving target that is the North Korea nuclear crisis moved once more. Though the terms 'roadmap' and 'CBMs' were not explicitly used, the agreement announced between the US and North Korea on 13 February 2007 looked an awful lot like a roadmap with CBMs. The announcement was made at the Six Party Talks in Beijing but had effectively been hammered out earlier at bilateral talks between Washington and Pyongyang in Berlin in discussions between US chief negotiator Christopher

Hill and the North's Vice Minister of Foreign Affairs Kim Kye-gwan which, according to the US side, 'teed up an agreement'. The deal appeared to have the support of the US president, who called it 'unique' and an important step in the right direction, while Seoul described it as 'far-reaching'. Press reports indicated that both Secretary of State Condoleezza Rice and Bush had given Hill a far greater flexibility to reach an agreement than previously.

That agreement did appear to be very similar to the 1994 Agreed Framework worked out under the Clinton administration. However, it was different in two regards – first, the DPRK does not receive the incentives offered, namely supplies of heavy fuel oil and other aid, until it disables its equipment at Yongbyon and allows inspections for verification and, secondly, this time the deal is not only with Washington, but with Beijing, Moscow, Seoul and Tokyo.

Still, it does appear that some at least in Washington have decided to agree with Beijing's analysts that Pyongyang has developed nuclear weapons in order to be taken seriously (primarily by Washington) and is now willing to bargain. In short, Kim's bomb is for sale and Washington appears to now recognise this.

The 13 February deal will require a lot of confidence-building, monitoring and enforcement on both sides but, in among the debate over whether Washington has blinked in the negotiations, it should be remembered that the deal can benefit the longer term aims of the pro-reform element in Pyongyang, become a catalyst for wider economic policy changes in the North and benefit regional security too. The Korean peninsula still has a long way to go until full denuclearisation, though. As Condoleezza Rice, a prime architect of the accord, has commented, it is just the beginning of a long process: 'This is not the end of the story.'

Notes

Introduction

1. G. McCormack, 'Putting Pressure on Rogues', Northeast Asia Peace and Security Network Special Report, Nautilus Institute, 15 January 2003, www.nautilus.org/fora/security/0231A_McCormack.html.
2. D. O' Hearn, 'The Second Economy in Consumer Goods and Services', *Critique* 15, 1981, p. 93.

Chapter 1

1. According to one expert on the DPRK, 'employment, food, medical care, housing and place of residence can be purchased illegally. Protection from arrest or release from jail is likewise for sale. Only if one's case comes to the personal attention of Kim Jong-il, who has everything, is bribery of no use.' Kongdan Oh Hassig, Political Classification and Social Structure in North Korea, Institute for Defense Analyses, Panel on 'Life inside North Korea', Testimony to the Subcommittee on East Asian and Pacific Affairs, US Senate Committee on Foreign Relations, Washington DC, 5 June 2003.
2. Electricity shortages are common even for priority locations. In the late 1990s the Russian embassy in Pyongyang reportedly went without electricity for a period. 'Russian TV Documentary Recounts How North Korea Became a Terrorist Nation', *Weekly Post*, 9 February 2003.
3. Korea Institute for National Reunification's White Paper on Human Rights in North Korea, Seoul, 2002.
4. J. Co and D. Struck, '"Dear Leader" Feted in North Korea, Kim's Birthday Features Displays of Loyalty, Military Readiness Themes', *Washington Post*, 18 February 2003.

5. Traffic police know the vehicles used by senior cadres as they reportedly carry the licence plate '216'. The figure apparently derives from Kim Jong-il's birthday – 16 February. According to Jasper Becker, in 1998 Kim Jong-il had two hundred S-500 Mercedes shipped in for the elite's use, costing US$20 million. J. Becker, 'How Kim Jong-il's Stalinist Policies Bred Starvation and Bled His Country Dry', *Irish Times*, 15 January 2003.

6. The professional North Korean Basketball League did produce one of the world's tallest players, Rhi Myong-hun (2 m 35) as well as Pak Chon-jong (1 m 86), dubbed 'the Michael Jordan of North Korea'.

7. 'North Korea Cracks Down on Border Area with China', Radio Free Asia, 5 December 2003.

8. The Catholic charity Caritas reports that Pyongyang has one Catholic church with around 800 members in Pyongyang and 3,000 nationwide, though with no resident priest. There are also two Protestant churches and a recently built Russian Orthodox church in Pyongyang. Before 1945, two-thirds of Korean Christians were based in the north, with 2,934 churches.

9. Several visitors to the DPRK have reported being victims of opportunistic theft. For example, see 'Cycling Tour of North Korea Like Time Warp', FDCH CEO Wire-Kyodo, 18 March 2003.

10. Although fertility statistics are unreliable, the DPRK does appear to have a low teenage birth rate at around 2 per 1,000 women aged between 15 and 19 in 2000. See *The Economist Pocket World in Figures, 2003 Edition*, Profile Books, London, 2003. A survey of rural women by Johns Hopkins University reported falling birth rates since the onset of the famine.

11. S.H. Choe, 'North Korea to Raise Nuclear Capabilities', Associated Press, 3 September 2003.

12. 'Influx of Western Culture Worrying North Korea', *Sankei Shimbun*, 2 May 2003.

13. 'Hamburger on the Menu at NK Universities', *Korea Times*, 17 December 2003.

14. Reported by *Xinhua* (Beijing), 28 April 2003. However, with subscribers having to pay the equivalent of US$825 to register and 2.5 US cents per minute to receive calls and 7.5 US cents to dial a call, ordinary citizens with an average income of US$13 per month will find the service ridiculously expensive. 'North Korea Progress at a Snail's Pace', *The Economist*, 9 October 2003. Many of these mobile phone owners are thought to be foreigners based in Pyongyang.

15. 'North Korea Launches "Secure Mail"', *CNETAsia*, 2 December 2003.

16. J. Gittings, 'North Korea Warms Elite while Sick Shiver', *Guardian*, 11 May 2001. It has been estimated that traditional medicines and herbs have replaced 70 per cent of medical supplies in recent years (S. Linton, Mansfield Center for Pacific Affairs NGO Symposium on North Korea, July 2002). See the report on Sariwon Hospital from M. Seddon, 'The Land that Time Forgot', *Guardian*, 11 March 2003. Seddon reported that staff complained of broken ambulances.

17. J. Larkin, 'Exposed – Kim's Slave Camps', *Far Eastern Economic Review*, 12 December 2002.

18. 'Country Reports on Human Rights Practices – Democratic People's Republic of Korea 2002', US Bureau of Democracy, Human Rights, and Labor, 31 March 2003, www.state.gov/g/drl/rls/hrrpt/2002/18249pf.htm.

19. On the breakdown of the informing system in China, see R. Terrill, *The New Chinese Empire*, Basic Books, New York, 2003, p. 151.

20. On the DPRK's political classifications see K. Oh and R. Hassig, *North Korea through the Looking Glass*, Brookings Institution Press, Washington DC, 2000, pp. 133–5; K. Oh and R. Hassig, 'Political Classification and Social Structure in North Korea', Institute for Defense Analyses, Panel on 'Life inside North Korea', Testimony to the Subcommittee on East Asian and Pacific Affairs, US Senate Committee on Foreign Relations, Washington DC, 5 June 2003.

Chapter 2

1. The concept of the Great Systemic Whole was used by China's emperors to claim that their rule encompassed 'all under Heaven'.

2. Comecon was the organisation responsible for the co-ordination of economic policy among the socialist nations. Comecon existed between 1956 and 1991 and did supply aid to North Korea.

3. E. Cornell, *North Korea under Communism*, RoutledgeCurzon, London, 2002; D. Oberdorfer, *The Two Koreas*, Warner Books, London, 1997, p. 229.

4. The DPRK's 1972 constitution omitted all mention of Marxism–Leninism; it claimed instead that 'North Korea is guided in its activity by the Juche idea'.

5. In 1921 Lenin declared that socialism could be built in Russia only on one of two conditions: if there was an international socialist revolution, or if there was a compromise with the peasant majority within the country. The essence of the NEP was a compromise with the peasantry, and the Bolshevik theoretician Riazanov labelled the NEP 'the peasant Brest'.

6. 1998 DPRK Constitution, http://210.145.168.243/pk/061st_issue/98091708.htm.

7. The term 'Yan'an' was taken from Mao's headquarters during China's War of Liberation (1945–49) in China's Shaanxi province.

8. The full story is retold in Oberdorfer, *The Two Koreas*, p. 21.

9. The Yi, or Choson, dynasty was the last and longest Korean imperial dynasty (1392–1910). Founded by General Yi Song-gye, who established the capital at Hanyang (now Seoul), the kingdom was named Choson after the state of the same name that had dominated Korea in ancient times.

10. Percentages from K. Oh and R. Hassig, 'Political Classification and Social Structure in North Korea', Institute of Defense Analyses, submission to the panel on 'Life inside North Korea', Testimony to the Subcommittee on East Asian and Pacific Affairs, United States Senate Committee on Foreign Relations, Washington DC, 5 June 2003.

11. Suh Dae-Sook, *Kim Il-sung: The North Korean Leader*, Columbia University Press, New York, 1988, pp. 305–6.

12. Hwang lives in South Korea in a guarded safe house. He remains active and in August 2003 applied for a visa to visit the US, visiting Washington in October 2003, despite DPRK threats to 'shoot his plane out of the sky'. Following his defection Hwang's wife and daughter reportedly committed suicide, while his other children and grandchildren are rumoured to be in prison camps.

13. Oberdorfer, *The Two Koreas*, p. 404.

14. K. Oh and R. Hassig, *North Korea through the Looking Glass*, Brookings Institution Press, Washington DC, 2000, p. 21.

15. Ibid., p. 16.

Chapter 3

1. Following the 'pygmy' remarks, the senators were reportedly 'stunned'. In interviews with the *Washington Post*'s Bob Woodward in August 2002, Bush stated: 'I loathe Kim Jong Il – I've got a visceral reaction to this guy.' B. Woodward, *Bush at War*, Pocket Books, New York, 2003, p. 340. Armitage's remark is from 'North Korea's Kim Not "Unstable" but "Canny": Armitage', *AFP*, 4 August 2003.

2. Mehmet Shehu (1913–81) rose to become Albania's minister of the interior, head of the secret police, and deputy premier. He opposed Hoxha's extreme isolationism, a power struggle ensued, and Shehu, accused of being a Yugoslav spy, reportedly committed suicide.

3. Lazar Kaganovich (1893–1991) was a member of Stalin's 'post-purge' Politburo. He rigorously opposed de-Stalinisation and was involved in the unsuccessful 1957 attempt to oust Khrushchev. He was expelled from office, and lived long enough to see the fall of the USSR.

4. He took the name Kim Il-sung after a legendary Korean hero.

5. The 1 March 1919 Declaration of Independence (*Samil*) proclaimed the independence of Korea and the liberty of the Korean people. During the 1919 demonstrations, 2 million Koreans participated 'non-violently'. The Japanese authorities killed 7,645 demonstrators, wounded 45,562 and arrested 49,811. Shortly after the Korean exile government was formed in Shanghai.

6. At the time Jilin, which is opposite Korea across the Yalu river, was a major settlement of 400,000 ethnic Koreans.

7. Kuo-Kang Shao, *Zhou Enlai and the Foundations of Chinese Foreign Policy*, Palgrave Macmillan, London, 1996.

8. 'Russian TV Documentary Recounts How North Korea Became a Terrorist Nation', *Weekly Post*, 9 February 2003.

9. Kim Tu-bong, alias Kim Sun and Kim Paik-yon (1905–58) fled to Shanghai in 1919 to join the Korean government-in-exile after participating in the Samil Movement and later went to Japan to study. He escaped death during the September 1923 Kanto Massacre of Koreans in Japan and returned to China, joining Mao's Long March. In August 1942, with Suh Sang-Il, Kim formed the Korean Independence League, which became the New Democratic Party in 1945. Kim held a number of high positions, including the initial presidency of Kim Il-sung University.

10. At the time Zhou Enlai was China's premier, Deng was general secretary of the Communist Party, Kosygin was first deputy chairman of the USSR Council of Ministers, and Kozlov was Soviet prime minister.

11. Suh Dae-sook, *Kim Il-sung: The North Korean Leader*, Columbia University Press, New York, 1988, p. 187.

12. North Korea Advisory Group, Report to the Speaker US House of Representatives, November 1999.

13. Kim Jong-il quoted in 'Let Us Accomplish the Revolutionary Cause of Juche under the Leadership of Kim Jong-il', *Rodong Sinmun*, 19 May 1996.

14. N. Kristof, 'Tunneling toward a Disaster', *Milwaukee Journal Sentinel*, 26 January 2003.

15. Fujimoto published a book in Japan in 2003 entitled *Kim Jong-il's Chef* that went into five editions and was partially serialised in *Chosun Ilbo* newspaper.

16. Lee Young-kook's book *Basic Knowledge on Kim Jong-il*, was translated into Japanese and sold over 300,000 copies.

17. A. Foster-Carter, 'Cook and Tell: Another Chef Spills the Beans', *Asia Times Online*, 2 July 2003, www.atimes.com/atimes/Korea/EG02Dg02.html.

18. Kim liked Choi and wanted to improve the North Korean film industry. After kidnapping Choi he later ordered the kidnapping of her husband, Shin Sang-ok, a dissident film director. Eight years later, after making several films in North Korea, Choi and Shin (who was also imprisoned for four years) escaped while visiting Vienna. The two later wrote a memoir, *Kidnapped to the North Korean Paradise*, which has not yet been translated into English. The use of funds from his personal gold mine concession to fund films is contained in S. Harrison, *Korean Endgame*, Princeton University Press, Princeton, 2002, p. 58.

19. 'Kim Jong-il – Playing a Poor Hand Skilfully', *CNN*, 14 January 2003, http://edition.cnn.com/2001/WORLD/asiapcf/east/06/13/bio.kim.jongil/.

20. P. Maass, 'The Last Emperor', *New York Times Magazine*, 19 October 2003; Kim quoted in Harrison, *Korean Endgame*, p. 54; Yazov quoted in ibid., p. 55.

21. In 2001 Castro declared: 'If tomorrow I have a heart attack, a stroke, a sudden death, then the person with more authority and experience in Cuba is Raul.' At the time the 74-year-old Fidel had reportedly suffered several health scares. Reported by M. Miranda, 'Cuban Succession', *Pravda*, 4 July 2001.

22. E. Cornell, *North Korea under Communism*, RoutledgeCurzon, London, 2002, p. 28.

23. Li Nam-ok, *The Golden Cage*, Macmillan, London, 1999.

24. B. Lintner, 'Dynastic Lies and Secrets', *Far Eastern Economic Review*, 10 July 2003.

25. Hwang, quoted in Kim Yeon-kwang, 'Second Son Being Groomed as Heir Apparent', *Chosun Ilbo*, 21 October 2003.

26. The Mansudae Grand Monument was erected in 1972. The monument with the gilded statue of Kim covers 240,000 square metres; it reportedly cost US$851 million. Deng's views on the statue in J. Becker, 'How Kim Jong-il's Stalinist Policies Bred Starvation and Bled His Country Dry', *Irish Times*, 15 January 2003. According to Becker the statue was later re-covered in less ostentatious bronze.

27. *New York Times*, 16 December 1997. North Korea reported the advertisement as an editorial praising Kim. Other official titles include Peerless Leader, Beloved Leader, Sun of Juche, Sun of Life, Sun of the Revolution, Fatherly Leader of All Koreans, Great General, Eternal Sun, and Sun of Socialism. 'N. Korea's Kim Has 1,200 Titles', *UPI News*, 2 December 2003.

28. B. Szalontai, 'The Dynamic of Repression: The Global Impact of the Stalinist Model, 1944–1953', *Russian History/Histoire Russe*, vol. 29, nos 2–4, Summer–Fall–Winter 2002, pp. 415–42.

29. *Suryong* means 'the greatest of the great'. Kim began applying the term to himself in the late 1960s, although he had used it previously to describe Lenin, Stalin and Mao, thereby elevating himself into the revolutionary pantheon of great leaders. Kim Jong-il's title of *yongdoja* (leader) is less exalted.

Chapter 4

1. For an extended excerpt from the 1998 meeting, see 'We Must Rationalise Prices and Accelerate Reform' in Deng Xiaoping, *The Selected Works of Deng*

Xiaoping, vol. 3, Foreign Languages Press, Beijing, 1990. The story of the DPRK delegation's visit to Deng is retold in J. Studwell, *The China Dream*, Profile Books, London, 2003. The comment that they were 'bemused' is Studwell's.

2. *Chollima* is a traditional Korean winged horse, capable of covering vast areas at high speed. The image is still common in the DPRK on everything from propaganda posters to cigarette packets.

3. The North Korean idea of permanent war preparedness, used to justify high military expenditure, the continuing nuclear programme and the rallying of mass crowds for 'spontaneous' demonstrations, is reminiscent of George Orwell's idea of 'permanent war' in his novel *1984*.

4. Only 18–20 per cent of North Korea is arable. Anthracite coal, with estimated reserves of 1.8 billion tonnes, is the most abundant of the country's mineral resources, along with an estimated 400 million tonnes of iron ore and 490 million tonnes of magnesite deposits. There are also deposits of lead (12 million tonnes), zinc (12 million tonnes), nickel, crystal and ceramic clay, tungsten (232,000 tonnes) and gold as well as production of approximately 5,000 TPM (total precious metals) of zinc ingot per annum.

5. Reverse engineering has been a major method of introducing technology to otherwise backward, poor or isolated countries. The Soviets had done this on a massive scale while the Chinese have now become global experts in reverse engineering, often double reverse engineering Soviet products that were themselves reverse engineered Western products.

6. According to Masahiko Nakagawa of the Japanese External Trade Organisation. 'History and Debts Cast Shadow over Investment in North Korea', *South China Morning Post*, 26 September 2002.

7. E. Cornell, *North Korea under Communism*, RoutledgeCurzon, London, 2002.

8. Adrian Buzo recalls one case, the Ryonsong Bearing Plant, built with Soviet assistance in 1985, which had a capacity for 10 million bearings annually, though produced nothing due to a lack of the correct steel and no market demand for the product. See A. Buzo, *The Guerilla Dynasty*, I.B. Tauris, London and New York, 2003, pp. 171–2.

9. Hua (1921–) was Minister of Public Security and deputy premier in 1975 and premier following Zhou Enlai's death in 1976 and chairman of the Communist Party when Mao died. Hua was eased out of power by Deng and replaced by Zhao Ziyang as premier in 1980, and by Hu Yaobang as Party chairman in 1981.

10. Edward Gierek (1923–2001), former Communist Party leader in Silesia, became president of Poland after Gomulka resigned following riots against economic deprivation in 1970. Gierek instigated an industrialisation programme that plunged the country into debt, and by 1980 Poland was suffering food shortages.

11. China has massive foreign reserves of over US$269.9 billion – fully 11 per cent of the world's total.

12. S. Green, 'Privatisation in the Former Soviet Bloc: Any Lessons for China?', *Royal Institute of International Affairs Asia Programme Briefing Note*, November 2003.

13. Equitisation involves SOEs transferring company stock into private hands with the authorities retaining a 20 per cent stake. It's a slow process – only 79 of the 1,800 companies identified for the first wave to be completed by 2003 achieved full transfer. Lack of managerial confidence, complicated procedures and worker resistance are some of the reasons given for the low success rate. The NEM in

Laos has encouraged more private household enterprises, FDI and new industries. However, Vientiane remains heavily dependent on international donors to
promote these initiatives and deal with the country's budgetary deficit. In 2003
a DPRK delegation visited Hanoi to study equitisation.

14. From S. Kotkin, *Steeltown, USSR*, University of California Press, Los Angeles, 1991,
    p. 10. It was estimated in the 1960s that in the Soviet machine tool sector four
    times as many workers were engaged in repairs as in production. US Congress
    Joint Economic Committee, *Economic Performance and the Military Burden in the
    Soviet Union*, JEC, Washington DC, 1970, p. 222; cited in H.H. Ticktin, 'Towards
    a Political Economy of the USSR', *Critique* 1, Spring 1973, p. 25.

15. From Kotkin, *Steeltown, USSR*, p. 9.

16. The 150-metre-tall, white granite Juche Tower was erected in 1982 to celebrate
    Kim Il-sung's seventieth birthday. It is capped by a 20-metre-high torch as a
    symbol of the 'rays of Juche', with a 30-metre-high group of workers, peasants
    and intellectuals at the base under the banner of the KWP. The 60-metre-high
    and 50-metre-wide Arch of Triumph was erected in 1982 to eulogise and glorify
    Kim Il-sung's exploits. It features over 10,500 pieces of white granite. The Grand
    People's Study House opened in 1982 as a 'centre for the project of intellectualis-
    ing the whole of society and a sanctuary of learning for the entire people'. The
    Study House has a floor space of 100,000 square metres and can house 30 million
    books. The 400,000-square-metre Kim Il-sung Stadium, which can hold 150,000
    visitors, opened with an 'international marathon' featuring runners from just six
    countries. The Kumsuman Palace reportedly cost US$900 million. The Thir-
    teenth World Festival of Youth and Students in 1989 was extremely expensive,
    costing an estimated US$4.5 billion. Although the facilities remain, the athletes'
    accommodation became desirable housing for the elite. There is also the cost of
    the massive celebrations that accompany major national dates and the leader's
    birthday. Apparently the celebrations for Kim Jong-il's fifty-seventh birthday in
    1999 cost US$90 million (*Joonang Ilbo*, 17 February 1999).

17. S. Harrison, *Korean Endgame*, Princeton University Press, Princeton, 2002, p. 49.
    North Korea's gold mines are located at Unsan, Sangnong and Hochon. While
    the scale of current reserves is unknown, it is assumed that outdated machinery
    and other problems are adversely affecting production of gold. Unsan was nearly
    developed by Israeli interests in a deal aimed at helping Pyongyang earn foreign
    exchange in return for ceasing to sell missile technology to Iran and Syria.
    However, the US applied pressure on Israel to halt the deal.

18. Ticktin, 'Towards a Political Economy of the USSR', p. 23.

19. Cornell, *North Korea under Communism*, p. 87.

20. The DPRK's alienation from the rest of the socialist world was almost total
    by the time of the Seoul Olympics. Only Cuba heeded Pyongyang's boycott
    call. Chinese and Soviet athletes attended. The Soviet attitude was considered
    uncharitable by Pyongyang, which had observed the Soviet boycott of the 1984
    Los Angeles Olympics.

21. See M. Gordon, ed., *The End of Superpower Conflict in the Third World*, Westview
    Press, Boulder CO, 1992.

22. In currency terms the shift was from roughly US$965 to U$1,954. Additionally,
    only 10 per cent of South Korean households were living below the poverty line
    by 1980.

23. The term 'dissipation of resources' is taken from Ticktin, 'Towards a Political Economy of the USSR', p. 32.

24. The effects of the ending of Soviet aid on the national diet are discussed in M. Noland, *Famine and Reform in North Korea*, Institute for International Economics, Washington DC, 2003.

25. JH. Williams, D. Von Hippel and P. Hayes, 'Fuel and Famine: Rural Energy Crisis in the DPRK', Nautilus Institute, 2000, www.nautilus.org/DPRK Briefing Book/energy/pp46.html.

26. Power maintenance is a key issue in the DPRK due to the fact that frequencies in the DPRK grid do not reach the standard of 60 Hz, fluctuating between 54 and 59 Hz and requiring maintenance to achieve an uninterrupted flow. For more details of the DPRK's power grid, energy standards and generating capacity, see M. Kozlov, 'The DPRK Energy Sector', *DPRK Business News Bulletin*, 1 September 2003, Korea Business Consultants, Beijing.

27. Miyazaki, J. 'North Korea: Anything Left to Revive?', *Asia Times Online*, 23 October 2003, www.atimes.com/atimes/Korea/EJ23Dg01.html.

28. P. Hayes, 'DPRK Energy Security without Rewarding Bad Behaviour', *Northeast Asia Peace & Security Network Special Report*, 2003, www.nautilus.org/fora/security/0230A_Hayes.html. It should be noted that other analysts estimate wastage to be lower, at around 30 per cent.

29. The share of thermal generated power fell to between 15 and 33 per cent by 2000. See Kozlov, 'The DPRK Energy Sector'.

30. Estimates of the DPRK's oil and gas reserves vary. Petroleum reserves are said to be between 5 and 50 billion barrels; natural gas reserves are reported by one exploration company, Singaporean Sovereign Ventures, to be approximately 1 trillion cubic feet.

31. Nor is this idea economically feasible, as the difference in power quality between the North and the ROK – the obvious grid to connect to, which has surplus output – would require a massive investment in conversion technology. There have also been suggestions that Russia and North Korea could connect their grids, although the same convertibility problems apply.

32. The most notable foreign investor in the energy sector is ABB, which has a US$200 million contract to supply equipment and services to KEDO and the DPRK government. The contract was in part negotiated by then ABB board member Donald Rumsfeld, who later denied knowledge of the deal, even though ABB has stated that 'board members were informed about this project' (R. Behar, 'Rummy's North Korea Connection', *Fortune Magazine*, 28 April 2003).

33. Rothman, quoted in D. Murphy, 'Economic Monitor: China – Two Track System', *Far Eastern Economic Review*, 19 December 2002.

34. O. Chung, 'The Role of South Korea's NGOs: The Political Context', in L. Gordon Flake and S. Snyder, eds, *Paved with Good Intentions*, Praeger, Westport, 2003, p. 87.

35. Statements have included Kim Jong-il's remark that 'The imperialist "aid" is a noose of plunder and subjugation aimed at robbing ten and even a hundred things for one thing given.'

36. See M. Schloms, 'The European NGOs' Experience in North Korea', in Flake and Snyder, *Paved with Good Intentions*, p. 163.

37. This situation is clearly embarrassing for Pyongyang. From 1997 the US labelled

each aid package with 'Gift of the People of the USA.' Over 30 million of these bags have entered the country. The Administrator of USAID described each bag as being a piece of 'informational contamination'. DPRK officials have been known to tell people that the aid is reparations for the Korean War. A. Natsios, Testimony to the Subcommittee on East Asian and Pacific Affairs, US Senate Committee on Foreign Relations, Washington DC, 5 June 2003.

38. CARE wished to move to 'sustainable rehabilitation and development programs in North Korea', though decided that the organisation would need 'significantly higher levels of access to people in need than it does currently'. MSF had run nutritional programmes in some of the worst affected provinces, while ACF operated nutritional programmes to support nurseries and training of staff in paediatrics and kindergarten care. Oxfam was organising water treatment programmes but was unable to conduct tests or assess the level of water-borne disease due to government interference.

39. This example is from Schloms, 'The European NGO Experience in North Korea', p. 51. Nampo is the main port for Pyongyang and the major inward route for aid from Inchon and Northern China. The government is keen to upgrade Nampo, which suffers from regular power cuts and can only accept 20-foot containers and has no cranes capable of unloading large containers. See 'Work Under Way on North Korea's First Box Terminal', *Lloyds List*, 1 December 2003.

40. Quoted in Schloms, 'The European NGO Experience in North Korea', p. 63.

41. Chung, 'The Role of South Korea's NGOs', p. 95.

42. It should also be remembered that Russia shares a border with the DPRK and that Russia is keen to be part of any overland route between South Korea and the Russian hinterland that could bring benefits to the ailing Russian Far East. The total number of North Koreans sent to work in Russia's Far East is unknown, though a delegation from the Primorsky region that visited North Korea in 2003 noted that 1,400 North Koreans were working in the province and that an additional 3,000 would be recruited in 2004. 'Maritime Kray Governor Describes 1–4 October Visit to North Korea', *Moscow Izvestiya*, 7 October 2003 (in Russian).

43. The Chinese leadership compound in Beijing adjacent to Tiananmen Square.

44. 'People Urged to Arm Themselves with Party Policies', *Korean Central News Agency KCNA*, 23 September 2002.

45. According to Sam Chambers, the East Asia Editor of *Lloyds List*, the ROK regularly builds 20,000 (deadweight) tonne ships as well as 300,000 (deadweight) tonne ships (large crude carriers) and sometimes 400,000 (deadweight) tonne tankers (ultra large crude carriers). In 2003 the ROK launched a 4,000-tonne-class 'stealth' battleship, and now plans to build three 7,000-tonne-class Aegis-equipped destroyers by 2012. Shipbuilding production statistics from the ROK National Statistical Office.

Chapter 5

1. A. Natsios, *The Great North Korean Famine*, US Institute of Peace Press, Washington DC, 2001, p. 245.

2. Trofim Lysenko (1898–76) was a Soviet biologist who developed a controversial

approach to biology. As head of the USSR Academy of Agricultural Sciences he declared genetics and cybernetics to be anti-Soviet. Lysenko also advocated the close planting of seeds and the heavy use of fertilisers, both policies that have caused long-term problems for the DPRK. In 1962 a group of Soviet scientists set out the case against Lysenko, following which Khrushchev dismissed him.

3. G.A.E. Smith, 'The Industrial Problems of Soviet Agriculture', *Critique* 14, 1981, p. 41.

4. According to R. Scalapino and Chong-Sik Lee, *Communism in Korea*, University of California Press, Los Angeles, 1972.

5. The South's land redistribution act was not popular with former landlords, who attempted to subvert the act by charging inflated prices for land. In 1953 when the Act was reintroduced, many tenant farmers exercised squatters' rights over the land they had been working. By 1956 tenancy had dropped from 49 per cent to 7 per cent according to J. Lie, *Han Unbound*, Stanford University Press, Stanford, 2002, p. 12.

6. Comparable ratios of arable to non-arable land in other similar countries include: Netherlands 27 per cent; Israel 17 per cent, Austria, 17 per cent, Belgium 25 per cent and China 13 per cent. *The Economist Pocket World in Figures, 2003 Edition*, Profile Books, London, 2003.

7. North Korea produced over 80 per cent of its own fertiliser needs prior to 1990. Fertiliser has normally been produced by synthesising ammonia, a method now considered outdated. Most fertiliser factories were built before the 1960s and have ageing machinery and scarce raw materials, meaning they produce only basic products. Humus soil, soot, human waste and animal manure are also commonly used. Fertiliser has come in as aid. The ROK Ministry of Unification estimates that an additional 300,000 tonnes can increase North Korea's food production by up to 600,000 tonnes. 'Fertilizer Will Be Sent – If North Asks For It', *Joongang Ilbo*, 16 April 2003.

8. *Chngbo* is a Korean unit of land area measurement. One *chngbo* equals about 2.45 acres, or 0.99 hectares.

9. E. Cornell, *North Korea under Communism*, RoutledgeCurzon, London, 2002, p. 44.

10. It is also true that one consequence of the increasing isolation Juche encouraged was a significant reduction in the genetic diversity of the seed stock, heightening its vulnerability to disease.

11. The description of the North Korean famine as a 'slow motion' famine is in M. Noland, *Avoiding the Apocalypse: The Future of the Two Koreas*, Institute for International Economics, 2000. It is attributed to Tun Myat, the WFP's director of transportation, following a visit to the DPRK's northeastern provinces.

12. 'Nutritional Survey of the DPRK: Report by the EU, UNICEF and WFP of a Study Undertaken in Partnership with the Government of the DPRK, UN/WFP', November 1998.

13. The government stuck firmly to the line that the famine was solely the result of natural disasters, even renaming the state organisation dealing with NGOs the Flood Damage Rehabilitation Committee (FDRC).

14. 'The Imperialists' Aid is a Tool of Aggression', *Rodong Sinmun*, 6 October 2000.

15. 'Hungry in North Korea', *New York Times*, 16 December 2003. The WFP's 2004 target is US$221 million.

16. Even here Pyongyang caused problems. John Gittings reported in 2001 that domestic coal purchased by Norway to provide fuel to hospitals had to be paid for with hard currency: 'The donors ask why they should have to buy coal from the government just to give it back to the government!' J. Gittings, 'North Korea Warms Elite while Sick Shiver', *Guardian*, 11 May 2001.

17. The Nautilus Institute has established wind generation equipment; the Rotarians provided a number of solar-powered sun ovens. Other examples of aid projects include bakeries set up by the Adventist Development and Relief Agency International; Mercy Corps International's model farms and orchards; and a number of noodle factories established by Korean-American charities.

18. P. Eckert, 'South Korea Tells North It Risks Aid in Nuclear Crisis', Reuters, 20 May 2003.

19. 'Scores of Children Dead in North Korea Famine', CNN Interactive, 8 April 1997, http://edition.cnn.com/WORLD/9704/08/korea.food.

20. R. Scalapino, *North Korea at a Crossroads*, Stanford University Press, Stanford, 1997, p. 2.

21. See S. Kotkin, *Steeltown, USSR*, University of California Press, Los Angeles, 1992, p. 69. G.A.E. Smith estimated that in 1980 Soviet agriculture lost 10 per cent of its potato crop, and that 'up to 30 per cent of fruit and vegetables were rendered worthless because of improper or inadequate storage.' G.A.E. Smith, 'The Industrial Problems of Soviet Agriculture', *Critique* 14, 1981, p. 49. Smith also estimates, in another statistic, which applies to the DPRK equally, that if the USSR had made the necessary investment in rural infrastructure it could have potentially improved crop output by 11–12 per cent annually. The FAO/WFP estimate is from Crop and Food Supply Assessment Mission to DPRK: Special Report, WFP, November 1998, p. 11.

22. 'Korea is Creating a "New Chollima Speed"', *KCNA*, 2 June 1998.

23. The 1998 Nutrition Survey of the DPRK conducted by the EU, UNICEF and the WFP, with Pyongyang's permission, found that in North Hamgyong province 62 per cent of children between six months and 7 years were chronically malnourished and a further 16 per cent severely malnourished.

24. North Korea Advisory Group, Report to the Speaker, US House of Representatives, November 1999.

25. According to Caritas, 'FAQ – Humanitarian Aid to North Korea', www.caritas-int.be/fr/actualite/archives/North per cent20Korea_oct2002_FAQ.doc.

26. These reports have appeared in many newspapers worldwide. For instance, 'Famine-Struck N Koreans "Eating Children"', *Sunday Telegraph*, 8 June 2003; 'The Poverty-Stricken World of North Korea', *The Age*, 29 October 2003.

27. The 220,000 estimate is from US Institute of Peace Special Report, 'Overcoming the Humanitarian Dilemmas in DPRK', Washington DC, July 2002, and is a 1999 DPRK government estimate, reiterated in 2001. For a more detailed discussion, see M. Noland, 'Famine and Reform in North Korea', Institute for International Economics, July 2003. The figures exceeding 2.8 million and as high as 3.5 million dead (equivalent to 10–12 per cent of the pre-famine population) are from statistics based on extrapolations from refugee interviews, notably surveys conducted by the Buddhist Sharing Movement, which conducted a combination of refugee interviews and personal observation.

28. These so called '927 Camps' (after their announcement on 27 September 1997)

were ordered by Kim Jong-il as reports of chaos increased and the internal travel permit system collapsed in the face of growing desperation. The camps also housed people returned by China. The 927 Camps were reportedly closed in 1999 and their functions subsumed by the existing prison camps.

29. A. Natsios, *The Great North Korean Famine*, US Institute of Peace, Washington DC, 2001, p. 6.

30. For more on this absorption of aid donations into the PDS, see Natsios, *The Great North Korean Famine*, F. Terry, 'Feeding the Dictator', *Guardian*, 6 August 2003.

31. Noland, 'Famine and Reform in North Korea'.

32. J.M. Kim, 'Economic Fallout', *Far Eastern Economic Review*, 20 March 2003. Japan–DPRK trade statistics from Korea International Trade Association (KITA).

33. This translates into expenditures of US$13,093,300,000 and US$5,217,400,000 respectively, for the ROK and DPRK. *CIA World Factbook*, www.cia.gov/cia/publications/factbook/index.html.

34. This overview of the economy is based on figures from the ROK's Ministry of Reunification, Bank of Korea and NGO estimates, as well as statistics from the DPRK Finance Ministry and PRC Customs Department. Per capita income statistics are from South Korea's National Statistical Office.

35. Conditions at Nampo Port are discussed in 'Work Under Way on North Korea's First Box Terminal', *Lloyds List*, 1 December 2003.

36. 'North Korea Steps Up Power Station Construction', *KCNA*, 15 December 2003.

37. 'South Korean Officials Say North's Energy Crisis Not Resolvable without Aid', *BBC International Reports*, 16 December 2003. Coal statistics from 'North Korea Reports 3 per cent Increase in Coal Production', *BBC International Reports*, 24 December 2003. Sino–DPRK electricity trade statistics are from 'Surge in North Korean Electricity Imports from China Reported', Yonhap, 30 November 2003.

38. *OCHA DPR Korea Situation Bulletin*, August 2003.

39. 'Port's Thriving North Korea Trade', *Far Eastern Economic Review*, 17 April 2003.

40. This boycott remains strong, notwithstanding stories circulating in 2003 that DPRK-made textile products had appeared in US retailers.

41. J. Miyazaki, 'North Korea: Anything Left To Revive?', *Asia Times Online*, 23 October 2003, www.atimes.com/atimes/Korea/EJ23Dg01.html.

42. A. Sen and J. Drèze, eds, *The Amartya Sen and Jean Drèze Omnibus*, Oxford University Press, Oxford, 1999.

43. See R. Conquest, *The Harvest of Sorrow: Soviet Collectivization and the Terror-Famine*, Oxford University Press, Oxford, 1987; J. Becker, *Hungry Ghosts: Mao's Secret Famine*, Henry Holt, London, 1998; B. Kiernan, *The Pol Pot Regime: Race, Power, and Genocide in Cambodia Under the Khmer Rouge, 1975–79*, Yale Nota Bene, New Haven, 2002.

44. Hwang Jang-yop, quoted in D. Oberdorfer, *The Two Koreas*, Warner Books, London, 1997, p. 405.

45. Quoted in Kim Jung-min, 'Economic Fallout', *Far Eastern Economic Review*, 20 March 2003.

Chapter 6

1. J. Miyazaki, 'Adam Smith Comes to North Korea', *Asia Times Online*, 22 October 2003, www.atimes.com/atimes/Korea/EJ22Dg01.html; S. Harrison, *Korean Endgame*, Princeton University Press, Princeton, 2002, p. 53.

2. *The Economist* cautiously welcomed the economic reforms with 'Stitch by Stitch to a Different World: Something Extraordinary Seems to be Happening in North Korea: The First Stirrings of a Proper Market', *The Economist*, 27 July 2002, and 'Open Sesame: Communist North Korea Appears to Have Taken Its First Small Step towards a Market System', *The Economist*, 27 July 2002. The *Far Eastern Economic Review* was more cautious, with J. Larkin, 'North Korea: Mysterious Reform', *Far Eastern Economic Review*, 7 August 2002.

3. This was the first time the word 'reform' (*kaehyok*) had officially been used in the DPRK.

4. Article 33 of the DPRK Constitution. This emphasis on costs, prices and profits was reminiscent of the 1965 Soviet industrial reforms that emphasised indices, sales and profits rather than gross output as the main criteria for SOE reform.

5. These wage increases were discussed in Cabinet resolutions 32, 128 and 129 in July 2002.

6. Adopted under Cabinet Directive No. 56, March 1952.

7. 'N Korean Daily Says Those Who Contribute Most to Society Should Be Rewarded Most', *BBC International Reports*, 15 June 2003.

8. CAP2004, p. 25. The average rations were: 300 grams per person per day between January and April 2003; 250 grams in May; 250/350 grams in June; and 380 grams in July, August and September. Also FAO/WFP, *Crop and Food Supply Assessment*, 2003, p. 19. *The Observer* reported that the daily ration in Songrim, an industrial town near Pyongyang, had fallen to 300 grams per day. J. Watts, 'North Korea is Slowly Starving. Yet It Won't Reveal Its Pain', *Observer*, 7 December 2003.

9. When the rations reached these levels NGOs reported rising instances of disease including beriberi, rickets and pellagra. Malnourishment combined with a lack of clean water also led to rising rates of gastrointestinal infections. In all these areas tuberculosis, malaria and hepatitis B are endemic.

10. See M. Noland, *Famine and Reform in North Korea*, Institute for International Economics, 2003. In 2001 the government claimed these markets were a temporary phenomenon to ease supply problems (see J. Gittings, 'North Korea Warms Elite while Sick Shiver', *Guardian*, 11 May 2001), while the FAO/WFP *Crop and Food Supply Assessment* in 2003 noted that the farmers' markets had been officially recognised since June 2003, p. 4.

11. 'Economic Reforms of 2002', Pyongyangsquare.com, 12 November 2003.

12. Despite their extension into other areas of supply the term 'farmers' market' is still applied, as opposed to 'private markets'. The level of government control of these markets remains high, including – in Pyongyang, at least – the areas they occupy. This is in contrast to the Soviet private markets, which though patrolled by the police, were far less controlled, and the Chinese practice, still seen regularly in large cities, of independent farmers and rural workers wandering the streets selling produce direct to consumers.

13. FDI in Cuba remained low and hampered by bureaucracy, though foreign investment laws allowed for up to 49 per cent foreign ownership in manufacturing, industrial, agricultural and tourism-related enterprises. Estimates of FDI in Cuba range from US$1.1 to 1.4 billion according to the *Cuba World Factbook* of the US Department of Commerce–National Trade Data Bank.

14. Cuba first opened *agropecuarios* in the 1980s, but they were shut down due to a sudden rise in rural inequality. They were reopened to ease food shortages

after Raul Castro, Fidel's brother, declared that food shortages were a matter of national security.

15. Noland quoted in J. Brooke, 'Talks Could Push North Korea Forward or Back', *New York Times*, 20 August 2003.

16. M. Ellman, 'Economic Crisis in the USSR', *Critique* 12, Autumn–Winter 1979–80, p. 10.

17. The only scheme attempted was the introduction of a national lottery in 1991 when ten million sheets of NKW50 'People's Lottery' tickets were issued and sold out in two months. The lottery was priced relatively high, given that ordinary North Korean workers earned NKW80 a month on average at that time.

18. Park quoted in A. Ward, 'N Korea Orders Dollars To Be Swapped for Euros', *Financial Times*, 30 November–1 December 2002.

19. Inflation is not a new phenomenon. In 1998 North Korea issued NKW500 notes, a sum five times a worker's average monthly pay at the time. Previously the highest notes were NKW100, indicating that the currency had undergone inflation.

20. Though Cuba has officially recorded growth in all sectors except sugar it is important to note the disproportionate importance of sugar to the economy. Inequality has continued to grow as Cuba divides between a have and have-not US dollar economy. Though tourism has brought in some revenues (as have the sex industry and crime), the command economy continues to drag down industrial and agricultural enterprises. Food, fuel and energy shortages remain chronic and promised wage rises have not materialised except for key constituencies, notably the police.

21. P.H. Yun, 'The Imperialists' Cunning Manoeuvre of Ideological and Cultural Infiltration', *Rodong Sinmum*, 24 May 1997.

22. The 1989 grain harvest in China was recorded at 408 million tonnes and in 1990 at 446 million tonnes – 52 million tonnes more than recorded in 1988.

23. A. Ward, 'Signs of Reform Seen in N Korean Bonds Plan', *Financial Times*, 29–30 March 2003.

24. C. Bennett, 'Hoeryong is Prepared to Wait for Ever for Kim Jong-Il to Visit His Mother's Birthplace, *South China Morning Post*, 16 March 2003.

25. See Yun-ho Chung, 'The Prospects of Economic Reform in North Korea and the Direction of Its Economic Development', *Vantage Point*, vol. 26, no. 5, May 2003, pp. 14–18.

26. North Korean exports were worth approximately US$1.95 billion (FOB) in 1998, US$1.24 billion in 1991, US$0.52 billion in 1999 and US$0.70 billion in 2001. Imports to the DPRK were worth US$2.85 billion in 1989, US$1 billion in 1991 and US$1.6 billion in 2001. In 2001 the DPRK's major export partners were Japan (28 per cent), ROK (21 per cent), China (5 per cent), Germany (4 per cent) and Russia (1 per cent). In 2002, following the problems over the Japanese kidnapping issue, China became the country's most important trading partner.

27. So-called by the defectors rather than by Pyongyang.

28. US$5 billion estimate from J. Solomon, and Hae Won-choi, 'Shadowy Business Arm Helps Regime Keep Grip on Power in Pyongyang', *Asian Wall Street Journal*, 14 July 2003.

29. North Korea Advisory Group, Report to the Speaker US House of Representa-

tives, November 1999.

30. In April 2003 a North Korean-owned ship, *Pong Su*, was captured near New South Wales by Australian special forces and police. The thirty crew members were arrested after allegedly unloading 50 kg of heroin worth US$50–80 million. Drug-trafficking seizures reported in R. Paddock and B. Demick, 'North Korea's Growing Drug Trade Seen in Botched Heroin Delivery', *LA Times*, 21 May 2003. Cultivation and refining statistics from US Governmental Affairs Subcommittee on Financial Management, the Budget and International Security (see 'North Defectors Tell of Drugs, Missiles', *Joongang Ilbo*, 23 May 2003).

31. Several Daesong officials have defected, although all deny involvement in illegal activities. See J.M. Kim, 'A North Korean Capitalist', *Far Eastern Economic Review*, 3 July 2003; and J. Solomon, and Hae Won-choi, 'Division 39 Helps Pyongyang Maintain Power', *Asia Wall Street Journal*, 14 July 2003.

32. Y. Li, 'Should Price Reform or Ownership Reform Come First?' *Shijie Jingji Dao Bao*, 3 October 1986 (in Chinese). Li (1930–) pointed out that China's primary task was ownership reform and developing shareholding.

33. The whole bonds programme even more closely resembles a lottery as there are twice-annual drawings with winners receiving their principal plus a prize. As Marcus Noland comments, 'The government's announcement states, without irony, that 'the bonds are backed by the full faith and credit of the DPRK government'. See Noland, *Famine and Reform in North Korea*. The share of GNP analysis is from D. Cooney, 'Many N. Korea Exports Go to Black Market', AP, 11 April 2003.

34. K. Zellweger, 'Caritas/FALU Monitoring Trip Report – Excerpts', Caritas–Hong Kong, 19 August–16 September 2003. The WFP has claimed that rural households are now spending up to 85 per cent of their income on food.

35. H.H. Ticktin, 'Towards a Political Economy of the USSR', *Critique* 1, Spring 1973. Ticktin reported that according to estimates by Soviet economists 7–22 per cent of the workforce could be made unemployed if 'scientifically based norms' were applied to the economy.

36. Quoted in R. Frank, 'North Korea: "Gigantic Change" and a Gigantic Chance', *Nautilus Institute*, 9 May 2003, http://nautilus.org/fora/security/0331_Frank. html.

37. The second devaluation was announced in several sources including the *Asahi Shimbun*. Even at NKW900/US$ the black-market rate must surely be higher (when the NKW was moved to NKW150 the black market rate was estimated to be NKW230/US$).

38. 'Price Reforms Force Poor to Eat Grass in North Korea', *The Times*, 18 September 2003. Marcus Noland also notes the extent of the price rises: 'when China raised the price of grains at the start of its reforms in November 1979, the increase was on the order of 25 per cent. In comparison, North Korea has raised the price of corn and rice by more than 40,000 per cent' (Noland, *Famine and Reform in North Korea*).

39. Frank, 'North Korea: "Gigantic Change" and a Gigantic Chance'.

40. Babson quoted in H.S. Khang, 'North Korea Slashes Exchange Rate', *South China Morning Post*, 7 October 2003.

41. Hyder quoted in 'UN Official Says North Korean Economic Reforms Creating New Class of Poorer Displaced Workers', AP, 2 December 2003; FAO/WFP, *Crop*

and Food Supply Assessment, 2003, p. 19.

42. J.M. Kim, 'Economic Fallout', *Far Eastern Economic Review*, 20 March 2003.

43. E. Cornell, *North Korea under Communism*, RoutledgeCurzon, London, 2002, p. 88.

44. R. Terrill, *The New Chinese Empire*, Basic Books, New York, 2003, p. 324.

Chapter 7

1. See 'E092003 – Basic Law of Sinuiju Special Administrative Region', *KCNA*, 20 September 2002.

2. The North Korean government displayed its plans for Sinuiju in the form of a model commissioned from an unnamed 'renowned architect' in France.

3. According to an interview quoting Iris Ying, president of Emperor Group's International Projects Department, *South China Morning Post*, 24 September 2002. However, Andrew Natsios reports gangs of abandoned children being sighted near Rajin–Sonbong in 1998, *The Great North Korean Famine*, US Institute of Peace, Washington DC, 2001.

4. D. Murphy, 'China Surprised by Plans for a Capitalist Enclave', *Far Eastern Economic Review*, 10 October 2002.

5. 'NK Rolls Out Rules for Industrial Zone amid Free-market Babbling', AP, 17 December 2003. Actually the minimum monthly wage will be US$57.50 a month, as there is also a compulsory social insurance premium of 15 per cent.

6. Coal was expected to be a major problem as the Chinese coal industry has been rationalizing over the last few years while the majority of DPRK coalmines are reportedly flooded.

7. 'China's 100 Richest 2002', *Forbes*, 24 October 2002, www.forbes.com/2002/10/24/chinaland.html.

8. Yang has described himself as a 'specialist in agriculture', although it is believed he has never received any formal training in the industry.

9. J. Kynge and A. Ward, 'Investors Eye North Korean Openings', *Financial Times*, 24 September 2002.

10. This was the HKSFC's first suspension in eighteen months, indicating how rare it is for the SFC to order a firm directly to halt trading. The authority declared: 'There is some price-sensitive information relating to the company that should have been disclosed. So we directed the company to suspend its share trading.'

11. Carrie Chan, securities analyst with Sun Hung Kai Securities Hong Kong, in an interview with the *Hong Kong Standard*, 25 September 2002.

12. At the same time a reshuffle occurred that saw vice-president Gu Zhuping promoted to deputy chief executive and Jacobus Lekkerkerk, Euro-Asia's former head of greenhouse technology, to the post of chief operating officer.

13. 'Yang Bin – The Perils of Flower Power', *Far Eastern Economic Review*, 10 January 2002.

14. All quotes from Kynge and Ward, 'Investors Eye North Korean Openings'.

15. 'North Denies South Korean, Japanese Reporters Entry to Sinuiju', AP, 30 September 2002.

16. Alice Chong, analyst with SG Securities (HK), quoted in 'Euro-Asia Shares All

to Record, *Joongnag Ilbo*, 26 September 2002.

17. J. Page, 'North Korea Combines Shenzhen with Hong Kong', Reuters, 22 September 2002.

18. The 1992 Southern Tour (*nanxun*) saw Deng visit several SEZs to restart the stalled reform programme and combat 'leftists' who opposed further reform by personally linking himself with the SEZ's activities. The Southern Tour effectively cemented the liberalization programme.

19. 'Axis of Trade', *EIU Business China*, vol. 28, no. 21, 14 October 2002.

20. Yang Rong is not related to Yang Bin. Yang Rong was head of China Brilliance Automotive, a Hong Kong-listed carmaker in China. Rong was the third richest man in China according to 'China's 100 Richest 2002', *Forbes*, 24 October 2002.

21. The *International Financial News*, a sister newspaper of the *People's Daily*, reported that Yang had used 66.7 hectares of farm land in Shenyang to develop property, a business that yields higher returns but attracts higher taxes.

22. Based on author's interview with Mark O'Neill, *South China Morning Post*, in Shanghai, August 2003.

Chapter 8

1. Histories of the Korean War include P. Lowe, *The Korean War*, Palgrave Macmillan, London, 2000; B. Catchpole, *The Korean War, 1950–53*, Constable & Robinson, Colchester, 2001; C. Malkasian, *The Korean War*, Osprey, Osceola, 2001; and W. Stueck, *The Korean War: An International History*, Princeton University Press, Princeton, 1997.

2. D. Oberdorfer, *The Two Koreas*, Warner Books, London, 1997, p. 7.

3. The *Pueblo* was seized on 23 January. The Tet Offensive started on 30 January. LBJ announced in March 1968 that he would not seek re-election. Despite the official histories it appears that the *Pueblo*'s capture was an accident that caused consternation in Pyongyang as at the time. The EC-121 spy plane was shot down in 1969 (on Kim Il-sung's birthday), with the loss of thirty-one US lives, in what was rumoured to be a last-ditch attempt by former guerrilla generals to prove their military capabilities and prevent their marginalisation by Kim after most had been purged by 1968.

4. The Nixon visit took place 21–28 February 1972 and resulted in the Shanghai Communiqué wherein both sides expressed their agreements and differences on bilateral and international issues.

5. Kissinger secretly visited Beijing to prepare for Nixon's visit, flying from Islamabad to Beijing, reportedly disguised as a woman.

6. The Nixon, or Guam, Doctrine, was announced in July 1969. Nixon stated that henceforth the US expected its Asian allies to take care of their own military defence.

7. The tree-cutting incident was confusing for all concerned as the chain of events was unclear. So far as can be established the Americans were unaware that the North Koreans had already challenged a group of ROK soldiers sent to trim the tree earlier. Whatever the cause it certainly angered Kissinger, who stated that the DPRK 'must pay the price' for the US dead and that 'North Korean blood must be spilled'.

8. Appointed in 1973, Hollingsworth had experience in World War II and Vietnam. He inspired confidence in Park, who supported his ideas of forward defence and allocated several million US dollars to build roads and other facilities closer to the DMZ supporting the strategy.

9. Carter had noted strong support for greater human rights in South Korea from senators and congressmen in April 1976 when the ROK government arrested and then imprisoned a number of protesting Christian leaders.

10. In 1975 a DPRK reconnaissance group was discovered photographing US airbases in the ROK, while in 1976 DPRK soldiers were apprehended south of the DMZ. In July 1977 a US army helicopter strayed into the Northern side of the DMZ and was shot down. Three Americans were killed and another imprisoned in the DPRK. Carter claimed the incursion was an error of navigation. The DPRK, keen to keep Carter 'on side', returned the bodies and released the captured American within three days.

11. Park was not missed in Washington as he had clashed with the US military command regularly, refused US entreaties to hold free elections and instituted political repression that embarrassed the US. From 1961 to 1967 the US had bugged Park's office despite the fact that Park had normalised relations with Japan, been consistently anti-communist and sent troops to fight in Vietnam.

12. The annual 'Team Spirit' was watched with trepidation by Pyongyang, which saw it as the prelude to a planned assault featuring amphibious landings, parachute drops and the deployment of nuclear-capable F1-11 fighter-bombers in the ROK.

13. When Deng visited Washington in January 1979 Carter reportedly asked him to help broker US–DPRK talks. Deng declined to do so. The normalisation of relations between the US and Beijing was enshrined in the January 1979 Sino–American Normalisation Treaty.

14. Chun (1931–) was a graduate of the Korean Military Academy, graduating in the American-, rather than Japanese-inspired, syllabus. He had spent time training with US forces and had worked for Park since 1961. He fought in Vietnam and led the pursuit of the DPRK agents that attempted to blow up the Blue House in 1968. Chun was initially appointed chief investigator into Park's assassination, where he came into conflict with army chief of staff Chung Seoung-hwa.

15. The 'Three Kims' were Kim Dae-jung; Kim Young-sam, who was expelled from the National Assembly in 1979, sparking riots in Pusan; and former Prime Minister Kim Jong-pil, DRP strategist and a founder of the KCIA.

16. A. Mansourov, 'The Reagan Solution to the North Korean Puzzle', Nautilus Institute, 3 March 2003, www.nautilus.org/fora/security/0315A_per cent20Mansourov. html.

17. P. Bracken, *Fire in the East*, Perennial, London, 1999, p. xxvii.

18. The biennial military exercise RIMPAC (Rim of the Pacific) 90 was held between April and June 1990 and included the controversial bombing of the Hawaiian island of Kaho'olawe. RIMPAC 90 involved 55 warships, 50,000 personnel and 200 aircraft. For the first time, a nuclear powered aircraft carrier, USS *Independence*, participated with vessels from Japan's navy.

19. This analysis of CIA reports is derived from J.D. Pollack, 'The United States, North Korea, and the End of the Agreed Framework', *Naval War College Review*, vol. 56, no. 3, Summer 2003, p. 73.

20. Articles 41 and 42 of the UN Charter authorise the Security Council to impose economic and diplomatic sanctions through the use of a militarily supported blockade.

21. The Atlanta-based Carter Center is a privately funded organisation established by Jimmy Carter that 'seeks to prevent and resolve conflicts, enhance freedom and democracy, and improve health'.

22. The Soviet graphite-moderated reactors were outdated and difficult to maintain, as well as – to Americans' concern – being capable of plutonium extraction for use in a nuclear weapons programme.

23. North Korea Advisory Group, Report to the Speaker US House of Representatives, November 1999.

24. The US inspection team visited the site five months later and found no evidence of nuclear activity. A second site visit took place in 1999 after another food deal was concluded. It later transpired that the DPRK had an undeclared facility inside Mount Chonma, 30 kilometres from Kumch'ang-ri.

25. See S. Harrison, *Korean Endgame*, Princeton University Press, Princeton, 2002, p. 65.

26. American policy documents identify 'rogue states' as those that pursue repression of their citizens, threaten neighbouring states, violate international treaties, seek to acquire WMDs, act as sponsors of terrorism, and generally reject 'American values'.

27. 'US to Bolster Military Alliance with South Korea,' *AFP*, 25 September 2003.

28. 'National Strategy to Combat Weapons of Mass Destruction', White House, Washington DC, December 2002.

29. C. Johnson, *Blowback*, TimeWarner, New York, 2000, p. 137.

30. Reported in P. Maass, 'The Last Emperor', *New York Times Magazine*, 19 October 2003.

Chapter 9

1. Officially the visit by Kelly had been delayed from July to October 2002, due to the deterioration in relations following the North–South naval skirmish in June 2002.

2. Evidence of WMDs in North Korea has been scant, though it has been alleged by the US State Department, the Defense Department, the Federation of American Scientists, the CIA and the US-based Center for Non-Proliferation Studies that in 1954 the USSR captured Japanese chemical agents and delivery technologies with the KPA, and that the DPRK has continued to develop these weapons. Further, the CIA has alleged that North Koreans have attempted to purchase biological warfare agents from Uzbekistan. The DPRK is not a signatory to any international conventions covering WMDs or CBWs. See L. O'Donnell, 'The Sinister Power Trip of the Dear Leader', *South China Morning Post*, 12 January 2003.

3. The three CIA concerns were presented to Bush by CIA director George Tenet a week before his inauguration. See B. Woodward, *Bush at War*, Pocket Books, London, 2002, p. 35.

4. Kim quoted in T.R. Reid, *Confucius Next Door*, Vintage, New York, 1999, p. 218.

5. L.V. Sigal, 'A Bombshell That's Actually an Olive Branch', *Nautilus Institute*, 23 October 2002, www.nautilus.org/fora/security/0208A_Leon.html.

6. All quotations from 'Meetings on DPRK Nuke Issue Held', *China Daily*, 19 October 2002.

7. 'White House Calls North Korea Admission "Troubling"', *Reuters*, 17 October 2002.

8. G. Vidal, 'The New War on Freedom' *San Francisco Chronicle*, 19 May 2002.

9. Woodward, *Bush at War*, p. 340.

10. Steve Kim, a naturalised US citizen, believed to have been born in North Korea, fired seven shots in front of the UN headquarters in New York, hitting several offices but injuring nobody.

11. P. Pomfret, 'China Embraces More Moderate Foreign Policy', *Washington Post*, 24 October 2002.

12. G. Kessler and K. DeYoung, 'N. Korea Puts Edge on Visit to Bush', *Washington Post*, 24 October 2002.

13. P. Hayes, 'The Agreed Framework is Dead: Long Live the Agreed Framework', Nautilus Institute, 16 October 2002, www.nautilus.org/fora/security/0204A_Peter. html.

14. V. Gilinsky, 'NK as Ninth Nuclear Power', Nautilus Institute, 22 October 2002, www.nautilus.org/fora/security/0210a per cent5Fvictor.html.

15. For more on the shift in US China policy, see J. Studwell, 'No More Mr Panda Hugger', *China Economic Quarterly*, Q3, 2002.

16. 'Report from the Icy Frontier', *The Economist*, 7 December 2002.

17. H. Restall, 'China's Little Help on North Korea', *Asian Wall Street Journal*, 22 October 2002. The Treaty of Westphalia brought to a close eighty years of religious wars in Europe with new rules of international law establishing the modern state system.

Chapter 10

1. 'US Beefs Up Forces Against "Reckless" North', *AFP*, 3 May 2003; D. Kirk, 'Seoul Reassured by US after Bombers Are Deployed in Guam', *New York Times*, 3 May 2003.

2. D. Cooney, 'US Planes in South Korea Will Remain as Deterrent', *Washington Post*, 2 April 2003.

3. J. Brooke, 'North Korea Watches War and Wonders What's Next', *New York Times*, 31 March 2003.

4. 'DPRK Vows to Build Up Military', *China Daily*, 2 January 2003; 'North Korea's New Year Message 2003', *KCNA*, 3 January 2004.

5. For example, 'Military-First Politics is a Precious Sword of Sure Victory for National Sovereignty', *Rodong Sinmun*, 3 April 2003.

6. Ibid.

7. Yonhap, 18 August 2003. Yonhap is the semi-official news agency of the ROK.

8. Chen Haosu, though the son of a former Chinese foreign minister, is not highly ranked, and the Association for Friendship with Foreign Countries is largely a relic of China's more belligerent and isolated days. Despite this the Chinese did

attempt to offset any snub by providing Chen with a letter of friendship signed by the leadership.

9. J. Fialka, 'Roots of North Korean Issue', *Asian Wall Street Journal*, 30 December 2002.

10. G. Gedda, 'North Korea Features Fearsome Military, AP, 27 March 2003; J. Bermudez, *Shield of the Great Leader*, Allen & Unwin, North Sydney, 2001.

11. Most of these CBWs are reportedly stored close to the Chinese border, making pre-emptive strikes politically problematic. Missile estimates are also problematic, some ranging as high as 600.

12. Article 27 of the DPRK Constitution states that the NDC decides military policy, methods of execution, organises and strengthens the military and directs all forces.

13. North Korea Advisory Group, Report to the Speaker US House of Representatives, November 1999.

14. M. Mazarr, *North Korea and the Bomb*, Macmillan, London, 1995, pp. 20–21.

15. Ibid.

16. 'US Military Starts Deploying High-Tech Weapons Near DMZ', Yonhap, 22 December 2003; 'New US Unmanned Spy Planes Deployed against North Korea', *AFP*, 23 September 2003; and B. Gertz, 'Rumsfeld Will Restructure US Military Forces in Asia', *Washington Times*, 13 November 2003.

17. G. Wehrfritz and R. Wolffe, 'How North Korea Got the Bomb', *Newsweek*, 27 October 2003. However, there were perks. It has been reported that when major breakthroughs were made at Yongbyon scientists would receive gifts of televisions and imported Japanese stereos (J. Solomon and Hae Won-choi, 'Division 39 Helps Pyongyang Maintain Power', *Asia Wall Street Journal*, 14 July 2003).

18. Wehrfritz and Wolffe, 'How North Korea Got the Bomb'.

19. Statement made in August 2000, when Kim met with a delegation of ROK media executives in Pyongyang.

20. A. Natsios, Administrator, USAID, Testimony to the Subcommittee on East Asian and Pacific Affairs, US Senate Committee on Foreign Relations, Washington DC, 5 June 2003.

21. This extremely high figure contrasts to the less than 3 per cent the ROK spends. The only country in Asia with relatively close levels of spending as a percentage of GDP is Myanmar with between 30 and 40 per cent. Statistics on budgeted expenditure for 2003 from 'North Korea Boosts Military Spending as Nuclear Crisis Persists', *AFP*, 27 March 2003.

22. Based on statistics from the International Institute for Strategic Studies and the Stockholm International Peace Research Institute.

23. 'US Military Starts Deploying High-Tech Weapons Near DMZ', Yonhap, 22 December 2003.

Chapter 11

1. The North Koreans evicted Canberra's Pyongyang mission. Bhutto believed he had influence, as relations between Pyongyang and Islamabad dated back to the 1970s when North Korea provided artillery, rocket launchers and other military assistance at the time of the 1971 Bangladesh war (see S. Goldenberg, 'Pakistan

Helped North Korea Make Bomb', *Guardian*, 19 October 2002; J. Carbaugh, 'Pakistan–North Korea Connection Creates Huge Dilemma For US', *Pakistan Facts*, 17 December 2003).

2. The NNSC was established following the armistice in 1953. However, no formal peace treaty was signed and so an armistice commission, the NNSC, was appointed to oversee implementation of the agreement. The UN, as a formal combatant, could not join. Eventually four 'neutral' nations were chosen: Sweden and Switzerland by the UN, Czechoslovakia and Poland by North Korea.

3. Stalin turned down Kim's request to invade the South in 1949, fearing World War III, though he finally agreed in 1950 as the situation changed and he was confronted with a combination of what he viewed as fortuitous circumstances. These included Mao coming to power in China, the USSR's recently achieved nuclear capability, the withdrawal of some US troops from Korea and US Secretary of State Dean Acheson's intimations that Korea was not an integral part of America's 'defence perimeter'. Stalin, wrongly as it transpired, assumed the US would not intervene in any conflict.

4. Kim, quoted in D. Oberdorfer, *The Two Koreas*, TimeWarner, London, 1997, p. 9.

5. S. Goncharov, J. Lewis and X. Litai, *Uncertain Partners*, Stanford University Press, Stanford, 1993, p. 130.

6. The assassination attempt was undertaken by a DPRK commando squad in January 1968. In the ensuing attack twenty-seven commandos were killed, three escaped and one was captured alive and admitted everything. The RPR was organised by Kim Chong-tae, a South Korean communist, along with DPRK intelligence. After the assassination attempt the RPR was effectively wiped out in 1968. Kim Chong-tae was executed in Seoul, though made a Hero of the Republic in North Korea, which also renamed a college and a railway locomotive factory after him.

7. Though officially meetings were between Red Cross officials, most of the participants were senior members of the KWP and KCIA.

8. The account of the meeting that does exist was recorded by the South Korean side and released seventeen years later.

9. The date of the signing of the South–North Joint Communiqué being that of American Independence Day is not believed to have been accidental.

10. A. Buzo, *The Guerilla Dynasty*, I.B. Tauris, New York, 2003, p. 148.

11. Roh was Chun's anointed successor and a retired general who had held various civilian posts including sports minister, home affairs minister, president of the Seoul Olympics organising committee and chairman of the Democratic Justice Party (Chun's own party). At the election he won 36 per cent of the vote, followed by Kim Young-sam with 28 per cent and Kim Dae-jung with 27 per cent. The other two candidates thus effectively split the vote and allowed Kim Young-sam into the Blue House. In 1992 Kim Young-sam again won with 42 per cent, against Kim Dae-jung with 34 per cent and the founder of Hyundai, Chung Ju-yung, with 16 per cent.

12. KAL 858 was blown up on 29 November 1987 by two DPRK agents apparently acting on direct orders from Kim Jong-il. The Abu Dhabi–Seoul flight exploded over Southeast Asia, killing all 115 passengers, mostly ROK citizens. The agents responsible were arrested in Bahrain. One died after taking a poisoned pill

but the other, a young woman called Kim Hyun-hui, survived. Kim, a former child actress in the DPRK and diplomat's daughter, was tried and sentenced to death in Seoul, though the sentence was eventually commuted on humanitarian grounds. She subsequently became something of a celebrity among many groups in the South both for her good looks and as a symbol of the repressions many wished to expose in the North.

13. It is also true, as the North Koreans point out, that the South Korean Armed Forces, which have set a total budget for 2004 of US$102 billion, a growth of 2.1 per cent over 2003, remain overwhelmingly under US military control and with a military command structure headed by a US general.

14. The term was taken from the Ostpolitik strategy of the West German Chancellor Willy Brandt, which centred on the concept of *Wandel durch Annäherung*, change through rapprochement.

15. Chung had planned to give the North 1,001 head of cattle. Pyongyang claimed that some of the cows died after being force-fed indigestible materials by the South Korean authorities in a bid to sabotage the donation (see 'Hyundai Founder Chung Visits North Korea', *Kyodo News*, 2 November 1998).

16. Thereby breaking the South's 1948 National Security Law, which forbids unauthorised contacts with the DPRK.

17. The EBRD was established in 1991 in London. The EBRD's 2003 disbursements were €2.4 billion.

18. These figures are cited from German sources in Park Young-kyu, 'Post Unification Challenges', in A. Jordan, ed., *Korean Unification*, Centre for Strategic and International Studies, Washington DC, 1993, p. 37.

19. M, Mazarr, *North Korea and the Bomb*, Palgrave Macmillan, London, 1995, p. 49.

20. Park, 'Post Unification Challenges', p. 37. Park also noted that the Korea Development Institute estimated in 1990 that US$140 billion would be required in the first three years of unification rising to between US$250 billion and US$300 billion by the end of the 1990s.

21. A curious analysis, as it goes hand in hand with describing the US economy as weak and unable to support its own people, while it can apparently create the world's twelfth largest economy in South Korea.

22. T.R. Reid, *Confucius Next Door*, Vintage Books, New York, 1999, p. 50.

23. B. Glosserman, 'North Korean Talks: A Tangled Web of Interests', *South China Morning Post*, 1 May 2003.

Chapter 12

1. Both Ceausescu and Honecker reportedly considered escaping to the DPRK in their final days.

2. C. Johnson, *Blowback*, Owl Books, London, 2000, p. 124.

3. Vollertsen was originally a German aid doctor with Cap Anamur. He was the only Westerner to be awarded the DPRK Medal of Freedom after donating some of his own skin to a burns victim. In December 2000 he was expelled after conducting a tour of Pyongyang for foreign media delegates accompanying Madeleine Albright. Since his expulsion Vollertsen has become an outspoken critic of the regime, encouraging a mass exodus campaign and undertaking other

actions. See N. Vollertsen, *Inside North Korea*, Encounter Books, San Francisco, 2003.

4. According to Tim Peters, an American missionary operating with DPRK refugees in China, in M. Kirkpatrick, 'Unwelcome Truths', *Asian Wall Street Journal*, 20 October 2003.

5. J. Pomfret, 'Portrait of a Famine', *Washington Post*, 12 February 1999.

6. Horowitz, quoted in M. Hiebert, 'Escape Valve', *Far Eastern Economic Review*, 14 August 2003.

7. A. Foster-Carter, 'When the Statues Are Toppled, *Asia Times Online*, 24 December 2003, www.atimes.com/atimes/Korea/ED17Dg01.html.

8. The elite comprises the extended Kim family, the between three and five thousand most senior KWP officials and their families, senior government officials and their families, as well as the military hierarchy and their families. There are also presumably a few trusted businessmen, sporting heroes, cultural workers, academics and secret police/intelligence service operatives whose social positions are in part owed to the leadership and who benefit from the regime directly.

9. K. Philo, 'The Sociopolitical Impact of the Food Crisis in North Korea', *Korea and World Affairs* 23, Summer 1999.

10. K. Oh and R. Hassig, *North Korea through the Looking Glass*, Brookings Institution Press, Washington DC, 2000, p. 37.

11. A. Natsios, *The Great North Korean Famine*, US Institute of Peace, Washington DC, 2001, p. 42.

12. The 1995 coup attempt is reported in D. Oberdorfer, *The Two Koreas*, Time-Warner, New York, 1999; the 1998 events in Natsios, *The Great North Korean Famine*, p. 218.

13. In 2003 reports emerged from China concerning criminal incidents along the border involving hungry and increasingly desperate KPA troops illegally crossing into China to steal food, rob banks and commit various other crimes, indicating that the army is starting to suffer from the same general depredations as the rest of the population.

14. 'North Korean Footsoldiers Could be Key to Revolution', Channel News Asia.com, 4 November 2003 www.channelnewsasia.com/stories/afp_asiapacific/view/55475/1/.html.

15. R. Terrill, *The New Chinese Empire*, Basic Books, New York, 2003, p. 80.

16. Kim Yeon-kwang, 'Second Son Being Groomed as Heir Apparent', *Chosun Ilbo*, 21 October 2003.

17. 'Former Bodyguard of North Korean Leader Interviewed', *BBC International Reports*, 13 October 2003.

18. Prime examples include the Stasi in the GDR and the Securitate in Romania, both of which acted a form of praetorian guard for their respective ruling regimes.

19. M. Noland, *Avoiding the Apocalypse: The Future of the Two Koreas*, Institute for International Economics, Washington DC, 2000; Natsios, *The Great North Korean Famine*.

20. *KCNA* reported in H. Greimel, 'Defiant North Korea Says "Sanctions Mean a War"', AP, 1 July 2003. Also J.S. Yoo, 'North Korea: Sanction Move Could Trigger War', AP, 30 April 2003, where an official DPRK spokesperson is quoted as declaring that sanctions would be 'the green light to a war'.

21. J. Takahashi, 'Rumsfeld Barb on Pyongyang Aid Earns Angry Rebuke from Fukuda', *Japan Times*, 18 April 2003.

22. Chinese shipments of oil to the DPRK were 317,000 tonnes in 1999, 389,000 tonnes in 2000 and 579,000 tonnes in 2001 ('China Sent 470,000 Tons of Oil to North Korea in 2002 – South Ministry', Yonhap, 9 October 2003).

23. J. Hari, 'Now North Korea Must Be Invaded and Liberated, for the Sake of Its People', *Independent*, 18 May 2003.

24. L. Flake, 'The Experience of US NGOs in North Korea', in L. Flake and S. Snyder, eds., *Paved with Good Intentions*, Praeger, Westport, 2003, p. 16.

25. O. Chung, 'The Role of South Korea's NGOs: The Political Context', in Flake and Snyder, eds, *Paved with Good Intentions*, p. 87.

26. S. Leys, *The Chairman's New Clothes*, Allison & Busby, London, 1978, p. 40.

Chapter 13

1. J. Studwell, *The China Dream*, Profile Books, London, 2002, p. 52.

2. Cover, *The Economist*, 17 June 2000.

3. J. Needham, *Science and Civilisation in China*, Cambridge University Press, Cambridge, 1956.

4. Peter Hayes, in J. Fialka, 'Roots of North Korean Issue', *Asian Wall Street Journal*, 30 December 2002.

5. H.H. Ticktin, 'Andropov: Disintegration and Discipline', *Critique* 16, 1983, p. 111.

6. A. Natsios, Administrator, USAID, Testimony to the Subcommittee on East Asian and Pacific Affairs, US Senate Committee on Foreign Relations, Washington DC, 5 June 2003.

7. Swenson-Wright, interview with the author, London, October 2003.

8. P. Maass, 'The Last Emperor', *New York Times Magazine*, 19 October 2003.

9. A. Mansourov, 'The Reagan Solution to the North Korean Puzzle, Nautilus Institute, 3 March 2003, www.nautilus.org/fora/security/0315A_ per cent20Mansourov.html.

10. Maass, 'The Last Emperor'.

11. Chen (1905–95) was the economic realist in Mao's circle, introducing measures to tame inflation after 1949 and again in the 1950s. He opposed the economic consequences of the Great Leap Forward and served under Deng, raising the importance of consumer goods, services and housing within the planning system. In the 1990s Chen warned Deng about inflation and opposed unplanned rapid economic growth for its own sake. He also opposed the use of force against the students at Tiananmen Square in 1989.

12. P. Bowring, 'North Korea: Relax', *Research-Works*, 20 February 2003.

Bibliography

Abrahmovitz, M. and Laney, J. (2000) *U.S. Foreign Policy toward North Korea: Next Steps*, New York: Council on Foreign Relations.

Amsden, A. (1989) *Asia's Next Giant: South Korea and Late Industrialisation*, Oxford: Oxford University Press.

An, T.S. (1983) *North Korea: A Political Handbook*, Wilmington: Scholarly Resources

Armstrong, C.K. (2002) *Korean Society: Civil Society, Democracy and the State*, London: Routledge.

Armstrong, C.K. (2002) *The North Korean Revolution, 1945–1950 – Studies of the East Asian Institute*, Ithaca: Cornell University Press.

Baum, R. (1996) *Burying Mao: Chinese Politics in the Age of Deng Xiaoping*, Princeton: Princeton University Press.

Becker, J. (1996) *Hungry Ghosts: China's Secret Famine*, London: John Murray.

Bedeski, R. (1994) *The Transformation of South Korea: Reform and Reconstruction in the Sixth Republic Under Roh Tae-woo 1987–1992*, London: Routledge.

Bermudez, J. (2001) *Shield of the Great Leader: The Armed Forces of North Korea*, Sydney: Allen & Unwin.

Blank, S. (1994) *Russian Policy and the Korean Crisis*, US Army War College: Strategic Studies Institute.

Bracken, P. (1999) *Fire in the East: The Rise of Asian Military Power and the Second Nuclear Age*, London: HarperCollins.

Breen, M. (1999) *The Koreans: Who They Are, What They Want, Where Their Future Lies*, New York: St Martin's Press.

Breen, M. (2004) *Kim Jong-il: North Korea's Leader*, Singapore: John Wiley.

Breuer, W. (1996) *Shadow Warriors: The Covert War in Korea*, New York: John Wiley.

Brown, G. (1974) *Korean Pricing Policies and Economic Development in the 1960s*, Boston: Johns Hopkins University Press.

Buzo, A. (2003) *The Guerilla Dynasty: Politics and Leadership in North Korea*, London and New York: I.B. Tauris.

Carranza Valdez, J. et al. (1998) *Cuba: Restructuring the Economy – A Contribution to the*

Debate, Institute of Latin American Studies.

Catchpole, B. (2001) *The Korean War 1950–53*, Colchester: Constable & Robinson.

Chamberlain, P. and Kihwan, K. *Korea 2010: The Challenges of the New Millennium*, Washington DC: Center for Strategic and International Studies.

Chung, J. (1974) *The North Korean Economy: Structure and Development*, Stanford: Hoover Institution Press.

Clifford, M.L. (1997) *Troubled Tiger: Businessmen, Bureaucrats and Generals in South Korea*, Armonk: M.E. Sharpe.

Clough, R. (1987) *Embattled Korea: The Rivalry for International Support*, Boulder: Westview Press.

Conquest, R. (1987) *The Harvest of Sorrow: Soviet Collectivization and the Terror-Famine*, Oxford: Oxford University Press.

Cornell, E. (2002) *North Korea under Communism – Report from an Envoy to Paradise*, London: RoutledgeCurzon.

Crabbe, M. and French, P. (1998) *One Billion Shoppers: Accessing Asia's Consuming Passions and Fast-moving Markets after the Meltdown*, London: Nicholas Brealey.

Crane, G. (1990) *The Political Economy of China's Special Economic Zones*, Boulder: M.E. Sharpe.

Cumings, B. (1998) *Korea's Place in the Sun: A Modern History*, New York: W.W. Norton.

Cumings, B. (1999) *Parallax Visions: Making Sense of American–East Asian Relations at the End of the Century*, Durham, NC: Duke University Press.

Dae, SS. (1995) *Kim Il Sung: The North Korean Leader*, New York: Columbia University Press.

Deng, X. (1996) *Selected Works of Deng Xiaoping*, Beijing: Foreign Languages Press.

Djilas, M. (1963) *Conversations with Stalin*, New York: Harcourt Brace.

Djilas, M. (1983) *The New Class: An Analysis of the Communist System*, New York: Harcourt.

Downs, C. (1998) *Over the Line: North Korea's Negotiating Strategy*, Washington DC: AEI Press.

Eberstadt, N. (1995) *Korea Approaches Reunification*, Boulder: M.E. Sharpe.

Eberstadt, N. (1999) *The End of North Korea*, Washington DC: AEI Press.

Eberstadt, N. and Ellings, R.J. (eds) (2001) *Korea's Future and the Great Powers*, Seattle: University of Washington Press.

Ellsworth Blanc, D. (2001) *North Korea – Pariah?*, New York: Nova Science.

Evans, R. (1997) *Deng Xiaoping and the Making of Modern China*, London: Penguin.

Flake, L. and Snyder, S. (eds) (2003) *Paved with Good Intentions: The NGO Experience in North Korea*, Westport: Praeger.

Goncharov, S., Lewis, J. and Litai, X. (1993) *Uncertain Partners: Stalin, Mao and the Korean War*, Stanford: Stanford University Press.

Gordon, M. (Ed) (1992) *The End of Superpower Conflict in the Third World*, Boulder: Westview Press.

Graham, E. (2003) *Reforming Korea's Industrial Conglomerates*, Washington DC: Institute for International Economics.

Halliday, J. and Cumings, B. (1988) *Korea: The Unknown War*, New York: Pantheon Books.

Han, Sung-joo (1974) *The Failure of Democracy in South Korea*, Los Angeles: University of California Press.

Hanson, C. (1988) *U.S. Nuclear Weapons*, New York: Orion Books.

Harrison, S. (2002) *Korean Endgame: A Strategy for Reunification and U.S. Disengagement*, Princeton: Princeton University Press.

Richard G. Head, R.G., Short, F.W. and McFarlane, R.C. (1978); *Crisis Resolution: Presidential Decision-Making in the Mayaguez and Korean Confrontations*, Boulder: Westview Press.

Henriksen, T. (1996) *Clinton's Foreign Policy in Somalia, Bosnia, Haiti, and North Korea*, Essays in Public Policy, No. 72, Stanford: Hoover Institution Press.

Hong, Y. (1999) *State Security and Regime Security: President Syngman Rhee and the Insecurity Dilemma in South Korea 1953–60*, London: Palgrave Macmillan.

Hong, Y.S. (1991) *A Sociolinguistic Study of Seoul Korean*, Seoul: Research Center for Peace and Unification of Korea.

Hough, J.F. and Armacost, M.H. (2001) *The Logic of Economic Reform in Russia*, Washington DC: Brookings Institution Press.

Humphrey, C. (2002) *The Unmaking of Soviet Life: Everyday Economies after Socialism*, Ithaca: Cornell University Press.

Hunter, H.L. (1999) *Kim Il-song's North Korea*, Westport: Greenwood Press.

Hwang Kyung-moon and Shin Gi-wook (2003) *Contentious Kwangju: The May 18th Uprising in Korea's Past and Present*, Lanham: Rowman & Littlefield.

Hyun, P. (1981) *Darkness at Dawn: A North Korean Diary*, Seoul: Hanjin.

Johnson, C. (2003) *Blowback: The Costs and Consequences of American Empire*, London: Owl Books.

Johnson, C. (ed.) (1973) *Ideology and Politics in Contemporary China*, Seattle: University of Washington Press.

Johnson, C. (1983) *Revolutionary Change*, Stanford: Stanford University Press.

Jordan, A. (1993) *Korea Unification: Implications for Northeast Asia*, Washington DC: Center for Strategic and International Studies.

Joyce, W., Ticktin, H. and White, S. (eds) (1989) *Gorbachev and Gorbachevism*, London: Frank Cass.

Kang Chol-Hwan and Rigoulot, P. (2002) *Aquariums of Pyongyang: Ten Years in the North Korean Gulag*, New York: Basic Books.

Kang, T.W. (1989) *Is Korea the Next Japan? Understanding the Structure, Strategy and Tactics of America's Next Competitor*, London: Macmillan.

Kie-Chiang Oh, J. (1999) *Korean Politics: The Quest for Democratization and Economic Development*, Ithaca: Cornell University Press.

Kiernan, B. (2002) *The Pol Pot Regime: Race, Power, and Genocide in Cambodia under the Khmer Rouge, 1975–79*, New Haven: Yale Nota Bene.

Kim Hak-joon (1977) *The Unification Policy of South and North Korea: A Comparative Study*, Seoul: Seoul National University Press.

Kim Jong-il (1982) *On Improving and Strengthening Judicial and Prosecution Work*, Pyongyang: Foreign Languages Publishing House.

Kim Jong-il (1990) *Accomplishing Juche, Revolutionary Cause, 1964–1971*, Pyongyang: Foreign Languages Publishing House.

Kim Jong-il (2003) *Our Socialism Centered on the Masses Shall Not Perish*, University Press of the Pacific.

Kim Il-sung (1975) *On Introducing New Systems of Economic Management*, Pyongyang: Foreign Languages Publishing House.

Kim Il-sung (1980) *Kim Il Sung's Works*, Volumes 1–38 and *Kim Il Sung's Selected Works*, Volumes 1–9, Pyongyang: Foreign Languages Publishing House.

Kim Il-sung (1983) *On the Korean People's Struggle to Apply the Juche Idea: Talks to the Delegation of the American Popular Revolutionary Alliance of Peru, June 30 and July 1 and 5, 1983*, Pyongyang: Foreign Languages Publishing House.

Kim Il-sung (2001) *For an Independent World*, University Press of the Pacific.

Kim Il-sung (2001) *On Socialist Pedagogy*, University Press of the Pacific.

Kim Il-sung (2001) *Juche! The Speeches and Writings of Kim Il-sung*, New York: Grossman.

Kim, S. (ed.) (2001) *The North Korean System in the Post-Cold War Era*, London: Palgrave Macmillan.

Kiska, F.J. (2003) *Korea: The Hard Way, Battling Invisible Trade Barriers – A Story from the Front Lines of America's Trade War*, Philadelphia: Xlibris.

Kong, T.Y. (2000) *The Politics of Economic Reform in South Korea: A Fragile Miracle*, London: Routledge.

Kotkin, S. (1992) *Steeltown, USSR: Soviet Society in the Gorbachev Era*, Los Angeles: University of California Press.

Krames, J. (2002) *The Rumsfeld Way*, New York: McGraw-Hill.

Kristoff, N. and Wudunn, S. (1995) *China Wakes: The Struggle for the Soul of a Rising Power*, London: Nicholas Brealey.

Kuo-Kang Shao (1996) *Zhou Enlai and the Foundations of Chinese Foreign Policy*, London: Palgrave Macmillan.

Kwak, T.W., Patterson, W. and Olsen, E.A. (eds) (1983) *The Two Koreas in World Politics*, Seoul: Institute for Far Eastern Studies, Kyungnam University.

Lankov, A. (2002) *From Stalin to Kim Il Song: The Formation of North Korea, 1945–1960*, London: C. Hurst.

Lardy, N. (1998) *China's Unfinished Economic Revolution*, Washington DC: Brookings Institution Press.

Lardy, N. (1994) *China in the World Economy*, Washington DC: Institute for International Economics.

Lardy, N. (1992) *Foreign Trade and Economic Reform in China, 1978–90*, Cambridge: Cambridge University Press.

LeBaron, D. (2001) *Mao, Marx, and the Market: Capitalist Adventures in Russia and China*, London: John Wiley.

Lee, C.S. (1978) *The Korean Workers' Party: A Short History*, Stanford: Hoover Institution Press.

Lee, H. (2002) *In the Absence of Sun: A Korean American Woman's Promise to Reunite Three Lost Generations of Her Family*, Nevada City: Harmony.

Lee, H.S. (2000) *North Korea: A Strange Socialist Fortress*, Westport: Greenwood Press.

Lee, K. (1993) *New East Asian Economic Development: Interacting Capitalism and Socialism*, Armonk: M.E. Sharpe.

Lee, S.H. (1996) *Outposts of Empire: Korea, Vietnam, and the Origins of the Cold War in Asia, 1949–1959*, Liverpool: Liverpool University Press.

Lerner, M.B. (2002) *The Pueblo Incident: A Spy Ship and the Failure of American Foreign Policy*, Lawrence: University Press of Kansas.

Levin, N. (1982) *Management and Decisionmaking in the North Korean Economy*, Santa Monica: Rand Corporation.

Lewis, L. (2002) *Laying Claim to the Memory of May: A Look Back at the 1980 Kwangju Uprising*, Honolulu: University of Hawaii Press.

Leys, S. (1977) *The Chairman's New Clothes: Mao and the Cultural Revolution*, London: Allison & Busby.

Li Nam-ok (1999) *The Golden Cage*, London: Macmillan.

Lie, J. (2000) *Han Unbound: The Political Economy of South Korea*, Stanford: Stanford University Press.

Lilley, J, (1998) *Over the Line: North Korea's Negotiating Strategy*, Washington DC: AEI Press.

Lim, R. (2003) *The Geopolitics of East Asia*, London: RoutledgeCurzon.

Lintner, B. (2003) *Blood Brothers: Crime, Business, and Politics in Asia*, London: Palgrave Macmillan.

Lowe, P. (2000) *The Korean War*, London: Palgrave Macmillan.

McFaul, M. and Perlmutter, T. (eds) (1995) *Privatization, Conversion, and Enterprise Reform in Russia*, Boulder: Westview Press.

Malkasian, C. (2001) *The Korean War*, Osceola: Osprey.

Mann, J. (1999) *About Face: A History of America's Curious Relationship with China, From Nixon to Clinton*, New York: Knopf.

Mao Zedong (1967) *Selected Works of Mao Tse-tung*, Beijing: Foreign Languages Press.

Mao Zedong (2002) *On Guerrilla Warfare*, Champaign: University of Illinois Press.

Mazarr, M. (1995) *North Korea and the Bomb: A Case Study in Nonproliferation*, London: Palgrave Macmillan.

Mesa-Lago, C. (1981) *The Economy of Socialist Cuba: A Two Decade Appraisal*, Albuquerque: University of New Mexico Press.

Minnich, JM. (2003) *The Denuclearization of North Korea: The Agreed Framework and Alternative Options Analyzed*, Mineville: 1st Books Library.

Mo, J. and Henriksen, T. (eds) (1997) *North Korea After Kim Il-sung: Continuity or Change?*, Washington DC: Hoover Institution Press.

Moak, S. (1974) *Marketing System of the Socialist Farms, North Korea*, Richmond: University of Richmond Press.

Nam Joo-Hong (1986) *America's Commitment to South Korea: The First Decade of the Nixon Doctrine*, Cambridge: Cambridge University Press.

Nathan, A. and Gilley, B. (2002) *China's New Rulers*, London: Granta.

Natsios, A.S. (2001) *The Great North Korean Famine: Famine, Politics, and Foreign Policy*, Washington DC: US Institute of Peace.

Needham, J. (1956) *Science and Civilisation in China*, Cambridge: Cambridge University Press

Noland, M. (2000) *Avoiding the Apocalypse: The Future of the Two Koreas*, Washington DC: Institute for International Economics.

Oberdorfer, D. (1999) *The Two Koreas: A Contemporary History*, London: TimeWarner.

Ogle, G.E. (1990) *South Korea: Dissent within the Economic Miracle*, London: Zed Books.

Oh, K. and Hassig, R. (2000) *North Korea through the Looking Glass*, Washington DC: Brookings Institution Press.

Pak, M.B. (1991) *The Patron of Public Health*, Pyongyang: Foreign Languages Publishing House.

Radzinsky, E. (1996), *Stalin*, London: Hodder & Stoughton.

Ree, E.V. (1989) *Socialism in One Zone: Stalin's Policy in Korea: 1945–1947*, New York: St. Martin's Press.

Reid, T.R. (1999) *Confucius Lives Next Door*, New York: Vintage Books.

Remnick, D. (1993) *Lenin's Tomb: The Last Days of the Soviet Empire*, New York: Random House.

Roper, S. (2000) *Romania: The Unfinished Revolution*, London: Routledge.

Rumer, B. (1989) *Soviet Steel: The Challenge of Industrial Modernization*, Ithaca: Cornell University Press.

Sardar, Z. and Wyn Davies, M. (2002) *Why Do People Hate America?*, Cambridge: Icon Books.

Scalapino, R. (1997) *North Korea at a Crossroads*, Stanford: Stanford University Press.

Scalapino, R. and Chong-Sik Lee (1972) *Communism in Korea*, Los Angeles: University of California Press.

Sen, A. and Drèze, J. (eds) (1999) *The Amartya Sen and Jean Drèze Omnibus: Comprising Poverty and Famines, Hunger and Public Action, and India: Economic Development and Social Opportunity*, Oxford: Oxford University Press.

Shmidt-Hauer, C. (1986) *Gorbachev: The Path to Power*, London: Pan Books.

Shrader, C. (1995) *Communist Logistics in the Korean War*, Westport: Greenwood Press.

Sigal, L.V. (1999) *Disarming Strangers: Nuclear Diplomacy with North Korea*, Princeton: Princeton University Press.

Simpson, J. (2003) *The Wars against Saddam: Taking the Hard Road to Baghdad*, London: Pan Macmillan.

Snyder, S. (1999) *Negotiating on the Edge: North Korean Negotiating Behaviour*, Washington DC: US Institute of Peace.

Song, C.Y. (2000) *The North and South Korean Political Systems: A Comparative Analysis*, Elizabeth: Hollym International.

Soon, OL. (1999) *Eyes of the Tailless Animals: Prison Memoirs of a North Korean Woman*, Bartlesville: Living Sacrifice.

Steers, R. (1998) *Made in Korea: Chung Ju Yung and the Rise of Hyundai*, London: Routledge.

Steinfeld, E. (1998) *Forging Reform in China: From Party Line to Bottom Line in the State-owned Enterprise*, Cambridge: Cambridge University Press.

Studwell, J. (2002) *The China Dream*, London: Profile Books.

Stueck, W. (1997) *The Korean War: An International History*, Princeton: Princeton University Press.

Terrill, R. (2003) *The New Chinese Empire*, New York: Basic Books.

Thornton, R. (2001) *Odd Man Out: Truman, Stalin, Mao and the Origins of the Korean War*, Virginia: Brassey's.

Van Vranken Hickey, D. (2001) *The Armies of East Asia: China, Taiwan, Japan and the Koreas*, Boulder: Lynne Rienner.

Vollertsen, N. (2003) *Inside North Korea: Diary of a Mad Place*, San Francisco: Encounter Books.

Wickham, J.A. (1999) *Korea on the Brink: From the '12/12' Incident to the Kwangju Uprising, 1979–1980*, Washington DC: National Defense University Press.

Wilborn, T.L. (1995) *Strategic Implications of the US–DPRK Framework Agreement*, US Army War College: Strategic Studies Institute.

Wo-Lap Lam, W. (1995) *The Era of Jiang Zemin*, London: Prentice Hall.

Woodward, B. (2002) *Bush at War*, London: Pocket Books.

Yang, S.C. (1994) *The North and South Korean Political Systems: A Comparative Analysis*, Boulder: Westview Press.

Yi, S.U. (1983) *The Security and Unification of Korea*, Seoul: Sogang University Press.

Yun, K.B. (1974) *North Korea As I Knew It: An Authentic Record*, Seoul: Buk-han Research Institute.

Index